WHEN
THE ALPS CAST
THEIR SPELL

Mountaineers of the Alpine Golden Age

WHEN
THE ALPS CAST
THEIR SPELL

Mountaineers of the Alpine Golden Age

TREVOR BRAHAM

www.theinpinn.co.uk

The In Pinn is an imprint of
Neil Wilson Publishing
303 The Pentagon Centre
36 Washington Street
Glasgow G3 8AZ

Tel: 0141-221-1117
Fax: 0141-221-5363
E-mail: info@nwp.co.uk
www.nwp.co.uk

A catalogue record for this book is available from the British Library.

ISBN 1-903238-74-9

Typeset in Aldine
Printed by CPD

CONTENTS

ACKNOWLEDGEMENTS

Royal Society, Edinburgh

The Royal Institution, London

Scott Polar Research Institute, Cambridge

Whyte Museum of the Canadian Rockies, Banff

John Wills for information and photographs from family archives

Alpine Museum, Bern (courtesy of Director, Urs Kneubühl)

Club Alpin Français, Paris (courtesy of Dominique Simon)

Alpine Museum, Chamonix

Heimatvereinigung, Grindelwald (courtesy of Samuel Michel)

Zentralbibliothek & Schweizer Alpen Club bibliothek, Zürich

Bibliotheque Cantonale et Universitaire, Lausanne

Musée Historique et Archives Communale, Lausanne

Bundesamt für Landestopographie, Wabern

Schweiz Tourismus, Zürich

Aargauer Kunsthaus, Aarau

Rotten Verlag, Brig

Gutenberg Verlag, Zürich

Frau Gozon-Amstutz for use of her late father's publications

The late André Roch and Albert Eggler for historical guidance

For use of illustrations, I am grateful to Rudolf Würzer (Linz), Martin
Moran, Roger Mear, Roy Ruddle and Erhard Loretan

PREFACE

An eminent eighteenth-century Bernese savant, Albrecht von Haller, expressed in poetic language the feebleness of the human mind to absorb the magnificence of mountains. For the early mountaineers, captivated by their mystical quality, the mountains cast a spell, arousing a challenge of adventure in a unique world. With today's crowding of once secluded places, some of the original enchantment appears to have diminished; and there have been radical changes in attitudes and practices. Amidst this transformation it is interesting to pry into the past for a closer glimpse of the pioneer mountaineers – particularly of those visitors from Victorian Britain who travelled out to the Alps where they introduced the new 'sport' of mountain climbing. Much has been written about them already, resulting in their activities having been judged fairly or unfairly based on past perceptions. It is perhaps a suitable time to look back at their conception of the mountain world, and to re-appraise the activities of some of the main actors during the period that the British labelled the Alpine Golden Age.

Unravelling of mysteries surrounding the origins of the Alps appealed strongly to the pioneer explorers, but the motives of later visitors from Britain were different. Leslie Stephen's definition would still seem fairly accurate for a majority of mountaineers: 'Mountaineering, in my sense of the word, is a sport which brings one into contact with the sublimest aspects of nature; and without setting their enjoyment before one as an ultimate end or aim, helps one to absorb and be penetrated by their influence. Still, it is a sport – and I have no wish to place it on a different footing'.

By the mid-nineteenth century interest in the new sport had been sufficiently aroused in Britain for the formation of a club in London. But the Alpine Club was barely eight years old when disaster struck after the deaths in 1865 of three British climbers and a leading French guide on the Matterhorn. The shock aroused by that event cast obloquy on the Club's *raison d'être*, threatening to set a ban on its activities. That the censorious attitudes to which the Club was then exposed were firmly resisted, is testimony to the commitment of a small group of amateur climbers for whom there was no turning back.

To pre-empt any censure concerning the limited range of my main actors, appearing in chronological order, I must add that I have emulated a principle favoured by Lytton Stachey in one of his biographical works: 'My choice of persons has been determined by no desire to construct a system or to prove a theory ... and it has been my purpose to illustrate rather than to explain'. If the names of other eminent pioneers appear only briefly, it is not because their contribution to the 'unveiling of the Alps' has been in any way less notable. It has been my aim, within a modest canvas, to illustrate the atmosphere of those far-off days, when every venture aroused a sense of wonder; and I have allowed the characters to speak for themselves, accurately recording facts, and seeking to avoid gratuitous opinions.

The writing of this book would not have been possible without the help that I have received from Bob Lawford, Librarian Emeritus of the Alpine Club London, who gave me unlimited access to the Club's valuable library and archives, which constitute the most complete source in the world of primary information about the Alpine Golden Age. I would like also to express my gratitude to several other sources and individuals – too numerous to mention – who have provided me so willingly with the benefit of their advice and assistance; and to apologise in advance if I have omitted to name them individually. I cannot conclude without conveying my appreciation of the support of my editors, Kate Blackadder and Sallie Moffat, for gently upbraiding me about inexactitudes and inconsistencies in my text, of which my enthusiasm for the subject left me oblivious.

PART ONE
12ᵀᴴ-18ᵀᴴ CENTURY

CHAPTER ONE
BEGINNINGS

Up there in the sky, to which only the clouds belong and birds and the last trembling colours of pure light, they stood fast and hard; not moving as do the things of the sky. They were as distant as the little upper clouds of the summer, as fine and tenuous; but in their reflection and in their quality as it were of weapons (like spears and shields of an unknown array) they occupied the sky with a sublime invasion: and the things proper to the sky were forgotten by me in their presence as I gazed. ... Since I could now see such a wonder, and it could work such things in my mind, therefore some day I should be part of it. That is what I felt. That is also which leads some men to climb mountain-tops.

Hilaire Belloc: on first viewing the Alps
from the Weissenstein (Jura), 1901

The developments that began to accelerate in the European Alps, culminating in the alpine Golden Age in the mid nineteenth century, were preceded by events less spectacular, but illustrating the existence of a spirit of keen enterprise long before the Alps became a playground for mountain climbers. During earlier ages the high mountains reflected aspects of terror as dwelling-places of the supernatural, while the hazards of approaching precipitous regions of rock and ice acted as a powerful barrier to access. The motives of the earliest explorers were different from those of today's mountaineers, but the challenges that they faced and overcame were no less intimidating.

The impressions of an English monk, John de Bremble, while crossing the Grand St Bernard pass in February 1188, typify the current of thought that prevailed among travellers in his day. 'Feeling myself so much nearer heaven that I was more sure that my prayer would be heard, I said "Lord, restore me to my brethren, that I may tell them that they come not to this place of torment".' That pass, which has been, and remains, one of the great thoroughfares across the Alps is believed to have been frequented prior to the Roman era. The first hospice was set up on its summit in 859AD, and was substantially rebuilt two hundred years later. The St Gotthard pass was of important use to the Romans, uniting the two portions of their province of Raetia, now embracing the cantons of Valais and Grisons. The Théodule pass, named according to legend after St Théodule, the first Bishop of Valais, from 381-391AD, flourished as a strategic route connecting the Rhône and Aosta valleys during a particularly mild climatic period in Europe between the tenth and sixteenth centuries, when the retreat of glaciers left the pass free of snow providing easy access to it for traders and feudal overlords with their horse and mule caravans. A major climatic change, described as the Little Ice Age, took place between the sixteenth and seventeenth centuries with the expansion of glaciers when the crossing of the pass involved a 'march on ice for a good eight miles'.[1] Apart from erratic spells of advance and retreat a general period of glacier-melt began by the mid nineteenth century and has continued ever since. (Note 1, see Notes to Chapters). The Alpine passes stretching across the southern borders of Switzerland retain their crucial importance as connecting links between northern and southern Europe, but serious environmental and social problems caused by the near-saturation of commercial and tourist road traffic have advanced research into major projects for the design and construction of underground railway routes.

EARLY TRAVELLERS

One of the earliest alpine travellers was the historian Aegidius Tschudi of Glarus (1505-72) who, between 1524-28, crossed several passes above the snowline, publishing in 1538 detailed accounts of his journeys illustrated with maps. His contemporary Josias Simmler (1530-76), professor of mathematics and history in Zürich, published in 1574 De Alpibus Commentarius which provided a good deal of practical advice for travel above the snowline, revealing surprisingly detailed knowledge about the use of alpenstock, climbing-irons, snow-shoes, dark glasses and rope. The English diarist and writer John Evelyn travelled from Italy across the Simplon pass on 16 May 1646 at the age of twenty-six when he encountered many difficulties,

[1]Scientists believe they have discovered evidence that during the Great Ice Age the Rhône glacier extended to the lake of Geneva from its source 150km away.

including freezing temperatures and snow. Reaching Switzerland, he recorded: 'The People ... rustikly clad, ... for the most part in blew cloth nor with almost any distinction twixt the gentleman and common sort, being exceedingly frugal: so as not one beggar amongst them: add to this their great honesty and fidelity, though exacting enough for what they part with. Every man gos with a sword by his side, and the whole country well disciplined and indeed impregnable which made the Romans have so little success against them.' (Note 2). During the early history of Switzerland it has been said that Swiss peasants governed themselves in the 'democratic' cantons, and were well governed in the 'aristocratic' ones.

SCHOLARS AND SCIENTISTS

Three eminent Swiss scholars who pioneered serious scientific investigations into the origins of the Alps were Johann-Jakob Scheuchzer of Zürich (1672-1733), Albrecht von Haller of Bern (1708-77), and Horace-Bénédict de Saussure of Geneva (1740-99). Scheuchzer, a professor of mathematics, physics, and natural science, was probably the first to undertake glaciological observations, carrying out nine exploratory journeys between 1702-11. His four-volume work, *Naturgeschichten des Schweizerlandes* published 1716-18, which included four map-sheets covering the whole of Switzerland, was dedicated to the Royal Society in London of which he was a Fellow. Haller, a specialist in natural sciences and a doctor of medicine, began his thirty-five-year involvement with the Alps at the age of twenty. He published works on botany, philosophy and theology; also a famous poem *Die Alpen,* a spare-time occupation of his youth, which earned him the title of 'the poet of the Alps'. (Note 3) Haller was elected to Fellowship of the Royal Society, and his work had a profound influence upon his successors. De Saussure, came from a noble family of scholars and intellectuals which had emigrated from Lorraine in the sixteenth century. He was a keen botanist, naturalist, geologist, and professor of natural philosophy at Geneva. At the age of twenty he began a long series of scientific travels in the mountains, for which he had developed a passion from early childhood, with a journey on foot from Geneva to Chamonix. He was fascinated by La montagne Maudite, as Mont Blanc was originally known, offering a monetary reward to anyone who succeeded in reaching its summit.

For thirty years, de Saussure's investigations led him through fourteen crossings of the main alpine chain by eight different passes, in addition to 16 other excursions to central parts of the chain. (Note 4) In 1788, he had a stone hut built on the col du Géant (3359m) first crossed by surveyors the year before, where he spent sixteen days with his son meticulously carrying out a series of geological and meteorological observations. His heroic efforts were not appreciated by his guides who apparently felt that enough was enough and destroyed his provisions, ensuring his return to the valley. In 1789 de Saussure visited Macugnaga in order to measure the height of Monte Rosa. In 1792 he camped for three days on the Théodule pass studying the Matterhorn and measuring its height. In 1787 de Saussure achieved his personal ambition when he climbed Mont Blanc, his motives being principally scientific. (Note 5) He is regarded as one of the founders of modern geology, and his monumental four-volume work *Voyages dans Les Alpes,* published 1779-96 combines geological observations with essays on natural science and mountain travel.[2]

ARTISTS

The Swiss painter Kaspar Wolf of Aargau (1753-98) was the first major interpreter of the alpine scene. He recognised the overpowering nature of this medium for giving expression to the grandeur of high mountains. His output includes over 150 oil paintings, which provide images of peaks and glaciers in their pristine isolation over 230 years ago. He was followed by Alexandre Calame (1810-64) of Vevey, distinguished for his magnificent portraiture of the Bernese Alps. JMW Turner (1775-1851) made six visits to Switzerland between 1802-44, painting over a hundred alpine watercolours. His impressionistic visions, acclaimed as the work of genius after his death, did not meet with universal appreciation during his lifetime. One of his great protagonists was John Ruskin, himself an artist and romantic worshipper of mountains, who referred to the Alps as 'the cathedrals of the earth'. First taken there by his parents at the age of thirteen, Ruskin's subsequent visits developed into an almost annual pilgrimage. On his last visit, he wrote at Chamonix: 'The only days I can look back to as rightly and wisely in entireness spent, have been in sight of Mont Blanc, Monte Rosa and

---

[2]An abridged version of the work was published in Geneva in 2003.

the Jungfrau'. The English lakeland poet William Wordsworth, at the age of twenty, spent most of his long vacation from Cambridge visiting the Alps, writing from Switzerland 'We are now upon the point of quitting these most sublime and beautiful parts; and you cannot imagine the melancholy regret which I feel at the idea'. (Note 6)

SCIENTIFIC RESEARCH

By the end of the eighteenth century curiosity was aroused by the unexplained presence of erratic blocks of massive proportions such as the *Pierre à Bot*, above the lake of Neuchâtel, the *blaue Stein* at Mattmark lake above Saas, and the *Pierre du Niton* on the bed of the lake at Geneva which raises its head close to today's familiar *jet d'eau*. (Note 7) In attempting to explain their presence, a number of theories were put forward. James Hutton, in his book *Theory of the Earth* published in Edinburgh in 1785, stated his belief that glaciers were the vehicles which carried erratic blocks into the valleys. Hutton's work was popularised by the Scottish scientist, John Playfair in his publication, *Illustrations of the Huttonian Theory of the Earth* published in 1802. A leading researcher during this period was Professor Franz Joseph Hugi (1796-1855) geologist, botanist, and professor of natural science at Solothurn, who carried out geological studies between 1827-30 from a cabin built on the lower Aar glacier, publishing in 1830 the result of his investigations in his book *Naturhistorische Alpenreise* (A Naturalist's Journey Across the Alps). Others were Jean de Charpentier (b1786) responsible for setting up the salt mines in Bex, whose publication in 1841, *Essai sur les Glaciers,* laid sound practical foundations to knowledge about the Ice Age; also Canon Rendu of Chambèry, who introduced some important glaciological theories. A series of studies from a base on the Aar glacier was carried out by Louis Agassiz (b1807) a leading Swiss scholar and doctor of philosophy at Neuchâtel. He was assisted by Edouard Désor, born in Germany in 1811, who later published several scientific papers on the Alps, and was made an honorary citizen of Neuchâtel. In 1841 Professor James David Forbes of Edinburgh was invited to visit them. (Note 8) The following year Forbes undertook an exploratory journey in the Valais accompanying the Bernese scientist Bernhard Rudolf Studer (b1794), who was responsible for important work on the geography of Switzerland during twenty years of research and travel. Eugène Viollet-le-Duc, born in Paris in 1814, gained wide fame as an artist, geologist and architect. He was responsible for restoration of the thirteenth-century Cathedral of Notre Dame in Paris and of the medieval city of Carcassonne, spending the last years of his life in Lausanne where he carried out restoration of the thirteenth-century cathedral, designed the Scottish Church, and the villa in which he lived; he died there in 1879. He spent the summers of 1868-75 in the Mont Blanc region where he was engaged in geophysical, geological and glaciological studies, besides producing a map of the massif. A genuine mountain lover, he was an original member of the Club Alpin Français. Over 125 years ago he was perhaps the first serious observer of mountain ecology with a clear perception of the natural laws that govern the environment. He sounded sharp warnings about the consequences resulting from failure to observe those laws by thoughtless exploitation of the resources of mountain regions – warnings which continue to be ignored, resulting in the increasing disappearance of wilderness areas. His book *Le massif du Mont Blanc,* was published in Paris in 1876. (Note 9) Present concern about the mountain environment is at best ambivalent, with growing misuse of resources generated by human and economic demands. A statement made recently by a university researcher in the USA, 'Mother Nature has a way of working against us', represents the sort of muddled thinking that occurs in sections of society which ought to know better.

EARLY MOUNTAINEERS

The Italian poet Petrarch (1304-74), achieving a long-cherished ambition, may have been the first to record, in a letter to his brother, sentiments of joy after his ascent of Mont Ventoux (1912m) in the Vaucluse on 26 April 1336, a mountain believed to have been climbed by shepherds in 1286.[3] On 1 September 1358 the pilgrim Rotario d'Asti climbed Rochemelon (3538m) near Susa, placing a bronze Madonna in a grotto below the top; a chapel was founded there, which has become the object of a summer pilgrimage. An artillery officer, Antoine de Ville, Seigneur of Domp Julien and Beaupré and chamberlain to Charles VIII of France, was the first to record the use

---

[3]Ventoux is invaded every summer by hordes of onlookers during the annual *Tour de France* bicycle race.

of mechanical aids when ascending Mont Aiguille (2086m) in the Vercors on 26 June 1492. Ten men scaled the cliffs employing warlike equipment designed to scale city walls, including ladders, ropes, pegs, hammers and stirrups. They spent three days on the meadow-like summit in order to establish convincing proof of their ascent. The second ascent of Mont Aiguille was made 342 years later by Jean Liotard, a local shepherd. Konrad Gesner (1516-65), doctor of medicine in Basel and of science in Zürich, expressed the true mountaineering spirit when he wrote to a friend in 1541: 'The soul is strangely rapt with these astonishing heights ... the abruptly soaring summits, the trackless steeps, the vast slopes rising to the sky, the rugged rocks, the shady woods.'[4]

The glaciers of Grindelwald had begun to attract travellers during the seventeenth century; but Chamonix, where a Bénédictine priory is known to have existed as early as the eleventh century, was not discovered as a goal for tourists until 1741 when William Windham of Felbrigg Hall, Norfolk, aged twenty-three, one of a group of young Englishmen studying in Geneva, and Dr Richard Pococke who had just completed an extensive study-tour of the Middle East, organised a journey to Chamonix with six others. They set out on 19 June along the wilderness of the Arve valley, carrying firearms as a precaution against possible attack by brigands. Travelling on foot they reached Chamonix after three days where they engaged a group of hunters as guides and porters. On 22 June: 'After climbing with great labour for four hours and three-quarters we got to the top of the mountain (Montenvers)[5]. It is impossible to give you a proper idea of what we saw from there because I know of nothing that bears the slightest resemblance to it.' Descending the steep and loose moraine slope with difficulty, Windham and Pococke's party reached the ice of the glacier, becoming the first tourists to set foot on the Mer de Glace where they spent half an hour. Laboriously re-ascending the moraine they had a short rest before returning to Chamonix at sunset. A granite boulder,

[4]See also Adolphus Warburton Moore Chapter 5, note 3.

[5]The present footpath from Chamonix to Montenvers provides a pleasant two-and-a-half hour ascent of 900m but in an age when crowds of tourists throng the railway, prospective walkers are greeted with expressions such as *'bon courage'* – freely translated as, 'feeling brave?' When it was inaugurated in 1908 the railway met with strong opposition from the men of Chamonix who foresaw the disappearance of their livelihood as guides for tourists.

where they are believed to have rested became known as *La Pierre des Anglais*. The stone seen today, near the pathway below the Montenvers cable-car station, inscribed 'Pococke et Windham 1741', is probably a replacement of the original 'ancient grey stone' which, it is believed, was damaged or destroyed. Although very few tourists are now aware of the stone's existence, the attention of the world at large was attracted to the unique features of the Chamonix valley and its glaciers by the account published shortly after Windham and Pococke's visit. It was nineteen years later that de Saussure visited Chamonix, and forty-five years were to pass before Mont Blanc was climbed.

The De Luc brothers of Geneva, who climbed the Brévent in 1754, ascended Mont Buet (3094m) in 1770. The elder brother, Jean-André, a geologist, meteorologist, and inventor of the hygrometer, was elected to Fellowship of the Royal Society and settled in England in 1772, where he died aged ninety. Mont Vélan (3731m) was climbed on 31 August 1779 by Abbé Laurent-Joseph Murith, prior of St Bernard hospice, with 'two hardy hunters', Moret and Genoud, only the latter accompanying him to the top; this was probably the hardest mountain ascent made at the time. Murith was a keen botanist, whose work *Guide de Botaniste* was published in 1810; a few days after his ascent he wrote to a fellow-botanist, de Saussure: 'I had too much difficulty, despite my hardihood, to gain this icy colossus'. He appears to have undertaken the climb purely as a sporting challenge. In 1784 JM Clement reached the main summit of the Dents du Midi (3257m) whose peaks dominate the village of Val d'Illiez, of which he was vicar; a keen naturalist, he possessed the richest library in the Valais, comprising over eight hundred volumes relating to natural history and languages. The explorations and climbs of Placidus à Spescha (b1752), a Bénédictine monk of Disentis, entitle him to a firm place among the early pioneers; T Graham Brown has described him as 'perhaps the first of the true mountaineers'. He loved both mountains and mountaineering, and took a keen interest in geography and geology. Between 1788-1824, he is credited with having made more than thirty mountain ascents, including the Rheinwaldhorn (3402m), Oberalpstock (3328m), Güferhorn (3383m), Piz Urlaun (3359m), Stockgrond (3422m), crossing a pass to its north which bears his name Porta da Spescha (3352m). At the age of seventy-two, he took part in the first ascent of the Tödi (3620m). A shrewd judge of men, he is reported to have remarked: 'In the choice of companion for a mountain expedition one cannot be too particular.' Spescha appears to have suffered a chequered fate: his monastery, said to have been founded in 614AD, was plundered and burnt, together with its valuable archives, by French troops during the military aggression following the Revolution; and, for a time, he was held prisoner by Austrian invaders. Something of an eccentric, he ended his days aged eighty-one as chaplain of his monastery.

The forerunners of the eighteenth century were the stage-setters for mountaineers at the start of the nineteenth century; who, in turn, inspired an interest that encouraged the arrival in the second half of that century of expanding numbers of tourists and mountain-climbers. The exploits of the latter encompass the history of the 'Golden Age' of alpinism.

TOPOGRAPHERS

The first complete map of Switzerland, stretching from the region of Mont Blanc to Lake Constance, comprising sixteen sheets on a scale of 1:108000, appeared between 1786-97, having been commissioned by an Aarau industrialist and politician Johann-Rudolf Meyer (1739-1813). During the fieldwork, which was carried out principally by Heinrich Weiss, an engineer and topographer from Strasbourg, assisted by Joachim Müller of Engelberg, several mountains were climbed, Meyer himself joining his surveyors on a few climbs including the third ascent of Titlis. In 1833 General Guillaume-Henri Dufour (1787-1875) Swiss soldier, statesman, and engineer, was appointed as head of the newly-formed Bureau Topographique in Geneva. (Note 10) Under his direction, between 1845-64, twenty-five copper-engraved sheets, which included twelve of the Alps, on the scale of 1:100000, were produced covering the whole of Switzerland. General Dufour was succeeded in 1865 by Col Hermann Siegfried (1819-79) who set the standards for the excellent Swiss maps that are published today. The Siegfried maps comprised 604 sheets, of which the alpine regions appeared on a scale of 1:50000. They continued to be published up to 1926, and remained in print until 1952.

Mont Blanc (4807m) and Monte Rosa (4634m)

Seven years before Mont Blanc was first climbed, an Englishman Thomas Bowdler, aged twenty-five, offered the princely sum of five guineas to the guides of Chamonix if they succeeded in finding a way to the summit. After the first ascent made by Dr Michel-Gabriel Paccard with Jacques Balmat on 8 August 1786, a second ascent was made on 5 July 1787 by three Chamonix men, Jean-Michel Cachat, Alexis Tournier, and Jacques Balmat. De Saussure made the third ascent on 3 August of the same year; and, six days later, a twenty-three year-old Englishman Mark Beaufoy made a fourth ascent, dressed in white ' ... that the sunbeams might be thrown off ... besides a pole for walking I carried with me Cramp Irons for the heels of my shoes ... a long rope, a hatchet, and a ladder'. Jean-Michel Cachat was his leading guide. Twenty-five years after the first ascent only ten parties had reached the summit. (Note 11) At the start of the Golden Age in 1854, the number of ascents had increased to forty-five. Nine years later an Englishman, Frederick Morshead, made a solo ascent in a single day. The first winter ascent was made in January 1876 by an Englishwoman, Miss Straton, accompanied by the guides, Jean Charlet, Sylvain Couttet, and Michel Balmat.

Ascents of the nine summits between 4046m and 4634m forming the Monte Rosa group were spread over a period of forty-four years. In 1819 and 1820 Joseph Zumstein and Johann Vincent from Gressoney climbed the Zumsteinspitze (4563m) and the Vincent Pyramid (4215m). Other peaks climbed were the Ludwigshöhe (4342m) in 1822 by Ludwig von Welden, an Austrian staff officer and the Signalkuppe (Pta Gnifetti) (4554m) in 1842 by G Gnifetti, a parish priest of Gressoney, with a party from Alagna.[6] The Grenzgipfel (4596m) was climbed in 1848 by Victor Puiseaux, and Dr Ordinaire, from Besançon. (Note 12) In 1855, 1861, and 1863 respectively three other main peaks of the group were reached by British climbers with their guides, the Dufourspitze (4634m), the highest peak in Switzerland, followed by the Nordend 4609m and the Parrotspitze 4432m. (Note 13)

---

[6]Fifty-one years later Queen Margherita of Italy, accompanied by a large escort, climbed the Punta Gnifetti where she was received by members of the committee of the Italian Alpine Club, and inaugurated the Margherita Hut, at which she spent the night. In recent years the Hut has been used as a research centre for the study of physiological problems arising at high altitudes.

MOUNTAIN ASCENTS (1800–50)

Mountaineering in Austria began over two hundred years ago with the ascent in 1800 of the highest peak of the Gross Glockner (3796m) by the brothers J and M Klotz, carpenters of Heiligenblut, who were members of an expedition promoted by Count Franz von Salm, Bishop of Gurk. In 1802, the physicist Ramond de Carbonnière (1755-1827), a pioneer of Pyrenean climbing, took part in the ascent of Mont Perdu (3355m); his guides, Laurens and Rondo, reaching the summit. In 1804 Josef Pichler, a chamois hunter from the Passeiertal, with two Zillerthaler, climbed the highest peak (3905m) of the Ortler group. The first to climb a Swiss mountain above 4000m were two brothers of the Meyer family of Aarau, sponsors of the first Swiss maps, and outstanding among the Swiss pioneers of mountaineering. Johann-Rudolf II and Hieronymus, with two chamois hunters, Alois Volker and Josef Bortis, reached the north summit of the Jungfrau (4089m) on 3 August 1811; and on 8 August 1812 the south summit of the mountain (4158m) was reached by Gottlieb, 19-year-old son of J-R Meyer II. In 1813, a French traveller Henri Maynard, accompanied by J-M Couttet of Chamonix, made the first ascent of the Zermatt Breithorn (4165m). On 10 August 1829 the Finsteraarhorn (4274m) was climbed by two guides accompanying the geologist Professor Hugi, who himself stopped short of the summit. Hugi, who reached the Strahlegg pass on 14 January 1832, became the first climber to accomplish an alpine winter ascent. Edouard Désor (Note 14), working with Louis Agassiz on the Aar glacier, climbed the Lauteraarhorn (4042m) in 1842, the Dossenhorn (3138m) in 1843, the Rosenhorn (3689m) in 1844 (Note 15), and the Galenstock (3583m) in 1845. During cartographic surveys connected with the Dufour maps, Johann Wilhelm Coaz of Chur climbed Piz Bernina (4049m) on 13 September 1850 accompanied by two brothers from the Grisons, Jon and Lorenz Tscharner. Coaz is credited with having made over thirty other ascents between the years 1845-50, including Piz Tchierva (3546m), Corvatsch (3451m), Kesch (3418m), Chapütschin (3386m) and Misaun (3249m). (Note 16) In the Austrian Alps, probably the first Tyrolean to climb out of a genuine love of mountains was Peter Carl Thurwieser (1789-1865) who is reported to have made seventy ascents including three first ascents during the years 1820-47.

PROMINENT SWISS MOUNTAINEERS

Edmund von Fellenberg of Bern (b1838) carried out a series of topographical expeditions in the Alps between 1856-83 which included first ascents of the Fiescherhorn (4048m), the first traverse of the Bietschhorn, and the second ascent (the first by the south-east ridge) of the Schreckhorn. Gottlieb Studer of Bern (1804-90), was a prodigious Alpine explorer whose campaigns commencing in 1823 extended for sixty years, and included 643 separate expeditions. Among his first ascents were the Studerhorn (3638m), which bears his name, the Gross Wannenhorn (3905m), Monte Leone (3553m), Sustenhorn (3503m) and Diablerets (3210m). His fame rests in his four-volume work *Uber Eis und Schnee* published between 1869-83, and in his output of engravings with over seven hundred Alpine panoramas. He was one of the founders of the Swiss Alpine Club (SAC), and in 1859 he became the first foreigner to be elected to honorary membership of the Alpine Club London. An active Swiss climber of the period was JJ Weilenmann (1819-96) of St Gallen, who is reputed to have climbed three hundred and twenty mountains in twenty years. He made the second ascents of the Dufourspitze in 1855, and of Monte Leone (solo) in 1859; and carried out a number of solitary climbs in the Oetztal Alps. On 11 September 1865 he made the first ascent of Mont Blanc de Cheilon (3870m). His climbs are recorded in a three-volume work *Aus der Firnenwelt* published in Leipzig 1872-77.

DEVELOPMENT OF TOURISM IN SWITZERLAND

Mountains, often the setting for major Biblical events, have exercised a powerful spiritual influence as symbols of supernatural power. They are universally revered by religious pilgrims supported by strong beliefs, who face unknown challenges in order to approach distant shrines; instincts that still prevail in many parts of the world. Indian pilgrims travel in thousands to the sources of holy rivers in the Himalaya; as Japanese pilgrims visit the shrine on top of Fujiyama. By the middle of the nineteenth century the importance of scientific research, which had provided the initial motive for alpine exploration, began to be displaced by the realisation that the beauty of the alps presented an almost untouched potential for tourism. The main alpine passes had become generally accessible to wheeled traffic, when new carriage-roads were opened across the Simplon in 1800-05, the Susten in 1811, and the St Gotthard in 1820-30, although until 1850 horse-drawn carriages faced steep descents not without danger, and were fitted with heavy wooden logs as 'drags'. Switzerland entered the railway age in August 1847 when the first rail-link was inaugurated between Zürich and Baden. The expansion of the system was among the key elements leading to the opening up of the alpine wonderland, accompanied by a rapid response to the needs of tourists with the construction between 1845-80 of a thousand new inns and hotels, one-third of which were situated above 1000m.

With the establishment of the Swiss Federal Constitution in 1848 the country introduced a national currency, a nationwide postal service, and the unification of weights and measures.[7] Swiss textile and watch industries had begun to flourish. Travel had become less tedious and difficult, the country was no longer an unknown or forbidding land. Mr Thomas Cook conducted his first alpine tour in 1863, which included Geneva and the Mont Blanc area; its success encouraged him to extend his visits in 1864 to Interlaken, Kandersteg and the Gemmi pass; thereafter the scale and popularity of Cook's annual tours gathered increasing pace. Three or four decades earlier, apart from scientists and artists, travellers had been limited to the wealthy upper classes carrying out a 'Grand Tour' of Europe. By 1868, when Queen Victoria rented a villa in Lucerne, visiting the Rigi, Pilatus and the Rhône glacier, tourism in Switzerland had taken a firm hold. The economic prosperity which had grown out of the industrial revolution in Great Britain created a growing class eager to escape from the narrowness of Victorian society to the splendours of the Swiss Alps. Most went there as curious travellers, but there was a small minority who, adapting readily to a different form of adventure which the mountains seemed to provide, evolved into a group of enthusiastic amateurs, forming the nucleus of the early British mountaineers.

Prior to 1854, occasional mountain ascents carried out in the course of scientific exploration were not generally recorded. Those who entered the field later made it perfectly clear by the manner and style of their activities that their interests were purely sporting. The magnificence of the setting cast the initial spell, but the new sport, demanding unusual physical and moral challenges, provided unique personal rewards. In its

---

[7] To the bewilderment of early travellers, currency values, even post charges, varied from one canton to another, as did internal customs regulations and levies.

infancy the activity was ridiculed; not long after, it was roundly condemned as dangerous. The centenary volume of the *Alpine Journal* has
recorded that: 'The first half of the 1860s may fairly be claimed to be the
greatest period in Alpine history.' To which it might be added that British
climbers, accompanied by their Swiss, French, and Italian guides, played
a dominant role in 'unveiling' the Alps and ascending its major peaks.

Interest in the alpine world was aroused in Britain by the
publication in 1843 of a book by Professor JD Forbes describing his
pioneer alpine journeys and glacier studies. Further stimulus was
provided by an extravagant lecture-show which ran for over six years
in London presented by Albert Smith, a congenial eccentric and gifted
showman, who made the fortieth ascent of Mont Blanc in 1851. A
few British amateurs had been visiting the Alps regularly by the mid
1840s. John Ball (1818-59), a man of private means, lawyer, politician,
and botanist, began his series of visits to the Alps in 1840. Travelling
through unfrequented regions for twenty-three years, he compiled
valuable records which led to his editorship in 1859 of *Peaks, Passes,
and Glaciers,* published by the Alpine Club London, and was followed
by the appearance between 1863-68 of three volumes of his *Alpine
Guide,* the forerunner of modern guide-books, titled The Western,
Central and Eastern Alps. Others prominent among the early British
mountaineers were William Mathews, and members of his family,
Edward Shirley Kennedy, Thomas George Bonney, Thomas
Hinchcliff and Alfred Wills; they were the leaders of a group who
spearheaded the formation of the first Alpine Club.

THE ALPINE GOLDEN AGE

The British invasion of the Alps which began in the early 1850s
spread swiftly over the next few decades. The men whose names fill
the next five chapters of this book were among the leaders of the first
wave of mountaineers. They belonged to a group whose ventures and
achievements often overlapped: the Reverends Charles Hudson,
Hereford Brooke George and James Robertson, members of the
Walker family, the brothers Parker, Pendlebury, Pilkington and
Smyth, Frank Gardiner, Francis Fox Tuckett, John Birkbeck, Florence
Craufurd Grove, Charles Taylor, Reginald Macdonald, Thomas
Stuart Kennedy, JJ Hornby, Reverend TH Philpott and several others,
including some notable lady climbers. Their ventures fill the records of

the early years. The Alpine Golden Age, so labelled by the English, which by vaguely defined tradition commenced with Alfred Wills' ascent of the Wetterhorn in 1854, opened a new era of sporting ascents of high peaks. It was followed a year later by the first ascent of Monte Rosa's highest summit by Charles Hudson, John Birkbeck, the Smyth brothers, and EJW Stevenson, and by the first guideless ascent of Mont Blanc by Charles Hudson's party. The 'eccentric' hobby developed into a new form of adventure, providing outdoor challenges and pleasures. During the first phase of the Golden Age, between the years 1854-65, thirty-six alpine summits above 4000m were reached for the first time, thirty-one of them by British parties, who were also largely involved in ascents of 120 other peaks, in addition to the crossings of new alpine passes during the same period. The measure of that achievement can be judged by comparison with the ascents of eight peaks above 4000m and 126 others during the preceding six hundred years.

The initial shock and horror aroused by the deaths of three British climbers and a French guide on the Matterhorn in 1865 briefly diminished, but did not end nor even halt, the expansion of alpine climbing. Fresh challenges were sought; new areas were discovered and developed, aspirations grew bolder, and mountaineering activities during the second phase of the Golden Age were no less impressive than those of the first. After the Matterhorn was climbed (Note 17) there remained other unclimbed peaks above 4000m, the Grandes Jorasses (Pointe Walker), the Grand Combin (Valsorey), the Lenzspitze, Mont Maudit, Aiguille de Rochefort, Les Droites, Aiguille du Géant, to name a few, apart from a wealth of challenging peaks above 3000m, while serious exploration of the Dolomites began only in 1870, and of the Dauphiné in 1873, providing rich opportunities for climbers who were active during the second phase between the years 1866-82. (Note 18) A new era began in 1882 with the adoption of mechanically-assisted climbing, when the Valtournanche guide Jean-Joseph Maquignaz hammered pitons into the rocks of the Aiguille du Géant and laid five hundred feet of rope between 26-29 July making the first ascent of the south-west summit with his employers, who were four young members of the Sella family. (Note 19) The use of mechanical aids was considered an aberration at the time.[8] Other mountaineers were successful without such aids,

[8]Although it was not unique – the first recorded use having occurred almost 400 years earlier when Antoine de Ville and his men climbed Mont Aiguille, see pages 10-11).

exploring difficult new routes on mountains which had been climbed. By the end of the nineteenth century the romantic age was over, and the way was open for new developments.

ALPINE CLUBS

The first Alpine Club was inaugurated at a meeting held in London on 22 December 1857, with John Ball chosen as President. The list of original members included the names of twenty-nine men whose alpine knowledge or experience had qualified them to join, an indication of the narrowly limited numbers in the beginning who were attracted to mountaineering. By 1865 membership had expanded tenfold, and in 1881 the membership register contained 444 names. The Club published two volumes of *Peaks, Passes and Glaciers* in 1859 and 1862; a third followed in 1932. Volume 1 of the *Alpine Journal* was published in 1863. The next Alpine Club was the Oesterreichischer Alpenverein set up in Wien in 1862. On 19 April 1863 the Swiss Alpine Club held its inaugural meeting in Olten attended by thirty-five members, with Dr Rudolf Théodor Simler, professor of geology and chemistry at Bern university, elected as President; membership by the end of that year grew to 257, grouped together in eight sections. In 1863 the first mountain hut, the Grünhorn, was built by the Club at a cost of 876 francs; over the years 152 others have been added, and membership has reached 100,000 in 2003 covering 92 sections. The Club Alpino Italiano was inaugurated on 23 October 1863 as the Club Alpino Torino, adopting its present name in 1866. Two of the club's chief founders were the politician Quintino Sella, and the geologist Felice Giordano, both of whom were associated with organising the first ascent of the Matterhorn from Italy in 1865; the Club set up its first primitive bivouac on the mountain in 1867. The Deutscher Alpenverein was founded in Münich in 1869, and the Club Alpin Français in 1874. The European clubs, unlike the London club, which laid down standards of eligibility for membership, attracted vastly greater numbers enabling them to finance the construction of pathways and huts in the heart of the Alps. In 1876 Le Centro Excursionista de Catalunya was founded in Spain, and in 1878 the Oesterreichischen Alpenklub in Austria. They were followed by the Belgian, Swedish, New Zealand and Slovenian Clubs in 1883, 1885, 1891 and 1893. The Royal Netherland, and American Alpine Clubs were established in 1902, and the Alpine Club of Canada in 1906. André Roch, a leading Swiss climber during the mid-twentieth century, wrote about this development, 'Alpine Clubs began to be established in several countries, the die was cast, and alpinism was born in the congenial form introduced by the English.'

It is considered fashionable now to deride the Victorian age. Clinton Dent, Alpine Club President in 1887, referred to the experiences of the Alpine pioneers from Britain as 'simple and wholesome pleasures'. They were serious men in a serious age, though their alpine activities sometimes tended to label them as eccentric or, at the least, as rather foolish. Their literature has been described as 'facetious and flippant ... but always alive'. They were individuals seeking a new form of personal satisfaction – aesthetic, spiritual, physical – which the mountains provided. Adapting to hardships unknown today, they were amply compensated by the privileges that were their lot – untouched natural beauty, kindly people eager to please, and 'the grand excitement of ascending an untrodden peak'. They were busy discovering the Alps: exploring secret places where an air of mystery still reigned. They were not bewhiskered embodiments of man's unconquerable ambition; nor peak-baggers blasting a path to personal fame and fortune. Poorly equipped, with scant knowledge of rope techniques, and climbing by 'fair' means, they were necessarily limited in their perception of what appeared to be feasible. They were phenomenal walkers.[9] No easy options were open to the pioneers. Mountain ascents were lengthy ventures beginning in the valley involving outings of up to twenty hours often followed by a cold night out, either on a glacier or in the draughty interior of a primitive shelter. There were no marked pathways, no alpine huts, no fixed aids attached to the mountains. There were no scientifically-based weather forecasts; and there was no rescue service. Reliance on guides does not detract from their achievements; it was they who provided the initiative; differences in skill between amateur and professional were readily accepted in a sport still in its infancy.

---

[9]The perceptions of the period are well illustrated by hints given to aspiring mountaineers in *Mountaineering* published in 1892 by the Badminton Library: 'It is the greatest mistake for the very young to indulge in mountaineering. Before the age of, say, eighteen, expeditions involving more than eight hours' walking are altogether unwise.'

At the beginning of the twentieth century Martin Conway reflected: 'each generation makes of the world more or less the kind of place they dream it should be, and each when its day is done is often in a mood to regret the work of its own hands and to praise the conditions that obtained when it was young.' Three decades later the ageless explorer and mountaineer, Tom Longstaff, expressed the thought that mountains were not giants to battle with, but great presences that fortunate people might come to know. Eric Shipton wrote in the 1960s: 'I do not claim that my dislike of competition was a virtue, since it stemmed largely from my failure to compete successfully; but it is certainly true that part of the attraction that I later found in mountaineering was that it could be practised without any sense of rivalry'. Charles Evans, addressing the Alpine Club in December 1970, struck a vital point: 'Mountaineering is more used than it was for ends not directly connected with mountains, – education, the winning of prestige, and the making of money ... interest seems to have moved towards prowess and technique and away from the setting, away from the mountains themselves.' (Note 20). The media was provided with its first big mountain story in 1865 after the Matterhorn accident. Ever since, it has exploited a fertile field by magnifying mountain drama in search of excitement, exposing climbers to its customary disregard for facts or scruples. For some, this results in stimulating a publicity cult, making a virtue of vanity and commercialism. While the latter is symptomatic of a materialistic society, the first is partly illusion – in what might still be considered a minority sport there is less interest than is generally supposed in the exploits of extreme climbers outside the community of extreme climbers.

The portraits in this book are limited to five leading mountaineers of the first period of the Golden Age, and two from the period that followed during the final quarter of the nineteenth century, when the freshness and romance of the early years were replaced by spectacular deeds. They helped to build the spirit and the traditions of mountaineering. Alfred Wills, an unambitious climber trusting to the skills and the safety standards of his guides, acquired a close intimacy with the alpine environment which he loved deeply. John Tyndall's mountain ventures tended to err on the side of daring, and he might have been judged by the conventions of his time as a risk-taker. Leslie

Stephen climbed with the best guides, accepting their supremacy on a mountain, but he would have drawn the line at what he might regard as unethical practice. Adolphus Warburton Moore, who had several fine ascents to his credit, was an explorer at heart, exercising a blend of prudence and daring, especially when in his judgement 'the game was worth the candle'. Edward Whymper, whose courageous, dogged, ambitious, colourful, and brief alpine career turned him into a legendary figure, was ever ready to exploit any means in order to achieve his ends. Albert Frederick Mummery, some of whose exploits are still regarded with awe, forged the spirit of modern mountaineering. He climbed for climbing's sake, delighting in the physical, mental, and moral challenges of his sport, and regarding the summit as a dispensable goal if its attainment demanded 'unfair' means. Emmanuel Boileau was an unknown star that shot brilliantly across the sky and disappeared from view. How similar were they in temperament to today's active performers? Examined closely, there are few real differences. There exist today mountaineers with Stephen's ethical standards, Moore's exploratory ardour, Mummery's pioneering spirit, Tyndall's taste for risk, Wills' trust in guides, Whymper's craving to predominate. With the possible exception of Whymper, all the pioneers were attracted by a love of mountains. Their portraits provide an insight into their individuality and aspirations within the context of a sport which they introduced and practised in a remotely different style, while creating the essential traditions of mountaineering which remain broadly in existence today.

PART TWO
19TH CENTURY
LEADING MOUNTAINEERS

CHAPTER
TWO
ALFRED WILLS
1828-1912

... did a sea
Of fire envelop once this silent snow?
None can reply – all seems eternal now.
The wilderness has a mysterious tongue
Which teaches awful doubt, or faith so mild,
So solemn, so serene, that man may be,
In such a faith, with nature reconciled -
Thou hast a voice, great Mountain, to repeal
Large codes of fraud and woe not understood
By all, but which the wise, and great, and good
Interpret, or make felt, or deeply feel!

Percy Bysshe Shelley, Mont Blanc, 23 July 1816

Although he was not the first traveller from Britain to undertake pioneering alpine journeys, and to publish an account of his adventures – he was preceded by such men as Professor James David Forbes, John Ruskin, John Ball and others – Alfred Wills was among the first to start visiting the alpine regions regularly, driven wholly by a love of the natural environment. It is a 'concession to an old tradition' to claim that climbing as a 'sport' began with Wills' ascent of the Wetterhorn in 1854, an honour that surprised and pleased him.[1] A few exceptional sporting ascents made earlier were those of the Jungfrau in 1811 by members of the Meyer family of Aarau; the Zermatt Breithorn in 1813 by H Maynard of Chamonix; ascents in the Monte Rosa group during 1819-20 by Italian priests; and the highest peak of the Wetterhorn group in 1845 by Stanhope Speer, a Scottish medical student. Alfred Wills was certainly one of the earliest Englishmen to discover the attractions of alpine travel for its own sake

---

[1]One hundred years later, a contentious Arnold Lunn declared the claim as 'absurd and now abandoned'.

27

when, in 1846, as a student at University College London, he visited the alps for the first time. He continued to do so yearly thereafter with few interruptions celebrating, in 1896 at Chamonix, his Golden Jubilee as an alpine traveller and mountaineer.

The previous chapter has shown that the desire to climb a mountain with no motive other than a sense of adventure was beginning to grow by the middle of the nineteenth century. Between 1820-53, eighty-six mountains were climbed, including five summits above 4000m. The year 1854 was probably regarded as a convenient starting point for the opening of the Golden Age because during the next eleven years to 1865 when the Matterhorn was climbed, practically every major alpine summit had been reached – a development in which British mountaineers played a prominent part. The centenary issue of the *Alpine Journal* contains a survey by DFO Dangar and TS Blakeney relating to the 1854-65 period, 'The Rise of Modern Mountaineering', a title designed to indicate that the new sport of mountain climbing had become firmly established. The first British climbers to ascend the Finsteraarhorn on 13 August 1857 – William St John Mathews, Edward Shirley Kennedy, John Hardy and JCW Ellis – were so encouraged by their adventure as to consider the formation of an Alpine Club, which they did, holding its inaugural meeting in London on 22 December 1857. A copy of the Club's first circular went out to twelve original members. With alpine climbing in its infancy, *The Times* noted the Club's formation with a waggish remark describing its members as men who 'seem to have a special fondness for regions which are suitable only as dwelling-places for eagles'. Alfred Wills, with six alpine journeys behind him, was one of the twelve members whose names were registered at the Club's inauguration; seventeen others were added in January 1858. Wills became the Club's third President in 1864. In a speech at the Club's forty-fifth Annual Dinner in 1903, he ventured to remark that he was one of only two original members left who had attended the first Dinner in 1858. He commented in 1892: 'I belong to a generation of mountain lovers already past, and have been rather a pioneer than one of the good soldiers by whom the triumphs of mountaineering have been won.' He must have been keenly aware that he was almost the sole surviving link between the Romantic Age and the dawn of a new mountaineering era. WE Davidson, Alpine Club President in 1912, speaking shortly after Wills' death, remarked that he had been intimately linked with the Club's early history, and his high principles and strong personality had exerted an important influence in shaping its traditions.

During Alfred Wills' Presidency, the Club was less than eight years old, and it was his direct intervention that persuaded Edward Whymper, three weeks after the disastrous loss of four lives on the Matterhorn, to break his self-imposed silence which was causing a good deal of public fury to be directed against the Club. In a letter to Whymper he wrote: 'Give your own account, let it be truthful, manly and unflinching – wherever blame is due (if blame there be) let it rest – but do not let people go on conjecturing the worst, when you could silence the greater part of it by your utterance. To some extent also the Club is on its trial. People are daily writing to abuse us and our doings.' In Wills' day, and particularly after 1865, the leaders of the Alpine Club, all of whom were responsible men, were sensitive to the public charge of foolhardiness which was heaped upon their activities. It was on Wills' initiative that a subscription was opened, and generously supported, for the dependent sisters of the Chamonix guide, Michel Croz, who had lost his life on the Matterhorn. Wills was a man of integrity, courage, and energy, always ready to act in matters about which he felt strongly. He was also a keen amateur naturalist deriving great pleasure from his travels through the upper alpine valleys, where he had the capacity to rid his thoughts of professional cares, identifying himself completely with the mountain environment and the people he encountered.

Alfred Wills was born on 11 December 1828, the second son of William Wills, a successful solicitor and Justice of the Peace in Birmingham. On completing his schooling at Edgbaston, he entered University College London where he took up mathematics, classics and legal studies. He obtained a scholarship in classics in 1849; and in 1851 a scholarship in law, and an LLB Following his father's profession, he was called to the Bar by the Middle Temple in 1851. He became a Queen's Counsel in 1872. One of Wills' significant cases as a QC in 1875 was his defence of a Mr Perkins against the Yorkshire Engineering Company concerning royalties for his newly-invented engine – the precursor of Perkins generators. It was a long case and Wills worked exceedingly hard on it, having to forego almost three weeks of his annual holiday to see it through to a successful conclusion, which enabled Mr Perkins to proceed with plans for developing his engine. In a letter to his wife, who had preceded him with their children on holiday, Wills wrote: 'Mr Perkins' engines will beyond all doubt revolutionise the construction of boilers and engines.' Another case, one which aroused wide publicity, was his sentence of two years imprisonment for Oscar Wilde in 1895. Wills was knighted in 1884 and was appointed Judge of the Queen's Bench Division of the High Court, a position which he held for twenty-one years. As a Judge, Alfred Wills has been described as 'just, patient, courteous, firm in the discharge of his duties, scrupulously careful in weighing his sentences, yet always ... making large allowances for the fallen'. (Note 1) Upon his retirement in December 1905, he was made a member of the Privy Council, with a seat on the Judicial Committee; and he was appointed for two years as President of Hartley University College, Southampton, near to where he lived during the last years of his life.

When Wills first travelled to Switzerland at the age of eighteen the journey occupied almost a week in a cumbrous diligence, half-smothered in dust, with nights spent at inns which provided, to say the least, variable standards in matters of food and lodging. Interest in the high mountains and glaciers, with few exceptions, was still largely centred around scientific research. Pioneer alpine investigations carried out by Professor Forbes and others had added substantially to general knowledge about glaciers, but several questions concerning the history of alpine regions remained unanswered. In 1846 Wills visited Chamonix, and was taken on an excursion to the Mer de Glace and the *jardin de Talèfre*, an island situated at about 2700m amidst the séracs of the *glacier de Talèfre* covered in summer with grass and flowers. (Note 2) If it was Professor Forbes' book *Travels Through the Alps of Savoy*, published in 1843 which exercised a strong influence upon the young Alfred Wills, it was his own first mountain journey which aroused his enthusiasm for the pristine wildness, the natural beauty, the wealth of botanical and geological interest in the upper alpine valleys.

In 1850, during his final year as a law student at University College, he visited the alps again. His journeys included visits to Lauterbrunnen, from where he made the first recorded ascent by a visitor to the Schynigeplatte where a hotel, built in 1902 and now approachable by cog-wheel railway, is a popular destination for tourists. He also visited the Val d'Aosta, and Zermatt, then a relatively unimportant village. He was gradually beginning to acquire a knowledge of the magnificent alpine regions where he found himself able to enjoy a sense of freedom in close communion with nature. As an enthusiastic amateur botanist, his writings are liberally sprinkled with descriptions of the richness of the alpine flora, such as his comments on '*leontopodium alpinum* [edelweiss] looking like a king among flowers, growing with remarkable profusion and vigour' on the slopes above Riffelberg. Observations which contrast starkly with those he made thirty-five years later when he wrote in 1885: 'It is a lamentable truth that, so far as some of the loveliest Swiss plants are concerned, their destruction is already an accomplished fact, while the entire flora of the country has undoubtedly undergone a palpable and grievous impoverishment during the last few years.' Among the causes of these sad depredations were the reckless gathering of plants by visitors, and their uprooting by the local population for sale to tourists.

As a young man of twenty-four, launched on his professional career, Wills increased the scope of his alpine wanderings. Accompanied by RC Heath, his holiday during the summer of 1852 included the crossings of four glacier passes. Short excursions were made around Chamonix, culminating in a walk across the foot of the aiguilles from Montenvers to the *glacier des Bossons*. The pair then travelled to Italy, visiting Macugnaga from where they crossed the Monte Moro pass to Saas. Wills was greatly attracted by the grandeur and isolation of the Saas valley, then very little known and rarely visited, regarding it as 'one of the most beautiful in the Alps', and he returned to it on several occasions. He appreciated the unspoilt splendour, the rich flora, and the almost untouched wealth of the larch and pine forests – which even today in certain areas present a luxurious appearance. Until the opening years of the twentieth century there were still in existence healthy larch trees believed to have been six to seven hundred years old, before they were cut down for buildings and roads. Two catastrophic avalanches occurred in the valley in March 1741 and April 1849, damaging several villages and causing serious loss of life; the second disaster is commemorated by a monument which stands in the centre of Saas-Fee. Wills walked up to

Fee – 'the sweetest pastoral valley that ever God created or man enjoyed' and from there to the Feegletscheralp: 'an island amidst a sea of ice [affording] excellent pasturage for the sheep and goats which are driven up ... from the chalets of Fee. ... After skirting the lower branch of the glacier, the track leads over a fatiguing bit of the lateral moraine underneath the foot of the upper branch. I found the two arms of the glacier about fifty or sixty yards apart. The path seemed ... a dangerous one, as the glacier is upon a considerable slope, and great blocks of recently fallen ice strewed the way in many places.' On a visit two years later he remarked that owing to the advance of the glacier the gap between its two arms had narrowed to fifteen or twenty yards. He was probably aware that in 1861, hardly ten years after his first visit, the glacier had advanced almost to the upper chalets of Fee village, when the inhabitants fixed a cross to mark the farthest point reached by the ice.[2] The great shrinkage of alpine glaciers which began in the second half of the nineteenth century has enabled the Längfluh hotel to be built above the Fee glacier on a rock platform at 2870m to which a cable-car transports crowds of skiers, climbers and tourists.

In 1852 Wills met the priest Johann-Joseph Imseng at Saas,[3] 'a notable personage in these parts who knows the mountains better than any man in the valley, and although far on the wrong side of sixty[4] can still walk for four-and-twenty hours at a stretch and make light of the achievement ... he is not deficient either in natural intelligence, or in the learning which belongs to his station and order. He is a good Latin scholar, and can talk Latin with an ease and fluency that would shame many a professed scholar; and he appears to be greatly beloved and respected by the inhabitants of his district'. Imseng's mountain ascents included the Lagginhorn, (first ascent), Fletschhorn, Weissmies and Ulrichshorn. This 'son of a peasant of Saas' who tended sheep and goats on the mountainsides in his youth, opened an *auberge* in Saas around 1836, and later owned a second hotel there, as well as a small inn at Mattmark lake.

---

[2]This was one of the relatively brief periods between 1850-1860 of glacial advance in the Alps, followed by a general retreat which gradually increased in scale over the next fifty years. According to official records, Switzerland's largest glacier the Aletsch currently measuring 23.2 km or 14.5 miles in length, has shrunk during the last 150 years by 3.37 km, 2.1 miles.

[3]Saas here refers to the village known today as Saas Grund.

[4]His appearance may have been deceptive; in 1852 Imseng would have been forty-six years old.

Imseng was a congenial and knowledgeable host who welcomed visitors to the valley, looking after their requirements, and often accompanying them on mountain trips. In 1852 Imseng guided Wills' party across the Allalin pass (3564m), situated between the Allalinhorn and the Rimpfischhorn, making the first direct crossing from Saas to Täsch. Two previous crossings had been made in the opposite direction from Täsch to Mattmark by a German scientist in 1828, and an English botanist in 1835.

After Imseng had guided Wills' group across the pass down to Täsch, he walked down that valley to Stalden and back up the Saas valley, arriving in time to conduct morning mass at his church there. Wills and Heath moved on from Täsch to Zermatt where they spent the night, setting out the following morning to cross the Théodule pass. Reaching the pass on 15 September, they were surprised to find a bronze weather-beaten old man, a grey beard falling over his chest, dwelling there with his wife in a small tent, who offered them bread, cheese, sour wine, and provided a mine of information about the Aosta region. The old man, whose speech and thought were those of an 'educated' person, was a nature-lover and admired, with Wills, the magnificent sunset and sunrise viewed from the pass. A rude structure of loose stones stood alongside; it was the old man's intention to set up a hotel there with four bedrooms. *'Je travaille pour l'humanité'* he said. (My work is intended for the benefit of everyone.) The structure was probably part of the remains of a shelter built for de Saussure who camped there in 1792 with his guides, one of whom was Jean-Pierre Meynet. This self-exiled mountain philosopher, who is thought to have been Meynet's grandson, set out in the winter of 1852-53 to travel on foot to Paris and London in order to collect funds for constructing his hotel; but he met with a tragic end, having been robbed and murdered in the Valtournanche soon after beginning his journey. Over a hundred years were to pass before the realisation of the old man's dream. (Note 3)

At the end of his travels that year Wills crossed the Tschingel pass from Lauterbrunnen to Kandersteg accompanied by two companions and the guides Christian Lauener aged twenty-three, younger brother of Ulrich Lauener the leading local guide, and their father aged about sixty.[5] The crossing involved a journey of fourteen hours, the last part

---

[5]During the next twenty years the former, like his brother Ulrich, gained a high reputation making four first ascents including the south-east face of the Dent Blanche with his English and Swiss clients, and accompanying FF Tuckett to the Engadine and Dolomites.

in stormy weather. Wills and his companions arrived at the Hotel de Helvétie in Frutigen at 7pm in drenched clothes, having walked through heavy rain during the final eight-mile stretch 'to avoid the bad quarters at Kandersteg.' The hotel was full: 'but the landlord not only gave up his own room to us, but supplied us with three complete suits of his own clothes. ... The landlord was very short and fat whereas two of us were spare, and one was six feet in his stockings. ... The task of allotting the various garments was no easy one, and the result beggared all description. ... When washed and dressed, we fell into long peals of laughter at one another; the prelude only to what burst forth – unsuppressible even by French politeness – from the other guests when we entered the *salle à manger*.' About his 1852 holiday Wills wrote: 'We were out nine weeks. We spent no small sum in guides and carriages, and although economical stinted ourselves in nothing. The trip cost us less than £40 each, everything included.' One pound sterling was then worth twenty-five Swiss francs!

Early in 1853 Professor Forbes, who had ceased his alpine travels a decade earlier, invited his guide Auguste Balmat (a great-nephew of Jacques Balmat of Mont Blanc) to England. Forbes suggested to young Wills that he might like to meet Balmat. The meeting which took place in London was the beginning of a close and lasting friendship between Wills and Balmat, greatly increasing the scope and pleasure of his subsequent alpine ventures. Then aged twenty-five, Wills was twenty years younger than Balmat. It was characteristic of him that he dedicated his book, *Wanderings Among the High Alps*, published in 1856: 'To my Guide and Friend Auguste Balmat, my tried and faithful companion ... with feelings of hearty respect and affectionate regard.' Balmat's association had begun in 1842 with Professor Forbes, whose assistant he became during the conduct of glaciological experiments on the Mer de Glace, Balmat himself controlling measurements and other data during Forbes' absences and during winter. Balmat possessed a natural sense of topography and, schooled by other scientists, he had acquired more than a passing knowledge of geology, botany and history. Wills wrote of him: 'Professor Forbes helped largely to make him the priceless treasure he was when I knew him ... a really good guide is a companion of a very different sort [possessing] refinement and intelligence [and] upon whose high character, disinterested kindness, and thorough

knowledge of the High Alps I can now always implicitly rely.' Auguste
Balmat had a modest and kindly nature, and a sense of generosity which
often led him into difficulties: 'If I could but teach you one
monosyllable – "Non!"', Wills often said to him, 'I should render you the
greatest of earthly services'. It was said that in appearance Balmat would
have passed more easily as an academic, or even a diplomat, than as an
alpine guide. Wills was probably the first of the pioneers to establish a
relationship with his guide based on mutual trust and friendship.

Wills' first alpine season with Balmat began in the summer of
1853. At that time the *Compagnie des Guides* founded at Chamonix in
1821, had forty names on its Register and exercised a set of strict bye-
laws enforceable legally, which included a rota system whereby
anyone requiring a guide was obliged to employ the next free name
on the list; character, competence, or previous service with the same
employer did not count, and there was one regulation tariff payable
for skilled or inefficient men. The rules, ostensibly designed to
provide every man with equal employment opportunities, resulted in
a monopolistic system, rewarding the 'gentry who hang about
Chamonix drinking places' without according due recognition to the
really reliable men. A case was known in 1853, when a party of three
wishing to climb Mont Blanc were allotted the regulation number of
six guides, not one of whom had ever climbed the mountain.
Persistent complaints from travellers were ignored, and it was not
until 1892 that the rota system was abandoned. CE Mathews, a
former President of the Alpine Club, wrote in 1898: 'Of the 300 men
now on the Chamonix Roll (of guides) those who could be relied on
in a grave emergency may be counted almost on the fingers of one
hand.' In Alfred Wills' day the bye-laws had one loophole; if a guide
was engaged outside the village limits, and arrived in Chamonix with
his employer by way of a col, the regulations did not apply. Wills was
able to evade the rules in August 1853 by arranging to meet Balmat at
Sallanches, from where they travelled over the Col de Voza to
Chamonix; Zachary Cachat, whom Wills already knew, was engaged
as a second guide. Bad weather limited their activity. After crossing the
Col du Géant from Chamonix to Courmayeur, the party moved to
Saas where Wills once again met the priest Imseng. 'On arriving ...
about seven in the evening we asked for some meat with our suppers.
It was readily promised, but was long in forthcoming; and the *curé* at

length came in with an apology, saying that the man was gone to kill a sheep for us, and we should not be kept waiting much longer ... when the poor beast which had, an hour ago, been bleating on the mountains did come up to table, we did as much justice to the fare as the generally tough nature of the repast would allow.' Imseng came up with the suggestion that they might cross to Zermatt over the Adler pass (3802m), between the Rimpfischhorn and Strahlhorn, which had been crossed only once before, in August 1849, when he had accompanied the Swiss scientist, Professor Gottlieb Studer from Mattmark to Zermatt in a journey which had taken sixteen hours.

The party, which included Alfred Wills' brother, left Saas on an afternoon in late August, spending the night on a bed of hay in a chalet situated at the head of Mattmark lake. Departing at 4.45 the next morning they began the ascent to the pass. 'Balmat, as usual, went grubbing about everywhere for stones, flowers, or anything else he could pick up. He found ... some stone rich in copper ore, some dolomite, some serpentine, and many beautiful wild flowers. No matter how hard the day's work might be, I never knew Balmat's interest to flag ... This made him a profitable companion ... for emulation kept me up to the mark myself. Balmat's knowledge is so considerable on many scientific subjects, and especially in all that relates to the structure and action of the glaciers, that one can seldom be long in his society without learning something ... he is always an instructive and agreeable companion.' Upon reaching the crevassed glacier at the foot of the final ascent to the pass: 'Balmat screwed into my boots four small double-headed pieces of iron ... and the guides did the same with their boots. These implements are a great assistance in ascending or descending banks of hardened snow, or slopes of ice, and are far easier to manage than crampons.' (Note 4) On top of the Adler pass the party discovered, very appropriately, an eagle's feather.[6] The descent on the Zermatt side turned out to be icy, giving the party an adventurous and exciting passage. Imseng seemed to show a preference for rock, and displayed no little skill in avoiding the ice. He 'wears today his oldest coat, a priest's coat, reaching down to his heels, patched in places innumerable, threadbare and so shiny that he might use it for a looking-glass ... it once was velvet; but what with darns, patches and rents, it is impossible to say whether thread, cloth or velvet predominates now'.

[6]*Adler* is the German word for eagle.

The two Chamonix men unanimously voted Imseng a '*véritable diable*' on rock.

In the summer of 1854 Alfred Wills married Lucy Martineau; shortly after their marriage, he took her to the alps where for the next few years she was his constant companion. On their first excursion they camped on the Mer de Glace as Wills had done eight years earlier, in order to visit the *jardin de Talèfre*. Balmat, charged with preparations for the trip, made a careful choice of equipment and provisions to ensure that Mrs Wills' first glacier visit should be comfortable. Later, during a few days' walking in the area around the thermal baths at Leuk, the Torrenthorn was climbed. This ascent, up a rather dull scree and stone slope, remains a popular tourist climb because of the view from its summit of the entire stretch of the Valaisian Alps. 'We stayed three hours at the top, for my wife to sketch ... but an unexpected difficulty occurred; the camel's-hair brush had dropped out of the sketching case and was gone ... In this emergency, I snipped off a bunch of my own hair, and cutting a little splinter of deal from the table, with the help of a piece of silk my wife had in her pocket, manufactured a paint-brush which ... was found sufficient for many a subsequent sketch.' The Gemmi pass was crossed and, travelling via Kandersteg, Interlaken was reached around the middle of September.

Wills admired the Jungfrau from there, meditating on the fact that he 'had crossed many a lofty col ... I had slept on the moraine of a glacier and on the rugged mountainside; but I had never yet scaled any of these snowy peaks'. Because of the relative lateness of the season, the guide Ulrich Lauener deemed the Jungfrau possible only from the Grimsel side, which would involve a lengthy approach. After the Finsteraarhorn had been ruled out for the same reason, Wills suggested the Wetterhorn. Lauener readily agreed, implying that the mountain had not been climbed; a curious claim in view of Lauener's later request for a second guide in the person of Peter Bohren of Grindelwald, who had taken part in recent attempts on the peak, one of which was supposed to have succeeded. Lauener and Bohren might have conspired to persuade Wills that the mountain had not been climbed because guides were then well aware that an employer would be likely to hand out a bonus for a first ascent; or they might have meant to indicate that no ascent from Grindelwald had yet succeeded (despite a previous claim, see below). An incident which might support the guides' story, was the eagerness with which two chamois hunters, both Grindelwald men, seemed to be surreptitiously engaged in an ascent of the mountain ahead of Wills' party. In the event, that did not prove to be the case, and the chamois hunters are likely to have known that previous attempts from Grindelwald were unsuccessful.

The heights of the three peaks forming the Wetterhorn group, and particularly their earliest ascents, had been the subject of controversy. The north-west peak prominent from Grindelwald, now known as the Wetterhorn, was originally known as the Haslejungfrau (3701m), first ascended on 30 August 1844 by two of Edouard Désor's guides, Melchior Bannholzer and Johann Jaun, from Rosenlaui. Another ascent, the first from Grindelwald, was claimed on 7 July 1845 by an Interlaken doctor, Gottfried Roth, with a forester Franz Fankhauser, accompanied by the guides Johann and Peter Bohren and Christian Michel. But their claim was doubted, and their ascent is believed to have ended on the Wettersattel. The second confirmed ascent was made from the Grimsel side on 31 July 1845 by Professor Louis Agassiz, A Vogt and P Bovet, accompanied by M Bannholzer, J Jaun and J Währen. On 13 June 1854, three months before Wills' arrival, an English climber EJ Blackwell made an attempt from Grindelwald, accompanied by Peter Bohren and four other guides. Blackwell reached a point about ten feet below the top, planting a pole there. About two weeks later, starting from Rosenlaui, Blackwell made the third confirmed ascent of the Haslejungfrau accompanied by the same guides. Wills' account of his ascent, includes a reference to 'a flag just like ours planted deep in the ice ... within ten feet of the summit' – providing evidence of the highest point reached by Blackwell in June during a snowstorm. Peter Bohren preferred to remain silent about his earlier climbs from Grindelwald and Rosenlaui. (Note 5) Wills was aware that doubts existed about the heights of the three peaks of the Wetterhorn group, also that some of them may have been climbed from the Grimsel side or Rosenlaui. But he had no reason to doubt Ulrich Lauener's assertion that the (Haslejungfrau) Wetterhorn had not been climbed, and he believed it to be the highest of the group. It is fair to add that the descriptive and moving account which Wills wrote about his climb exercised a powerful influence on young men who were not yet fully aware of the attractions of mountaineering, bringing about a rapid surge in its growth and popularity. It is typical of his fair-mindedness that, despite Ulrich Lauener's swagger and the expense that stemmed from the elaborate preparations which he deemed necessary for the expedition, Wills praised him generously for the success of the climb.

Ulrich Lauener (1821-1900) won a high reputation as a guide; his three younger brothers Christian, Jakob and Johann all adopted the guiding profession. Wills first met him at Interlaken two days prior to his ascent of the Wetterhorn. 'We saw a tall, straight, active, knowing-looking fellow, with a cock's feather stuck jauntily in his high-crowned hat, whom I recognised at once as possessing the true Lauener cut, perched on the railings in front of the hotel, lazily dangling his long legs in the air.' Balmat, on meeting at Interlaken a Chamonix colleague Auguste Simond, persuaded Wills to appoint him as an additional guide. Wills also agreed to Lauener's request for a porter to carry the party's needs for an overnight bivouac, and a fourth guide was engaged on the morning of their departure when Lauener 'called me aside, and begged permission to retain another guide, one Peter Bohren of Grindelwald, who he said had been three times this season to the plateau out of which the peaks of the Wetterhörner spring.' A mutual respect developed between the Chamonix and Lauterbrunnen guides. 'Balmat always called Lauener, *le capitaine,* and a very hearty feeling of regard evidently existed between them. I was a little staggered at the magnitude [of the preparations] and at the serious air of the men, who were far more grave and quiet than is usual on such an occasion; and I heard so much on every side of the difficulties and dangers we were to encounter, that I almost began to fear we were bent on a rash enterprise. ... The Chamonix men who do these things in a more quiet and business-like manner were quite disgusted with the noise and confusion. Balmat said they made his head ache.' At the moment of departure, the landlord wrung Balmat's hand. '"Try", said he, "to return all of you alive."'

Wills' party of six set out from Grindelwald on the afternoon of 16 September 1854. Leaving the last chalets behind, they began to ascend a path overhanging the Upper Grindelwald glacier, and within five hours they reached a hunter's shelter, near the site where the first Gleckstein hut was placed twenty-six years later. 'Our sleeping den consisted of a low arched cave formed by two or three rocks one of which had fallen upon the others so as to make a vaulted roof.' It was a perfect shelter with only one narrow entrance. After a frugal but cheerful supper had been prepared and eaten around a log fire outside in darkness relieved only by the white of the glacier beyond, the party retired for the night inside the cave. But the presence of six persons in a confined area proved too much for Wills. 'I waxed restless and feverish and all chance of sleep deserted me. ... at length I could endure it no longer.' Balmat appears to have been equally affected, and both of them made their escape at 2am. 'How grateful was that fresh air ... the stars were shining as I never saw them before in the soft light of the waning moon, and a bracing air blew briskly.' Before the fire was rekindled for breakfast the next morning, Wills had a wash in the glacier stream. 'It was icy cold, but did me more good than the weary night in the hole.' They set out at 4.30, groping their way up the moraine with a lantern. At about 10 o'clock, halting at the edge of the upper plateau: 'We had been surprised to behold two other figures creeping along the dangerous ridge of rocks we had just passed ... they were dressed in the guise of peasants ... one carried on his back a young fir tree, branches, leaves and all.' While Wills' party were having a second breakfast, the two men were seen again 'on the snow slopes, a good way ahead, making all the haste they could. ... After all our trouble, expense, and preparations, this excited the vehement indignation of my Chamonix guides ... and they at length roused our Swiss companions to an energetic expostulation'. Peace was restored when it became clear that the intruders had no competing ambitions. 'Balmat's anger was soon appeased ... he declared that they were *bons enfants*, and presented them with a cake of chocolate.' The two men fully established their innocence, and became the best of friends. While it is true that three previous ascents had been made of the Wetterhorn from the east – and a fourth had been claimed from Grindelwald – Wills' party was the first to follow the rock-ridge from the Gleckstein, since referred to as the 'Willsgrätli', which led them up to the Wettersattel 200m below the top of the Wetterhorn and separating it from the Mittelhorn which became the standard route up the mountain.

Feelings such as Wills expressed upon reaching the summit of the Wetterhorn in 1854, are less easily admitted now than they were then. 'I am not ashamed to own that I experienced, as this sublime and wonderful prospect burst upon my view, a profound and almost irrepressible emotion ... as in the more immediate presence of Him who had reared this tremendous pinnacle, and beneath the 'majestical roof' of whose deep blue heaven we stood, poised as it seemed half-way between the earth and the sky.' (Note 6) Wills was fascinated by the view. 'We were so high that we could trace the course of pass after pass in several directions from the foot of their ascent to the crest or col to which they led; many of them wound through valleys, both sides of which we could see from top to bottom. I never, from any other point, got so good an idea of the grouping of mountains, and of the manner in which the passes lie amongst them.' His reactions were typical of the impressions created by the breathtaking splendour of the alpine universe viewed from a high peak which only few, at the dawn of the Golden Age, had been privileged to experience.

Wills' four guides cannot escape a charge of faint-heartedness and neglect when, before starting to descend, his proposal that the party should rope up as they had done for the ascent was turned down. 'They told me afterwards, that an accident to any one would, in that case, have involved the destruction of the whole party.' (Note 7) Wills had made the fourth (perhaps the fifth) ascent of the Wetterhorn, the first (perhaps the second) from Grindelwald. He described the climb as 'the greatest and grandest expedition of my life'. Six hours after leaving the summit Wills rejoined his wife, who had walked up the valley to Engi to meet him. On their return to Grindelwald they were greeted by such a triumphal welcome that Wills might be forgiven for believing that they had been the first to climb the highest peak in the group. His concluding comments were: 'The expedition cost me, in the whole, nearly £10. I think it might be done for between £6 and £7.'

Christian Almer, aged twenty-eight, was one of the *bons enfants* who planted his young fir tree beside Lauener's *flagge* on top of the Wetterhorn; his brother-in-law, Ulrich Kaufmann, was the other. The latter was one of the guides, with the brothers Christian and Peter Michel, who accompanied Leslie Stephen on the first ascent of the Schreckhorn in 1861; not to be confused with Ulrich Kaufmann (1846-1917), also of Grindelwald, who with Emil Boss accompanied Reverend WS Green to New Zealand in 1882, and climbed with WW Graham in Garhwal and Sikkim in 1883. Christian Almer went on to become one of the leading guides of the Golden Age; his great qualities were his upright character and calm temperament; he was specially valued for his sound judgement, and resourcefulness. He had several first ascents to his credit, including the Monch and the Eiger; and the first winter ascents of the Wetterhorn, Jungfrau, and Schreckhorn. His successes with Moore, Whymper and Coolidge are related in later chapters. Almer commemorated the thirtieth anniversary of his ascent of the Wetterhorn by conducting one of his sons up the mountain in 1884. In January 1885, after a winter ascent of the Jungfrau with WW Graham, they had a desperate struggle through a storm to arrive at the Bergli hut in darkness; Almer's feet were frostbitten, and he subsequently lost all his toes. He resumed climbing, accompanied by his sons, well-known among whom were Ulrich (1849-1940), and 'young' Christian (1859-1939). One of his later employers remarked upon the aura of confidence that Christian Almer seemed to reflect, which arose from his long experience and his exceptional courage and toughness exceeding that of many younger guides. On 22 June 1896, when he was seventy and his wife Margareta seventy-two, they celebrated their golden wedding by ascending the Wetterhorn, behind two of their younger sons, Hans and Peter, and their eldest daughter; the climb took six hours twenty minutes from the Gleckstein Hut; it was his wife's first ascent of a large snow mountain. Almer made his last ascent of the Wetterhorn in 1897, a year before he died. Charles Pilkington, (a pioneer of guideless climbing two decades earlier with his brother Lawrence and Frederick Gardiner) as President of the Alpine Club, described him as: 'that prince of guides, who for so many years led the fathers of the Alpine Club to victory, and never to disaster, and who, even in his old age, was able to guide their sons and show them how boldness could be allied with discretion, and that determination and experience were two of the greatest factors in mountaineering success.'

During the winter of 1854-55, Wills invited Balmat to England; and in the summer he continued his regular visits to the Alps, climbing Monte Rosa, (probably a second ascent of the Dufourspitze) accompanied by Lauener, and making several other ascents. In 1857 he traversed the Fenêtre de Saleinaz, which had been crossed only once before, in 1850 by Professor Forbes. During Wills' ascent of Mont Blanc with John Tyndall in 1858, described in another chapter, an iron rod was erected at the summit as a lightning-conductor, 'in the hope of seeing what the electricity would do with the bar'. Meeting a friend who had climbed Mont Blanc a few weeks later, Wills enquired whether the iron rod was safe. 'Oh yes' he replied, 'I was determined to leave some memento of my presence and I stuck a glass bottle on the top of it.' An amusing tale. But a portent of the disfigurement of the alpine environment which would begin to proliferate with mass tourism a century later. In 1864 Wills climbed the Grandes Jorasses, and in 1866 he ascended Mont Blanc by the Bosses ridge. He made his last ascent of a major mountain when he climbed Mont Blanc on 30 September 1873, accompanied by his wife and daughter and by the French painter Gabriel Loppé and his daughter.[7]

In August 1857, Wills' association with the alps entered a new phase. After climbing Mont Buet in the Haute Savoie, north-west of Chamonix, an area visited by very few travellers, he descended its south-west slopes and arrived at the Plateau des Fonds situated on an isolated meadow and surrounded by luxurious forests above the village of Sixt. He was immediately attracted by the idea of having a chalet built there. A day or two later he decided to revisit the spot, and the initial 'passing thought ... began to assume the character of a definite wish'. Strong opposition by the village council to the sale of the land to a foreigner did nothing to weaken Wills' resolve. One of the principal objectors was the *curé* who refused to accept that the property was intended to serve as a place for summer recreation, suspecting that a vein of gold ore had been discovered, and that the surrounding forests would be turned into fuel for smelting furnaces.[8] When the matter came up for a final decision, seven out of the fourteen councillors present voted in favour of the sale, and seven against. It was the Mayor's casting vote as chairman which carried the day. The initial price of the land was eight pounds per acre, and the overall cost worked out at twenty pounds. In August 1858, when Wills and his wife Lucy went to take possession of the property, they

---

[7]Gabriel Loppé, 1825-1913, who dwelt in Chamonix was a pupil of Alexandre Calame (see Chapter 1, page 5). He acquired fame for his wide range of paintings, emphasising the beauty of Mont Blanc and the valley of the Arve. He became a close friend of Alfred Wills and Leslie Stephen, and was married to a sister of the active British climber James Eccles. In 1865 he was elected to honorary membership of the Alpine Club London. The Alpine Museum in Chamonix used to hold a number of his paintings, of which about half were destroyed by a fire in 1999.

[8]It was in an isolated region above the Glacier des Fonds that Jacques Balmat of Mont Blanc disappeared in 1834 or, as some said, was murdered while reportedly searching for deposits of gold.

received an unexpected welcome from a deputation representing the village of Sixt who, in the friendliest spirit, assured them of their full support and co-operation. On 29 September Lucy and Alfred Wills drove pegs into the ground to mark the area of the property. The only architect in the construction of the chalet was Lucy Wills, who sketched the plans and prepared the scale drawings. Balmat laid out a winding path to the chalet from the Giffre stream below the forest surrounding the property. During Wills' enforced absence of almost two years, he appointed Balmat to take sole charge of the construction of the chalet which provided a welcome source of employment for the people of the valley. In April 1860 Wills' father died; and barely a month later Wills was heartbroken by the death of his wife Lucy. He dwelt at his Surrey home at the age of thirty-one with his two small children, Edith and Jack, helped for a time by his sister Mary. The chalet which Lucy had designed, but which she was never to see, was completed later; Alfred Wills dedicated his book, *The Eagle's Nest in the valley of Sixt: a summer home among the Alps,* to her memory.

The chalet enjoyed a long and interesting history. A large house, with polished wooden ceilings and floors and a magnificent carved wooden staircase, it included a dining room, drawing room and large kitchen and boiler room downstairs, with two upper floors filled with bedrooms, and a bathroom with running hot and cold water. It became a captivating summer residence for Wills, his large family, and numerous friends. In 1862 Wills married Bertha Taylor, and there were altogether seven children and numerous grandchildren. Wills possessed a genius for friendship, and the Eagle's Nest with the whole surrounding area became a familiar playground for young and old. Bertha Wills presided over the overflowing hospitalities with a kindness and attention that created lasting memories among those who had the privilege of sharing in them. It was not uncommon for the main building, with an annexe added later, to lodge about two dozen people during the height of summer. Excellent relations existed between the family and the inhabitants of the valley.

Wills' eldest son, John Tayler Wills (1858-1922), was a keen mountaineer. At thirteen he climbed the highest peak of the Dents du Midi in a day from Champéry. Accompanied by his younger brother, William Alfred Wills (1862-1924), he climbed most of the classic Alpine routes, and made a few excellent guided ascents with Thomas

Stuart Kennedy. He guided the family's guests on climbs of all grades surrounding the chalet, about which he used to remark facetiously, 'the footholds are good enough to step on, but not to stand on'. It was at the Eagle's Nest that he gave his nephew, Wills' grandson Edward Felix Norton, his first lessons in mountaincraft. He joined the Alpine Club as did his brother, the latter serving as Honorary Secretary from 1897-1900. Wills' daughter, Frances, and both her sons, Jerome and John, also inherited the family's mountaineering interests.

After an illness lasting six weeks, Balmat died in 1862 at the age of fifty-four, 'before one trace of old age could be detected or one physical or mental power had begun to fail'. Wills devoted much time to nursing him at the Eagle's Nest. His affliction, brought on by severe mental depression, was referred to as 'softening of the brain', but was more likely to have been the result of a broken spirit. Of a sensitive and remorseful character he was a model of honesty and generosity, never taking any interest in personal gain. He had been imposed upon by unscrupulous contractors connected with the construction of the chalet, resulting in a serious misappropriation of money, for which he held himself personally responsible.

Suffering from ill-health in 1871, Wills spent five months in the spring and summer of 1872 convalescing at the Eagle's Nest accompanied by his daughter Edith, aged sixteen. He had begun to reduce his mountain expeditions, deriving greater satisfaction from exploring the region around his chalet, and he obtained a good deal of pleasure from devising pathways through the forests, entertaining friends, and conducting parties up newly discovered climbs. With his interest in geology, he was fascinated by the marine fossils which he found in the vicinity of the Col d'Anterne, accumulating a collection which he donated later to the British Museum.

In 1902 Wills spent his final summer at the Eagle's Nest, gifting the property to his daughter Edith, Mrs Edward Norton, in 1904. (Note 8) She spent fifty-five summers at the chalet with her family, and died there in August 1936, aged eighty-one; her grave lies in a corner of the churchyard at Sixt. The Eagle's Nest was sold in 1958, ending the family's long association with the area which had extended for almost a century. It is occupied every summer by its present French owners. In 1995 I noticed framed portraits of Lucy Wills who designed the building, and Edith Norton who inherited it, still attached to a wall below the staircase. Some distance above, situated at 1200m on the main route to the Col d'Anterne, is the Refuge Alfred Wills, a convenient halting place for walkers on the way to and from Chamonix. The track passes below the Rochers des Fys whose towering cliffs had profoundly impressed John Ruskin (see AF Mummery chapter heading). The col, overlooking Chamonix and Mont Blanc, is a spectacular viewpoint. At the *Maison de la Reserve,* the local museum in Sixt, an interesting panel of photographs can be seen relating to the Eagle's Nest, and to Sir Alfred Wills and his family. Nothing indicates more vividly the remoteness of that age than the faded photograph of six stalwart men carrying a piano up a forest track to the chalet at the Plateau des Fonds.

Three years before his retirement in 1905, Wills ceased to visit the alps. His life had spanned a significant period of alpine history. In 1828, alpine climbing was in its infancy; by the turn of the century the pioneering days were over, and difficult new routes were being ascended without guides. If Wills' ascent of the Wetterhorn in 1854 was said to mark the opening of the Alpine Golden Age, his life also spanned the opening of a new mountaineering era. A genuine lover of the wildness and isolation of mountain country, the magnificent alpine flora and fauna provided him with added delight. His book *Wanderings Among the High Alps* was published in 1856, the same year in which Charles Hudson and Edward Shirley Kennedy's *Where there's a Will there's a Way* appeared. Both books, together with *Summer Months Among the Alps* by Thomas Hinchcliff published in 1857, were among the earliest to be devoted exclusively to alpine travel and mountaineering. Wills' book reflected a different outlook from the other two, describing several of his early alpine ventures between 1852 and 1854, and a second edition with additions came out in 1858. Apart from the last chapter, which contains a description of the Wetterhorn ascent, there are wide-ranging accounts of mountain travel, illustrated on a broad canvas and covering every aspect of his journeys which came within range of his careful observation. Wills' style is neither lyrical nor literary but forthright and practical, depicting the country and the people with candour and enthusiasm. To his observations on flowers, birds and butterflies, he adds frequent human touches. 'I was occupying a few spare moments ... in the arrangement of my collection of wild flowers among the pages of my book when the woman of the inn, after expressing considerable admiration, went out, and brought me several large dahlias ... some camomile, fennel, and other garden herbs. In order to avoid giving her bitter disappointment, I was obliged to carry them with me, till I got out of sight of the house.' *Wanderings Among the High Alps* is essentially a faithful record of early alpine travel, written by a sensitive observer who, driven by no scientific or professional motives, obtained complete satisfaction from his wanderings whether exploring new country, crossing a high pass, or ascending a mountain. It is not surprising that opinions expressed about the book, barely thirty years after its first appearance, referred to its 'rare' and 'refreshing' qualities, which seemed to categorise it as belonging to an age that had passed.

When Wills first visited the Saas valley in 1852, he found it neglected by travellers, and regarded its isolation as one of its chief attractions. Following his third visit in 1854 he remarked: 'These valleys ... are becoming so much more visited than they were a few years ago, that I have little doubt that, before long, all ... discomforts will have been remedied. Already, at Zermatt, you may live almost as well as at Chamonix; and I have been told that, last year, there was little to complain of at Saas.' Today, the bustling town of Saas Fee vies in importance as a tourist centre with Zermatt, Grindelwald and Chamonix. The basic element of change has been the shift in emphasis between the respective attractions of winter and summer. Lord Schuster, writing in the 1930s, named two inter-related factors responsible for the great changes, namely the introduction of skiing, and a difference in outlook by tourists emerging from an increase in private wealth. Those perceptions have advanced by leaps and bounds with the present proliferation of mechanical facilities, transforming the character of the environment[9]. In the spring of 1894 Arthur Conan Doyle, who used skis to travel across the Maienfelder Furka pass (2442m) from Davos to Arosa, described his journey in the *Strand Magazine*. 'Granted that a man has perseverance and a month to spare ... he will then find that ski-ing opens up a sport for him which I think is unique. This is not appreciated yet, but I am convinced that the time will

---

[9] Tourism remains as important to the Swiss economy as ever, with annual earnings of about nine billion US dollars, directly employing 170,000 persons and contributing over five per cent to the gross national product of the country. Present visitors hail mainly from Europe, and there are signs that future growth is likely to come from Japan and China.

come when hundreds of Englishmen will come to Switzerland for the ski-ing season in March and April. I believe that I may claim to be the first, save only two Switzers, to do any mountain work ... on snow shoes [sic] but I am certain that I will not by many a thousand be the last.'[10]

Glimpses of a bygone age can be found inside the Saas Fee Museum, which contains interesting relics of the previous two or three centuries, housed in a well-preserved wooden chalet of the period. Not far from the Museum stands a prominent statue of Johann Imseng, '*Pfarrer* [priest] and alpine guide'. Wills records that Imseng was: 'greatly beloved and respected by the inhabitants of his district, ... [who] loves the mountains most passionately; but not so exclusively as to overlook even the little flowers of the Alps. ... whenever he is mentioned [amongst his people] *c'est un brave homme*, escapes from the lips of one or another.' Imseng hosted visitors at the Hotel du Mont Rose, one of only two establishments then available to travellers in the Saas valley, and guided parties on climbs around the area. A man of vitality and courage, he met with a mysterious and tragic end at the age of sixty-three when he was apparently killed, and his body thrown into Mattmark lake. Several legends have grown around his death. It was thought that Imseng had aroused resentment among the professional guides of the valley by his increasing services to tourists. A judicial enquiry after his death ended inconclusively owing to lack of evidence. Rumours linked the name of Alexander Burgener (then aged twenty-three at the start of his guiding career) and his companion, both chamois hunters, with Imseng's murder, because of his supposed disclosure of their unauthorised hunting activities. Burgener, who stated on oath that he was not guilty, is reported to have said that if he were guilty he would meet his own death in the mountains.[11]

During the Little Ice Age, the Allalin glacier spread its broad tongue across the width of the Saas valley, damming the upper streams and giving rise to the Mattmark lake. After over a century of shrinkage the glacier finally receded above the valley floor in 1950, and now

---

[10]In 1895 Conan Doyle was chiefly behind the organising of what was probably the first 'Ski Race' in Switzerland, when a group of predominantly English competitors were given 'judicious handicaps' and participated in a race which took place on the slopes of Clavadel south of Davos.

[11]He did so forty-one years later, when an avalanche below the Bergli hut swept him and one of his sons to their deaths.

terminates high above, revealing the steepness of its former rocky bed and lateral moraines. The construction of a rock-and-boulder dam almost one kilometre long has created a water reservoir of greater size and depth than the original lake, submerging the ancient Mattmark hotel and the famous Blue Stone, which John Tyndall referred to as 'two magnificent boulders of green surpentine'. Work on the dam, which began in 1951, was not completed until 1969. On 30 August 1965 during a catastrophic avalanche, the most disastrous in alpine history, three million cubic metres of ice from the protruding tongue of the glacier fell in thirty seconds filling the valley floor with compacted blocks up to ten metres deep, killing eighty-eight site-workers. Thirty-five years later there was a fresh collapse of ice from the glacier poised high above. An automatic warning system set up by the Swiss Glacier Commission enabled advance precautions to be taken, which helped to avert a calamity when, between 30-31 July 2000, one million cubic metres of ice comprising almost the whole of the visible tongue of the glacier crashed into the valley without loss of human life.

Wills' account in *Wanderings Among the High Alps* of his fifteen-hour crossing in September 1852 of the Allalin pass from Saas to Täsch provides a vivid picture of the atmosphere of those far-off days. In appreciation of Johann Imseng's guiding services during that expedition, Wills presented him the following year with a silver snuff-box inscribed: '*per nives sempiternas et rupes tremendas*' (Across mighty rocks and eternal snows).

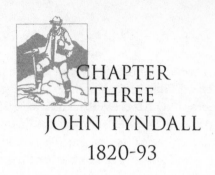

CHAPTER THREE
JOHN TYNDALL
1820-93

Happy the traveller who ... established in some mountain shelter with his books, starts on his first day's walk among the alps in the tranquil morning of a long July day, brushing the early dew before him and, armed with his staff, makes for the hill-top – begirt with ice or rock as the case may be – whence he sees the field of his summer campaign spread out before him, its wonders, its beauties, and its difficulties, to be explained, to be admired, and to be overcome.

James David Forbes, 1842

Among the earliest British mountaineers in the Alps were John Ball, Edward Shirley Kennedy, members of the Mathews family, and Thomas Hinchcliff. John Ruskin was an ardent alpine traveller, who glorified rather than climbed mountains, expressing his belief that scientists and climbers by ascending the peaks desecrated them. Professor James David Forbes, born in 1809, was the son of a banker, Sir William Forbes, seventh Baronet of Pitsligo, and of his wife Williamina Belsches (Sir Walter Scott's first love). To satisfy his father's wishes he began to study law at Edinburgh but expressed preference for a scientific career, in which he began to take courses. Attracted to mountains as providing a wonderful field for scientific research, he first visited Switzerland in 1826. Between 1832-44 he travelled extensively through every alpine district between Provence and Tirol not as a climber but as a pioneer explorer and glaciologist. His visits to remote alpine regions involved crossings of numerous glacier passes including the Oberaarjoch and the Col du Sellar in 1841; the Col du Géant, Col d'Hérens, Col de Collon, and the Théodule pass in 1842; he made the first crossing of the Fenêtre de Saleinaz in 1850; and was probably the first British traveller to visit the little-known hamlet of La Bérarde in the Dauphiné Alps. His mountain ascents included the Jungfrau (4158m) in 1841, the Stockhorn (3595m) in 1842, and the Wäsenhorn (3245m) in 1844. He was one of the most distinguished scientists of his day, elected to Fellowship of the Royal Society at the age of twenty-three, and appointed, a year later, to the Chair of Natural Philosophy, as science was then called, at Edinburgh University, a post which he held until 1859 when he resigned in order to accept an appointment as Principal of United College, St Andrews University. In 1868 he was offered the Presidency of the Royal Society of Edinburgh, an honour which he was obliged to decline owing to a deterioration in his health. Forbes' alpine explorations formed a link between the scientific investigations of H-B de Saussure whose work he much admired, and the mountain climbers of the Golden Age, for many of whom his writings had been an inspiration. In 1841, Forbes was invited to visit a research camp set up on the Unteraar glacier by Professor Louis Agassiz of Neuchâtel. In 1842 he pioneered a systematic study of glaciers, and carried out detailed observations on the Mer de Glace. His book *Travels Through the Alps of Savoy*, published in 1843, became an important reference work as much for men of science as for mountaineers. In 1859 the newly formed Alpine Club in London made Forbes its first honorary member. (Note 1)

Tyndall occupied an important place, as a scientist and mountaineer, in the history of the period that succeeded Forbes. It was scientific enquiry that originally drew him, as it had drawn Forbes, to the alps. The valleys, glaciers and peaks contained a vast reservoir of concealed knowledge which had been barely touched, studies so far having given rise to conflicting theories about their origin and structure. Tyndall's alpine travels did not begin until 1856, and continued for the next fifteen years enabling him to carry out investigations from which he developed his theories that erosion was one of the principal factors whereby the mountains were sculpted, and glacier action the main agent in the excavation of the valleys. In his activities and writings a gradual shift is discernible between his scientific and mountaineering interests. But never quite. While fellow mountaineers wrote extravagantly of the striking prospect from a mountain top, and of the beauty of the sky at dawn or sunset seen from a high ridge, Tyndall the scientist, deeply moved by Nature's magnificence, felt impelled to define the colours, analyse the cloud formations, explain the cause and effect of their patterns, and induce reasons for the phenomena of glacier motion and the composition of ice and rock. Yet in 1862 he wrote: 'You ... know how light a value I set on my scientific labours in the alps. Indeed, I need them not. The glaciers and the mountains have an interest for me beyond their scientific ones. They have been to me well-springs of life and joy. They have given me royal pictures and memories which can never fade. They have made me feel in all my fibres the blessedness of perfect manhood, causing mind and soul and body to work together with a harmony and strength unqualified by infirmity or *ennui* ... This has been the bounty of the Alps to me. And it is sufficient. ' Although he was a scientist first and foremost, Tyndall was also a mountain-lover, demonstrating courage and daring in his mountaineering ventures, an activity in which he began to indulge for its own sake.

Forbes and Tyndall were involved in a bitter controversy, disagreeing over the composition and motion of glaciers. On the Mer de Glace in 1842, Forbes recorded daily, even hourly, changes in the motion of the ice enabling him to determine facts that we now take for granted, showing that glacier movements resemble those of a river, being faster in the centre than at the sides; and are continuous, although slower, in winter. He provided proof of the plasticity of glacier ice, affirming that a glacier is a viscous body, urged down its bed by pressure – views that were not generally accepted at the time. Tyndall, among others, believed in the rigid composition and sliding motion of glaciers. A further point of controversy which damaged relations between the two professors concerned Tyndall's insistence on emphasising that the conclusions reached by Forbes were not original, having been proposed in a scientific paper published in France in 1840 by a Savoyard priest Louis Rendu, later Bishop of Annecy. On the latter point, Tyndall chose to ignore the fact that Rendu's observations were of a general character, included among other possible theories, none of which, Rendu admitted, had been proved; while Forbes' conclusions resulted from careful field observations to which accepted scientific principles had been applied. Forbes had a meeting with Bishop Rendu at Annecy in 1846. In a letter to his wife he wrote: 'Nothing could be more gratifying than my reception, or more pleasing and engaging than the Bishop himself. He was so cordial, so unselfish as to his own claims on the plasticity theory, so much interested in my present undertaking, that I was quite delighted with him.' (Note 2) In 1873, five years after Forbes' death, Tyndall wrote: 'The more (Forbes) labours are compared with those of other observers, the more prominently does his intellectual magnitude come forward ... the book of Professor Forbes is the best book that has been written on the subject; the qualities of mind, and the scientific culture invested in that excellent work are such as to make it ... outweigh all other books upon the subject taken together. ' (Note 3)

It can be fairly said that Tyndall rose to fame from the humblest beginnings through ability and determination. Speaking at a dinner given in his honour in the closing years of his scientific career he said: 'I have climbed some difficult mountains in my time ... but ... the hardest climb by far that I have accomplished was from the banks of the Barrow to the banks of the Thames, from the modest Irish roof under which I was born to ... [these] Rooms. Here I have reached my mountain top.' Tyndall's grandfather was William Tyndall, a descendant of William Tyndale of Gloucestershire who had crossed to Ireland during the seventeenth century and settled at Leighlin Bridge in Co Carlow. His father, John Tyndall, a member of the Royal Irish Constabulary, a man possessing an open and independent character, married Sara McAssey, a farmer's daughter, who was a devout and gentle mother to their five children. Both parents set a high value on providing within their limited means the best education for their children. Their son John, born on 2 August 1820, inherited many of his parents' qualities, which exercised a strong influence on him during his boyhood and youth. Between the ages of sixteen and eighteen, he attended the National School at Ballinabranagh four miles from his home, where he showed above average skills for solving problems in algebra, geometry and trigonometry. At the same time he was strongly attracted by the study of English grammar, 'a discipline of the highest value, and a source of unflagging delight'. Although Tyndall became a successful lecturer during his professional career his literary work, while never lacking clarity, tended towards heaviness. Dedication rather than humour marked his style, as it seemed to mark his character.

At the age of twenty, Tyndall began work with the Ordnance Survey in Co Cork on a salary of £1 per week, half of which he paid out for his board and lodging. He learnt to handle a theodolite and lay a chain in the traditional manner of pioneer surveyors. His chief was Lieutenant (later General) George Wynne, with whom he maintained a close friendship for over forty-five years. Employed in remote areas on rough and lonely survey work which he apparently enjoyed, he wrote to his father: 'I'm nearly as strong as an ox, every nerve has its proper tone; and every sinew is braced.' His father, a man of some intellectual capacity himself, believed strongly in his son's ability, writing to him: 'The only thing that prevented you from going through the degrees of college was my poverty.' The support and sympathy provided by his father were a source of strength to Tyndall in his efforts at self-education, and in his fight to overcome the difficulties that lay ahead of him during the depressing years of famine, poverty, and unemployment in Ireland which began in the 1820s and continued for over two decades. In 1842, attracted by the major surge of railway expansion taking place in England, Tyndall moved there, and was able to obtain work as a draughtsman with the Ordnance Survey in Preston.[1] The following year he was dismissed with eighteen others who had appealed for improvements in their deplorable working conditions. With unbounded confidence he attempted to calm the alarm which this gave to his father writing, 'Let not my dismissal trouble you or my mother; the situation was a paltry one. My salary ... was little better than £50 per year.' At that age, Tyndall was described as 'a gallant youth with a burning zeal against injustice and oppression'. Still without work two months later despite strenuous efforts, and with only twenty-five shillings in his pocket, he went home to Leighlin where he pursued his studies in mathematics and French. He returned to England in 1844, when with his mathematical training and surveying experience he was able to obtain a post with an engineering company in Manchester on a salary of three guineas a week. Working variously in field and office, often almost ten hours a day, on the Chester-Stockport and West Yorkshire railway expansions, he began to draw heavily on his nervous and physical energy. In 1846 Tyndall returned to Ireland for a brief holiday but, finding his father grievously ill, he spent most of the period nursing him. When his father died a few months later he

---

[1] In 1841 Britain had 1600 miles of railway track, which ten years later had grown to 6890 miles.

wrote from England, 'one of the strongest links between me and life is broken'.

This harsh spell of his early manhood in the mid and late 1840s, with poverty and distress in England, and the potato famine raging in Ireland, could well have been the origin of Tyndall's seeming austerity of outlook in later life. His difficulties began to ease when he took up an appointment in August 1847 as a lecturer at Queenwood, a college founded in Hampshire in 1841. While instructing juniors and youths in classroom and field in mathematics and surveying, Tyndall simultaneously pursued a course of study in chemistry. On the staff of the same college was Edward Frankland, a fellow scientist. Tyndall resigned his teaching post after a year and, supported largely by his savings, he decided to study for a degree in Germany. Frankland joined him with the same object. Starting at Marburg University in October 1848, Tyndall accomplished in two years a three-year course in mathematics, physics and chemistry, in a language with which he was then imperfectly acquainted. He lodged on the top floor of a house in two rooms, one a study the other a bedroom. Frankland wrote of him: 'At Marburg he was, as a student at the age of 29, a very conspicuous figure; the most juvenile of undergraduates in his leisure moments, but at the same time extremely industrious, genial, good-tempered and unconventional.' After passing his examinations in September 1849, Tyndall took a short holiday in Switzerland. His first impressions appear to have been mixed. He enjoyed the sunset view from the Rigi, but disliked the crowds; after visiting the Rhône glacier, then one of the largest in the country, he lost his way between the Furka and Grimsel passes. 'My remarks on this scramble would make a climber smile possibly with contempt for the man who could refer to such a thing as difficult. The language of my journal, however, is, "By the Lord, I should not like to repeat this ascent."' He climbed to the Kleine Scheidegg and watched avalanches falling from the Jungfrau. It was a Spartan journey, travelling on foot from Basel to Zürich on the way in, and from Bern to Basel on the way out. 'Trusting to my legs and stick ... eating bread and milk, and sleeping when possible in the country villages where nobody could detect my accent, I got through amazingly cheap.' Returning to Marburg, he worked on his thesis, and was awarded a PhD in 1850. When leaving Marburg, he noted courageously in his journal: 'I am a poor man, but

I have no fear of poverty. If I return with a lighter purse, I return with a clearer head and a stronger heart. I feel no anxiety about the future.'

In 1851, Tyndall resumed his post as a lecturer at Queenwood. A year later, he was elected to Fellowship of the Royal Society. Following an immensely successful lecture which he delivered to the Royal Institution in February 1853 on the principles of magnetism, he was appointed in September of that year Professor of Natural Philosophy at the Institution. During his thirty-four-year career with the Royal Institution he was responsible for a very wide range of experimental work.[2] He worked with Michael Faraday, then Superintendent and thirty years his senior in age, whom he regarded as his 'great Exemplar'. They worked side by side for over fourteen years in harmony, their ideas rarely differing, except on religious matters. In a letter to Faraday in 1861 Tyndall wrote: 'the fact of your being here was my chief motive in coming to this place, and it has continued to be my chief privilege ever since.' On Faraday's death in 1867, Tyndall was appointed to succeed him as Superintendent, a position which he held until his retirement in 1887. It was a period of brilliant pioneering work in a variety of scientific fields. When William Gladstone met Faraday he asked him whether his work on electricity would be of any use. 'Yes, sir' responded Faraday with prescience, 'One day you will tax it'.

Tyndall's fame as a man of science rests on his contribution to studies in physics and biology: principally on an important series of experiments connected with his discovery of the transmission of radiant heat through gaseous bodies; also in the fields of light, sound, electricity and magnetism; and on the cleavage of rocks. His investigations into living organisms floating in the air, proceeded in parallel with the work of Pasteur and Lister on bacteriology; and he carried out trials on the use of discontinuous heating as a sterilisation technique. It should be remembered that it was a time when events now in the past were still in the future. Tyndall, and the Victorian giants of over 125 years ago, were pioneers probing scientific secrets that are now common knowledge and taken for granted. Science moves on, delving ever more deeply into uncovered knowledge about the universe. Even now, with outer planetary systems still unexplored, fresh scientific evidence could reveal hitherto unknown matters

[2]Founded in 1799, the RI remains one of the leading scientific societies in Britain.

relating to the origins and foundations of the earth's mountains and glaciers. One wonders how Tyndall and his contemporaries would have viewed current scientific developments, such as the adoption of therapeutic systems which suppress one physical affliction while generating another; and exploration into genetic fields which involve questions about the very meaning and purpose of human existence.

Tyndall refused to acknowledge anything that could not be proved by experiment. 'We deal with physical laws ... but when we ... pass from the region of physics to that of thought we meet a problem beyond our present powers ... the real mystery of existence still looms around us.' As a scientist, occupied with experimental physics and the origins of matter, Tyndall was unable to accept the Biblical concept of the Creation. He was not irreligious; but, like Leslie Stephen, he was agnostic. In his view there was a boundary where science ended and speculation began. 'Let us lower our heads and acknowledge our ignorance, priest and philosopher, one and all.' He was not one to withhold his opinions, his outspokenness sometimes causing offence. Unlike other eminent scientists, including Faraday and Forbes, who believed that no man could apply reasoning or science in order to find out God, Tyndall felt unable to accept traditional religious doctrines. He and Thomas Henry Huxley were prominent as early movers of agnosticism, which they regarded as the method of following the intellect fearlessly, and of not pretending that conclusions were certain which were not demonstrable. Tyndall's skill in illustrating principles established in the laboratory, combined with a gift for clarity of expression, won him renown as a lecturer. Tyndall, and his friend Huxley: 'as exponents of science ... were unrivalled. When they lectured at the Royal Institution, the theatre was unable to hold all who wished to come. In style they were very different. Huxley convinced his audience and compelled their assent. Tyndall carried them with him. They could not help agreeing with Huxley, even if they did not wish to do so; they wished to agree with Tyndall, if they could. ... Tyndall's outspoken utterances contrasted with Huxley's [supposed] reticence ... and a somewhat uncharitable illustration of Huxley's wisdom and Tyndall's recklessness [was] the simple fact that while Professor Tyndall most incautiously entered the crater of Vesuvius during an eruption, Professor Huxley, on the contrary, took a seat on the London School Board!' (Note 4) Tyndall's style had the power of attracting a general audience, so that people who knew little about his subject felt interested, and came away having assimilated food for thought. In later years, his wife gave an amusing picture of his preparations for a lecture on rainbows, in which he referred to the 'white mist bow which every man can see for himself on a sunny morning when the dew is heavy on the grass. ... John spent most of the day clothed in a large waterproof, his head enveloped in a south-wester, standing in the midst of showers of water, paraffin, turpentine, petroleum, until the whole place reeked of smells, producing rainbows of surpassing glory which have never before been seen by the human eye.'

Among his friends, Tyndall's company was never less than stimulating. Later in life, recognised as an eminent scientist, he was also a social success. He had a leaning towards scientific controversy, and when roused by a principle he stood resolute. He held courageously to his views, and was sensitive to criticism. His persistence in an adopted cause was sometimes misguided, and led him into three public controversies, none of which related in any way to his own advancement – sometimes to his disadvantage – but in defence of one whom he believed had suffered some injustice. Besides his admiration for, and friendship with, leading literary figures, particularly Alfred Tennyson, and Thomas Carlyle (whose monument on the Thames Embankment he unveiled in 1882 after Carlyle's death), Tyndall's close personal and scientific friends were Michael Faraday, Thomas Henry Huxley, Sir Joseph Hooker, Sir John Lubbock and Charles Darwin. His lifelong friend was Thomas Archer Hirst, whom he met in 1846 as a young apprentice working on the railways in Halifax. Hirst, a Fellow and Medallist of the Royal Society, became Director of Studies at the Royal Naval College Greenwich in 1873, and ten years later was appointed Principal. He was a man of high principles, perceptive, gifted and intelligent. He did not hesitate to censure his friend when the opportunity demanded. He was the only person able to do so, Tyndall invariably accepting his criticism in good spirit: [you have] 'held up a glass before me, which revealed myself to myself in a manner in which I had not appeared to myself previously ... I have no doubt that your observations are perfectly correct.' It was to Hirst that the Preface to his book *Hours of exercise in the Alps* was inscribed in May 1871. 'The name of a friend whom I taught in his boyhood to handle a theodolite and lay a chain, and who afterwards turned his knowledge to account on the glaciers of the Alps, occurs frequently in the following pages. Of the firmness of a friendship, uninterrupted for an hour, and only strengthened by the weathering of six-and-twenty years, he needs no assurance. 'Hirst predeceased Tyndall by one year, their friendship having endured for over forty-five years.

In 1856, at the age of thirty-six, Tyndall set out on his second visit to Switzerland, from which sprang his subsequent interest in mountaineering. A spare frame disguised his physical toughness and strength. His stamina and powers of endurance enabled him to carry out long expeditions subsisting on little in the way of physical nourishment. Given his limited climbing experience some of his mountaineering achievements testify to an exceptional degree of determination. Huxley, a professor who shared Tyndall's eagerness to investigate a number of theories relating to the origins of the Alps, joined him on his 1856 journey. They visited the Guggi, Grindelwald, Unteraar and Rhône glaciers; and Tyndall later travelled to Austria, where he attended a scientific convention in Vienna and visited a small glacier above the Gepatsch alp. The investigations resulting from these travels opened up for Tyndall a decade and a half of alpine exploration and climbing. An explanation for his motives, expressed in ponderous language, leaves no doubt about his genuine love of mountains. 'I have returned to [the alps] every year, and found among them refuge and recovery from work and the worry – which acts with far deadlier corrosion on the brain than real work – of London. Herein consisted the fascination of the Alps for me; they appealed at once to thought and feeling, offering their problems to one and their grandeur to the other, while conferring on the body the soundness and purity necessary to the healthful exercise of both.' In 1857, based at Montenvers, Tyndall spent six weeks studying the Mer de Glace and its tributary glaciers. Accompanied by a boy, Edouard Balmat, he rashly undertook an excursion to the Col du Géant, having no knowledge of the route, unequipped with rope, and miraculously escaping from an avalanche and a fall into a crevasse. 'Once or twice, while standing on the summit of a peak of ice, and looking at the pits and chasms beneath me, ... I experienced an incipient flush of terror.' His companion expressed himself in plainer language, '*N'avez-vous pas peur?*' (Aren't you frightened?) Tyndall was joined at various times by Huxley and Hirst. Later, Tyndall and Hirst, with the guide Edouard Simond, climbed

Mont Blanc. Deep snow slowed and exhausted the party, and seventeen hours were required for the round trip from the Grands Mulets. At one stage during the ascent of an ice slope, when their guide showed signs of fatigue, Tyndall took over the work. 'I hewed sixty steps upon this slope, and each step had cost a minute ... I always calculated that the *will* would serve me even should the muscles fail, but I now found that mechanical laws rule man in the long run; that no effort of will ... can draw beyond a certain limit... The soul, it is true, can stir the body to action, but its function is to excite and apply force, and not to create it.' This was Tyndall's first major mountain climb. He had demonstrated a fearless determination, and a neglect of precautions against natural forces which he had not yet learned to control.

In 1858, after crossing the Strahlegg pass from Grindelwald to Grimsel, Tyndall climbed the Finsteraarhorn, 'spurred by a desire to make observations from its summit'. He was accompanied by the guide Johann-Joseph Bennen, based at the Eggishorn hotel, whom he later employed regularly. Bennen, probably uncertain of Tyndall's capacity, demurred at first, implying the need for a second guide, and requesting a porter to carry the provisions required for a night at the Faulberg cave near the present site of the Concordia Hut. A porter was engaged, but not a second guide; Tyndall carried his boiling-water apparatus and telescope on his own back. The night's bivouac by the glacier stirred Tyndall's imagination. 'Surely, if beauty be an object of worship, those glorious mountains, with rounded shoulders of the purest white – snow-crested and star-gemmed – were well calculated to excite sentiments of adoration.' During the ascent of the peak, [Bennen] 'strong as he was sometimes paused, laid his head upon his mattock, and panted like a chased deer. He complained of fearful thirst, and to quench it we had only my bottle of tea: this we shared loyally, my guide praising its virtues, as well he might.' The summit was reached without incident, and without the use of a rope; not a bad achievement for a man who had previously ascended little more than the ordinary route up Mont Blanc. Tyndall placed a thermometer near the highest point of the Finsteraarhorn, hoping to record the low winter temperatures.[3] Prior to commencing their descent Bennen asked

[3]One year later, accompanying four English climbers to the summit, Bennen found Tyndall's thermometer. Swinging it round in triumph, he is likely to have disturbed the position of the index, and its lowest reading of -32°C was considered to be of uncertain accuracy.

Tyndall: 'whether we should tie ourselves together, at the same time expressing his belief that it was unnecessary. Up to this time we had been separate, and the thought of attaching ourselves had not occurred to me till he mentioned it. I thought it ... prudent to accept the suggestion. "Now" said Bennen, "have no fear; no matter how you throw yourself, I will hold you." Afterwards, I repeated this saying of Bennen's to a strong and active guide, but his observation was that it was a hardy untruth, for that in many places Bennen could not have held me.' Bennen's views about the security of the rope on the descent were in sharp contrast to those of Sir Alfred Wills' guides four years earlier, prior to commencing their descent of the Wetterhorn (see page 41). With safety techniques almost unknown, many of the early guides avoided using a rope when descending. Bennen evidently had meant to impress his employer; but it is fortunate that his exaggerated claims in the event of a slip were never put to the test thanks to Tyndall's consistently steady performance. As events turned out, during a voluntary glissade on hard snow: 'Bennen's footing gave way; he fell, and went down rapidly, pulling me after him. I fell also, but turning quickly, drove the spike of my hatchet into the ice, got a good anchorage, and held both fast; my success assuring me that I had improved as a mountaineer since my ascent of Mont Blanc.' On reaching the crevassed snow-covered glacier the rope was unwisely cast off, and it was providential that when Bennen, in front, fell into a crevasse he managed to extricate himself without endangering the life of his employer.

On 10 August 1858 Tyndall climbed Monte Rosa in seven hours from Riffelberg with the Lauterbrunnen guide Christian Lauener. On this climb once again Tyndall and his guide were not roped during the ascent; but before starting the descent, Lauener tied the rope around Tyndall's waist and 'forming a noose at the other end slipped it over his arm ' – an action as astonishing as it was unsound.[4] Six days later, Tyndall set out from the Riffelberg hotel to make his second ascent of Monte Rosa; he was accompanied by a reluctant local guide to the foot of the climb, where the guide was paid off. Tyndall continued alone. 'Whether my exercise be mental or bodily, I am always most vigorous when cool. During my student life in Germany, the friends

---

[4]According to J Simler's writings, this appears to have been the method applied by sixteenth century trackers and hunters who guided travellers across snow-covered passes.

who visited me always complained of the low temperature in my room, and here among the Alps it was no uncommon thing for me to wander over the glaciers from morning till evening in my shirt-sleeves ... My object now was to go as light as possible, and hence I left my coat and neckcloth behind me.' For sustenance he carried a ham sandwich and a bottle of tea. He seems to have embarked on this venture in a strangely rash and over-confident mood, driven not by any scientific curiosity but by: 'the unspeakable beauty of the morning [which] filled [him] with a longing to see the world from the top of Monte Rosa.' Fortunately it was a day of perfectly calm weather. During the ascent Tyndall occupied his mind observing physical phenomena; he was fascinated by the circular zones of colour which formed around the sun caused by light veils of cloud. 'The sense of weariness is often no index to the expenditure of muscular force ... if the nervous excitant be feeble, the strength lies dormant, and we are tired without exertion. But the thought of peril keeps the mind awake, and spurs the muscles into action.' On arriving at: 'the base of the last spur of the mountain I once had occasion to stoop my head, and, on suddenly raising it, my eyes swam as they rested on the unbroken slope of snow at my left. The sensation was akin to giddiness, but I believe it was chiefly due to the absence of any object upon the snow upon which I could converge the axes of my eyes' – a scientist's explanation for feelings commonly experienced by those who lack a 'head for heights'. While seated alone on the summit, Tyndall's ice-axe slipped out of his grasp, 'the thought of losing it made my flesh creep, for without it descent would be utterly impossible. I regained it and looked upon it with an affection which might be bestowed upon a living thing, for it was literally my staff of life.' During the descent he 'came to a place where the edge was solid ice which rose to the level of the cornice ... The place was really perilous, but encouraging myself by the reflection that it would not last long, I carefully ... hewed steps, causing them to dip a little inward, so as to afford a purchase for the heel of my boot, never forsaking one till the next was ready, and never wielding my hatchet until my balance was secured.' He returned safely to the Riffelberg hotel within ten hours after a courageous climb, having made the first solo ascent of Monte Rosa. Tyndall then moved to Saas, where he spent a few days based at the Mattmark hotel in order to examine the Allalin glacier. His proposed attempt on the Dom guided by the *curé* Imseng had to be abandoned owing to bad weather. Imseng then conducted him to a spacious cavern under the Fee glacier, roofed by immense slabs of rock. Seated inside, a singular group comprising the *curé* and his followers, including a young theological student, recited an appropriate poem from one of Schiller's plays – Tyndall, in fluent German, heartily joining in with the others. Travelling to Chamonix, he made another ascent of Mont Blanc accompanied by Wills, Balmat and five porters, with the object of planting a thermometer in the summit snows, and carrying out other observations. Balmat used his bare hands to dig a hole for the thermometer; the labour that this involved in a temperature of -12°C was cut short after a warning from Wills about the danger of frostbite to Balmat's hands. Tyndall had been too deeply absorbed by his work to attend to the efforts of others. 'Balmat pinched and bit his fingers ... but there was no sensation ... seeing him thus produced an effect upon me that I had not experienced since my boyhood, – my heart swelled and I could have wept like a child. The idea that I should be in some measure the cause of his losing his hands was horrible to me.' Beating and rubbing by Wills and Tyndall, accompanied by Balmat's exclamations ' *N'ayez pas peur, frappez toujours, frappez fortement!'* (Don't be afraid, keep on beating as hard as you can!) finally produced the excruciating pain preceding the restoration of the blood-flow to Balmat's hands which were saved. Tyndall obtained for Balmat from the Royal Society a reward of twenty-five guineas, which was used, at Balmat's request, for the purchase of a 'photographic apparatus'.

During the winter of 1858-9, Tyndall spent a few days at Montenvers measuring movements on the Mer de Glace, assisted by two guides and four porters. To reach the semi-deserted village of Chamonix from Geneva by horse-drawn sledge it was necessary to battle through deep snowdrifts, which sometimes concealed all traces of the road. From Chamonix, the seven-man expedition struggled up trackless slopes of snow, the guides wearing 'pattens', (*patin* in French) comprising wooden planks 16 inches long and 10 inches wide. The half-submerged shelter at Montenvers was reached five hours later. (Note 5) Known as the *Temple de la Nature*, it was originally built around 1795 and twice renovated in 1819 and 1840, having been used by Professor Forbes during his studies of the Mer de Glace in 1842. It can still be seen today, a symbol of a former era, on a promontory above the Montenvers hotel. The shelter provided primitive accommodation; wind and snow penetrated through gaps in the doors and windows, resulting in an indoor temperature of -2°C, with -11°C recorded outside. Bad weather and heavy snowfall often intervened. 'At times the glacier was swept by wild squalls. The men were sometimes hidden from me by the clouds of snow which enveloped them, but between those intermittent gusts there were intervals of repose, which enabled us to prosecute our work.' Tyndall's investigations enabled him to confirm, as Professor Forbes had done earlier, facts about glacier movements in winter. The following summer Tyndall ascended Mont Blanc for the third time, accompanied by his friend Edward Frankland, Auguste Balmat, and two other guides. A number of scientific objectives were planned, and a large party was organised which included twenty-six porters, twelve of whom went to the summit. Six porters were retained there, which resulted in eleven men spending twenty hours packed inside a tent ten feet in diameter in an air temperature of -15°C. Understandably, the porters 'showed a temper very like mutiny'. The oxygen-reduced atmosphere resulted in feeble candle-light, and muted the report from a pistol-shot intended for listeners at Chamonix. Six maximum/minimum thermometers were placed in the snow at six different points of elevation. Tyndall was greatly moved by the stupendous view at sunrise, but he was prevented by strong winds from making observations on solar radiation. Bad weather the following season defeated all attempts to retrieve the thermometers buried in the summit snows.

Tyndall's book, *The Glaciers of the Alps,* published in 1860, and inscribed to Faraday, recorded most of the experimental work which he had carried out during the previous four years, and included accounts of his mountain ascents in 1858-9. 'In 1859 I had bidden the Alps farewell, purposing in future to steep my thoughts in the tranquillity of English valleys, and confine my mountain work to occasional excursions in the Scotch Highlands, or amid the Welsh and Cumbrian hills. But ... the mere thought of the snow-peaks and glaciers was an exhilaration; and to the Alps, therefore, I resolved once more to go.' Tyndall the scientist had developed a craving for fresh alpine adventures. In August 1860, he made the first crossing of the

Lawinentor, a difficult and rarely used pass from Lauterbrunnen to the Eggishorn, with F Vaughan Hawkins and the guides Christian Lauener and Kaufmann. After a period of work on the Aletsch glacier, he travelled to Breuil in order to join Vaughan Hawkins, who had planned to make an attempt on the Matterhorn. Their guides were Bennen and Jean-Jacques Carrel, a leading chamois hunter of the Valtournanche, who had taken part in the first attempt on the mountain in 1857. The difficulty and length of the climb were underestimated, and the failure of the attempt below the Great Tower on the south-west ridge underlined the need for placing an upper bivouac prior to launching a serious summit attempt.

The following year was an important one for Tyndall, in which he made his first acquaintance with Belalp, which he continued to visit almost yearly for the next thirty-two years, establishing his summer home there in 1877. At Belalp he is recorded as having once said: 'Some people give me little credit for religious feeling. I assure you that when I walk here and gaze at these mountains, I am filled with adoration.' In 1861 Tyndall succeeded in making the first ascent of the Weisshorn, one of the most beautiful mountains in Switzerland, and one of the most sought-after summits. That success opened a new phase in his alpine career. The ascent, which had no specific scientific aims, was a fine achievement. A bivouac was set up on a ledge at the foot of the east ridge on 16 August, and during the afternoon Tyndall and Bennen: 'skirt[ed] the mountain until the whole colossal pyramid stood facing us. When I first looked at it my hope sank, but both us of gathered our confidence from a more lengthened gaze ... Bennen decided on the route ... A chastened hope was predominant in both our breasts as we returned to our shelter.' The following morning at 3.30 under a clear moon Tyndall, accompanied by Bennen and the Oberland guide U Wenger, began their ascent. After two hours they roped up. 'The ridge became gradually narrower, and the precipices on each side more sheer ... upon the wall of rock was placed a second wall of snow, which dwindled to a pure knife-edge at the top. It was white, of very fine grain, and a little moist ... I did not think a human foot could trust itself upon so frail a support. Bennen's practical sagacity ... came into play. He tried the snow by squeezing it with his foot, and to my astonishment began to cross it. Even after the pressure of his feet, the space he had to stand on did not exceed a hand-breath.

... It is quite surprising what a number of things the simple observation made by Faraday in 1846 enables us to explain. Bennen's instinctive act is justified by theory. The snow was fine in grain, pure and moist. When pressed, the attachments of its granules were innumerable, and their perfect cleanness enabled them to freeze together with a maximum energy. It was this freezing which gave the mass its sustaining power. ... My guide ... unaided by any theory did a thing from which I should have shrunk, though backed by all the theories in the world.' After ascending the ridge for about six hours: 'we found ourselves apparently no nearer to the summit ... Bennen laid his face upon his axe for a moment ... remarking *"Lieber Herr, die Spitze ist noch sehr weit oben".'* (Sir, the top is still a good way above.) Bennen's words convey the impression that, had his remarks received the merest hint of an echo from his employer, he would have counselled retreat. A halt was made for food and drink: 'mightily refreshed [Bennen] exclaimed *"Herr! wir müssen ihn haben"* (We've got to make it.) and his voice, as he spoke, rung like steel within my heart.' An 'eminence now fronted us, behind which, how far we knew not, the summit lay. We scaled this height, and above us, but clearly within reach, a silvery pyramid projected itself against the blue sky ... we passed along a knife-edge of pure white snow [which] ran up to a little point, ... and instantly swept with our eyes the whole range of the horizon.' Standing on the summit, 'I had never before witnessed a scene which affected me like this ... An influence seemed to proceed from it direct to the soul; the delight and exultation experienced were not those of Reason or Knowledge, but of Being: I was part of it, and it of me and in the transcendent glory of Nature I entirely forgot myself as a man ... I opened my notebook to make a few observations, but I soon relinquished the attempt. There was something incongruous if not profane in allowing the scientific faculty to interfere where silent worship was the reasonable service.' The simple and moving account of his first major alpine achievement, illustrates Tyndall's growing sense of identity with the mountains, and reveals the existence of deeper instincts seemingly in conflict with his professed agnosticism. His thoughts were of a different order from those expressed in simpler language by Reverend Leslie Stephen three days earlier when seated on the summit of the Schreckhorn, 'a delicious lazy sense of calm repose was the appropriate frame of mind'. Tyndall and his guides descended to Randa the same evening after an outing of almost twenty hours. They were told that until their summit banner was seen: 'nobody in Randa would believe that the Weisshorn could be scaled – least of all by a man who for two days previously had been the object of Philomène, the waitress', constant pity, on account of the incompetence of his stomach to accept all that she offered for its acceptance.' (Note 6) Three days after the ascent, Tyndall sent Bennen ahead to Breuil to examine whether a bivouac site could be found on the south-west ridge of the Matterhorn with a view to launching a summit attempt. Tyndall followed him there, making a solitary journey from Riffelalp across the Gorner glacier and the Theodule Pass. He was deeply disappointed to receive Bennen's negative verdict which, with the complete faith that he placed in Bennen's judgement, he accepted unquestioningly. After this failure Tyndall retreated to Saas from where he and Bennen crossed the Monte Moro pass descending to Macugnaga. Here Tyndall proposed returning to Zermatt via the Weisstor pass, first crossed earlier that year by FF Tuckett with Bennen. During the climb Bennen missed the way and the party of three, including a porter, narrowly avoided disaster in a stone-swept couloir by escaping on to a steep face, which terrified the porter and severely tested the other two. Traces of chamois were observed, which altered Tyndall's previously held belief that where chamois could go men could go too. Emerging on to the pass after a struggle brought immense relief. 'For a long time the snow cornice hung high above us; we now approach its level; the last cliff forms a sloping stair with strata for steps. We spring up it, and the magnificent snow-field of the Gorner glacier immediately opens to our view. The anxiety of the last four hours disappears like an unpleasant dream, and with that perfect happiness which perfect health can alone impart, we consumed our cold mutton and champagne on the summit of the old Weissthor [sic].'

In July 1862 Tyndall, accompanied by Huxley and John Lubbock, climbed the Galenstock. They then visited the Aletsch glacier, but an accident to one of their porters, who had to be rescued after falling into a crevasse, frustrated their intended attempt on the Jungfrau. On 27-28 July Tyndall made another attempt from Breuil to climb the Matterhorn, accompanied by Bennen, with Anton Walter as a second guide. Jean-Antoine Carrel and his cousin César were engaged as porters. Carrel, with members of his family and others, had taken part in four, perhaps five, previous attempts to climb the Matterhorn; no other person was better acquainted with the difficulties, or possessed a better mental and physical capacity to deal with them. Carrel probably agreed to accept the subordinate role of porter out of curiosity, arising from the proprietary interest which he felt in the mountain. At Breuil they: 'found that a gentleman, whose long perseverance merited victory, was then on the mountain ... At night Mr Whymper returned from the Matterhorn, having left his tent upon the rocks. In the frankest spirit, he placed it at my disposal, and thus relieved me from the necessity of carrying up my own.' Whymper waited below at Breuil, 'filled with anguish', while Tyndall's strong party carried out their attempt on the mountain. (Note 7) After a night spent on the Col du Lion, Tyndall's party of five started up the ridge at 4am. The climbing was hard, and Bennen's early elation over the chance of success evaporated as the difficulties multiplied. Tyndall's descriptive comments about the physical aspect of the south-west ridge of the Matterhorn indicate that his scientific curiosity was not in the least restrained by what must have seemed a very testing climb. 'We adhered as long as possible to the weather-worn spine of the mountain, until at length its disintegration became too vast. The alterations of sun and frost have made wondrous havoc on the southern face of the Matterhorn; but they have left brown-red masses of the most imposing magnitude behind – pillars, and towers, and splintered obelisks, grand in their hoariness – savage, but still softened by the colouring of age. The mountain is a gigantic ruin; but its firmer masonry will doubtless bear the shocks of another aeon.' Tyndall provided Bennen with unfaltering support during several hours of strenuous work. By the early afternoon the party reached the Shoulder at the top of the south-west ridge, since called Pic Tyndall (4242m), where they planted a flag. From there, following a 'hacked and extremely acute ridge [with] ghastly abysses on either side,' they faced a 'deep cleft' separating them from the final cliffs, with the summit rising 232m above. Tyndall wrongly estimated his position as being 'within almost a stone's throw' of his goal, but his party had overcome some of the most difficult sections of the climb, succeeding in reaching a point higher than anyone had been before.

'As on other occasions, my guide sought to fix on me the responsibility of return, but with the usual result, "where you go I will follow, be it up or down". It took him [Bennen] half an hour to make up his mind. But he was finally forced to accept defeat.' Whymper's account of this incident, as reported to him by the Carrels, indicates that when appealed to for their opinion at this point the Carrels replied, 'We are porters, ask your guides'. If true, this would underline Jean-Antoine Carrel's understandable, if arrogant, refusal to lend any support to a 'foreign' guide, determined as he was to reserve for himself the prize of final success.[5] Tyndall's account differs substantially, 'Bennen spoke of danger, of difficulty, never of impossibility; but this was the ground taken by the other three men.' However, Tyndall described Carrel in his book *Hours of exercise in the Alps* as 'an extremely handy and useful companion [whose] climbing powers proved very superior', and wrote in Carrel's record-book before leaving Breuil on 29 July 1862: 'Jean-Antoine Carrel accompanied me up the Matterhorn in the 27-28 of July 1862. He proved himself an extremely good man on this occasion. He is a very superior climber and, I believe, an excellent guide. ... I can express without reserve my entitre satisfaction as regard Carrel's conduct through a very difficult day.' (Note 8)

Tyndall did not relinquish his interest in the Matterhorn. He had been in correspondence with Carrel following the latter's ascent to the Italian summit in 1865. In 1867 Tyndall visited Breuil; but owing to Carrel's unreasonable demands, and a spell of exceptionally bad weather, no arrangements were made. Not long after his return from Switzerland that year, Tyndall was appointed Superintendent at the Royal Institution to succeed Faraday, who had died on 30 August of that year; the appointment was one which Faraday himself had wished.

In the summer of 1868 Tyndall returned to the Alps, to make the seventh ascent of the Matterhorn (the fifth from Breuil) and the first complete traverse of the mountain from Italy to Switzerland. He was accompanied by the brothers Jean-Pierre and Jean-Joseph Maquignaz. (Note 9) Tyndall and his guides set out from Breuil on 26 July: 'scaling the crags and rounding the bases of those wild and

[5]In 1863 Carrel was summoned to Biella by Quintino Sella, a leading politician and one of the chief founders in Turin of the Club Alpino, who selected him as leader of an all-Italian party to achieve the ascent of the Matterhorn from Breuil which he did when he reached the Italian summit (4478m) on 17 July 1865 three days after Whymper's ascent of the Swiss summit (4477.5m) from Zermatt.

wonderful rock-towers, into which the weather of ages has hewn the southern ridge of the Matterhorn. The work required knowledge, but with a fair amount of skill it is safe work. I can fancy nothing more fascinating to a man given by nature and habit to such things than a climb alone among these crags and precipices. He need not be theological, but if complete, the grandeur of the place would certainly fill him with religious awe.' Tyndall's personal emotions seemed to be at odds with his spiritual attitudes, while apparently responding impassively to the challenging nature of the ascent. A night was spent at the *réfuge* erected at the '*cravate*' the year before, and a final start for the top was made at 6 am the next day.[6] On arriving at the place from where he and his guides had turned back six years earlier Tyndall expressed feelings familiar to climbers embarking on the unknown. 'I think there must have been something in the light falling upon this precipice that gave it an aspect of greater verticality when I first saw it than it seemed to possess on the present occasion. ... It looks very bad, but no real climber with his strength unimpaired would pronounce it, without trial, insuperable. ... It was probably the addition of the psychological element to the physical, ... that quelled further exertion.' On the final cliffs, the rope fixed by the Maquignaz brothers the year before was found partly iced-over, and 'it required an effort to get to the top of the precipice'. The summit was reached at 11 o'clock. There, the two guides, with the 1865 disaster fresh in their minds, may have entertained some misgivings about the descent into Switzerland, requesting Tyndall's confirmation of his wishes, which he had no hesitation in giving them. Fresh footsteps were found in the snows of the Swiss summit, made two days earlier by JM Elliott, who was the first to sweep aside the three-year shroud of fear guarding the upper part of the Swiss route by making the second ascent from Zermatt on 25 July 1868 with the guides J-M Lochmatter and Peter Knubel. (Note 10) Tyndall and his guides, roped together, exercised great caution on commencing their descent of the Swiss side of the mountain when they discovered a glaze of ice on the upper rocks of the north face, scene of the fatal accident. 'No semblance of a slip occurred in the case of any one of us, and had it occurred I do not think the worst consequences could have been avoided. ... Joseph Maquignaz was the leader of our little party, and a brave, cool, and competent leader he

[6]The Hut on the Great Tower was built in 1885.

proved himself to be. He was silent, save when he answered his brother's anxious and oft-repeated question, *"Est-tu bien placé, Joseph?"* (Are you quite secure?) Along with being perfectly cool and brave, he seemed to be perfectly truthful. He did not pretend to be *bien placé* when he was not, nor avow a power of holding which he knew he did not possess.' Tyndall and his guides reached the foot of the Hörnli ridge after dark, arriving in Zermatt at 2am on 28 July after an outing of twenty hours.

Tyndall applied the same degree of determination to his climbing as he did to his scientific work, and he was no idealist. 'These stones and ice have no mercy in them, no sympathy with human adventure; they submit passively to what man can do; but let him go a step too far, let heart or hand fail, mist gather or sun go down, and they will exact the penalty to the uttermost. The feeling of "the sublime" in such cases depends very much ... on a certain balance between the forces of nature and man's ability to cope with them: if they are too strong for him, what was sublime becomes only terrible.' Tyndall possessed physical and mental qualities which kept him unruffled in the face of danger; and he could be counted upon to demonstrate an added resolve if his guides' spirits showed signs of wavering. Despite a slender frame, he possessed the vitality and will which made him a good mountaineer. At the age of sixty-two he wrote: 'I think no more of a march of twenty miles in cool weather than a walk across the room.'

On 3 August 1868, one week after Tyndall had traversed the Matterhorn from Breuil to Zermatt, two Swiss climbers, F Thioly and O Hoiler, made the third ascent from Zermatt and the first traverse from Zermatt to Breuil, guided by Jean-Joseph and Victor Maquignaz and Elie Pession. On 4 September of the same year Felice Giordano who, with Quintino Sella, had played a large part in planning the first Italian ascent of the Matterhorn in 1865, achieved his ambition by climbing the mountain accompanied by Jean-Antoine Carrel and Jean-Joseph Maquignaz, and making the second traverse from Breuil to Zermatt. In a letter from Florence dated 31 December 1868, Giordano wrote to Tyndall: *'Quant à moi, je dirai que vraiment j'ai trouvé cette fois le pic assez difficile. ... J'ai surtout trouvé difficile la traversée de l'arête qui suit le pic Tyndall du côté de l'Italie. Quant au versant suisse, je l'ai trouvé moins difficile que je ne croyais, parce que la neige y était un peu consolidée par la chaleur.'* (I personally found the mountain quite difficult, particularly the section of the ridge beyond Pic Tyndall on the Italian side. I found the Swiss side less difficult than expected, because of the consolidated state of the snow.) (Note 11)

Johann-Joseph Bennen, from the village of Lax in Upper Valais, was killed in an avalanche together with one of his employers during a winter attempt on the Haut de Cry in February 1864. Tyndall had a high regard for Bennen's loyalty and courage, referring to him as the 'Garibaldi' of guides. Although he generally received high praise from a number of English climbers including FF Tuckett, F Vaughan Hawkins and J Birkbeck, Bennen does not seem to have possessed the initiative and judgement of some of the great guides. On the Weisshorn and Matterhorn, with Tyndall providing the driving force, he appeared to fix on his employer the responsibility of whether to continue. On the Aletsch glacier in 1862 it was Tyndall's quick reaction and not Bennen's cries of despair which saved the life of a porter who had fallen into a crevasse. Since the party's entire supply of rope lay at the bottom of the crevasse with the porter, coats, waistcoats, and braces were knotted together to fashion a rope before Tyndall descended with Bennen into the crevasse and helped to rescue the unfortunate man who was half-buried under layers of ice débris, but was not seriously hurt. On the Haut de Cry Bennen, whose experience of snow conditions far exceeded that of the local guides, failed to place greater trust in his own judgment by agreeing to adopt their route across snow-slopes which he had instinctively recognised as dangerous. Bennen was under forty-five when he died. Upon receiving news of his death, Tyndall organised a collection in England for his dependent mother and sisters, and, with Tuckett and Vaughan Hawkins, sponsored the raising of a monument to his memory in Ernan churchyard near his home at Lax, where it can still be seen. (Note 12)

From 1863 to 1870, Tyndall continued his annual summer excursions in the Alps, with a growing appetite for mountaineering combined with scientific enquiry. In August 1863 he climbed the Jungfrau in six hours from the Faulberg cave, with Dr JJ Hornby, Reverend TH Philpott, Christian Almer and Christian Lauener. The following year he carried out a series of measurements on the Roseg glacier, and climbed Piz Morterasch; on the descent, his roped party comprising three Englishmen and two guides was caught in an avalanche on an icy stretch of the Morterasch glacier, resulting in an 'uncontrollable slide of 1000 feet' which luckily ended on the brow of a crevasse without causing serious harm to anyone. 'I thought of Bennen on the Haut de Cry and muttered "It is now my turn" ... I experienced no intolerable dread ... the excitement of the rush was too great to permit of the development of terror.' Later in that year, Tyndall visited the Via Mala, because he 'had heard that it was a striking illustration of the fissure theory' – an unproven theory to explain the origin of the Alps.[7] In 1866 Tyndall examined the eroded gorge of the Finsteraarlucht, and crossed a number of passes, generally with a scientific objective. After ascending the Titlis and the Diablerets, he visited the Italian lakes. In 1867 he climbed the Eiger in seven-and-a-half hours from Wengernalp; and, in 1869, the Wetterhorn from Grindelwald to 'within 15 minutes from the top' before being driven back by a storm.

Tyndall's appointment to the post of Superintendent at the Royal Institution in 1867, did not bring to an end his annual summer pilgrimages to the Alps, but his major alpine ventures were by then virtually over. In 1869, he ascended the Aletschhorn accompanied by a member of the staff at the Belalp hotel. 'It was the first time the mountain had been attempted with a single guide, and I was therefore careful to learn whether he was embarrassed by either doubt or fear. There was no doubt or fear in the matter: he really wished to go with me. His master (the proprietor of the hotel) had asked him whether he was not undertaking too much. "I am undertaking no more than my companion" was his reply.' Tyndall returned to the hotel with his 'guide' after an expedition lasting fifteen hours feeling 'as fresh as after a stroll up Primrose Hill'. For sustenance during the ascent Tyndall had carried 'a crust of bread and a bottle of milk.' Typical of his spartan régime were his laconic comments on the subject of food. 'It is not good to go altogether without food on these climbing expeditions, nor is it good to eat copiously.' His views contrasted sharply with those of Francis Fox Tuckett who, on the eve of the first ascent of the Aletschhorn in 1859, carried an apparatus of his invention to enable him to prepare soup at his bivouac on the Mittelaletsch glacier. Clinton Dent, in a jocular speech in 1907, a

[7]A very different purpose from the 'passion' that the crags of the Via Mala aroused in AF Mummery seven years later!

Jubilee Year for the Alpine Club, said of Tuckett, by then an honorary member of the Club: 'that volatile youth whose devotion to science was such that, being desirous of studying the expansion of gaseous bodies under a diminished atmospheric pressure, he carried with him to the top, [of the Aletschhorn] from purely scientific motives, a bottle of champagne.'

Shortly after the Aletschhorn climb Tyndall was laid low by a trifling accident. 'It was a great delight and refreshment to me, whenever I felt heated, to choose a bubbling pool in some mountain stream, roll myself in it, and afterwards dance myself dry in the sunshine. Each morning I had a tub in a rivulet, a header in a lake, or a douche under a cascade. The best of these was half a mile or more from the [Belalp] hotel, but there was an inferior waterfall close at hand to which I resorted when time was short. On a bright morning towards the end of August, I was returning from this cascade to my clothes, which were about twenty yards off. They might have been reached by walking on the grass, but I chose to walk on some slippery blocks of gneiss, and using no caution I staggered and fell. My shin was urged with great force against the sharp crystals, which inflicted three ugly wounds; but I sponged the blood away, wrapped a cold bandage round the injured place, and limped to the hotel. I was quite disabled.' After five days confined to bed Tyndall felt better and resumed walking, but he returned in the evening with a much inflamed leg. He persisted at Belalp without medical help for two weeks, by which time the wounds had turned gangrenous. He was then carried down to Brig, travelling from there to Geneva where he finally submitted to medical attention. 'Despite all the care, kindness, and real skill bestowed on me, I was a month in bed at Geneva.' He spent a few weeks convalescing by the shores of the lake, at the home of Lady Emily Peel.[8] It was several months before Tyndall was able to resume his normal activities.

The mountains seemed wholly to satisfy two of Tyndall's greatest passions: they were a laboratory for his scientific research, and an arena that stimulated him physically and spiritually. Occasionally, he undertook solitary excursions. 'As a habit going alone is to be deprecated, but sparingly indulged it is a great luxury ... at rare

[8]Her husband Sir Robert Peel was twice Prime Minister of Great Britain between 1834 and 1846.

intervals it is good for the soul to feel the full influence of that society where none intrudes. When the work is clearly within your power, when long practice has enabled you to trust your own eye and judgement ... if the real climbers are ever to be differentiated from the crowd who write and talk about mountains it is only to be done by dispensing with professional assistance.' The dawn of a new era, with AF Mummery as one of its foremost exponents, was not far away. By 1870, in his fiftieth year, and recognised as one of the leading scientists of the day, overwork and ill-health compelled Tyndall to reduce the scope of his alpine activities. His personal circumstances were at last comfortable. From the proceeds of a successful lecture tour of America, he established a sum of £2500 to found three Tyndall Fellowships at the universities of Harvard, Columbia and Pennsylvania. For a while, he was an occasional weekender in the mountains of North Wales. Once, in a group that included Huxley, Tuckett and FC Grove, Tyndall battled through stormy weather in knee-deep snow to make a winter ascent of Snowdon. Other alpine climbers, including CE Mathews, A Adams-Reilly and AW Moore, occasionally spent weekends walking in Welsh and Cumbrian hills. But even under their winter snows British hills were not regarded then as able to offer any 'real' mountaineering: an attitude which began to alter, particularly in regard to serious rock-climbing, after the ascent in 1886 by WP Haskett-Smith of the Napes Needle in Cumberland.

Tyndall had been invited to join the Alpine Club as an original member in 1857, but he did not do so until a year later. Perhaps as a scientist he took a cynical view of a club which bore a stigma of eccentricity. Around that time, Charles Dickens had castigated the Club as a: 'society for the scaling of such heights as the Schreckhorn, the Eiger, and the Matterhorn [which] contributed about as much to the advancement of science as would a club of young gentlemen who should undertake to bestride all the weather-cocks of all the cathedral spires in the United Kingdom.' Leslie Stephen, who, in a jocular speech at an Alpine Club dinner in 1862 satirised science as an adjunct to mountaineering, rubbed Tyndall up the wrong way. Tyndall, smarting under Stephen's remarks which 'reflected on the value of science', resigned in a huff from the Club, of which he had been elected Vice-President only six weeks earlier. The breach between the two men healed later, and on Faraday's death Tyndall agreed to Stephen's request to write an article about him. Mrs Tyndall agreed to a similar request from Stephen to write about her husband after his death: both articles appeared in the *Dictionary of National Biography* under Stephen's editorship. Tyndall was appointed to honorary membership of the Alpine Club in 1888. He had been elected an honorary member of the SAC in 1865 (the first foreigner to be so honoured) and of the Club Alpino Italiano in 1876. In 1892, a year before his death, he was made an honorary member of the Sierra Club of America.

For years Huxley had chaffed his bachelor friend about marriage, hoping to 'discover one competent to undertake the ticklish business of governing you.' In February 1876 at the age of fifty-six, Tyndall married Louisa Hamilton, whom he had known for four years, having become a friend of the family and a frequent visitor at their home Heathfield Park. She was thirty-one, the eldest daughter of Lord Claud Hamilton brother of the first Duke of Abercorn, and of Lady Elizabeth Proby daughter of the third Earl of Carysfort The marriage was solemnised by Dean Stanley of Westminster in the Jerusalem Chamber of the Abbey. Lord Lansdowne and Thomas Carlyle signed the Register and Thomas Hirst was best man; among others present were Huxley, Sir Joseph Hooker and Edward Frankland. Telling his friend Hirst and others of his engagement he wrote: 'I have made known to her my birth and education, and all the little escapades which might influence her feelings against me. Greater tenderness, truth, and natural nobility I have never seen ... [she] has chosen to forsake her own beautiful home and share my modest rooms here at the Royal Institution.' The marriage resulted in seventeen years of 'perfect companionship and co-operation.' In many ways Tyndall's happiest years were those following his marriage. He described his wife as 'strong, tender, entirely womanly and utterly self-renouncing'. By relieving him of many tedious and monotonous tasks, she contributed in no small way to the amount of work he was able to do during the early years of their married life. In addition she made a home for him, where they were able to entertain friends, and she 'filled the house with the sunshine of perfect health and immeasurable love'. In the summer of 1876, Tyndall took her, as he himself had gone every summer since 1861, to Belalp. They stayed at the hotel, situated at 2137m, which had opened in 1858 as a wooden chalet containing ten rooms. In 1861 Gervais Klingele of Naters acquired an interest in it, and five years later he became the sole proprietor, extending the original building and adding a new one.[9] A room, known as the Tyndall *zimmer*, has been retained in the original section of the hotel, furnished in Victorian style and probably not very different in appearance from the days when Tyndall occupied it. Summer visitors to the hotel used to include a variety of British tourists, and traces are still discernible of a tennis-court perched above the snout of the Aletch glacier. Lady guests originally travelled up from Brig in a *chaise* (chair) carried by four porters. Belalp is accessible today by cable-car from Blatten in an airy ascent of about eight minutes.

In 1882 when the Tyndalls bought a piece of land in Hindhead he wrote: 'This region is of unrivalled beauty. Heather knee-deep, gorse lately ablaze; far horizons with ... hills intervening. If the air and scenery fail to heal my [ailments] they are incurable.' A little hut was occupied on a hill nearby while their home, Hindhead House, was being built. The house was ready in December 1884. Water drawn from a well, sunk to a depth of 220ft, was 'soft as the dew and clear as crystal.' A stretch of adjoining land measuring thirty-six acres in the Nutcombe valley where he loved to walk was added later to the property; it became known as Tyndall's Wood, and was donated by Mrs Tyndall to the National Trust after her husband's death. Upon Tyndall's retirement from the Royal Institution in 1887, he entered a new life. He had neither pension nor salary, and was dependent on his savings and on what he could earn from his pen. Yet he was generous, and donated money freely to various causes in which he took an interest.

The 'alpine wildness' of Belalp appealed strongly to Tyndall, and he sought permission from the *commune* (village council) of Naters to build a house on Lusgen alp situated above the Belalp Hotel. Tyndall

[9]Provisions for the hotel were delivered on mule-back from Brig 1560m below, the track winding through rich forests of larch and pine. For over a hundred years the Klingele family ran the hotel, which enjoyed an exceptionally prosperous period between 1870-1900 when it became a favoured refuge for mountaineers. Accessible from the lower Aletsch glacier the hotel's Visitors' Book contains the names of almost all the alpine pioneers of the period. One by AW Moore, written on 19 July 1864 states, 'From Zermatt in a day. Not too long, starting early. Hope to ascend the Aletschhorn tomorrow and descend to the Lötsch Thal by the Birch [sic] Grat. Everything here very good.' Moore had arrived from Zermatt with Christian Almer after his pioneer crossing of the Moming Pass with Edward Whymper and Michel Croz two days earlier.

was no stranger to the community of Naters, having shown much friendship and generosity to the people over several years. Permission to acquire land for building was granted on 13 August 1876 by a vote of eighty-eight ayes against six noes. The price fixed for an area of 2800 square metres was 900 francs, and the Sale Deed included a donation of 2512 francs to the local school. The proceeds provided a valuable contribution to the community of the then under-developed village. The house, which was ready for occupation in November 1877, became the Tyndalls' summer home. Henceforth, Tyndall's visits to Switzerland were dominated by a search for health and relaxation from the stress and worry of his professional work, and he cherished Villa Lusgen as his 'spiritual ' home. In an environment that he loved, he would walk on the glacier, work, read, meditate, entertain friends. He took a keen interest in the village people, sometimes visiting the sick in their homes, and providing medical aid to the many who flocked to his villa. There is a story of a brave little boy with life-threatening burns, his fortitude deeply touching Tyndall who nursed him back to health, personally dressing his terrible wounds twice a day for five weeks. During his final visits to Belalp it was clear to the local people that Tyndall was in poor health. His wife wrote: 'It spoke well for their friendly feeling that ... when they knew he was ill [their visits] almost entirely ceased, the few that came apologising for their intrusion.'

Villa Lusgen, built in the pedestrian style of a seaside cottage, is a misfit in the rugged beauty of Belalp. But its isolated position, perched above a wide sweep of the lower Aletsch glacier, commands a magnificent alpine panorama stretching from the Simplon Pass, Monte Leone and the Fletschhorn to the Mischabel group, the Matterhorn, and the Weisshorn – a prospect that must have warmed Tyndall's heart. During his last years, his body much enfeebled by ill-health and his mind wearied by overwork, he was greatly supported by the devotion of his wife. In 1887 the *Burgerschaft* (civil authorities) elected Tyndall an honorary citizen of Naters. On 31 July 1893 Tyndall, then much weakened in health, arrived at the Villa with his wife, benefiting physically during the weeks they spent there until 21 October. He died at Hindhead House on 4 December, and was buried at St Bartholomew's churchyard, Haslemere, in a part of the Surrey countryside for which he had developed a deep affection. Louisa Tyndall survived her husband by nearly forty-seven years, reaching the age of ninety-five before her death in 1940. Her great ambition during her widowhood had been to write a life of her husband, having collected and arranged a vast amount of material during the last years of his life with the object of joint authorship. But it was not to be. 'I cannot pretend to be impartial. I am speaking of one whom my whole being adores, whom I am utterly incompetent to criticise. His foibles were few, but the beauty of his nature was of a quality that the world will not see again.' An official biography was published five years after Louisa Tyndall's death, based on the material meticulously put together during her lifetime. She continued to visit Villa Lusgen every summer. On 10 August 1911, with assistance from the authorities at Naters, a memorial to her husband was raised on an isolated knoll above the Villa, comprising a tall granite stone drawn from a nearby glacier bearing the simple inscription 'to mark a place of memories'. On a grey autumn morning in 1993, to commemorate the 100th anniversary of Tyndall's death, a bronze plaque was unveiled on the memorial at a ceremony supported by the local authorities as a gesture of respect to a former honorary citizen. Almost at the moment of the unveiling, a break in the clouds provided a fleeting glimpse of the Weisshorn and the Matterhorn, two mountains which had witnessed Tyndall's greatest alpine exploits. Belalp, a green balcony perched above a forest belt overlooking Brig and the Aletsch glacier, still retains something of its pristine character, which was one of its principal charms in Tyndall's day.

On his retirement in 1887, Tyndall was made an Honorary Professor of the Royal Institution. He was awarded Honorary LLD degrees by Cambridge and Edinburgh Universities and by Trinity College Dublin; and a Fellowship of Trinity College London. He was Rumford Medallist of the Royal Society in 1864, and a member of its Council. He was granted honorary membership of several scientific, philosophical and literary societies at home and abroad, including the Institution of Civil Engineers, and was awarded an MD degree from Tübingen University. His published writings between 1851 and 1892 comprise twenty-seven scientific works and four relating to the alps; several of the former were authorised for translation. Tyndall's alpine writings include *The Glaciers of the Alps* (1860), *Mountaineering in 1861* (1862), and *Hours of exercise in the Alps*, first published in May 1871, the year in which Leslie Stephen's and Edward Whymper's books appeared.

A second edition of *Hours of exercise in the Alps* was issued in July 1871 and a third in 1873. In 1899, a new edition was published, edited and indexed by Mrs Tyndall, which was twice reissued in July and October 1906. This is Tyndall's best-known alpine work, combining the quality of a travel book with that of a climber's journal, and portraying mountains with the dual vision of a mountaineer and a disciple of nature eager to explain some of its wonders. In the Preface, Tyndall describes the book as illustrating 'the mode in which a lover of natural knowledge and of natural scenery chooses to spend his life. Much as I enjoy the work, I do not think that I could have filled my days and hours in the Alps with clambering alone. The climbing was in many cases the peg on which a thousand other 'exercises' were hung. The present volume, however, is for the most part a record of bodily action, written partly to preserve to myself the memory of strong and joyous hours, and partly for the pleasure of those who find exhilaration in descriptions associated with mountain life.' Tyndall's love of mountains was unqualified. During periods of overwork or ill-health, particularly in his later years, he was able to benefit from their power to restore his spirits.

The mystery of the Matterhorn's formation fascinated Tyndall. 'It is not a spurt of molten matter ejected from the nucleus of the earth; from base to summit there is no truly igneous rock. It has no doubt been upraised by subterranean forces, but that it has been lifted as an isolated mass is not conceivable. It must have formed part of a mighty boss or swelling, from which the mountain was subsequently sculptured.' Tyndall provides a lively account in *Hours of exercise in the Alps* of his traverse of the Matterhorn from Italy to Switzerland in 1868 with Joseph and Pierre Maquignaz, which illustrates something of the mood of his 'strong and joyous hours'. He was then at the height of his physical and mental powers, and the narrative, which makes light of the seriousness of the climb, is accompanied by an almost clinical examination of the mountain's structure, and of the impressive aspect of destruction brought about by the powerful forces of nature.

CHAPTER FOUR
LESLIE STEPHEN
1832-1904

If we, being otherwise for the most part persons of moderate
respectability, and not more obviously mad than most people,
continue in these unremunerative pursuits merely for the sake
of pleasure, and proclaim that our climbing days have been
among the best days of our lives, we ought to be able at least to
define that pleasure in an intelligible way.

AD Godley

The Alpine Golden Age revives memories of amateur mountaineers
of the Victorian era, among whom Leslie Stephen was one of the
foremost. His mountaineering exploits reached their crowning point
during the early period of the Golden Age, and his alpine writings,
like those of Edward Whymper, inspired the beginnings of many a
notable alpine career. While the technical standard of his climbs, one
hundred and fifty years on, might seem ordinary, his reputation as an
alpine pioneer rests on his exceptional number of first ascents of
major peaks, and on the quality of his mountain writing. As a young
man, Stephen admits to having been influenced by John Ruskin,
whose accounts of his alpine journeys combined analytical
descriptions of the structure and form of mountains with
impassioned impressions of their majesty and beauty. Stephen wrote,
'When long ago the Alps cast their spell on me, it was woven in a great
degree by the eloquence of *Modern Painters*. I might have followed him
from the mountains to picture galleries, and spent among the stones
of Venice hours which I devoted to attacking hitherto unascended
peaks, and so losing my chance of becoming an art critic. I became a
fair judge of an Alpine guide, but I do not even know how to make a
judicious allusion to Botticelli or Tintoretto. I can't say I feel the
smallest remorse. I had a good time and at least escaped one temptation
of talking nonsense.' Ruskin has been called: '... one of the most

voluminous and ... one of the most miscellaneous of writers [whose] thought is sometimes dressed in royal purple and adorned with gold embroidery, ... in opinion, one of the least consistent. Convictions expressed with the utmost confidence in the first edition of a book are scornfully renounced in the second. Yet Ruskin will never be understood unless the truth be grasped that there is a unity underlying all his diversity, and that, in spite of contradictions on this point and on that, no writer, in essentials, is more consistent'. (Note 1) Stephen found Ruskin's attitude to mountains unacceptable. His own passion, unlike Ruskin's which was confined to contemplating mountains as objects to be worshipped from below, drove him to explore the upper valleys and passes, and to reach unclimbed summits, activities that Ruskin vigorously condemned. Stephen admired the works of the French philosopher and writer Jean-Jacques Rousseau, whom he thought was 'the first to set up mountains as objects of human worship'. Rousseau was probably the second to do so; a poem, *Die Alpen*, published in 1732 by the Bernese scientist Albrecht von Haller, glorifying the beauty of the Alps and the lives of those who dwelt there, was widely acclaimed in Europe, and began slowly to transform the former perception of mountains as unapproachable and sinister regions.

Stephen was born into a family that formed part of what has been called the 'intellectual aristocracy' of Victorian England. His father, Sir James Stephen (1789-1859), was a successful lawyer, colonial administrator, and member of the Privy Council who, after his retirement in 1849, was appointed Regius Professor of Modern History at Cambridge. His mother was Jane Venn, daughter of Reverend John Venn, Rector of Clapham. His elder brother, Sir James Fitzjames Stephen (1829-94) an eminent jurist, was appointed as a judge in 1879. In his boyhood, Stephen was small and fragile, and his brother's image loomed above him, strong-minded, competent and forthright. It was his delicate physique that dictated his removal from Eton at the age of fourteen. Both brothers were unhappy in the unreformed Eton of their day, which was dominated by the teaching of classical languages, and by the need for juniors to endure the semi-brutal rule over them by senior boys. The two brothers and their sister were brought up in a strict evangelical home, in which a strong patriarchal influence imbued them with the principle that life was a continual effort to do one's duty to other people. The family lived in Hyde Park Gate, and their playground was Kensington Gardens where in later years Stephen would walk regularly with his dog, accompanied perhaps by one of his daughters, and would recall how as a little boy he and his brother, when walking in the gardens, had 'made beautiful bows to young Queen Victoria, and she had swept them a curtsey' ... and had 'once saluted the Duke of Wellington'. Stephen developed an interest in literature and poetry at an early age; he was instructed by private tutors, and spent a few terms at King's College London, where he studied mathematics, modern languages and history.

In December 1850 Stephen entered Cambridge. At the end of his first year he won a scholarship at Trinity Hall. The hard work, far from breaking his health, caused it steadily to improve. Though he rowed badly, he triumphed as a rowing coach for his college, which enabled him slowly to acquire the self-confidence which he lacked. He became a formidable walker, and something of an athlete, once challenging a friend to run three miles while he walked two, and won. In 1854 he obtained a Mathematical Tripos, and in December of that year was elected to a Fellowship at Trinity Hall. This required him to take Holy Orders, which he did in 1855 at the age of twenty-three, and was appointed to a Junior Tutorship in mathematics at his college. A tall (he was 6ft 3ins), gaunt, shy don, Stephen was thought to be a rather modern clergyman, concerned more with ethics than theology. His enthusiasm for rowing, athletics, and in organising thirty-mile Sunday walks, often enabled undergraduates to overlook his clerical status. He was ordained in 1859. In 1861 he was appointed to examine the newly-created Moral Science Tripos. He had been steadily reading philosophy, a subject that was to become the focus of some of his important literary work later. The following year, troubled by the difficulty of reconciling modern thought and the discoveries of modern science with traditional beliefs, a phenomenon that was beginning to seep more deeply into some sections of Victorian society, he felt unable to continue his regular religious practice, and renounced holy orders in 1862. Under the requirements of his Fellowship, he was obliged to resign his teaching post, sacrificing for a principle his position as a College Tutor. Stephen remained in residence at Cambridge until 1864, where he had also begun writing, and publishing anonymously, a series of light articles entitled 'Sketches from Cambridge by a Don', containing portraits drawn from life and essays on history, politics, philosophy, and theology, which he referred to thirty years later as the outpourings 'of a pert young journalist written with a certain flippancy'. Stephen's abandonment of Christianity in 1875 was an expression of his intellectual honesty and moral courage, the action seeming paradoxical for a man who was deeply radical and who, during the remainder of his life, inwardly displayed uniquely religious attitudes. He appeared to separate ethics from religion, writing to a friend: 'I now believe in nothing, to put it shortly, but I do not the less believe in morality. I mean to live and die a gentleman, if possible.' Leslie Stephen adopted what one of his biographers has called 'a combination of evangelical morality and Victorian rationalism'. (Note 2) His was an upright character, filled with what are nowadays referred to as 'Victorian' virtues – self-discipline, a sense of responsibility, and an obligation towards one's community. His attitudes and actions accorded with his belief that the moral health of society was founded on the institution of the family. 'Revenge or malice were beneath him; he despised personal gain and all devious ways of influence or persuasion; and if this magnanimity took him a pace or two out of the world, it invested his character with a noble simplicity.' (Note 3)

In 1855, shortly after obtaining his Fellowship at Trinity Hall, Stephen spent a few weeks walking in Bavaria and the Tyrol, reaching a glacier at the foot of the Gross Glockner. His next alpine visit took place during the course of a month's holiday in 1857; his companion wrote about him during his ascent to the Col du Géant from Courmayeur, 'he was irrepressible, and in the highest spirits'. Stephen had been smitten by mountains at the relatively late age of twenty-five. That holiday opened up a phase in his life when for the next decade, which covered his most active alpine years, mountaineering seemed almost to dominate his other interests. Sir Alfred Wills' book, *Wanderings Among the High Alps* published in 1856, containing a graphic account of his ascent of the Wetterhorn in 1854, provided an initial impulse. It was not long before Stephen became identified with the alpine world, joining the Alpine Club in 1858 a year after it was established, and once walking fifty miles in twelve hours from Cambridge to London to attend the Club's Annual Dinner. He soon earned a place in the hierarchy of Victorian mountaineers.

In 1858, in the course of wide-ranging journeys, Stephen crossed thirteen passes including the Gemmi, Adler and Strahlegg, and climbed the Wildstrubel, Galenstock and Monte Rosa; it was in that year that he met Melchior Anderegg, regarded by many as the leading guide of the Golden Age, with whom he retained a close association. Between 1855-94, Stephen spent twenty-five summer and eight winter holidays in the Alps. His record of first ascents includes five mountains above 4000m, and five other major peaks; he also crossed several new passes, including the Col des Hirondelles, Eigerjoch, Fiescherjoch, Jungfraujoch, and made the first ascent from Lauterbrunnen of the Jungfrau. Edward Whymper, on his first visit to the alps in 1860, refers in his diary of 12 August to his meeting with Stephen who had just come down from the Riffel to Zermatt in thirty-five minutes, a descent which had taken Whymper four hours the previous evening lost in mist and darkness. Four days later Whymper met Stephen with Thomas Hinchcliff at Fiesch from where they walked up to the Eggishorn hotel, Stephen arriving one hour ahead of the other two. During an age still occupied with enquiry into the origins and structure of mountains and glaciers, Stephen adopted a cynical attitude towards those who encumbered themselves in the mountains with scientific paraphernalia. He had no scientific pretentions himself; for him alpine climbing was a recreation.' He was an individualist, regarding mountains as aesthetically satisfying, and providing a magnificent field for adventure demanding both physical and moral challenges.

One of Stephen's earliest alpine successes was his ascent of the Bietschhorn on 13 August 1859. He was accompanied by Felix Lehner aged fifty-seven, prior of Kippel village in the Lötschental, at whose house he stayed, and who had made an attempt to climb the mountain in 1858; also by: 'two very queer-looking guides. The latter appeared in ... dress coats and chimney-pot hats. ... A certain air of shabby respectability was thus communicated to the party in singular contrast to the wild scenery around; and with our clerical guide, in shorts and a shovel hat, we had the appearance of being on our way to some outlandish Young Men's Christian Association, rather than the ascent of a new mountain.' The party, which numbered six including a porter and the prior's 'footman', left Kippel at 4am and ascended the Nestgletscher to reach the north ridge of the mountain. When the serious climbing began, the prior, who was showing symptoms of distress, dropped out with his footman and the porter. Stephen continued the ascent with his guides, the brothers Johann and Joseph Siegen, whom he referred to oddly as Zügler, and Joseph Ebener, described as Appener. Johann Siegen, whom Stephen regarded as a 'good mountaineer', became one of the leading guides in the valley. The party found the north ridge composed of loose, crumbling rock, '… sometimes walking upright over an easy bit, sometimes using our hands, knees, and eyelids'. The summit was reached at 12.30, 'a ridge some hundred yards or so in length, with three great knobs, one at each end and one in the middle'. Three cairns were raised on the three rival summits. Disappointingly, clouds blotted out the view. On the descent: 'I was rather out of training, and was conscious of a strong disposition in my legs to adopt independent lines of action … I felt rather nervous on commencing the snow arête, and made a stumble nearly at the first step. Old Appener, emitting a fiendish chuckle, instantly gripped my coat-tails, – with the benevolent intention, as I am willing to believe, of helping me, and not of steadying himself. If so, his design was better than his execution … whenever I made a longer step than usual, the effect of his manoeuvre was to jerk me suddenly into a sitting position on the ice. I denounced the absurdity of his actions, both in German and dumb-show, but, as I only elicited more chuckles and a firmer grip on my coat-tails, I finally abandoned myself to my fate.' Rope was not used, and security, to say the least, was illusory.

Prior to the Bietschhorn ascent, the first crossing of the Eigerjoch was made on 7 August 1859 from Wengern Alp to the Eggishorn. Stephen, accompanied by the 'gigantic and picturesque' Ulrich Lauener, the leading guide of Lauterbrunnen who was Wills' guide on the Wetterhorn five years earlier, was joined by William and George Mathews with their Chamonix guides Jean-Baptiste Croz and Jean Charlet. Lauener's 'rule is apt to be rather autocratic … he has certain views as to the superiority of the Teutonic over the Latin races'. The sun had reached the huge masses of ice during the ascent of the heavily crevassed glacier. 'The Chamonix guides declared it to be dangerous, and warned us not to speak. On my translating this well-meant piece of advice to Lauener, he immediately selected the most dangerous looking pinnacle in sight, and mounting to the top of it sent forth a series of screams loud enough … to bring down the top of the Monch.' Owing to the need for long spells of step-cutting during their ascent of the steep and broken glacier, the climb to the pass had taken much longer than expected, and the party stepped thankfully on to its crest fourteen hours after leaving Wengern Alp. Descending to the Aletsch glacier, which was bathed in sunset colours, the party was forced to bivouac under a sinking moon short of the Faulberg cave, approximate site of the Concordia hut. 'Having drunk my wine, and made a perfectly futile effort to swallow a piece of bread, I put on a pair of dry stockings which I had in my pocket over my wet ones, stuck my feet into a knapsack and sat down on some sharp stones under a big rock. My companions most obligingly sat down on each side of me, which tended materially to keep off the cold night wind, and one of them shared my knapsack. My seat may very easily be imitated by someone who will take the trouble to fill one of the gutters by the side of a paved street with a heap of granite stones prepared for macadamising. If he will sit down there for a frosty night, and induce a couple of friends to sit with him, he will doubtless learn to sympathise ... I fully expected to get up in the morning stuck all over with pebbles, like a large pat of butter dropped into a sugar basin. In other respects I believe I really enjoyed the night.' An enthusiastic account by a twenty-seven-year-old Fellow of Trinity Hall who, in that year, had become the Reverend L Stephen. The 1859 season, one of his most successful, included the first ascent of the Rimpfischhorn (4198m), and the second ascent of the Dom (4545m). In those days Stephen always wore, whether boating or mountaineering, grey flannel trousers with a large purple patch in the seat, and he recalls, 'with something like a sense of shame, how on one of the loftiest peaks of Switzerland I spent the precious moments [on the summit] in having my trousers mended by a guide, who happened to be also a tailor'.

In 1861, Stephen set his sights on the unclimbed and rather repellent-looking Schreckhorn, (Mountain of Fear). 'Many a noble peak, which a few years before had written itself inaccessible in all guide-books, ... had fallen an easy victim to the skill and courage of Swiss guides, and the ambition of their employers. ... I was strongly attracted by the charms of this last unconquered stronghold of the Oberland. ... On the night of August 13, I found myself the occupant of a small hole under a big rock near the northern foot of the Strahlegg. Owing to bad diplomacy, [this brief remark conceals

Ulrich Lauener's flat refusal to attempt the Schreckhorn] I was encumbered with three guides – Peter and Christian Michel, and Ulrich Kaufmann – all of them good men, but one, if not two, too many. ... An early start is always desirable before a hard day's work, ... swallowing a bit of bread, I declared myself ready. ... but old Peter Michel sat opposite me for some half-hour, calmly munching bread and cheese, and meat and butter, at four in the morning, on a frozen bit of turf, as if it were the most reasonable thing a man could do, and as though such things as the Schreckhorn and impatient tourists had no existence.' Stephen and his guides got under way at 4.30am. There followed several hours of slow but steady progress up the southern ridge on steep rock occasionally glazed with ice; Christian Michel 'a first-rate cragsman' led the way. 'We were frequently flattened out against the rocks, like beasts of ill-repute nailed to a barn, with fingers and toes inserted into four different cracks which tested the elasticity of our frames to the uttermost.' Creeping along the final rock ridge with deep cliffs beneath, 'the scene was ... significant enough for men of weak nerves'. At 11.40 they finally stepped on to 'the little level platform which forms the allerhöchste Spitze [the highest point] of the Schreckhorn'. An hour was spent on the summit: 'There is something almost unearthly in the sight of enormous spaces of hill and plain ... spell-bound by an absolute and eternal silence.... On that perfect day on the top of the Schreckhorn, where not a wreath of vapour was to be seen under the whole vast canopy of the sky, a delicious lazy sense of calm repose was the appropriate frame of mind.' Two years after the Bietschhorn ascent, Stephen's mountaineering skills had clearly advanced, and his account does not reveal any misgivings about the difficulties or the outcome of the climb. When the descent began the guides, probably to impress upon him the hazards, lowered him down on a tight rope from one ledge to the next, until: 'the idea dawned upon the good fellows that I might be trusted to use my limbs more freely – "a little less zeal", reflected the Reverend LS, 'is occasionally a good motto for guides as well as for ministers.' His reactions on the summit, unlike those of some of his contemporaries, were not spiritual, or even philosophical. He appears to have been absorbed wholly by a sense of inner contentment. Thirty-six years later, Thomas Hardy, viewing the Schreckhorn during a visit to Grindelwald, provides enlightening evidence of his friendship with

Stephen. 'I suddenly had a vivid sense of him flattened out against the rock "like a beast of ill-repute nailed to a barn". His frequent conversations on his experiences in the Alps recurred to me, experiences always related with high commendations of the achievements of others, which were really no greater than his own.'

In 1862 starting from Wengern Alp with a large party of thirteen including six guides and a porter, Stephen made the first crossing of the Jungfraujoch, accompanied by the Reverend HB George, AW Moore (aged twenty-one), Reverend John F Hardy, JR Liveing and Reverend Dr HA Morgan (later, Master of Jesus College Cambridge). Their guides included three leading Grindelwald men, Christian Almer, Ulrich Kaufmann and Christian Michel. 'As the sun rose whilst we were climbing the huge buttress of the Mönch, the dullest of us – I refer of course to myself – felt something of the spirit of the scenery. The day was cloudless, and a vast inverted cone of dazzling rays suddenly struck upwards into the sky through a gap between the Mönch and the Eiger". In the critical approach to a gigantic crevasse: 'Rubi [the porter] appeared to think it rather pleasant than otherwise in such places to have his head fixed in a kind of pillory between two rungs of a ladder, with twelve feet of it sticking out behind and twelve feet before him'. Very steep slopes of séracs were encountered before the final rise to the joch. 'A clinometer, which showed various symptoms of eccentricity throughout the day, made some specially strong statements at this point. By interrogating one of these instruments judiciously, the inclination of Holborn Hill may be brought to approximate to 90°.... It would be very hard to give to any but Alpine readers the least notion of what the task before us was like. I reject unhesitatingly Morgan's statement that it was exactly similar to the ascent of the Glydirs from Llyn Ogwen.... The top of the Jungfraujoch ... rises so gently above the steep ice-wall ... that instead of giving three cheers ... we calmly walked forwards as though we had been crossing Westminster Bridge.' The party split up there; George and Moore descended to the Aletsch glacier, while the others including Morgan, who had been singing Welsh songs, turned left to ascend the snow-slopes towards the gap between the Mönch and Trugberg. While passing the huge icy masses: 'rising from the centre of one of the noblest snowy wastes of the Alps, Morgan reluctantly confessed for the first time that he knew nothing exactly like it in

Wales.' If Stephen was sentimental about mountains, he disguised his sentiment in satire. During the course of that season Stephen had also made a crossing of the Viescherjoch, the first ascent of Monte della Disgrazia, and the second ascent of the Weisshorn (4506m), which John Tyndall had climbed a year earlier.

Stephen's ascents in 1864 included the Eiger, Aletschhorn and Jungfrau, as well as the first traverses of Mont Blanc and the Lyskamm. His most notable climb during that season was the first ascent of the Zinal Rothorn (4221m) accompanied by FC Grove and Reginald Macdonald (the latter had to drop out before the final ascent), guided by Melchior Anderegg and his cousin Jacob. At 'the little village of Zinal' they stayed at the Hotel Durand, the first travellers' inn to be opened there in 1859, where 'M Epinay an excellent cook provided us daily with dinners which – I almost shrink from saying it – were decidedly superior to those of my excellent friend M Seiler at Zermatt'. Of the history of the Zinal valley, Stephen added, 'I know little, with the exception of two facts – one, that till lately the natives used holes in their tables as a substitute for plates, each member of the family depositing promiscuously his share of the family meals in his own particular cavity; the other, that a German traveller was murdered between Zinal and Evolena in 1863.' The party was forced by the weather to spend three days at Zinal, where their arrival 'rather more than doubled the resident population'. To relieve the boredom Stephen and his friends played cricket in the high street, 'with a rail for a bat and a small granite boulder for a ball'. Stephen sent the first ball crashing through the window of the chapel. No one could be found in the village to accept the payment that was offered for the damage.

The weather looked better when they left Zinal to start the climb on 22 August at 1.50am but on halting for breakfast four hours later 'a heavy mass of cloud clung to the ridge between the Dent Blanche and the Gabelhorn, and seemed to be crossing the Col de Zinal under the influence of a strong south wind.' Melchior Anderegg had spoken confidently about their chance of success. But when they reached the foot of the mountain's North ridge he: 'began to take a gloomy view of his prospects, and to confide his opinion to his cousin Jakob in what he fondly imagined to be unintelligible *patois* [dialect]. I understood him only too well. "Jakob", he said, "we shall get up to that rock, and then – ". An ominous shake of the head supplied the remainder of the sentence.' Their progress to within a short distance of the anticipated difficulty was fairly rapid. 'We were at a great height, and the eye plunged into the Zinal valley on one side, and to the little inn upon the Riffel on the other. ... We cowered under a rocky parapet which ... guarded us from the assaults of a fierce southern gale ... My hands were numb, my nose was doubtless purple, and my teeth played involuntary airs, like the bones of a negro minstrel.' They continued up a narrowing ridge with steep cliffs on either side. 'Melchior led us with unfaltering skill – his spirits, as usual, rising in proportion to the difficulty. Three principal pinnacles rose in front of us, each of which it was necessary to turn or surmount.' The first was outflanked by means of a gully in which a sheet of hard ice covered the steep slabs. On the second the: 'method of progression was not unlike that of caterpillars ... doubled up into a loop and then stretched out at full length.' The third was approached *à cheval* 'the rock was so smooth and its edge so sharp that ... I crept along it, supported entirely on my hands ... In front of us the rocks rose steeply in a very narrow crest rounded and smooth at the top ... I was scrambling desperately upwards, abandoning all thoughts of doing my task in "good form" or of refusing any kind of assistance ... I found myself fumbling vaguely with my fingers at imaginary excrescences, my feet resting upon rotten projections of crumbling stone, whilst a large pointed slab of rock pressed against my stomach, and threatened to force my centre of gravity backwards. My chief reliance was upon the rope ... Suddenly Melchior, who had left the highest ridge to follow a shelf of rock on the right, turned to me with the words, "in half an hour we shall be on the top". My first impulse was to express an utter scepticism.' After climbing the third pinnacle their difficulties were over. In less than Melchior's half-hour they reached 'I had almost said the top, but the Rothorn has no top. It has a place where a top manifestly ought to have been ... It ended in a flat circular area a few feet broad, as though it had been a perfect cone, with the apex cleanly struck off. Melchior and Jacob set to work at once to remedy this deficiency of nature by building a suitable cairn.' Twenty minutes later, at 11.15, unsheltered from the bitter wind, they turned to descend. 'At one point I conceived myself to be resting entirely on the point of one toe upon a stone coated with ice, and fixed very loosely in the face of a tremendous cliff, whilst Melchior absurdly told me I was "absolutely secure" and encouraged me to jump (jump!!!).' Melchior and Jacob were in high spirits, and seemed perfectly at ease. In under two hours they were back at the foot of the rocks. 'The next traveller who makes the ascent will probably charge me with exaggeration.... I must therefore apologise beforehand and only beg my anticipated critic to remember two things: one, that on the first ascent a mountain, in obedience to some mysterious law, is always more difficult than at any succeeding ascent; secondly, that nothing can be less like a mountain at one time than the same mountain at another.' Racing down towards the track leading to Zinal, they halted to luxuriate on a patch of mossy turf, where Melchior 'pointed out eleven different ways of ascending the hitherto unconquered Grand Cornier', a mountain which Whymper and his guides climbed the following year.

Stephen climbed usually with the best guides, and he was completely frank about their superior skills and experience. 'I utterly repudiate the doctrine that alpine travellers are or ought to be the heroes of alpine adventures. The true way at least to describe all my alpine ascents is that Michel or Anderegg or Lauener succeeded in performing a feat requiring skill, strength, and courage, the difficulty of which was much increased by the difficulty of taking with him his knapsack and his employer ... other travellers have been more independent: I speak for myself alone.' Remarks characteristic of his dislike of boasting, and his habit of playing down his own accomplishments. He added: 'Amongst the greatest of alpine pleasures is that of learning to appreciate the capacities and cultivate the goodwill of a singularly intelligent and worthy class of men.' Stephen, nevertheless, gives the impression of having retained rather more formal relations with his guides than some of the other pioneers, such as Wills and Tyndall. In 1866 he wrote: 'I quite agree that it is impossible to extract the full amount of pleasure from mountaineering until you are able to dispense with leading-strings, and learn to feel yourself at home in the wildest parts of the Alps. But at the same time I must say that, in my opinion, if ever it becomes fashionable for English travellers to attack the high Alps without guides and without due experience, the era of bad accidents will begin'. During the early years of the Golden Age, British climbers in the Alps invariably employed professional guides, and accidents were rare. Stephen predicted future developments correctly. According to

Swiss Alpine Club records, over a period of twenty-seven years from 1859-85 there were 134 deaths in the Alps; while in six years between 1886-91, when the practice of guideless climbing had become more widespread, 214 deaths were recorded, a seven-fold increase, attributable perhaps in equal measure to increased activity as well as the search for more difficult routes.[1] Mountaineering, as he practised it, attracted Stephen because it involved physical danger, manliness in pursuit of an objective, and the sensation of being one with nature. His tall, spare frame, and long reach gave him some advantage, while his self-possession and calm gave confidence to those near him. Friends described him as a careful and skilful cragsman, as much at home on rocks as he was steady on ice. Anderegg told Clinton Dent that he regarded Stephen as an eminently safe climber, recognising his excellent snowcraft, and remarking on his tendency to belittle his own powers. Peter Baumann, a Grindelwald guide, once told a client: 'Ach, der Herr Stephen! Der *ist* Ein Herr! Er kann Alles und weiss Alles so gut wie ein Führer, und sagt doch nie; Wir sollen hier oder dort gehen, macht keinen Tritt vor einem Führer – das ist Ein Herr.'[2] Another guide remarked that Stephen was a master in every department of mountaineering, except as a weather-forecaster.

Like other mountaineers of the period, Stephen had a high regard for Melchior Anderegg whose home was in the Haslital, where as a boy he tended his father's cattle and learnt the art of wood-carving in which he later excelled. In his youth he took on odd jobs at the hostel on the Grimsel pass, and at the Schwarenbach inn on the Gemmi pass. At Grindelwald in 1858 he and Christian Almer were the first two men to be issued with an official Guide's badge and a Führerbuch[3]. One of Melchior's earliest guiding engagements was with Thomas Hinchcliff. Later, he met Frank Walker, and thereafter he accompanied him and his son Horace and daughter Lucy on all their Alpine expeditions. Melchior's other regular employer was Charles

[1]With vastly increased Alpine activity nowadays mostly by guideless climbers, the annual death-toll was ninety-three and ninety-four for the years 1999 and 2000 respectively; those numbers increased to 133 for 2001 and 102 for 2002. Fatalities would almost certainly have been higher were it not for the speed and efficiency of the hundreds of helicopter rescues carried out every year.

[2]He is a master. He has as much knowledge and skill as a guide, but he will never give an unreasonable order to his guides nor push himself out to the front. He is a true master.

[3]*Führerbuch* in German and the French equivalent, *Livret*, are the official terms for guide's Record-book.

Edward Mathews, a nephew of William Mathews, one of the chief founders of the Alpine Club of which Charles was an original member, and its President from 1878-81; he was also one of the founders in 1898 of the Climbers' Club and its first President. Mathews said of Melchior: 'To say that I owe him a debt impossible to pay is not to say much ... He first taught me how to climb. For more than 20 seasons he has led me ... Year after year I have met him with keener pleasure. Year after year I have parted from him with a deeper regret.' Anderegg's integrity and sense of justice are revealed in a story relating to the Boer War. Swiss sympathies were mainly with the Boers, and at a meeting organised in Meiringen to collect funds on their behalf Melchior listened quietly to a number of speeches. Then he rose and said: 'I am in favour of opening a subscription to help the Boers, but only after we have repaid the British all the money they subscribed to help us after our disastrous Meiringen fire in 1899.' Stephen invited Melchior to England, and he and Thomas Hinchcliff met him at London Bridge station in a thick fog. The tale, which may be apocryphal, goes on that some days later, at London Bridge once again, Hinchcliff said, 'Melchior, you will lead us home', which he did unfalteringly with only one minor pause. His cousin Jakob, who later became AW Moore's regular guide and was highly praised by him, frequently acted as joint guide with Melchior, accompanying Stephen, Moore and the Walker family. He also climbed with FC Grove and GE Foster, leading the latter on the first ascent of the Gspaltenhorn in 1869. Jakob was Melchior's equal in technical skill, and there are several instances of the great dash and initiative shown by him at critical moments during an ascent. Jakob's daring contrasted with Melchior's prudence, providing a perfect balance when both were acting as joint guides.

Stephen's active mountaineering years, which began when he was twenty-five and spanned over a decade, virtually came to an end after his marriage at the age of thirty-five. In 1866 he moved from Cambridge to London to embark on a career as a writer, and in 1867 when he returned to Switzerland he was accompanied by his wife. Although his carefree climbing days were over, he retained a deep interest in the alps, and his love of mountains remained undiminished throughout his life: they were, for him, 'the elixir of life, a revelation, a religion'. He visited the alps in summer and in winter until he was over sixty-two. He remained closely involved with alpine affairs, and in 1864 the Alpine Club appointed, on his suggestion, a committee to advise on more practicable designs for ice-axes, sleeping-bags, and climbing rope. He was elected President in 1866, and edited the *Alpine Journal* from 1868-72, producing volumes 4 and 5, having been preceded by HB George who edited the first three volumes. For thirty years the heartiness of his speeches at the Annual Dinners of the Club, won a high reputation with their sudden and unexpected transitions from sentiment to humour, which never failed to delight. On his last visit in 1901: 'I went to the AC Dinner and made them a sort of farewell speech. ... I only went there because I wanted my son to hear me speak there for once. It was not very cheerful (by then Stephen was rather deaf) ... But they seemed to like my speech.' On a rare visit to the Club about three decades after his presidency he wrote: 'It was queer enough to go to the old place, and feel that I was regarded with curiosity like a revived mammoth out of an iceberg.'

After 1867 Stephen's visits to the mountains, generally accompanied by his wife, took the form of more leisurely excursions and walking tours, with a tacit prohibition on ventures that were not risk-free. On one such journey, in the autumn of 1869, he visited the peaks of Primiero: 'situated, geographically speaking, on the headwaters of the Cismone, a tributary of the Brenta. It lies, however, to be more precise, at a distance of some thousand miles, more or less, and two or three centuries from railways and civilisation.' The area provided access, through alpine meadows and forests, to groups of rock peaks, small glaciers, and snow-clad summits, few of which had ever been approached. In this unfrequented fairyland Stephen indulged in some solitary walking and scrambling. 'I stood silent before the peaks of Primiero, and saw in them a new land, still untouched by the foot of the tourist, and opening vast possibilities of daring adventure and deathless fame for some hero of the future.[4] To me, alas! those possibilities were closed.' There were other striking contrasts. 'The Swiss, unlike their neighbours ... have travelled on railways, they understand addition and subtraction, and can make out bills to perfection. They have some notion of the use of a tub, and many of them dimly perceive that the ultimate end of man is to climb snow peaks ... a kind of human amalgam has been formed by the

---

[4]It was not many years after Stephen's visit that the region, with its wealth of unexplored mountains, began to attract the attention of a new wave of rock climbers.

steady infiltration of British tourists. ... It is pleasant, for a change, to be amongst a more primitive race [and to see] a peasant with a national costume.' At 6.45am on a brilliant morning in August Stephen found himself: 'in the quiet street of the lovely little town of Primiero. I was prepared indeed for a day's mountaineering, but a day how unlike to those when, with alpenstock in hand and knapsack on back, with a little core of faithful guides and tried companions, I had moved out to the attack of some hitherto unconquered peak! ... There is this great advantage about walking without guides – namely, that it is easy to get into real difficulties on places where it would be apparently impossible to do so on the ordinary system. Thus, for example, on the Sovretta there is only one cliff on the mountain where anything like a scramble is conceivable, and that cliff is perfectly easy to cross except after a fresh fall of snow. It is entirely out of the way of any sensible route to anywhere. But by abstaining from guides, I succeeded in placing myself on the face of this cliff the morning after a heavy snowfall, and had two hours of keen excitement in a climb which was ultimately successful.' Although acutely aware of the transition between his early years on big mountains accompanied by competent guides, and his solitary efforts in an unknown region, he appreciated the compensations. 'It is delightful to lie on one's back on a glorious day, to watch the gleaming snow-line against the cloudless sky, and to say, If I was doing my duty, I should be toiling up a slippery ice staircase on that tremendous slope. To be doing nothing when every muscle in your body ought to be at its utmost strain, is to enjoy a most delightful sensation.' In 1869 he engaged a local guide Colesel Rosso. Stephen was skilful in blending his flippant style with a remark earnestly intended: 'Colesel is very poor and very deserving. He is willing, exceedingly cheerful, full of conversation which I regret to say was imperfectly intelligible to his companion, a good walker and a mighty bearer of weights. In short he has every virtue a guide can have consistently with a total and profound ignorance of the whole theory and practice of mountain climbing.' Colesel faithfully followed Stephen's footsteps as far as the base of the Cima di Ball, where he collapsed while Stephen completed the climb alone. Like John Ball and Francis Fox Tuckett, Stephen was an early British visitor to the Dolomites. In addition to the Cima di Ball in the Sass Maor, he climbed solo the Cima di Fradusta, in the San Martino area.[5] Stephen engaged a

[5]The main peak of Sass Maor (2816m) was climbed in 1875 by CC Tucker with F Devouassoud.

guide to climb the Konigspitze (3859m), or Gran Zebru, the second highest mountain in the Ortler group: 'The expedition reminded me of former days in Switzerland. It was not particularly difficult, ... It took me eight hours to get to the top, and four to return, which ... astonished my guide, who declares that I am the best walker he has ever seen.'

With the object of avoiding the annual invasion of the alps by summer tourists Stephen, like AW Moore earlier, was one of the few British mountaineers who began to visit the Alps in winter. In January 1877 he went to Grindelwald where he was joined by the French painter Gabriel Loppé, who became one of his close alpine friends accompanying him on all his subsequent winter trips. His winter climbs included the Titlis, and an attempt on the Galenstock frustrated by a storm and by the illness of a member of his party; also the crossings of a number of glacier passes. During his last few visits he would content himself merely with the assurance that he still possessed the physical capacity to experience the magical atmosphere of the mountains which he loved. In a letter to a friend in February 1877 he wrote: 'I went for a visit to the Winter Alps, partly for the sake of a holiday, which I can get nowhere else, partly because the Oberland is to me a sacred place. ... I could not describe to you a tithe of the tender, melancholy, inspiriting glories of the Alps in January.' In March 1879 he wrote: 'I took it into my head to make a little pilgrimage to the Alps the other day, and revisited some of my favourite haunts ... I take an indefinable pleasure in seeing the old places all asleep in the quiet snow. I don't know anything of the kind that gives me such keen pleasure.' (Note 4) In Stephen's day, the journey to Grindelwald took two hours by horse-drawn sleigh from the railway terminus at Interlaken. But there were already signs of change. In 1874, the young WAB Coolidge and his aunt Meta Brevoort, encouraged by good weather and the promptings of their guide, Christian Almer, climbed the Wetterhorn on 15 January from Grindelwald, following that with an ascent of the Jungfrau on 22 January. Two days later Professor F Bischoff and R Bohren accompanied by four guides climbed the Mönch; and in January 1879, Coolidge, accompanied by Almer with two of his sons and a porter, climbed the Schreckhorn. In the winter of 1888, after Stephen had sat down to dinner at Grindelwald with twenty others, he began to feel that his winter visits had lost a great deal of their charm. By the early 1890s, the funicular line from Lauterbrunnen to Mürren was almost ready, and tunnelling for the construction of the Jungfraujoch railway began in 1896. (Note 5) Not everyone was happy with this 'modern' development condemning it as a 'desecration of Nature and a vulgarisation of the playground of Europe'. Those who feared at the time that the project's financial future was dubious could not have guessed that by the year 2000 Jungfraubahn Holding would be a thriving public company putting up a good performance on the Swiss stock market. At the time, however, such schemes were regarded as the first steps on the slippery slope leading to the disfigurement of the Alps – a continuing trend, with seemingly endless variations. (see Note 15 for Chapter 1)

In the summer of 1871, accompanied by Loppé and Frederick Anthony Wallroth, Stephen made the first ascent of Mont Mallet, which he referred to as 'that child of my old age'. On 20 August 1872, he returned to the Bietschhorn to make the fifth ascent of the mountain, fulfilling his resolve to obtain the view from the summit which had eluded him thirteen years earlier. In a letter to his wife he wrote: 'I am pretty well decided that this shall be my last big mountain'. Accompanied by Charles Mathews, Morshead and Wilson, and by the guides Melchior and Peter Anderegg and Christian Lauener, the party walked across from Lauterbrunnen over the Petersgrat to spend a night at the Nesthorn Hotel, a comfortable inn in Ried built in 1865, the first to be established in the Lötschental. In the original Visitors' Book I found the signatures of Stephen's party. (Note 6) In August 1873, having been advised to take an alpine rest-cure, Stephen wrote to a friend that he had: 'just come back in the soundest of health ... I went up Mont Blanc once more, invented a new pass from Chamonix to Courmayeur ... it was the well-known, often contemplated, but never executed Col.' Although he had 'long abandoned difficult and dangerous expeditions' Stephen agreed to join TS Kennedy, Loppé, and JG Marshall, accompanied by the guides Johann Fischer, Ulrich Almer, and Henri Dévouassoud, to make the first crossing of the col. After a night spent at Montenvers, they found at the foot of the pass 'the poor little bodies of some twenty swallows ... Ten minutes' flight with those strong wings would have brought them to the shelter of the Chamonix forests, or have taken them across the mountain wall to the congenial climate of Italy ... We proposed at the time to give to our pass the name of the Col des Hirondelles'.[6] An ascent of six hours from

---

[6]*Hirondelle* is the French word for swallow.

Montenvers took the party to the top. 'The summit of a new pass is a pleasure which can be but rarely enjoyed ... I always love these recesses of the great chasm, where the spirits that haunt solitudes have not yet been finally exorcised.' Notwithstanding his retirement from mountaineering, Stephen had not lost his attachment to the 'sacred places' of the Alps, to which his senses responded as acutely as ever. The party descended to Courmayeur, returning later to Chamonix over the Col du Géant. The ascent to the latter Col, which had been Stephen's first serious alpine climb in 1857, was also his last. By then his term as editor of the *Alpine Journal* had ended; his editorship had coincided with a lull in alpine activity, an aftermath of the Matterhorn accident in 1865, causing him to remark ruefully that the *Alpine Journal* 'might perish for want of contributions'. Before Douglas Freshfield succeeded him as editor in 1872 such pessimism had vanished, following the vigorous advance of alpine activity.[7]

Stephen paid his last visit to the Alps in 1894. Deeply affected by the death of his second wife in 1895, he regretfully declined an invitation to visit Chamonix in 1896 to celebrate with Wills and Loppé their joint golden jubilee as mountaineers. Stephen's letters to Loppé, always written in flowing French, evoked the following comment from the latter: '*Stephen m'écrivait toujours dans ma langue natale. Ses lettres étaient si claires, si délicatement exprimées que ses paroles écrites rapidement, souvent traduites mot à mot de l'anglais, donnaient toujours un charme particulier à sa pensée.*'[8] It was Loppé who once remarked, '*Il n'y a pas des montagnes dangereuses; il n'y a que des personnes qui sont dangereuses sur les montagnes*'.[9]

While alpine mountaineering had occupied an important place during Stephen's earlier years, his later life was dominated by literary

---

[7]Addressing the Alpine Club as President in 1888 Clinton Dent commented about the *Alpine Journal*: 'Twenty-five years ago the first number was introduced in somewhat modest fashion. Little was predicted for the new venture, save that death from starvation was not an imminent probability. Such a mode of extinction is at least as unlikely now as it was then. As a matter of fact the *Alpine Journal*, profiting by the occasional use of stimulants in the form of adverse criticism, has thriven and waxed fat ... the *Alpine Journal* so far as its subject matter is dealt with, constitutes the most trustworthy guide-book to the Alps and work of reference on general mountaineering exploration that exists in any language'.

[8]Stephen always writes to me in French. His letters are so clear and so daintily expressed that his style scribbled word for word from English, expresses his thoughts in an unusually attractive way.

[9]There are no dangerous mountains, only dangerous mountaineers.

and family interests. After moving from Cambridge to London he lived at first with his mother and sister. Encouraged by his brother Fitzjames, 'a rising barrister, and a risen journalist he was 'busy learning to become a journalist', finding his way to literature, like many others, through journalism. It was not long before he became a regular contributor of articles to leading London periodicals, the *Saturday Review, Cornhill Magazine*, and *Pall Mall Gazette* founded respectively in 1855, 1860 and 1865. Stephen's literary output spread over forty years, brought him recognition and fame, and fell into three main periods, the last two of which partly overlapped. As a journalist, or 'penny-a-liner', he wrote three or four articles a week, sometimes doing eight thousand words at a sitting, 'limited to the inoffensive ... which excludes politics and religion'. Several notable literary figures contributed articles to the same magazines, among whom were John Ruskin, Matthew Arnold, Charles Kingsley, Anthony Trollope and Stephen's brother Fitzjames, who wrote in the *Saturday Review* a scathing criticism of Charles Dickens, then enjoying immoderate popularity. In 1871 Stephen was appointed editor of the *Cornhill Magazine* (founded by the novelist WM Thackeray) a position which he held until 1882. His contribution to the magazine was characterised by common sense, seeing facts as they really were, a dislike for anything false or artificial, and by his particular brand of humour. An incident relating to a letter he wrote to Thomas Hardy in November 1873 bears retelling. Hardy received the letter from the hands of a farm labourer who found it lying in a puddle near his cottage; it contained a request for a contribution to the *Cornhill Magazine*. Hardy was then aged thirty-three, his literary fame not yet won, and Stephen became for a period, his mentor. Hardy agreed to provide in serial form 'a pastoral tale' which, under the title 'Far from the Madding Crowd ' became, upon publication a year later in book form, the first of Hardy's famous Wessex novels. Stephen's request marked a turning-point in Thomas Hardy's life from a struggling writer to a successful author. During his editorship, Stephen encouraged contributions from fledgling authors, among whom were Robert Louis Stevenson and Edmund Gosse. After the death of Thackeray in 1863 and of Dickens in 1870, Stephen once remarked in the *Cornhill Magazine* that he considered George Eliot to be 'the greatest living writer of English fiction ... one of the very few writers of our day to whom the name great could be conceded with any plausibility'.

Stephen's second literary period began when he accepted an appointment in 1882 as the first editor of the *Dictionary of National Biography*. His place in the literary world had been established by the publication in 1876 of his major philosophical work in two volumes, *History of English Thought in the Eighteenth Century*, and in 1882 of *The Science of Ethics*. The dictionary (or DNB) was conceived in the early 1880s by George Smith, founder and owner of Smith Elder, publishers of the *Cornhill Magazine*, also of Ruskin, the Brontës, Trollope and other writers. Smith discussed his ideas with Stephen and they agreed that the work should provide 'full, accurate, and concise biographies of all noteworthy inhabitants of the British Isles and colonies (excluding living persons) from the earliest historical period to the present time'. Starting the work singlehanded, Stephen realised that the challenge was more arduous than he expected, and in 1883 Sidney Lee aged twenty-four, fresh from Oxford, joined him as an assistant, later as joint editor. Stephen's work is said to have 'caught a sense of purpose and quiet national pride, which assumed rather than asserted'. His elegant writing style was distinctive, emphasising interest, variety of coverage, and liveliness. Sidney Lee, the perfect assistant, was methodical, exceptionally accurate, and enthusiastic. Stephen had a motto which he imposed on contributors, 'No flowers by request'. The first volume was published in 1884, and was prepared serially starting with 'A', subsequent volumes appearing each quarter. A work of such colossal dimensions without the benefit of modern technology would seem inconceivable today, and the success of the DNB is a tribute to the joint skills and commitment of Stephen and Lee. In 1891 after a decline in Stephen's health ('it was impossible with his nature for him to do half-work'), Stephen decided to retire from the editorship. His personal contribution to the DNB had amounted to 378 articles covering over a thousand pages, which 'cost a slice of (his) life'. Lee succeeded Stephen, continuing to edit the series until 1900. (Note 7)

Stephen met his first wife Harriet Marian Thackeray in 1865, two years before their marriage, when his mother invited her and her sister along with other friends to a dinner party; the sisters lived alone in Kensington after the death of their father WM Thackeray. Upon becoming engaged Stephen wrote to one of his closest friends in

December 1866: 'I am not such a don but that I can fall in love ... I love Miss Thackeray with all my heart and soul ... [I am] unreasonably and absurdly happy.' Directly after their marriage their travels included visits to Grindelwald, Martigny, Zinal and Zermatt. 'I wander at the foot of the gigantic Alps and look up longingly to their summits which are apparently so near and yet know that they are divided from me by an impassable gulf.' In his essay, 'The Regrets of a Mountaineer', written in that year, he muses wryly, and with characteristic humour, about the end of his active climbing career. Established in the world of letters, he settled in London with his wife and their daughter Laura, born in 1870. But tragedy struck when his wife died in 1875, plunging him into a period of deep melancholy, from which family and friends found it difficult to draw him out. Julia Prinsep Jackson had been for years his wife's close friend; with her beauty and personal charm she was much sought after in the intellectual and artistic society to which she belonged. In 1867 she married a friend of Stephen, Herbert Duckworth, who died in 1870, leaving her widowed at the age of twenty-four with three small children. Stephen, with his five-year-old daughter, and Julia Duckworth were close neighbours, and he began to rely increasingly upon her advice and friendship. She was fourteen years younger than Stephen, and although she refused him when he first proposed marriage in 1877, they were married on 26 March 1878. Unselfish, able and kindly, Julia made Stephen a congenial and caring wife during eighteen years of a very happy marriage, presiding over her family with a calm and competent efficiency, always available to everyone, especially to her husband who adored and revered her. Between 1879-83, two sons were born, Thoby and Adrian, and two daughters, Vanessa and Virginia. Leslie Stephen, then over fifty years old, lived with his wife, eight children, and seven maidservants, at 22 Hyde Park Gate, where he worked, and where he and Julia entertained their friends, among whom were several of the prominent literary figures of the day. By then Stephen's great days in the mountains and on the river were over. His daughter Virginia has written: 'Relics of them were to be found lying about the house – the silver cup on the study mantelpiece; the rusty alpenstocks that leant against the bookcase in the corner; and to the end of his days he would speak of great climbers and explorers with a peculiar mixture of admiration and envy.'

He worked daily and methodically in his large book-lined study situated on the fourth floor of their tall, dark house, books scattered around him in a circle. In 1882 Stephen bought Talland House, in Cornwall, a holiday home near St Ives, where the family, including guests, spent summer after summer for over a decade. His daughter Virginia recaptures the atmosphere of that period in her novel *To the Lighthouse*. When starting to write the book in May 1925 her diary records: 'This is going to be fairly short; to have father's character done complete in it; and mother's; and St Ives; and childhood; and all the usual things I try to put in – life, death, etc. But the centre is father's character.' The picture that she drew of an unfeeling, somewhat eccentric, paternal tyrant, was unflattering; reflecting, perhaps not inaccurately, the 'Victorian' attitudes he displayed. When the book was published in 1927, her husband Leonard Woolf wrote that the central character Mr Ramsay was 'a pretty good fictional portrait of Stephen ... and yet there are traces of unfairness in Ramsay'. Five years later when Virginia Woolf wrote an essay for *The Times* to mark the centenary of her father's birth on 28 November 1932, she provided a rather different picture, emphasising his genuinely human qualities, and his intellectual integrity. In a diary entry dated 22 December 1940, less than a year before her death, she wrote about her parents: 'How beautiful they were, those old people – I mean father and mother ... [he] had such a fastidious delicate mind, educated, transparent.' Virginia grew interested in literature at a very early age. Her father had a system of issuing her with books from his library, and she became an avid reader. 'Gracious child, how you gobble,' her father would exclaim as he got up from his seat to take down fresh volumes from the shelves. At the age of fifteen she was given the free run of her father's large library. She wrote later: 'Read what you like [he said] ... To read what one liked because one liked it, never to pretend to admire what one did not – that was his only lesson in the art of reading. To write in the fewest possible words, as clearly as possible, exactly what one meant – that was his only lesson in the art of writing.' Leonard Woolf describes his first meeting with Stephen, which took place at Cambridge in 1901: 'When [Thoby's] father, Sir Leslie Stephen, came up to stay a weekend with him, Lytton [Strachey] and I were had in to meet him. He was one of those bearded and beautiful Victorian old gentlemen of exquisite gentility and physical and mental distinction. He was immensely distinguished as a historian of ideas, literary critic, biographer... He had immense charm and he obviously liked to meet the young and Thoby's friends.' He has been described variously as a purely literary man of the best type; silent, patriarchal with a look, in his later years, of benignity and sadness.

Stephen inherited from his father and grandfather an instinctive opposition to the practice of slavery which, although abolished throughout the British Empire in 1833, was still present in other parts of the world. He visited America three times; on his first visit in 1863 during the Civil War he campaigned for the abolition of slavery, championing the cause of the North. Of his three close American friends, the nearest in thought and spirit was Charles Eliot Norton, poet, writer and publisher, to whom Stephen dedicated one of his books; also James Russell Lowell, poet and leading man of letters, godfather to his daughter Virginia, and for a time US Minister at the Court of St James's London; and Oliver Wendell Holmes the great American essayist, whose son OW Holmes Jr, three times wounded as an army captain during the Civil War, subsequently became Chief Justice of the US Supreme Court.

In 1879 Stephen founded a society called the Sunday Tramps, of which he was a leading participant until 1891; the rule of the Order was High Thinking and Plain Living. Among its sixty members were Douglas Freshfield, Martin Conway and Clinton Dent, three future Presidents of the Alpine Club; others included the Scottish scientist RB Haldane, the poet Robert Bridges, and the novelist George Meredith. Each Sunday, for eight months in the year, a group of them would walk twenty miles across country, generally in Surrey, Kent and Hertfordshire, in all weathers, 'through hedges, over ditches and fallows, ... sustained by bread and cheese at the village ale-house'. George Meredith has left a thumb-nail sketch: 'When that noble body of scholarly and cheerful pedestrians, the Sunday Tramps, were on the march, with Leslie Stephen to lead them, there was conversation which would have made the presence of a shorthand writer a benefaction to the country. A pause to it came at the examination of the leader's watch and Ordnance map under the western sun, and word was given for the strike across country to catch the tail of a train offering dinner in London.' Occasionally the Sunday Tramps broke the last lap of their journey home, to dine with Tyndall at Hindhead House, or with Meredith at Box Hill. Stephen and Meredith, both redoubtable pedestrians, were close friends. In Meredith's novel *The Egoist*, published in 1879, Vernon Whitford was recognised as an intended portrait of Stephen. In later days they never forgot their mutual enjoyment of mighty walks over hill and dale. Shortly before his death in 1904 Stephen, confined to a hospital bed, wrote to thank Meredith for a gift that he had sent: 'My very dear friend, I must make the effort to write to you once more with my own hand. I cannot trust to anybody else to say how much I value your friendship, and I must send you a message, perhaps it may be my last, of my satisfaction and pride in thinking of your affection for me.' (Note 8)

Stephen was nearly forty before his name became familiar to the public. He occupied the fringe of a circle of prominent men of letters during a brilliant period in English literature. Among them were Charles Darwin, Henry James, Alfred Tennyson, Matthew Arnold, John Ruskin, George Eliot and TH Huxley. He had a strange empathy and friendship with Thomas Carlyle, Scottish historian and philosopher whose social and political ideas exercised some influence in nineteenth century Britain; but it was of a different character in depth and spirit from Tyndall's relationship with Carlyle; Stephen and Tyndall were, of course, very different men. Stephen described his relations with Carlyle thus: 'I can't help loving the old fellow ... of all the literary professionals, he is the manliest and simplest. ... Besides the difference in age and point of view, he impresses me with the feeling that he thinks me hot-headed, misguided ... he always rails at me, more or less directly, and makes me feel uncomfortable, ... I am convinced that he disapproves of my writing, and thinks me an irreverent creature; and I think further that he does not like me personally.' Typical of his self-deprecatory habit was Stephen's verdict, expressed in his last years, about himself: 'I think that I had it in me to make something like a real contribution to philosophical or ethical thought. Unluckily, what with journalism and dictionary-making I have been a jack-of-all-trades; and instead of striking home, have only done enough to persuade friendly judges that I could have struck.'

Stephen was elected an Honorary Fellow of his old college, Trinity Hall, Cambridge; and he was awarded honorary degrees by the universities of Oxford, Edinburgh and Harvard. In the Coronation honours, to mark the accession of Edward VII in 1902, he was appointed a Knight Commander of the Bath. 'I had settled to refuse the KCB as such things are quite against my principles. But the children cried out, and I knew that they would think my principles absurd' – not appropriate to a literary gent, was how he felt. Stephen's literary output covers about thirty volumes over a period of forty years. His first book, published in 1861, was a translation of a German book by HA von Berlepsch entitled *The Alps*. Thereafter his writings fell mostly within the sphere of literary criticism; and he was skilled as a writer of literary biography. His weightiest books were his contributions to philosophy. These included *History of English Thought in the Eighteenth Century*, regarded as probably his most important work, about which his biographer, Noel Annan, commented in 1951: 'It still stands as a major contribution to scholarship and in a sense will never be superseded in its scope.' His other philosophical writings included *The Science of Ethics* (1882), and *The English Utilitarians,* three volumes (1900). His biographical works included *English Men of Letters*, series of five volumes (1880-1904), *Studies of a Biographer*, four volumes (1898) and *Hours in a Library*, three volumes (1874-6) which shows him at his best as a literary critic. In *The Science of Ethics* Stephen expressed the belief that: 'the greatest literature is the best source for understanding the ideas of an age ... even minor writers and pamphleteers must be studied for understanding the configurations of the times.' In 1895 Stephen wrote a biography of his brother Sir James Stephen, who had died the year before. If Stephen's literary interests dominated his later years over-riding, but never subduing, his love of mountains, those interests had been in existence as a strong background influence throughout his active years as an alpine pioneer. In 1875 he wrote: 'I will confess to preferring the men who have sown some new seed of thought above the heroes whose names mark epochs in history. I would rather make the nation's ballads than give its laws, ... I would rather have written Hamlet than defeated the Spanish Armada, ... I would rather have been Voltaire or Goethe than Frederick or Napoleon.' (Note 9)

When Stephen's wife Julia died in 1895, their eldest daughter Vanessa was sixteen, and their youngest son Adrian twelve. He wrote to Loppé: *Je suis à peu prés écrasé. Je ne sais pas comment je regagnerai un peu de courage, mais il faut essayer de faire ce que je puis pour mes enfants.* (I feel shattered. I don't know how I shall ever regain my courage. But I must try to do what I can for the sake of my children.) The depth of his grief was something that he could never quite shake off. He had relied excessively on Julia's affection and support; her death left him with a feeling of emptiness. The burden of her mother's household duties was taken over by his stepdaughter Stella Duckworth, but two years later she died after a short illness, when Vanessa took her place. Bitterness and ill-health saddened Stephen's last years, and he became specially demanding of his children. In 1902 abdominal cancer was diagnosed. Surgery provided a short period of relief; but his health slowly went into decline. He continued writing until shortly before his death, working on a course of lectures entitled English Literature and Society in the Eighteenth Century, which introduced a study supporting his belief that a work of art has a life of its own in time, and is subject to different kinds of perception in each age – the communication between author and reader constantly changing. The exercise of the intellect was a passion with Stephen, and it was always his dread in old age, lest he should lose his power of thought.

About one month after Stephen's death on 2 February 1904 his daughter Virginia, then twenty-two, wrote to a friend: 'I have the curious feeling of living with him every day. I often wonder as we sit talking what it is I am waiting for, and then I know I want to hear what he thinks. It was a most exquisite feeling to be with him, even to touch his hand – he was so quick, and that one finds in no one else.' A few months later she wrote to her sister Vanessa: 'I have been thinking a great deal about father ... I believe he was really very modest. He was certainly not self-conscious in his work; nor was he an egoist.' The insularity of Stephen's character was quintessentially English. His integrity, rectitude, and high moral standards, were among the qualities that Victorian England venerated. George Mathews wrote of Stephen: 'Under a somewhat brusque exterior, he concealed one of the sweetest and kindest hearts ever given to the sons of men.' It had been said of him that he was 'unworldly without being saintly, unambitious without being inactive, warm-hearted without being sentimental; he loved his friends, and scorned to injure his enemies'.

In 1870, Stephen wrote to Whymper, well established by then as an illustrator of alpine scenes: 'I am going to publish a little book about the Alps. ... Longman says that I ought to have an illustration, and asks me to apply to you. Can you devise a good subject for a frontispiece? ... If a view of scenery, ... it would have to be something in the Oberland – the Eiger or Schreckhorn or thereabouts. This sounds to me rather stale, and I should prefer some picture of self and friends hanging on by our eyelashes. ... The book is to come out at Christmas. When do you appear?' Whymper, at work then on the final stages of his *Scrambles amongst the Alps*, was able to meet Stephen's request, and the latter expressed himself 'thoroughly well pleased' with Whymper's proofs; but it is interesting that he offered a few suggestions intended to render the illustrations historically more accurate.[10]

Both Whymper's book and Stephen's *The playground of Europe*, appeared in 1871; although of an entirely different character, they remain among the great classics of mountaineering literature. The two books played a vital role in restoring a degree of respectability to alpine mountaineering at a period when the sport had not fully recovered from disrepute after the Matterhorn accident in 1865. Shortly before the publication of his book, Stephen wrote to his American friend, James Russell Lowell: 'Perhaps I may send you a little reminder of myself in a little book on the Alps, ... It is a very humble performance in literature; and you needn't read it. Only accept it as a token of my regard and of my wishes that I could send you something better.'

In an Introduction to a reissue of *The playground of Europe* in 1936 Geoffrey Young wrote: 'A pause followed upon the successful conquest of all the greater Alps. It even seemed possible that climbing might end where it had begun, among academics and leisured intellectuals. ... It was due very largely to Leslie Stephen's *Playground* that this gap was safely bridged. The estimation in which he was held as writer, thinker, and equally as mountaineer gave him the position to speak with authority of this new world of discovery. The mountaineering elect could welcome him wholeheartedly as their representative, and delight in all he found to say in justification of their private hobby.' The title of his book does not seem to express appropriately what Stephen really thought and felt about the alps. Douglas Freshfield rightly remarked: 'The Alps were for Stephen a playground, but they were also a cathedral.' Stephen's 'worship' of the mountains is reflected in his writings which reveal how deeply sensitive he was to their beauty and power. 'To me the Wengern Alp is a sacred place – the holy of holies in the mountain sanctuary, and

---

[10]In illustrating his own book Whymper appears occasionally to have allowed drama to triumph over accuracy – a practice which nowadays is not regarded as unusual.

the emotions produced when no desecrating influence is present and old memories rise up, ... belong to that innermost region of feeling which I would not, if I could, lay bare.' But Stephen was not content merely to admire. The view from the Wengern Alp included the challenging aspects of the Jungfraujoch and the Eigerjoch, both of which he was the first to cross. The physical challenges that the mountains demanded, increased the power of their attraction; the disciplines necessary for the enjoyment of his pastime were clearly part of something that appealed to Stephen's abstemious nature. His book reveals a good deal about his mountain philosophy. He tended to say exactly what he felt, expressing his feelings with a mixture of dry humour and satire. Descriptions of his climbs are blended with philosophical musings, illustrating his thoughts during moods of deep enjoyment – a literary don projecting his personality and style on to a much-loved subject. He had once written: 'A man may worship mountains, and yet have a quiet joke with them when he is wandering all day in their tremendous solitudes.' He had a profound dislike of ornate language. Here is how he reacted to Ruskin's purple passages: 'Mr Ruskin has covered the Matterhorn with a whole web of poetical associations which, to a severe taste, is perhaps a trifle too fine ... most humble writers will feel that if they try to imitate Mr Ruskin's eloquence they will pay the penalty of becoming ridiculous.' Stephen's mountain writing was natural, unaffected and straightforward. According to Clinton Dent, Stephen wrote: 'without effort, evidently for the sheer pleasure of experiencing again the delights of a pursuit which was, to him, in the truest sense of the word a pure recreation.' Of Stephen as a mountaineer, someone had said that he strode from peak to peak like a pair of compasses. Whymper spoke of him as 'the fleetest of foot of the whole Alpine brotherhood. ... Of all the men I have met in the Alps, no one attracted me so much as Leslie Stephen. It was not so much because he was an athlete and a conspicuous mountaineer as from the fact ... that he towered head and shoulders above the rest. As time went on, one found that to the physical and intellectual qualities were united tenderness of heart and generosity. 'A mutual respect for their respective exploits appears to have developed between Whymper and Stephen who, in reviewing Whymper's book, wrote: 'His career in 1865, up to its most disastrous end, was by far the most brilliant ever carried out in the Alps; and we, who remained behind and heard the reports of his successive triumphs, can well remember the admiration, not unmingled with jealousy, with which we received them. He would leave us, we thought, nothing to conquer.' (Note 10) The alpine careers of Stephen and Whymper were both brilliant. Between 1861-65 Whymper made four first ascents of 4000m peaks, and four of 3000m peaks. Stephen made altogether five first ascents of 4000m peaks, new routes on three others, and five first ascents of 3000m peaks, as well as explorations of glacier passes. Both climbed with guides, but their attitudes towards them contrasted sharply: Whymper relied on their superior skills, but exercised a dominating authority, Stephen acknowledged his appreciation of their contribution to his successes.

In 1894, the year in which Stephen paid his last visit to the Alps, a new edition of *The playground of Europe* was published, in which two of the original chapters were suppressed, and substituted by three others. As editor of the *Alpine Journal* in 1871, Stephen had refused to allow a review of his book to appear when it was first published. In reviewing the new edition the *Alpine Journal* remarked: 'The reissue of this Alpine classic will be a great boon to the younger generation of mountain lovers, many of whom have doubtless unsuccessfully endeavoured to procure copies of the first edition, long since out of print. ... Whilst regretting the loss of any of the contents of the original edition we welcome the additions, and especially the "Sunset on Mont Blanc" where once again the great peak's supremacy is affirmed and an admirable word picture given of one of the glorious effects which this mountain provides.' (Note 11) That chapter, which achieves a peak of literary artistry, was described by Stephen in 1895 as 'the best thing I ever wrote'. The chapters omitted from the 1894 edition related to The Old School and The New School, in which Stephen, qualified as he was by his voracious reading and his own exploits, traced the transition from a fashionable horror of mountains to a fashionable worship of mountains. The 1894 edition contained a dedication to Loppé, with whom, on the morning of 6 August 1873, he had set out from Chamonix, climbing through the lower pinewoods, the séracs of the glaciers, lingering on the Dôme du Goûter, and the Bosses ridge, calculating their time carefully, and 'stepping upon the culminating ridge about an hour before sunset ... to prepare for the grand spectacle'. Loppé, seated on the summit snows, worked furiously in an attempt 'to fix upon canvas some of the

110

magic beauties of the scene'. (Note 12) At the end of a brilliant sunset display in faultless weather they raced down from the summit, passing the Corridor and the Grand Plateau 'between day and night', reaching the shelter at the Grands Mulets by the light of a full moon. Stephen recalls the experience in his dedication: 'Twenty-one years ago we climbed Mont Blanc together to watch the sunset from its summit. Less than a year ago, we observed the same phenomenon from the foot of the mountain. The intervening years have probably made little difference in the sunset. If they have made some difference in our powers of reaching the best point of view, they have, I hope, diminished neither our admiration of such spectacles, nor our pleasure in each other's companionship.' Stephen's book had set a standard for mountain literature which few could surpass. Three further editions appeared during the next five years. In 1903, Stephen gave two old ice-axes and an alpenstock to the Alpine Club, writing in a letter to Sir Martin Conway, then President: 'Those quaint old poles reminded me of some of the pleasantest days of my life. My membership of the Club has been a source of unmixed pleasure.'

There is great diversity to be found in *The playground of Europe*. Apart from accounts of classic ascents, there are glimpses of tranquil Bernese villages in winter and of two solitary climbs one of which, entitled 'A Bye-day in the Alps', describes an ascent of the Dent d'Oche (2220m), a rocky mountain situated above the 'quiet old town' of Evian, now a thriving tourist resort. 'The climb is perfectly easy, though I tried to complicate matters by going the wrong way. ... Indeed, to confess the truth, a former attempt on the mountain had failed altogether by reason of my ingeniously attacking it by the only impracticable route. It was with all the more satisfaction that I found myself on the present occasion rapidly approaching the summit. ... Few views in the Alps or in Europe can be more impressive ... At my feet lay the huge crescent of the Lake of Geneva – 44 miles in length on the Southern shore and 55 along the Northern – ... Here was a fitting place to invoke the shades of Byron and Shelley and Rousseau, of Gibbon and Voltaire, and of all the great men ... whose names are indissolubly associated with the loveliest lake in Europe. ... Had I been a bona fide anchorite, I might possibly have remained on the summit of the Dent d'Oche till my nails grew into my flesh. ... Thoughts of dinner and speculations about a certain short cut became irresistible, and before long I descended from my peak and my poetising.' An earlier visitor, Sir Samuel Romilly, who in 1781 made an 'excursion to the summit of the Dent d'Oche' 'provided a lofty impression of the view from this very high mountain of Savoy on the southern bank of the lake of Geneva. The ascent is very difficult and for that reason, perhaps, it is seldom visited by strangers; but the prospect it affords is the most beautiful and the most sublime that I ever beheld ...' Choices from the many gems which fill *The playground of Europe* can only be subjective. I derive particular enjoyment from Stephen's account of the sunset view from the top of Mont Blanc in 1873; the solitary descent of an unknown Dolomite ridge in 1869; and the introspective essay, 'The Regrets of a Mountaineer', written in 1867 shortly after his first marriage, which contains an element of sadness, but also of humour – feelings which are likely to raise an echo for all who, because of increased responsibilities, infirmity or age, have had to abandon their active mountain days.

CHAPTER FIVE
ADOLPHUS WARBURTON MOORE
1841-87

> Mountaineering is a pursuit in which the deepest motives
> behind it are a longing for adventure, a love of nature, and a
> sentiment that can only be called mystical. The traditional
> mountaineer matches himself against the forces of nature, and
> does not seek to vie with other men in the sort of competition
> that requires regulations and rewards.
>
> CF Meade, 1940

Adolphus Warburton Moore is remembered in alpine history as
having been the first to conceive the possibility of a route up Mont
Blanc from Italy by its impressive Brenva face, which his party
succeeded in climbing in 1865. An account of the ascent of the Route
Moore, or the Old Brenva route as it is now called, appears in his
book *The Alps in 1864* published in 1867. Subtitled 'A private journal',
the book was little more than an extension of Moore's climbing
diaries covering his remarkably successful alpine campaigns in 1864,
to which was added a supplement to include his account of the
Brenva climb. The book was not intended for general publication,
and only a limited number of copies were printed. With the
permission of Moore's family, it was first made available to the public
in a fine edition published by David Douglas of Edinburgh in 1902,
fifteen years after Moore's death. The book is a model of an explorer's
testament, an unpretentious and faithful record of Moore's
mountaineering activities during the Alpine Golden Age. Douglas
Freshfield summed it up as: 'perhaps the most authentic, exact and
vivid record of what climbing was to early explorers of the High Alps.'
It reads like an autobiography of one of the most active mountaineers
of the Victorian era, revealing Moore's wide knowledge of the
western and central Alps, which gave him extensive scope for
undertaking between 1860-75 a remarkable series of pioneering
expeditions.

A quotation from Theocritus, once suggested as a motto for the early Alpine Club, 'One must be doing something while the knee is green', was said to have been applied aptly to the young Moore during his early alpine journeys. Having first visited the alps at the age of nineteen, he was twenty-three in 1864 when during an alpine campaign of six weeks he planned and carried out a series of bold ventures which included twelve glacier passes (three crossed for the first time), and six mountain ascents. The following summer his alpine activities included the crossings of eight passes and the ascents of seven peaks. His close friend and climbing companions was Horace Walker, older than him by three years, whose sister Lucy was one of the leading lady climbers of her day. Moore climbed with the best guides, initially employing Christian Almer, and later Jakob Anderegg. Crossing passes might seem a pedestrian form of alpine activity; but the passes that Moore crossed were mostly pioneered by him, approached with an element of uncertainty, and without the assurance of a descent on the other side – feelings not unlike those experienced by early Himalayan explorers half a century later. Moore's expeditions were planned with an attention to detail that exemplified his character; his topographical skills provided him with unlimited opportunities for the pioneering journeys in which he delighted. He expressed the view that 'no one really knows a group until he has been up and down all its valleys'. Geoffrey Winthrop Young summed up his qualities: 'In charm of presentment Moore is only second to Stephen. In skill and daring as a climber he would seem to have been surpassed only by the Reverend Charles Hudson among his contemporaries, and as a mountaineer of intimate vision ... he overtopped them all'. (Note 1)

Moore served his alpine apprenticeship in 1860 and 1861 under Reverend Hereford Brooke George, editor of the first three volumes of the *Alpine Journal*, and author of a book published in 1866, *The Oberland and its glaciers explored and illustrated*. Two early journeys were confined to glacier travel and the crossings of cols, including the Anterne, Théodule and Géant. A few minor ascents were made, such as the Strahlegg, Titlis and Buet; and attempts were made to climb the Lyskamm and Galenstock. Several regions of the Alps were visited enabling Moore to accumulate a store of knowledge upon which he was able to draw when planning subsequent expeditions. In 1862 he began to undertake more serious mountaineering. With George, he made the first ascent of the Gross Fiescherhorn (4048m), attempted the Mönch, and was a member of Stephen's party during the first passage of the Jungfraujoch. The Sesiajoch was traversed from Italy to Switzerland for the first time, and ten other passes were crossed, including the Oberaarjoch, the Mönchjoch, and the Adler pass. In 1863, Moore climbed the Dom, and the Lyskamm (third ascent), also the Aiguille du Gouter and Dome du Gouter, but was unable to continue over the Bosses ridge to the top of Mont Blanc. He also attempted Piz Roseg, made his third ascent and second crossing of the Strahlegg, and crossed the Alphubeljoch from Saas to Täsch. During a visit to Courmayeur that year in a party including George, RJS Macdonald, and F Morshead, with the guides Melchior Anderegg, Christian Almer and Peter Perren, a study was made of the possibility of an alternative way of ascending Mont Blanc from the Brenva glacier. After examining the face, the balance of opinion among the guides was unfavourable because of its steepness, the difficulty of the glacier, and the danger of avalanches. Anderegg and Perren ruled the idea out altogether: Almer alone, although less despondent, was non-commital. The following year Moore and Almer were able, as will be seen, to take a more optimistic view. Four active summers in the Alps had whetted Moore's appetite, encouraging him to start planning his own ventures.

Moore drew up a number of interesting objectives for his alpine holiday in the summer of 1864, almost all of which were achieved. Accompanied mostly by Horace Walker, he was able to engage as sole guide Almer whose qualities he had learned to appreciate during three previous seasons with George. Almer, the chamois hunter from Grindelwald who stood on top of the Wetterhorn with Sir Alfred Wills ten years earlier, commenced his guiding career in 1856 and had several first ascents to his credit, winning a reputation for calmness, amiability and reliability. Edward Whymper who, like Moore, was introduced to the Alps in 1860, had arranged to join Moore's party for their first week's campaign in the Dauphiné, with his guide Michel Croz of Chamonix. Although not widely known then, Croz had been highly praised for his strength and courage on previous expeditions with Francis Fox Tuckett, Thomas George Bonney, and William Mathews, with whom he had made the first ascents of Monte Viso, the Grande Casse, and Mont Pourri in 1860-61. Moore had some apprehensions about how the two guides might combine, writing to Mathews a few days before his departure from England: 'We are slightly wondering how Almer and Croz will get on, each being ignorant of a word of the other's language.' Moore need not have worried. The contrasting temperaments of the two men seemed to complement their relationship, Croz being excitable and impetuous with Almer always cool and measured. The Dauphiné region was off the beaten track and relatively unknown. Bonney summed it up. 'Everything is of the poorest kind; fresh meat can only be obtained at rare intervals, the bread and wine are equally sour, the *auberges* are equally filthy, and the beds entomological vivaria!' The joint campaign began on 21 June, when the party crossed the Col des Aiguilles d'Arve descending to La Grave. Departing from there on 23 June, and ignoring local advice as to its inaccessibility, they made the first crossing of the Brèche de la Meije. Moore commented: 'The great southern face of the Meije, overhanging this arm of the glacier, is a wonderful object; a long line of cliff, totally unlike anything I have seen in any other part of the Alps. The range of crags forming the left bank of the glacier is seamed by several snow couloirs, leading up to gaps in the ridge.' (Note 2)

Descending from the Brèche de la Meije into the 'wilderness' of the Vallon des Etançons, Moore's party battled their way through a howling gale down a valley 'covered with stones of all sizes from that of a cricket-ball upwards without the faintest sign of a path', to reach La Bérarde after a journey of fourteen and a half hours. There, they 'entered the house of young Rodier, who always receives the casual visitors to this out of the way spot'. After a frugal dinner, comprising ham and eggs prepared by Moore and Walker, they were ready to retire for the night. Rodier showed them to their sleeping quarters. 'He led us to a capacious barn close by, where there was an abundance of clean straw, held a candle while we arranged ourselves for the night, not a very long operation, and then took his departure.' (Note 3) The baggage had been sent round by the valley; the porter, probably counting upon their failure to cross the pass, turned up a day late and it was found that two-thirds of the cigar supply had disappeared. Walker asked, "*Monsieur Pic, je pense que vous avez fumé beaucoup hier*", (I suppose that you smoked quite heavily yesterday) to which the fellow replied with an air of surprise and total innocence quite delightful, "*Moi, je ne fume jamais, jamais*" (What, me? I never smoke.) Of course, after that nothing more could be said, but we mentally resolved that if he did not smoke, he chewed, and that pretty vigorously.' Departing from La Bérarde, the party including the porter Pic set up a bivouac on the glacier de la Bonne Pierre. The following morning it was discovered that four-fifths of the wine was missing. Moore, Walker and Whymper had not touched any, while Croz and Almer were quite emphatic that they had not done so; Pic again professed his complete innocence. Whymper offered a solution: 'the dryness of the air was responsible: one method of preventing such evaporation is to use the wine-flask as a pillow.'

On 25 June the party, minus the porter, set out early from their bivouac to ascend the unclimbed Les Ecrins. Within two hours, at 5.55, they reached the Col des Ecrins, descending to the Glacier Blanc below the north-east face of the mountain. Encouraged by an apparent lack of any real difficulty, Moore 'hazarded the opinion that by 9.30 we should be seated on the highest point'. Whymper was less sanguine, and 'on hearing my opinion, offered to bet Walker and myself two francs that we should not get up at all, an offer which we promptly accepted'. Two years earlier, Croz had taken part in two previous attempts to climb the mountain. (Note 4) On reaching the *bergschrund*[1] opinions were divided between the two guides as to the best route. Croz suggested climbing the icy face to a point directly below the summit, while Almer preferred to try the rock ridge to the left. Croz did not trust the rocks and began cutting steps up the ice. The work was arduous, and after half-an-hour doubts began to be raised about whether the face should not be abandoned in favour of the rocks for which Almer had shown a preference. This caused a momentary rumpus. 'Now, up to the present time no two men could have got on better ... than Croz and Almer. ... Almer displayed such an utter abnegation of self, and such deference to Croz's opinion, that had the latter been the worst-tempered fellow in the world, instead of the really good fellow that he was, he could not have found a cause of quarrel. Upon this occasion, although Almer adhered to his own opinion that it would be better to keep to the rocks, he begged us to follow the advice of Croz. ... Croz protested emphatically against the

[1]A crevasse or gap separating a glacier from the base of a mountain.

rocks, but left it to us to decide ... The position was an awkward one. ... So convinced, however, were we that the rocks offered the most advisable route, that we determined to try the experiment on Croz's temper, and announced our decision accordingly. The effect was electric; Croz came back again in the steps which he had cut ... requesting us to understand that, as we had chosen, we might do the work ourselves.' The threatened storm blew over: Croz returned to his task, and four and a half hours later, after overcoming a troublesome couloir, the party emerged from the face reaching the upper part of the north-east ridge, which they then followed. '[When] we were close to the top, the guides tried to persuade us to go in front, so as to be the first to set foot on the summit. But this we declined; they had done the work, let them be the first to reap the reward.' The climb had taken nine and a half hours from their overnight bivouac.

Twenty minutes were spent on the summit. Doubts were raised about the choice of a suitable descent route, serious misgivings having been raised about attempting to climb down the icy face. It was decided to traverse the ridge in the opposite direction. Almer led the way, proceeding slowly and with great care along the unknown ridge. Suddenly he stopped short, looked about him uneasily, and began to discuss the nature of the difficulty with Croz. 'Under any other circumstances we should have been amused at Almer's endeavours to communicate his views to Croz in an amazing mixture of pantomime, bad German, and worse French ... we soon made out that the point at issue was whether we could get over this particular place, or whether we must return to the summit, and go down the way we had come. Croz was of the latter opinion, while Almer obstinately maintained that ... we *could* get over it. ... Croz was unconvinced, and came back to us, declaring plainly that we should have to return. We shouted to Almer, who was still below, but he evidently had not the slightest intention of returning, and in a few moments called upon us to come on, an injunction which we cheerfully obeyed, as, in our opinion, anything would be preferable to a retreat, and Croz perforce followed. ... We crept along the cliffs, sometimes on one side of the ridge, sometimes on the other, frequently passing our arms over the summit, with our feet resting on rather less than nothing. Almer led with wonderful skill and courage, and gradually brought us over the worst portions.' There is a striking engraving in *Scrambles amongst the*

Alps of this traverse, illustrating a daring leap by Almer across a notch in the ridge. Moore, the last man on the rope, evidently did not see the leap nor does his narrative mention it. The point was seized upon by the meticulous alpine chronicler Coolidge, giving rise to a heated correspondence between him and Whymper, and leading to years of strained relations between the two men. Although it appears that Moore and Whymper read each others' accounts before publication, (each quoted short passages from the other) there are differences in their respective descriptions of the descent. Whymper highlighted Almer's leap across a fault in the ridge, while Moore dwelt upon the sharpness and exposure, with progress only possible in places by straddling the ridge. It is clear that the traverse of the ridge and the descent of the face below tried the skills and patience of everyone. A lengthy route down the Glacier Blanc followed in the gathering dusk, and the party reached the valley at 9.40pm in rainfall and complete darkness. Moore, Walker and Almer decided to bivouac under 'a huge mass of rock as big as a house' which served as a shelter, sharing between them a stick of chocolate for supper. (Note 5) Whymper and Croz pushed on for another half-hour spending the night in a rhododendron forest, hungry but warmed by the glow of a fire. Both groups apparently slept soundly after their trying twenty-hour day. Early the next morning they walked down the valley via Ailefroide to Vallouise for breakfast.

Two days after the Ecrins ascent, the same party, joined by Whymper's friend Jean Reynaud, a surveyor of roads from La Bessé, pioneered an adventurous crossing from the Val d'Entraigues over the Col de la Pilatte situated between Les Bans and the Crête des Boeufs. Guided by Almer's route-finding skills, the ascent to the pass was long and fatiguing, its final part involving a steep and narrow rock couloir, partly iced, and threatened by falling fragments. Cloud and snowfall greeted their arrival on the Col, but not before Croz had obtained a brief glimpse of the Pilatte glacier below, and the direction they would need to follow. A brilliant lead by Croz through fog took them down to the *bergschrund*. The only way forward from there required a jump of fifteen feet across a gap of about ten feet. After Croz, Walker and Whymper had landed safely, it was Reynaud's turn. 'Monsieur Reynaud advanced to the edge, looked, hesitated, drew back, and finally declared that he could not jump it ... We encouraged him, but without effect, and at last proposed to lower him down, when the others would hook hold of his legs somehow and pull him across. Almer and I therefore made our footing as secure as possible, anchored ourselves with our axes, and made ready to lower our friend, but his courage failed him at the last moment and he refused to go. We were now obliged to use stronger arguments, as it was snowing fast, and time was passing, so we pointed out that, if we wished to return ever so much, we could not get the others back across the *schrund* and that, in point of fact, there was no choice – over he must go. Again did he advance to the edge, again draw back, but finally, with a despairing groan, leaped, and just landed clear of the chasm, but instead of letting his rope hang loose, he held it in one hand, and thereby nearly pulled me over, head foremost.' Whymper provides a colourful account of this incident, immortalised by an engraving in his book: 'I do not believe that he [Reynaud] was a whit more reluctant to pass the place than we others, but he was infinitely more demonstrative, – in a word, he was French. ... How he came over I do not know. We saw a toe – it seemed to belong to Moore; we saw Reynaud a flying body, coming down as if taking a header into water; with arms and legs all abroad, his leg of mutton flying in the air, his bâton escaped from his grasp; and then we heard a thud as if a bundle of carpets had been pitched out of a window. ... When set upon his feet he was a sorry spectacle; his head was a great snowball; brandy was trickling out of one side of the knapsack, chartreuse out of the other.' The jump proved to be their last obstacle, and after a walk of about three hours down the Vallon de la Pilatte, the party returned to M Rodier's front door at La Bérarde late in the afternoon.

Moore carried out one other expedition with Whymper that summer, accompanied by their respective guides Almer and Croz. Moore was eager to discover a new way from Zinal to Zermatt via the Moming glacier, possibly shorter than the known routes across the Triftjoch and the Col Durand. He was confident that one could be found in spite of Melchior Anderegg's conviction to the contrary. 'You may make the attempt, and you may lose your life but, take my word for it, you will never get over it: it is impossible.' A night was spent on the Arpitettaz alp above Zinal in a leaky, foul-smelling hovel occupied by a cheese-maker. Moore described it as 'an exaggerated pig-sty'. (Note 6) Moore's party, discouraged by a heavily clouded morning, left the alp doubtfully on 18 July to search for their pass at the head of the glacier. The cheese-maker told them that they need not distress themselves about the weather, as it was not possible to get to the point for which they were aiming. The complexities of the Moming glacier gave rise, once again, to divided opinions between the two guides. Here is an extract from Whymper's account. 'I advocated that a course should be steered due south, and that the upper plateau of the Moming glacier should be attained by making a great detour to our right. This was negatived without a division. Almer declared in favour of making for some rocks to the south-west of the Schalihorn, and attaining the upper plateau of the glacier by mounting them. Croz advised a middle course, up some very steep and broken glacier. Croz's route seemed likely to turn out to be impracticable, because much step-cutting would be required upon it. Almer's rocks did not look good; they were, possibly, unassailable. I thought both routes were bad, and declined to vote for either of them. Moore hesitated, Almer gave way, and Croz's route was adopted. 'But before he got very far, (Whymper again): 'Croz suggested the abandonment of his own and the adoption of Almer's route. No one opposed the change of plan, and ... [Croz] proceeded to cut steps across an ice-slope towards the rocks. ... The part [which Croz originally] intended to traverse was, in a sense, undoubtedly practicable. He gave it up because it would have involved too much step-cutting. But the part of this glacier which intervened between his route and Almer's rocks was, in the most complete sense of the word, impracticable. ... It was executing a flanking movement in the face of an enemy by whom we might be attacked at any moment. The peril was obvious. It was a monstrous folly. It was foolhardiness. A retreat should have been sounded.' (Note 7) Throughout twenty minutes of the ice-traverse the party was in danger; Moore's reference to it is more restrained, but no less expressive. 'I am not ashamed to confess that during the whole time we were crossing this slope my heart was in my mouth, and I never felt relieved from such a load of care as when ... we got on to the rocks. ... I have never heard a positive oath come from Almer's mouth, but the language in which he kept up a running commentary, more to himself than to me, as we went along, was stronger than I should have given him credit for using. His prominent feeling seemed to be one of *indignation* that we should be in such a position, and self-reproach at being a party to the proceeding.'

Shortly after completing the crossing: 'We saw one of the immense masses of ice, underneath which we had crept in fear and trembling, lurch over, totter for a moment as if struggling against the resistless pressure which was urging it on, and then fall with a crash, straight down upon the slope we had traversed.' The dividing ridge at the head of the Moming glacier was eventually reached and the party found themselves standing on a depression between the Rothorn and the Schalihorn. There are differences between Whymper's and Moore's accounts of the events that followed. Whymper first: 'A steep wall of snow was upon the Zinal side of the summit (of the pass); but what the descent was like on the other side we could not tell, for a billow of snow tossed over its crest by the western winds, suspended o'er Zermatt with motion arrested, resembling an ocean wave frozen in the act of breaking, cut off the view. Croz – held hard by the others, who kept down the Zinal side – opened his shoulders, flogged down the foam, and cut away the cornice to its junction with the summit; then boldly leaped down, and called on us to follow him.' (Note 8) There is an impressive illustration of Croz in action with his ice-axe, magically poised on the very edge of a large cornice. Moore writes: 'It was not easy to discover what lay between us and the [Hohlicht] glacier, for at the point at which we had hit the ridge an immense snow cornice impended over it, and it was impossible to venture far enough on this to get a look down. However, advancing along the ridge towards the Rothorn for a few yards, we found a point where the breadth of this overhanging fringe was not so great, and the guides, having cut away a portion of it, disclosed a wall of snow, which, so far as we could judge through the fog, though exceedingly steep was of no great height, that is to say, not more than a hundred feet. Anyhow, Croz led the way through the hole in the cornice, and we followed, Almer bringing up the rear. The descent was more formidable in appearance than reality, the snow being soft but good, and floundering down we were soon on the comparatively level surface beneath.' The facts from Moore: a touch of drama from Whymper. The passage of the party from the Arpitettaz alp to Zermatt had taken twelve hours, proving that although the new pass was more direct it was not any shorter; and, owing to the hazards of the Moming glacier, it turned out to be much more arduous. It has never become a popular route. Moore concluded: 'Most fortunate was it

Professor FJ Hugi (1796-1855) and scientific team on Rottal, by Martin Disteli, 1830.

Approaching the Furka Pass (2431m) in 1925; note huge mass of Rhône glacier and unsurfaced motor road. Photo: P de Rivaz.

Rhône Glacier from Gletsch in 1848, by Eugène Cicéri.

Rhône glacier in 1998.

La Meije (northern aspect) from La Grave. Brèche de la Meije is the col on far right.

La Meije (southern aspect) from Châtelleret.

P à Spescha (1752-1833).

A von Haller (1708-77).

J-J Scheuchzer (1672-1733).

General G-H Dufour (1787-1875).

Horace Bénédict de Saussure
(1740-99), by J Iuel, 1777.

Mont Aiguille (Vercors), 1993

Chamois hunter, by G
Lory, 1825.

Alfred Wills in 1854.

View from the Torrenthorn.

Grindelwald and Wetterhorn, by J-J Wetzl, 1820.

The Eagle's Nest, Sixt, 1995

Matterhorn and
Weisshorn from
Riederalp, with
Villa Cassel.

Ascent of East ridge, Weisshorn.

Belalp Hotel (right), Villa Lusgen (above far left), with shrunken Aletsch glacier, 1985.

Tyndall Memorial on Lusgen alp.

Bietschhorn and Nest glacier.

Wengernalp, by S Corrodi, 1840.

Traverse of Lyskamm ridge.

Pierre Gaspard Memorial at
St Christophe village.

Leslie Stephen at Grindelwald 1889.
Photo: Gabriel Loppé

British Climbers and guides at Chamonix in 1863. Back row (left to right): F Morshead, P Perren, AW Moore, HB George and R Stephenson. Front row (left to right): M Anderegg, R Macdonald and C Almer.

Professor John Tyndall, by G Richmond, 1864.

Professor James David Forbes, by J Watson Gordon, 1860.

Dychtau from the south. Mummery's route followed the rock rib just left of centre.

that we had as guides two of the first ice-men in the Alps, to whom ignorance of the ground was of very trifling consequence as, with incompetent or second-rate men, I doubt whether we should have extricated ourselves.'

An important climb made a fortnight earlier by Moore, accompanied by Almer, was a traverse of Mont Blanc on 2 July from the Pavillon de Bellevue above Les Houches, over the Aiguille and Dôme du Goûter, where they were greatly slowed by steep ice, then along the Bosses ridge. 'At 3.5pm [3.05pm] two proud and happy men grasped each other's hands on the summit of Mont Blanc. We had been rather more than thirteen hours from the Bellevue ... but under ordinary circumstances the distance might be accomplished in certainly two hours less time, as we were detained quite that [by step-cutting] on the Aiguille du Goûter. The sky was still cloudless, and the atmosphere retained the marvellous clearness by which it had been characterised all day. We therefore saw the view under such favourable circumstances as fall to the lot of few.' They descended from the top of Mont Blanc via the *Mur de la Côte,* (a feature on the north-east side below the top of Mont Blanc) near the edge overlooking the Glacier de la Brenva. 'I had expected in this direction a very considerable precipice ... but I was completely astounded to see the trifling depth at which the upper *névé* [consolidated snow] of the Brenva glacier appeared to lie, and was at once firmly led to believe [in] the accessibility of Mont Blanc from that side, if the head of the glacier [could] only be reached from Courmayeur.' The pursuit of that objective became the focal point of Moore's plans for 1865. Moore and Almer were benighted in the forest during their descent of Mont Blanc, arriving in Chamonix after a pre-dawn walk of twenty-five minutes the following morning.

Moore's other climbs, during his remarkably successful 1864 season, included the Rimpfischhorn (second ascent) on 12 July with Morshead and Almer, Lucy Walker, her father Frank, and their guides Melchior and Jacob Anderegg. Their times are worth mentioning; starting from the Monte Rosa hotel Zermatt at 2.15am, they reached the top at 11.10am, returning to the hotel at 4.15pm. (No chair-lift in those days!) Moore and Almer then traversed the Biesjoch from Randa to the Turtmann Tal, where they spent a night at an inn on the lonely and isolated Gruben Alp. From there they crossed the ridge by a pass that divides the Turtmann Tal from the Val d'Anniviers near the peak of Bella Tola, a panoramic viewpoint popular today with walkers. They reached Zinal in the late afternoon to be met by Whymper and Croz for the journey up the Moming glacier. On 19 July Moore and Almer travelled from Zermatt to Belalp, where they halted at the hotel for a day. 'Enforced idleness in such a position as that of this most charming inn was not a matter of regret. ... As I lay on the grass slopes, in a state of bliss, I looked straight up the Aletsch glacier for many miles. ... The evening was one of the finest I ever remember in the Alps, and the sunset on the Dom and Weisshorn was a thing to be dreamed of, so unearthly beautiful was it.' On 21 July they climbed the Aletschhorn by its southern slopes and south-east ridge, then crossed the Beichpass to the Lötschental. This was followed on 22 July by the first passage of the Wetterlücke to Lauterbrunnen and Grindelwald. On 25 July, a large party, comprising Moore and C Wigram with Frank, Lucy and Horace Walker, accompanied by six guides among whom were Almer, Melchior and Jakob Anderegg, climbed the Eiger (third ascent) from Wengernalp. Two days later, Moore and Horace Walker, accompanied by Almer and Rudolph Boss, started from Grindelwald at 12.15am, reaching the top of the Wetterhorn at 9.45am. The party traversed the mountain, descending to Rosenlaui from where they crossed the Grosse Scheidegg returning to Grindelwald at 8.20pm. Moore described this as 'one of the most glorious excursions I ever had the pleasure of making' adding, 'we had fairly earned our dinner'. *The Alps in 1864* contains colourful accounts of these expeditions.

It was during the Rimpfischhorn climb that Moore first met Jakob Anderegg, 'a fine, handsome, fair man, with a profusion of beard, and apparently as strong as a horse'. At the relatively late age of thirty-seven he had taken up guiding as a profession, in 1864. In August he was engaged by Stephen, as a joint guide with his cousin Melchior for the Zinal Rothorn ascent, and received high praise from Stephen. Jakob Anderegg henceforth accompanied Moore on almost all his future climbs until the year of his death in 1878. During his most active years, between 1864-76, he made a number of first ascents of exceptional quality. In the opinion of one of his many employers, he 'reached the highest rank of his profession, with a reputation for brilliant and daring enterprise'.

In 1865 Moore and Jakob Anderegg began their first season together, joined by Horace Walker, with the ascent and the first traverse of the Tödi. Then, travelling further east, they climbed and traversed the Rheinwaldhorn. That was followed with the first ascent of Piz Roseg. One week later, on 6 July from Zermatt they made the first ascent of the Ober Gabelhorn. They continued their travels with the first crossing of the Col de Bertol and, after making the first ascent of the Pigne d'Arolla, descended to Chanrion making the first crossing of the Col de Breney. At Aosta, in bad weather, they paid a brief visit to the Val Grisanche, then retreated to Courmayeur. Backing his discovery made the year before from the *Mur de la Côte,* Moore had set his heart on attempting Mont Blanc from the Brenva glacier. At Courmayeur on 13 July, they 'were joined by Mr George Mathews, and also received a fresh recruit in the person of Mr Walker senior, who brought with him a tower of strength in the shape of Melchior Anderegg'. The latter was regularly employed by the Walker family; Frank, father of Lucy and Horace, was then aged fifty-nine. It was agreed that the combined party would commence the big venture the following day. 'Horace Walker, Jakob and I, animated by the uninterrupted series of successes ... during the previous month, considered the thing as good as done ... Mr Walker was also fairly sanguine, and Mathews was willing enough to concur in the roseate view we took of things. Melchior alone declined to share our confidence ... Jakob, who notwithstanding his almost idolatrous respect and admiration for his cousin, ventured to deride his fears, and to chaff him generally in a free, not to say irreverent manner.'

Starting from Courmayeur on 14 July the party ascended the moraine of the Brenva glacier camping that afternoon at about 2800m, somewhat below the present fixed bivouac of the Club Alpino Italiano. At 2.45am the following morning, working their way through the icefall of the Upper Brenva glacier, and crossing the depression now known as Col Moore, they reached the foot of their chosen ridge. Two hours of scrambling along a rocky buttress brought them to a: 'formidable ice *arête* (ridge) ... I have always considered it a providential circumstance that at this moment Jakob, and not Melchior, was leading the party. In saying this, I shall not for an instant be suspected of any imputation upon Melchior's courage. But in him that virtue is combined to perfection with the equally necessary one of prudence. Had he been in front, I believe that in seeing the nature of the work before us we should have halted, and discussed the propriety of proceeding, and I believe further that, as a result of that discussion, our expedition would have then and there come to an end. Now in Jakob, with courage as faultless as Melchior's and physical powers even superior, the virtue of prudence is conspicuous chiefly from its absence, and on coming to this ugly place it never for an instant occurred to him that we might object to go on.' The icy and exposed passage, which Moore traversed mostly à cheval, (straddled) occupied almost an hour. Steep slopes of névé followed, leading to the great sérac (ice-cliff) barrier above. 'After careful scrutiny, Melchior thought it just possible that we might find a passage ... The ice here was steeper and harder than it had yet been. In spite of all Melchior's care the steps were painfully insecure ... Melchior had steered with his usual discrimination, and was now attacking the séracs at the only point where they appeared at all practicable. Standing over the mouth of a crevasse choked with débris, he endeavoured to lift himself on to its upper edge, which was about fifteen feet above ... At last, by a marvellous exercise of skill and activity, he succeeded, pulled up Mr Walker and Horace Walker, and then cast off the rope to reconnoitre, leaving them to assist Mathews, Jakob and myself in the performance of a similar manoeuvre. We were all three still below, when a yell from Melchior sent a thrill through my veins "What is it?" said we to Mr Walker. A shouting communication took place between him and Melchior, and then came the answer, "He says it is all right." That moment was worth living for.' Moore's words reflect his intense relief over the feasibility of the route, and the vindication of his judgement in suggesting it. They also illustrate graphically the atmosphere of those days when pioneering ventures faced an uncertain outcome. To Moore attaches the principal credit for having visualised the route, and for backing his convictions. His account of the climb has been described as 'among the finest in mountain literature' of the period. The climb was made on the day following the Matterhorn accident. Five years were to pass before a second ascent was made, by Coolidge guided by Almer, who adopted a variation to the left above the great sérac barrier. Twenty-nine years later Mummery, Norman Collie and Geoffrey Hastings, made the fifth, and the first guideless, ascent after a very cold bivouac below the final sérac barrier. At the end of the nineteenth century only two further ascents of the Brenva route were made; and up to 1926, two years before Graham Brown began his explorations on the

Brenva face, a total of nineteen ascents had been recorded, five of which were guideless.

Although Professor John Tyndall spent a couple of days at Montenvers in December 1859 studying the Mer de Glace, and TS Kennedy in January 1862 reached the foot of the Hörnli ridge of the Matterhorn, Moore was the first British mountaineer to spend a winter holiday in the Alps – one of his reasons being a desire to avoid the crowds of summer tourists! His first venture was characteristic. On 23 December 1866, Moore and Horace Walker, accompanied by Melchior Anderegg, Christian Almer, and Peter Bohren left Grindelwald at 3am and, benefiting from moonlight, crossed the Finsteraarjoch and the Strahlegg, returning to Grindelwald by 1pm the next day. They also made an ascent of the Faulhorn. In December 1867, during a visit to the Dauphiné, the Brêche de la Meije (3358m), the Col de la Lauze (3512m), and the Col du Goléon (2880m) were crossed.

In January 1869 Moore and Walker, TS Kennedy and GE Foster, accompanied by Melchior Anderegg walked to the Grands Mulets; they attempted the Balmhorn, and climbed the Plattenhörner. In the summer of 1870, Moore accompanied by Jakob Anderegg and Hans Baumann, joined occasionally by Horace Walker, traversed four passes including the Winterjoch making the first direct crossing from the Göschenen valley to the Grimsel hospice. Moore's other climbs included the Jungfrau, Monte Rosa, Cima di Jazzi, and the first ascent of the north summit of the Aiguille de Trélatête.

In July 1871 Moore and Foster, accompanied by J Anderegg and H Baumann, ascended Monte Leone, the Balfrinhorn, Galenstock, Wildstrubel and Diablerets. Then they made the first crossing of the Tiefenmattenjoch south-west of the Dent d'Hérens. Moore, always a seeker of new passes, was interested in finding an alternative to the Col de Valpelline as a route from Zermatt to Prarayé. Moore's definition of a 'perfect' pass was that it should involve some difficulty, that its actual top should bear the true character of a pass, and that it should provide the most direct route between the two places which it connects. The Tiefenmattenjoch seemed to fulfil those requirements. In his numerous crossings of passes Moore was acting on his belief that there was no better way of getting to know a mountain range than by crossing over from one valley to the next. The party left Zermatt on 17 July at 1.35am, stopping at the foot of the Stockje at 5.50am for breakfast. Passing from the Z'mutt glacier towards the icefall of the

Tiefenmatten glacier they were threatened by possible avalanches from the giant ice-terrace poised 1000m above them on the north face of the Dent d'Hérens. 'The danger was palpable, and theoretically we ought not to have incurred it; but, fortunately for the success of the majority of expeditions, people in the Alps do not allow theory to blind them to facts – at least when theory runs counter to the wishes of the moment – and we satisfied ourselves that, great as was the theoretical risk, the practical danger of a fall occurring at the precise moment of our passage was small. If it did, of course we deserved our inevitable fate; if it did not, we probably made our pass ... The game may not have been worth the candle – at any rate we thought it was, as hundreds have thought before under similar circumstances, and I hope hundreds will think again.' Never reckless, very rarely overstepping his personal limits, but with an explorer's eye for an intriguing objective, Moore seemed in his alpine ventures to achieve a fine balance between prudence and daring. The speed and skill with which the two guides overcame the difficulties and dangers of the Tiefenmatten icefall enabled the party to reach the sharp crest of the Tiefenmattenjoch eight hours after leaving Zermatt. From there they traversed the Tsa de Tsan glacier, crossing over the Col du Mont Brulé (3213m) to the Arolla glacier. Descending the Arolla valley they reached Evolène at 8pm, after an outing of eighteen and a half hours.

Moore visited Switzerland again in 1872, joined for some of the time by Walker, and accompanied by Jakob and Melchior Anderegg. During June and early July his climbs included the Oberalpstock, Studerhorn and Gross Nesthorn (the last two by new routes) and Fletschhorn. On an afternoon in early July Moore, accompanied by Walker and the Andereggs, set up a bivouac at 2600m on the Bies glacier above Randa in order to attempt the north-east face of the Weisshorn. Starting at 2.40am the next day they headed for the *névé* plateau at the foot of the face. 'For some distance we made good progress. We were stopped, however, rather suddenly by a line of ice-cliffs, breaking into *séracs*, which completely barred the way on the line we were following. Jakob did indeed point out what seemed to him a practicable breach in the fortress, but neither to Melchior nor to us did it at all commend itself – on the contrary, we agreed that a more repulsive-looking place could not be, ... we struck to the right where the ice-fall, though more broken, was less steep, ... we were soon brought up by a crevasse which, though perhaps not beyond a jump, required some looking at. ... we were calmly discussing the feasibility of the suggested leap, when all of a sudden, from no cause I can call to mind, I tripped and fell. I had merely to let myself fall and no harm would have ensued, ... as I fell I instinctively threw my left arm out, it caught over the edge of the crevasse, to which I naturally clung, and as I swung round on my side with unexpected heaviness, the arm was exposed to a sudden and very violent strain. The pain for the moment was intense, but I did not on the instant realise the full extent of the disaster; it was only when I found myself unable to move the limb that the horrid truth flashed on me that my shoulder was dislocated. ... Melchior has, in his time, had some experience of this sort of accident, and flattered himself that he would be able to repair the injury, but his operations merely caused me great agony without other result.' An English doctor present in Zermatt reset the joint, and Moore was then consigned to a sling in order to immobilise the arm. With his left arm strapped to his body Moore occupied the remaining three weeks of his holiday crossing four cols, and ascending the Wildstrubel, Rinderhorn, Mettenberg, Rosenhorn and Mönch, the last climb taking seventeen hours, starting from the Kleine Schiedegg and finishing in Grindelwald. Writing in 1872 Moore commented: 'Nowadays there is a growing tendency to gauge the merits of an expedition, not by its intrinsic interest, but by the risks attending it, and to overlook the broad general distinction between difficulty and danger.' Evidently a matter worthy of comment then, although commonplace now. In 1873, Moore climbed the Grivola and Finsteraarhorn; then on 18 July, joined by Foster and U Kelso, and accompanied by J Anderegg and H Baumann he climbed the highest point of the Grandes Jorasses, following Walker's 1868 route, in a round trip of nineteen and a half hours from Courmayeur. Starting again from Courmayeur on 21 July at 12.20am with his guides and the same companions, Mont Blanc was climbed from the Miage glacier and the glacier du Mont Blanc, and a descent was made to Chamonix, which was reached at 10.40pm. Moore clearly had a special liking for lengthy expeditions. This was the second ascent from the Miage glacier via the Rocher du Mont Blanc which was first climbed the year before by TS Kennedy accompanied by Jean-Antoine Carrel and Johann Fischer.

Moore visited the Caucasus twice. In 1868, he accompanied Douglas Freshfield, Tucker and F Dévouassoud of Chamonix who was Freshfield's regular guide and the first alpine guide to visit any of the distant ranges. Kazbek (5033m) was climbed, and the east (lower) summit of Elbruz (5621m): both were first ascents. The party also traversed several passes. Describing that expedition, Freshfield revealed a disagreeable feature of their journey. 'There were dangers other than the perils of mountaineering ... the people were very hostile. Our things were stolen and then sold to us again. We only got away after a violent row, revolvers in hand, and it was fear of our firearms alone which prevented our being plundered. The walk down the valley of Ingour was a series of disputes with the man who led our baggage horse, and who did all in his power to delay us and to expose us to the violence and extortion of his compatriots.' (Note 9) Moore visited the Caucasus again in 1874, when he came 'with regret at the dismal conclusion that the campaigns of the last four years had to a great extent exhausted for me the attractions of the Swiss Alps'. Apparently undismayed by the prospect of fresh encounters with unfriendly tribes, Moore organised an expedition which included Horace Walker, Frederick Gardiner and Florence Craufurd Grove, with Peter Knubel from St Niklaus. Gardiner, a friend of the Walker family and of Coolidge became one of the most active climbers of his day, making a number of guideless ascents with the brothers Charles and Lawrence Pilkington, notably of the Grand Pic of La Meije in 1879, and between 1896-98 of the Matterhorn, Zinal Rothorn and Finsteraarhorn.

Moore's diary of the Caucasus journey reveals the often delicate relations with the inhabitants over porters and transport, as well as difficulties arising from the generally slender resources of the country. His diplomatic skills appear to have smoothed out more problems than the official documents which he carried, particularly in regions remote from political and military control, 'where the "tourist" is utterly unknown; where a European (even a Russian) is rarely seen, his object in travelling an inexplicable mystery to the people, and himself regarded as a curious novelty to be stared at open-mouthed'. The tribesmen who populated the Georgian region around the areas bordering Daghestan, Abkhazia and Grozny, were seemingly even less predictable then than they are now. A complicated twelve-day journey was involved between London and Tiflis (Tbilisi), capital of Georgia, by a variety of railways and steamboats via Odessa and Yalta. At Tiflis, Moore encountered 'Goumilevsky, whose acquaintance I had made on the Black Sea in 1868. His astonishment at my appearance was quite real: "I can understand a man coming once to these parts, – but a second time! that is indeed inexplicable."' At dinner, two young cavalry officers, Bernoff and Kwitka, expressed a sufficiently keen interest in the expedition to request their participation in an ascent of Elbruz. A meeting place was accordingly agreed, and a date fixed for their arrival at the party's camp below the mountain. 'We gave [them] all sorts of good advice as to their mode of life in the interval ... and enjoined on them as much walking exercise as possible ... The purchase of a pair of snow spectacles commenced Bernoff's equipment that very night, and was, at all events, an evidence of zeal on his part, which encouraged us to hope that he, at any rate, would come up to time, as to which young Goumilevsky was profoundly sceptical.'

Accompanied by local porters and pack-animals Moore's party travelled for over a month through the mountains dogged by persistent rain, crossing five passes, traversing the Bezingi and other glaciers and climbing a 3200m peak, Tau Sultra. One day in advance of the deadline given to the two Russians, they reached the agreed meeting point south of Elbruz, and the weather had suddenly taken a turn for the better. The next day Moore and his friends set out for their first bivouac, leaving a message for the Russian officers. Swelled by a group of fifteen followers seated in a circle round a fire, their bivouac that evening was 'of a kind impressive to all of us ... there was a romance and a spice of adventure in the situation such as in the Alps is no longer possible'. Late the next day at their final camp below Elbruz a note arrived from Bernoff and Kwitka, begging the party not to start the climb without them. With the fine weather showing signs of breaking up, this was awkward. Moore quickly came to a decision. 'I announced to my companions that the only course was for them to carry out the programme ... and for me to remain behind ... and try the mountain on the following day.' An unselfish act which was to result in deep personal disappointment. Grove, Walker, Gardiner and Knubel set out at 1am on 28 July, and reached the west summit of Elbruz, at 5642m some 21m higher than the summit which Moore had climbed in 1868. The next day Moore and Knubel, joined by the two Russians, set out to repeat the climb. The last two turned back exhausted after two hours; Moore and Knubel, with 'Achia' a local porter-cum-guide, pressed on for another two hours. 'We were already on the very outskirts of the *tourmente* [storm] which was raging over Elbruz: snow was falling and the cold was scarcely endurable ... I asked Knubel for his opinion ... he replied that we might be able to advance for another hour, but then we should certainly have to retreat ... Achia, I believe, was willing and rather desirous to persevere.' Perhaps wisely, they turned to descend. 'The moment was one of the bitterest of my life. The dream of the past six months was dissipated, an unlooked for opportunity gone, never to recur.' (Note 10) Achia, or Akhia Sottaev, 'the most accomplished hunter in the [Urusbieh] valley' had been to the east summit of Elbruz with Moore in 1868 when his age was said to have been getting on for seventy years. (Note 11)

After 1875 there is little record of Moore's Alpine visits; although in 1878, between 25 May and 29 June, he and Horace Walker accompanied by Melchior and Jakob Anderegg 'wandered from Geneva to the Ortler' during long spells of very poor weather. After this journey Moore wrote in Jakob's *führerbuch*, ' his health is ... not so good ... but he is still up to a good deal of hard work ... I hope to see him again next year.' A hope that was not fulfilled. Jakob Anderegg, who was born near Meiringen in 1827, died there on 17 September 1878. Moore's unpublished diary contains the following tribute to him. 'He had been my personal guide ever since 1865. Great physical strength and a keen mountaineering instinct combined to place him in the first rank of path finders. In addition to these qualities he was endowed with a particularly sweet and equable temper, considerable sense of humour, ... As a companion and friend, no less than as a guide, I shall ever deplore his loss.' Jakob Anderegg who possessed great courage and strength was one of a handful of great guides during the early period of the Golden Age. His record includes several noteworthy ascents and new climbs during his relatively short career of fourteen years. On his first season in 1864, accompanying his cousin Melchior on the first ascent of the Zinal Rothorn, Leslie Stephen wisely predicted in his *führerbuch* 'when he has gained knowledge of more districts he will be one of the best guides for

difficult expeditions to be met with in the Alps'. His other notable
'firsts' were Piz Roseg, Ober Gabelhorn and the Brenva route on
Mont Blanc in 1865 with Moore, and the Gspaltenhorn with Forster
in 1869, also the first and second ascents from the Rottal of the
Jungfrau. In 1876 he made first ascents of Les Courtes, the south-east
arête of the Finsteraarhorn, and the Argentière face of the Aiguille
Verte, the last with Thomas Middlemore and Henri Cordier.

Like most diarists of the period, Moore carefully recorded details
of his daily activities. In his alpine writings, several passages can be
found which express unaffectedly his genuine love of nature, and his
appreciation of mountains. Here is one: 'As we made our way towards
the central part of the glacier, the sun rose. In all my Alpine
wanderings I have never witnessed so gorgeous a daybreak, or such
wonderful effects of colour. The eastern sky was an absolute green,
the depths of the crevasses all round us were yellow, the shadows on
the surface of the ice were a misty blue, while simultaneously the
summits of the Weisshorn, Dom and Monte Rosa were suffused with
a roseate tint, of delicacy unparalleled in my experience of similar
scenes.' Perceptive and sensitive to beauty, he was able to put into
words, simply and vividly, his reactions to what he saw and
experienced, giving a lively picture of a bygone age in the Alps with
accounts of what Leslie Stephen has called ' innumerable other
pleasures of the old scrambling days'. Moore's alpine diaries covering
the years 1860-69 are now held by the Alpine Club, who purchased
them some years after his death. They comprise substantial bound
volumes, containing carefully handwritten pages radiating with a
descriptive power which is effective because of its sincerity. The diary
of his 1874 Caucasian expedition was presented to the Alpine Club in
1954 by the daughter of Lady Throckmorton who was Moore's sister.

Horace Walker (1838-1908), Alpine Club President 1889-92, and
Moore's frequent climbing companion wrote: 'on all occasions when
we were together, my part was that of *fidus Achates* to his *Aeneas*.
Indeed, I was well content to follow such a leader, for his knowledge
of the Western and Central Alps was for long unsurpassed, and his
ingenuity in planning new and interesting routes inexhaustible.'
(Note 12) Walker was educated privately partly in Switzerland and
Germany; at the age of nineteen he joined his father in Liverpool
where the latter conducted an active business in the lead trade. His

alpine career which, like his sister's, began at the start of the Golden Age, included practically all the great climbs of the day as well as several first ascents and crossings of passes. He was a very competent climber, and on 30 June 1868 in a climb of four and a half hours from a bivouac above the glacier des Grandes Jorasses he reached the highest peak of the Group, the Pointe Walker, with Melchior Anderegg, Johann Jaun and Julien Grange. An active mountaineer for over fifty years, his first alpine ascent was made at the age of sixteen when he climbed Mont Vélan; and his last when he climbed Pollux at the age of sixty-seven in 1905. Although a keen collector of books, he himself wrote very little, and only rarely about his expeditions in the Alps. Horace and his sister Lucy began their climbing careers accompanied by their father, who was one of the earliest and most active of the alpine pioneers. One of the latter's last ascents at the age of sixty-four, a year before he died, was of the Matterhorn, which he climbed with his daughter and Melchior Anderegg in 1871.

A model secretary of the Alpine Club, Moore was energetic in his duties and his two-year term of office beginning in 1872 was one which marked a turning point in the fortunes of he Club. The romance of the opening years of the Golden Age was almost over, and a few of the earlier members were no longer active. The impetus vital to the health of the Club was beginning to recover after the shock of the Matterhorn accident; but a stigma lingered around the Club's activities, which were still regarded in many circles as weird and dangerous. During this crucial phase, Moore 'nursed the Club through a difficult period, and laid down the main lines on which it has been conducted ever since'. It was probably owing to his tact and energy that membership, which had begun to sag at around 290 after 1865, leapt up by fifty per cent during the early 1870s at the end of his term as Secretary. His animated and amusing after-dinner speeches were much applauded. He was twice offered the Presidency of the Club; although deeply appreciative, he considered that his official duties compelled him to decline the honour. Moore's father, Major JA Moore, was a director of the East India Company in London. His eldest brother was John Arthur Moore, father of Lord Brabazon[2]. Very

---

[2]Politician, pioneer aviator and winter sports enthusiast, who became one of the pillars of the Cresta Run at St Moritz after World War One.

little has been revealed about Moore's early life. Upon leaving Harrow, he joined the East India Company at the age of seventeen. It was the beginning of a distinguished career lasting twenty-seven years in the civil and political service where his work and his character were held in high esteem. He occupied various positions of responsibility, being appointed, at the age of thirty-four, Assistant Secretary and, from 1876-8, Acting Secretary in the Political Department of the India Office. On his retirement in 1885 he was awarded a CB. Soon after, he was offered, and accepted, a post as Private Secretary to the then Conservative Prime Minister Lord Salisbury. But it was considered that his services would be more valuable at the India Office where he took up a position as Private Secretary to Lord Randolph Churchill. In January 1887 Moore accepted an offer of an important appointment as Political Secretary at the India Office. Before assuming his duties he applied for two months' leave. He died in Monte Carlo on 2 February 1887 aged forty-six. During the previous two years his friend, Horace Walker, had repeatedly urged him to take a break from his work in order to restore his weakening health. Walker wrote, 'it was the only subject on which I ever found him unreasonable. When he did take rest it was too late. The proximate cause of his death appears to have been typhoid fever, probably contracted at Hastings, where he spent a week before leaving for the Riviera; but the real cause was, no doubt, overwork. It is sad to think of his career, cut short by too scrupulous adherence to supposed duty, just as his merits had been recognised, his services rewarded and a full opportunity afforded him of displaying his ability and sagacity'. Moore's character, enriched by a liveliness and wit, attracted many friends; it was said that his best friends were those who knew him best. With a rare independence of thought, temperate, setting forth his views, relishing frank discussion, his company was always stimulating. During his alpine expeditions, spread over a period of more than fifteen years Moore was a mountaineer pure and simple. Throwing aside official cares, he gave himself up to his passion for mountains. He was a true lover of Nature, and there was no kind of mountain scenery that did not appeal to him. As an alpine pioneer, although acutely aware of the dangers involved in his ventures he was never daunted by them. His exploits reveal his talent for exploration. As a climber he was utterly reliable. He was a sound judge of a situation, and he very rarely stepped beyond what he considered a justifiable risk.

Only one of Moore's diaries, that covered his successful campaigns of 1864, was published during his lifetime, when about a hundred copies were privately printed in 1867 for circulation among his friends. By the 1890s, occasional copies of that edition were said to have fetched up to ten guineas at second-hand booksellers in London. In the preface introducing the first edition Moore wrote: 'My object in originally writing it was to compile a narrative, the subsequent perusal of which might recall to my own recollection various details of my mountaineering campaign of that year. ... I recorded at full length all the trivial incidents which form the staple of such a tour and constitute its charm ... these details will be very dull reading to other people, and had I at the time had any idea that the narrative would ever emerge from the obscurity of manuscript, I should have omitted most of them. Want of time has prevented me rewriting the book on an entirely different principle, and it is therefore printed almost word for word as it originally stood. ... I have only further to add, with reference to my speculations as to the accessibility of various mountains, most of which have been falsified by subsequent events, that I have allowed them to remain as written in order to show how worthless is the opinion on such points of even a fairly experienced observer.' An example of the book's record of 'trivial incidents' provides a rare illustration of alpine travel during Moore's era. 'We were received with the utmost cordiality by the two honest-looking women in charge, and were shown for night-quarters a large clean barn with an abundance of soft hay. Having deposited our traps, we went into the chalet, a model of cleanliness, to superintend the making of tea, and during the operation endeavoured to get some information about the country. ... We fared sumptuously on tea and quantities of milk, hot and cold, helped down by bread and butter from our own stores, and nothing could have surpassed the civility with which we were attended to. Tea over, I went to the edge of the grassy knoll overhanging the gorge, the black shaly cliffs on the other side of which were remarkable, and sat there for some time, returning to witness a most gorgeous sunset. ... The air soon became chilly, so we retired to our barn, and burrowing in the soft hay were with the addition of our plaids shortly warm enough, and soon slept the sleep of the just.' Moore's diaries include his own sketch-maps which, although most areas were imperfectly mapped at the time, marked the routes described in his narrative enabling the reader to follow his journeys. In 1902, when permission was obtained from Moore's family to reissue *The Alps in 1864*, Professor Alexander Kennedy FRS, an ardent climber and a distinguished engineer, edited the work and expanded it, adding from Moore's journals accounts of five later expeditions; also providing a well-researched Notes section and several illustrations. Copies of the finely produced 1902 edition, originally priced at thirty-six shillings, are now rarely available. A new edition in two volumes was published in 1939, edited and annotated by EH Stevens. The original review in the *Alpine Journal* of *The Alps in 1864* described it as 'one of the most vivid and fascinating books of Alpine travel which has ever been written'. The style, which is free from drama or heroics, reflects the openness of Moore's character, his lively powers of observation, and something of the genuine pleasure that he derived from his mountain adventures.

Moore's account of the ascent of the Brenva face of Mont Blanc on 15 July 1865, which he read to members of the Alpine Club on 6 March 1866, provides one of the most engrossing chapters in his book. Of the four amateurs and two guides who made the ascent only the latter carried ice-axes; the others had alpenstocks; no crampons were used. Two porters accompanied the party as far as the first night's bivouac at 2800m, one of whom, young Julien Grange, later acquired fame as a guide. The outcome of the climb was in doubt until the end. The final ascent which commenced from a bivouac on the glacier ended in Chamonix twenty hours later at 10.30pm. Professor Graham Brown, a pioneer of major new routes on the Brenva face of Mont Blanc sixty-five years later, commented on Moore's 1865 ascent: 'The climb was far in advance of the standards of its time ... It is still to be classed amongst the great climbs of the Alps.'

CHAPTER SIX
EDWARD WHYMPER
1840-1911

What power must have been required to shatter and to sweep away the missing parts of this pyramid, for we do not see it surrounded by heaps of fragments; one only sees other peaks – themselves rooted to the ground – whose sides, equally rent, indicate an immense mass of debris which, in the form of pebbles, boulders, and sand, fills our valleys and our plains.

Horace-Bénédict de Saussure:
impressions on viewing the Matterhorn
Voyages dans les Alpes, 1792

The events of the early 1850s, heralding the opening of the Alpine Golden Age, occurred when Edward Whymper was a schoolboy. They reached a peak in the mid 1860s when he was a young man at the height of his powers, and in the forefront of the leading mountaineers of the day. As the only English survivor of the accident that followed the first ascent of the Matterhorn in 1865, and as the driving force behind one of the most daring mountain climbs then achieved, Whymper was thrown dramatically into the limelight. The Matterhorn disaster dwelt like a cloud over the rest of Whymper's life, extinguished his ambition for further alpine adventures, and 'brought [his] scrambles among the alps to a close'.

Whymper was born in London on 27 April 1840, the second of eleven children in a family which had emigrated from Holland and settled in Suffolk in the mid seventeenth century – the original family name was Wimper which is Dutch for eyelash. Edward's grandfather, Nathaniel Whymper (1787-1861), was a brewer in Ipswich, a career adopted by one of Edward's brothers Henry, who went out to India quite young, became manager of Murree Breweries, and received an award for public services. Edward's father, Josiah Whymper, an artist and painter, established in 1829 at Lambeth what was to become a growing business as a wood-engraver. At the age of fourteen, Edward was apprenticed to his father's factory where, with a natural intelligence and a clear, well-informed mind, he quickly developed skills as a professional engraver. His diaries of the period, beginning when he was fifteen, reveal common sense, self-reliance, and egotism – qualities which he retained throughout his life. The following entry appears on 18 March 1856. 'Went errands, cut up wood and began some shields of heraldry. No news. Raining. I have long wished to compete for some of the prizes which are offered for the best designs and plans for building. I intend to try one at least soon ... Competition is certainly the best way for getting new designs in architecture, and I should say it was in many other things also.' His observations, which are strikingly mature, ranged widely over political, social, moral, economic and military issues, including views about the Crimean war which England joined in 1854, and the Indian Mutiny in 1857. Certain glimpses of Victorian life in an entry dated 13 November 1856, which relate to insecurity on the streets of London, and the discovery of large-scale fraud, might be applicable today. A note dated 16 February 1859 illustrates an emerging taste for authorship. 'John Cassell has offered some premiums for the best tales for his journals ... I am at present trying to concoct a story, getting material, etc.' The diary reveals a degree of loneliness and discontent. Under a firm patriarchal rule, hard work and thoroughness were qualities that the young Edward learnt to develop; yet he seemed to crave for work 'where my head might be worked as well as my hands' and to escape from 'the everlasting round ... one day not varying at all from the other'. In July 1855 holidaying in Eastbourne, he reports 'nearly broke my neck trying to climb a cliff' on Beachy Head. He indulged in long walks, once covering thirty-five miles in a day. In August 1858 he 'formed the nucleus of the North Lambeth Cricket Club which I hope may last many years'. Earlier that year he had attended Albert Smith's Mont Blanc extravaganza, then entering its seventh and final year. 'I found myself quite satisfied and more.' Filled with ambitious dreams, he was unable to feel any enthusiasm for the monotonous tasks at the factory. Curiously, when his father relinquished the business in 1882 he agreed to take it over, paying his father an annuity of £350 for almost twenty years. The outlook for engraving by the turn of the century was clearly under threat owing to advancing developments and lower costs in photography. Whymper began to take a keen interest in the new 'science', the basic principles of which were conceived as early as 1840 by using wet glass plates spread with collodion before exposure in order to produce a negative. He did some pioneering work later with the Ilford Company on developments with dry plates.

At the age of twenty Whymper received a commission from the publishing firm Longmans Green to prepare a series of mountain sketches for use as illustrations in a forthcoming publication of the Alpine Club in London. William Longman was a member of the recently formed Club, of which he became President in 1872, and his firm published on the Club's behalf two volumes of *Peaks, Passes and Glaciers*, a few early volumes of the *Alpine Journal*, and two of the earliest mountaineering books, *Summer Months Among the Alps* by Thomas Hinchcliff, and *Where there's a will there's a way* by Charles Hudson and Edward Shirley Kennedy.

On 23 July 1860, Whymper, who had 'neither seen not set foot upon a mountain', sailed across the English Channel bound for the alps, perhaps little realising that he was launched on a short but meteoric alpine career, which would shape the course of his future life. His book *Scrambles amongst the Alps*, first published by John Murray in 1871, remains one of the great classics of alpine literature. Whymper, always fastidious and precise, rewrote, altered, and added to the text in some of the later editions. Aiming at perfection, he is known to have remarked in later life to the alpine historian Coolidge that he felt his book was not free from mistakes, which he ascribed to a combination of 'printer's errors and author's faults.' The book, superbly illustrated with over a hundred engravings, almost all of which were reproduced from Whymper's own drawings, contains graphic accounts of six years of travel and mountaineering in Switzerland, France and Italy, in a series of carefully planned journeys. From 1860 onwards, as the book unravels, the callow youth of twenty grows to the stature of a determined and experienced mountaineer, climbing and exploring in unknown corners of the alps; observant and enquiring, ultimately driven by a single ambition; returning again and again to the scene of his endeavours until the fateful day on 14 July 1865 when he achieved his ambition to be the first to stand on top of the Matterhorn. Almost 140 years later the Matterhorn retains its mystique, and Whymper remains an essential part of its history.

From very early during his first alpine journey, Whymper demonstrated the resolve that was characteristic of his five subsequent expeditions when, undaunted by the desertion of a Valpelline guide from 'Prerayen' (Prarayer) on top of the isolated 'Va Cornère' pass (Col de Valcournera), he undertook a solitary descent into the unknown Valtournanche, arriving at Breuil the same evening without his knapsack and sketching materials. This 'shorter' route to Breuil had been chosen by him instead of the normal approach via Aosta to Chatillon. It has been said, with some truth, that Whymper lacked a sense of humour; but the accounts of some of his early alpine experiences contain passages that could only have been written by someone with a sense of fun, and are often overdrawn to add flavour.

Whymper ranged far and wide between 23 July to 15 September 1860, mostly alone, with sketch book in hand, intent on the purpose of his commission – the Bernese mountains, the Gemmi pass, the Visptal, the Saas valley, 'the three-peaked Mischabel, hopelessly inaccessible from this direction', the Weisshorn, 'the noblest (mountain) in Switzerland', which became, with the Matterhorn, one of his two future objectives. On the road above Stalden three weeks after his arrival in Switzerland, Whymper records a chance meeting with Alfred Wills' former guide from Saas, the priest Johann Imseng. 'I asked if I had the honour of speaking to Monsieur le Curé Imseng ... I told him how much I had heard of him and how glad I was to see him.' The valley between Stalden and Zermatt he considered 'a perfect paradise for an artist'. After his first view of the Matterhorn from Zermatt, he wrote in his diary: 'Saw of course the Matterhorn repeatedly; what precious stuff Ruskin has written about this, as well as about other things. When one has a fair view of the mountain as I had, it may be compared to a sugar-loaf set up on a table; the sugar-loaf should have its head knocked on one side. Grand it is, but beautiful I think it is not.' Eleven years later, with an eye on his public image, Whymper transformed the prosaic sugar-loaf into a more sublime object when he wrote, 'generations will gaze upon its awful precipices and wonder at its unique form ... none will come to return disappointed.' At Zermatt he met Leslie Stephen, Thomas Hinchcliff and several other 'Alpine men' from England, which probably formed the nucleus of an idea for the famous engraving in his book titled 'The Club-Room of Zermatt in 1864'. A few days later at Fiesch he walked up to the Eggishorn hotel with Stephen and Hinchcliff, the former 'bolted away' to arrive one hour ahead of the others. Whymper climbed the Eggishorn in mist, probably his first mountain top, on which he was unable to resist cutting his initials on the summit cross and painting them red. Always rigidly practical, Whymper recorded during his travels: 'I do not believe in the pretty views in which Switzerland is represented in the conventional manner. Everything here is *fine*, but I have not seen any *pretty* views.'

Travelling extremely light, he performed some prodigious walking feats – from Martigny to the Grand St Bernard 'a tiring walk of 32 miles ... and very glad when the hospice appeared in sight. I got a comfortable tea with very hard bread and went to bed'. After making his first sketch of the Italian side of the Matterhorn, he walked thirty-five miles in seven hours from Aosta to Courmayeur. Throughout Whymper's diary of his 1860 journey, an impassive tone fails to reveal any deep sense of attraction to the beauty of mountains. Chapter One of *Scrambles amongst the Alps* concludes: 'on this tour I was introduced to the great peaks and acquired the passion for mountain scrambling, the development of which is described in the following chapters.' Whymper's passion was of an ambitious kind. His style, always clear and sometimes dramatic, compels attention; but only rarely does his book contain passages resembling the literary skill of Stephen, the freshness of Wills, or the transparency of Moore.

The sketches produced by Whymper for Longman in 1860 were recognised as work of great merit resulting in further commissions. Whymper was quick to recognise the opportunities that had opened, enabling him to combine his artistic abilities with mountain 'scrambling'. Although he never acquired wealth during his lifetime, Whymper's fame grew as an illustrator of mountains, a writer, a lecturer, and as an enigmatic figure associated with the mystery of the alps. With an intuitive skill in the art of self-promotion, he was able to enjoy fairly comfortable means during his advancing years. In August 1861 Whymper visited the little-known Dauphiné mountains in France, and it was there that his climbing adventures really began when, accompanied by Reginald Macdonald, he made an ascent of the highest summit of Mont Pelvoux about which he wrote: 'I look back upon this, my first serious mountain scramble, with more satisfaction, and with as much pleasure, as upon any that is recorded in this volume.' Whymper believed that he had made a first ascent, but learnt that Victor Puiseaux, whom he contacted later, had preceded him in 1848. A visit to Monte Viso followed, accompanied by a local porter, which took place two weeks prior to the first ascent of that mountain, made on 30 August by William Mathews and FW Jaccomb, guided by Jean-Baptiste Croz of Chamonix and his brother Michel, with whom Whymper was to share many later adventures. Having learnt that Tyndall had succeeded in climbing the Weisshorn on 19 August, Whymper lost further interest in that mountain, revealing one of the principal factors that motivated his future plans. The magnificence of an alpine peak was not by itself of intrinsic interest, unless it could satisfy his ambition to be the first to climb it. It was the year in which he began his long and relentless series of campaigns to climb the Matterhorn. Towards the end of August 1861 he travelled to Chatillon, and was introduced to Jean-Antoine Carrel, then aged thirty-two, who 'was the first to doubt [the Matterhorn's] inaccessibility ... the only man who persisted in believing that its ascent would be accomplished. It was the aim of his life to make the ascent from the side of Italy for the honour of his native valley'. Jean-Antoine, a *chasseur* (hunter) who enjoyed a certain local status, was known as the *bersaglier*, having acquired fame as a soldier in the *bersaglieri,* a special *corps* of mountain infantry, whose men wore a cock's feather in their hats as an insignia of the elite formation to which they belonged. An ardent patriot, he had fought for his country against Austrian invaders in the Italian wars of liberation, when their armies suffered a defeat at Novara in 1849; and again in 1859, when he won his sergeant's stripes during their victory at Solferino. (Note 1) Jean-Antoine's uncle, Canon Carrel of Valtournanche, was the first to promote an interest in the mountain locally known as *La Becca*, which dominated the head of their valley, when in July 1857 an attempt to climb it was strongly supported by him. It was led by, Jean-Antoine's cousin, the experienced *chasseur* Jean-Jacques Carrel accompanied by Jean-Antoine himself and a young theological student (later *Abbé*) Aimé Gorret who set out from the village of Breuil (now the tourist-dominated town of Cervinia) to launch their attempt. Reaching the Col Tournanche (3479m), the three pioneer climbers gazed for the first time on the Tiefenmatten glacier, about 500m below them on the Swiss side of the mountain. From the Col, they climbed to the top of the Tête du Lion (3715m); the Col du Lion lay at their feet, and they saw that it would provide a springboard to the south-west ridge which formed the backbone of the giant peak. Jean-Antoine was involved in several attempts to climb the mountain between 1858-60 with members of his, the Gorret, and the Maquignaz families during which a high point of about 3850m was reached on the south-west ridge. Whymper's relations with Jean-Antoine Carrel dominate the history of his attempts to climb the Matterhorn, and illustrate the developing rivalry between two resolute men. Their first meeting ended in disagreement. The *bersaglier* would not accompany Whymper in an attempt to climb the mountain without a second man of his choice, whom Whymper refused to engage. Carrel and Whymper carried out separate attempts the following day, when Whymper set up his first camp on the Col du Lion. Whymper left Breuil in 1861, 'longing, more than before, to make the ascent, and determined to return, if possible, with a companion, to lay siege to the mountain until *one or the other was vanquished* (my italics). In December 1861, on the strength of his ascent of Mont Pelvoux that summer, Whymper was elected to the Alpine Club.

A bolder Whymper returned to Breuil in 1862 with Macdonald his companion on Pelvoux. He had designed a tent which weighed 20lbs and cost four guineas; (mountain tents of the same general pattern, made of lighter fabrics, continued to be used for about eighty years). Whymper had also brought a cast-iron hook for use as a rock-belay, and rings to secure roped descents. He was quick to recognise any methods which might assist his efforts, including steel grapnels for ascending steep rock. That year, Whymper made a series of attempts to climb the Matterhorn. The first with Macdonald and the Zermatt guides Johann zum Taugwald and Johann Kronig; two days later, he was accompanied by J-A Carrel and Pession, 'one of his relatives, a strong and able young fellow'. Ten days later from his camp on the Col du Lion a solo attempt on the ridge was not unexpectedly defeated and he was forced to descend. While negotiating a narrow rock-ledge overlaid with hard snow below the Col, Whymper slipped and 'fell nearly 200 feet in 7 or 8 bounds'. A description of this incident in his book is preceded by six pages of comment on foolhardiness, accidents, and the distinction between difficulty and danger. He was badly cut and bruised, lost a lot of blood, and was fortunate to have escaped without serious injury. By 'a combination of luck and care' he managed to descend '4800 feet' (1463m) safely to Breuil. As he lay alone recovering within sight of the mountain, he 'vowed that if an Englishman should at any time fall sick in the Valtournanche, he should not feel so solitary as I did during this dreary time'. Five days later his courage and powerful will drove him up the mountain again to make his fourth attempt on 23-24 July, accompanied by Jean-Antoine and César Carrel with Luc Meynet, the hunchback of Breuil, as a porter. A further attempt was made on 26 July accompanied by Luc Meynet, when a new high point of about 4000m was reached on the ridge at what 'appeared to be the most difficult part of the mountain'. (Note 2)

On 27-28 July, two days after that attempt, Whymper watched from below, 'with envy and all uncharitableness' while Tyndall with his Swiss guides J-J Bennen and Anton Walter, accompanied by Jean-Antoine and César Carrel as porters, reached the top of the Matterhorn's south-west shoulder, Pic Tyndall, 232m below the summit. Tyndall's failure has been attributed to lack of collaboration between his foreign guides and the two Italians. In the second edition of his book, *Hours of exercise in the Alps* published in July 1871, and in later correspondence published in the *Alpine Journal,* Tyndall referred to an incident which Whymper omitted from *Scrambles amongst the Alps*. Meeting Whymper in Breuil on the evening of 26 July 1862, Tyndall invited him to join his party, emphasizing that the climb would be conducted under Bennen's leadership, a condition which Whymper was apparently unwilling to accept. He had spent eleven days on the mountain during various attempts over two seasons, having only the day before reached a point higher than anyone else; while Bennen had spent just one day each on the lower part of the south-west ridge in 1860 and 1861. Swiss guides of the period considered themselves superior to men from the Italian valleys, and Bennen was no exception. He probably regarded Whymper, then aged twenty-two, as a rash and impetuous youth. A clash of wills between the two men on the mountain was something not to be contemplated. After discussions with Bennen, whose judgement he trusted completely, Tyndall withdrew his offer. Disagreement between Tyndall and Whymper was perhaps inevitable, and their respective accounts of this incident, published at the time, differ materially.

Whymper, who had left his tent on the Col du Lion, returned to it the following morning before the departure of Tyndall's party from Breuil. Climbing alone and unladen he moved fast, and waited on the Col until their arrival, having offered Tyndall the use of his tent. Might there have been a different outcome to Tyndall's attempt had the discussions at Breuil on the evening of 26 July resulted in Whymper's participation? Whymper's influence as a member of the party is likely to have been deeply divisive, given his personal ambitions and those of the experienced and ambitious J-A Carrel, who had accepted the subordinate rôle of porter under Bennen's leadership.

Whymper returned to Breuil in 1863 to renew his attempt on the Matterhorn, equipped with a set of folding ladders for scaling steep rock sections above his previous high point. During a period of bad weather, accompanied throughout by J-A Carrel, he crossed a new pass, the Breuiljoch, and completed a circuit of the Matterhorn. An attempt was made on the Dent d'Herens. 'We were divided in opinion as to the best way of approaching the peak. Carrel, true to his habit of sticking to rocks in preference to ice suggested the long rocky western ridge.' Whymper proposed a south-west approach via the Tsa de Tsan glacier. Carrel's route turned out to be dangerous, owing to the loose nature of the rock, and their attempt had to be abandoned. 'Four days afterwards a party of Englishmen ... including my friend R Macdonald ... under the skilful guidance of Melchior Anderegg made the first ascent ... by the route which I had proposed.' Later, Whymper made his sixth attempt on the Matterhorn, accompanied by J-A and C Carrel, and Luc Meynet. His tent had been carried 350m higher up the south-west ridge, and his seventh night on the mountain was enlivened by a violent electrical storm, depicted by a spectacular illustration in *Scrambles*. The storm plastered the rocks with fresh snow, dictating a retreat the following day.

Four seasons of extensive travel, combined with increased opportunities for work with his sketchbook, had provided Whymper with a wide background of alpine experience, financial independence, and heightened ambitions. At the age of twenty-four he had acquired a reputation as a courageous and determined mountaineer. His 1864 season began with a successful ten-day campaign in the Dauphiné when he joined forces with Moore and Walker. They had secured the services of Christian Almer, established by then as one of the leading guides of Grindelwald, while Whymper was able to engage Michel Croz of Chamonix, whose skills had been praised highly by several well-known mountaineers including Francis Fox Tuckett and William Mathews. Much new ground was covered, and some fine successes were achieved (see Chapter 5); but none of them brought Whymper any nearer to his principal objective. After the Dauphiné expedition Whymper joined Anthony Adams-Reilly, who was busy preparing a map of the Mont Blanc region, which was published the following year by the Alpine Club. Adams-Reilly had agreed in return to join Whymper later in order to try a new route on the Swiss side of the Matterhorn from the east. Their partnership was very fruitful. On 8 July the Col de Triolet was crossed for the first time. Three first ascents were made, Mont Dolent on 9 July, the Aiguille de Trélatête (south peak) on 12 July, and the Aiguille d'Argentière on 15 July. The last two peaks were described by Whymper as the fourth and fifth highest still unclimbed after the Grandes Jorasses and the Aiguille Verte – two peaks which he noted for inclusion in his plans for the following year. After his climbs with Adams-Reilly, Whymper and Croz teamed up with Moore and Almer to make an adventurous crossing from Zinal to Zermatt over the Moming pass as described in the previous chapter. On arrival at Zermatt, Whymper found an urgent message recalling him home, bringing his alpine season to an abrupt end, and causing the abandonment of his immediate plans for the Matterhorn.

In 1865 Whymper reached the crowning point, and the end, of his triumphant alpine career in a remarkable series of campaigns. He had conceived an ambitious set of plans, aiming to ascend all the major unclimbed peaks, having acquired the fullest information about them in order to profit from the reasons for previous failures. His successes were the result of careful forethought and calculation, and his ascents were made almost on the very days for which they had been targeted months earlier. The routes he selected took into account his growing preference for snow, which was a reversal of his previous belief in the greater security of rock. The Matterhorn remained his principal goal. Since his preferred guide Michel Croz was available for only part of the time, Whymper also engaged Christian Almer and Franz Biener.[1] During a period of twenty-four

---

[1]Whymper's spelling is retained, although the accepted form is Biner.

days between 13 June and 7 July, Whymper and his guides climbed five peaks (four were first ascents), and crossed eleven passes (four were new), ascending in the process 30,500 metres and descending almost 30,000 metres, an unmatched record.

On 17 June Whymper made a near ascent of the Dent Blanche (4357m).[2] Apparently he was unaware of the earlier ascents made by Finlayson and Kennedy. (Note 3) Whymper described the Dent Blanche as a 'mountain of exceptional difficulty' and his ascent as 'the hardest that I have made'. This was prior to his ascent of the Matterhorn, but about the latter climb he wrote of the lower part that there was 'no occasion for the rope' and even of the upper part that 'it was a place over which any fair mountaineer might pass in safety'. The ascent and descent of the Dent Blanche from a bivouac at Bricola alp at 2415m occupied seventeen hours; Kennedy had taken sixteen hours for his ascent in 1862, and Finlaison with better weather in 1864 took fourteen hours. An icy wind swept the upper part of the final ridge, numbing the fingers of Whymper's party. When Whymper saw through the clouds 'about twenty yards off' the outline of a cairn on the summit, providing visible proof that he was not the first, his reaction illustrated his primary motive for the ascent. 'It was needless to proceed further. I jerked the rope from Biener, and motioned that we should go back. He did the same to Almer, and we turned immediately.' Whymper and his three guides returned to their bivouac on Bricola alp in heavy mist shortly before midnight.

The following day they set out to cross the Col d' Hérens in order to descend to Zermatt. 'The walk is of the most straightforward kind ... all you have to do, after once getting upon the ice, is to proceed south ... in two hours you should be upon the summit of the pass.' Roping up, Croz and Almer placed Biener in the lead 'as he had frequently crossed the pass'. After advancing about halfway mists descended. 'For some time little Biener progressed steadily, making a tolerably straight track; but at length he wavered, and deviated sometimes to the right and sometimes to the left. Croz rushed forward directly he saw this, and taking the poor young man by his shoulders gave him a good shaking, told him that he was an imbecile,

---

[2]The first ascent was made on 18 July 1862 by TS Kennedy and Reverend W Wigram with Michel Croz's elder brother Jean-Baptiste, and J Kronig; a second ascent was made in 1864 by J Finlaison, Christian Lauener and F Zurfluh.

to untie himself at once and go to the rear. Croz led off briskly and made a good straight track for a few minutes. Then, it seemed to me, he began to move steadily round to the left. ... the others thought the same and we pulled up Croz ... He took our criticism in good part ... Almer went to the front. He commenced by returning in the track for a hundred yards or so, and then started off at a tangent from Croz's curve. We kept this course for half an hour, and then we were certain that we were not on the right route ... We were greatly puzzled ... The mists had thickened and were now as dense as a moderate London fog.' Dithering in this way, lost in the fog, and in fading light, Whymper and his little group, comprising two of the leading guides of the day, were compelled to find their way back to the bivouac at Bricola for a third night. The next morning in fine weather, they were able to study the follies that had been committed. 'Biener's wavering track was not so bad; but Croz had swerved from the right route from the first, and had traced a complete semi-circle ... Almer had commenced with great discretion; but he kept on too long, and crossed the proper route. Our last attempt was ... right ... we were actually upon the summit of the pass, and in another ten yards we should have commenced to go down hill!'

For his seventh attempt on the Matterhorn, Whymper had decided to investigate a different route – via a gully on the less steep east face, where the dip of the rock strata seemed more favourable for climbing. (Note 4) A route on the east face, further to the right, had been tried twice, in July 1860 and 1861 from Zermatt, by the brothers Alfred, Charles and Sandbach Parker, who had ascended without guides to about 3600m, having encountered no real difficulties, but their high point was a long way below the steep upper part of the mountain. In a letter from Zermatt after their 1861 attempt Charles Parker wrote: 'We saw our way for a few hundred feet further; but beyond that the difficulties seemed to increase.' (Note 5) In the summer of 1858, and again in 1860, Kennedy viewing the Matterhorn from Breuil did not rate very highly the chances of an ascent from that side. In the winter of 1862 he took a serious look at the north-east (Hörnli) ridge and after a night spent at the Schwarzsee with his guides, Peter Perren and Peter Taugwalder, the party proceeded up the ridge to a point near the present site of the Hörnli hut, where they erected a huge cairn before being driven down by bitter winter winds. In an account of his climb

Kennedy wrote: 'The only route offering a chance of success [is] the Northern or Hörnli ridge', which turned out to be the route of the first ascent three years later. (Note 6) Whymper's attempt from the east, approached via the Breuiljoch, had to be abandoned after the initial gully was found to be dangerously exposed to stonefall. Nevertheless, his plans were firmly set on the Matterhorn. 'The men advocated leaving the mountain alone. Almer asked, with more point than politeness, "Why don't you try to go up a mountain which *can* be ascended?" "It is impossible," chimed in Biener. "Sir," said Croz, "if we cross to the other side [Breuil] we shall lose three days, and very likely shall not succeed. You want to make ascents in the chain of Mont Blanc, and I believe they can be made. But I shall not be able to make them with you if I spend these days here, for I must be at Chamonix on the 27th."'

Croz was right, and Whymper agreed to move over to Courmayeur from where, on 24 June, the Grandes Jorasses (Pointe Whymper, 4180m), was climbed. (Note 7) In the course of a twenty-one-hour outing on 26 June the Col Dolent was crossed. The descent to the Argentière glacier was a *tour de force* involving seven hours of step-cutting by Croz on a slope of hard ice upon which a slip by any member of the party would have been impossible to hold. After Croz left the party at Chamonix to keep his engagement with John Birkbeck, Whymper, with Almer and Biener, climbed the Aiguille Verte (4122m) on 29 June by what has since been called the Whymper Couloir. Starting at 3.15am from a bivouac under a 'great rock' on the Talèfre glacier, where the old Couvercle Hut was later placed, the summit was reached at 10.15, and a descent was made to Chamonix, which was reached at 8.15pm. The Chamonix guides were furious on hearing about the ascent made by 'outsiders' on their much-tried mountain. They refused to believe it, and when Whymper's party descended to the village three *gendarmes* had to be summoned to quell a near-riot. Charles Hudson and Kennedy made the second ascent of the Aiguille Verte one week later via a new route. (see Note 3 above) Whymper now turned his thoughts resolutely to the Matterhorn; on his way there he crossed a new col, the Talèfre, and made the first ascent of the Ruinette (3875m).

Returning to Breuil on 7 July, Whymper once again questioned his guides about the Matterhorn. Almer once again declined. 'He did not speak of difficulty or of danger, nor was he shirking *work*. He offered to go *anywhere*; but he entreated that the Matterhorn should be abandoned.' Almer's reluctance stresses the awe in which the Matterhorn was held prior to 1865, even by the best Swiss guides. Almer entered the history books in Alfred Wills' account of his Wetterhorn ascent in 1854, as the Grindelwald hunter inspired by a personal desire to reach the top of that mountain; he went on to become one of the two leading guides of the Golden Age with more first ascents to his credit than any of the others. (Note 8) While acknowledging that 'no two men ever served me more faithfully or more willingly', Whymper decided to release Almer and Biener on 7 July, having sought out Jean-Antoine Carrel to propose a fresh attempt from the east on 9 and 10 July. Carrel refused to abandon his original route: an understandable reaction, given his long-standing determination to make the ascent from the Italian side. He appears to have proposed joining Whymper in an attempt on his old route, if Whymper should find the east side impracticable. Carrel was at that moment making final and furtive preparations for the major attempt on the Matterhorn that he was due to launch on behalf of his Italian sponsors, and it could hardly be expected that he would pre-empt those plans, to which he was firmly pledged since 1863, by contributing to the fulfillment of Whymper's ambitions. At this point, at least eighteen attempts had been made to climb the Matterhorn since 1857 all, except three, from the Italian side. Whymper had been involved in seven, Carrel in at least as many, the Parker brothers and Tyndall in two each, apart from Kennedy's winter reconnaissance.

Stormy weather prevailed on 8 July, and continued on the 9th. On that day Whymper, in fulfillment of a resolution he had made three years earlier when recovering alone at Breuil after his fall on the Matterhorn, descended the valley to succour a sick Englishman, Reverend AG Girdlestone at Valtournanche. He encountered Carrel, ascending the valley with a mule and several laden porters, who now told him that he would be unable to serve him after 11 July owing to a long-standing engagement. Whymper returned up the valley late that evening, when he met Carrel again; they spent an apparently congenial evening together at the inn in Valtournanche recounting past adventures over a bottle of wine. On 10 July when Whymper returned to Breuil the weather was still unfavourable. Early on the morning of 11 July, Carrel was seen ascending the lower slopes of the Matterhorn at the head of a large and heavily laden party. Whymper reacted with anger and surprise. Anger was appropriate, but hardly surprise. Carrel had warned him two days earlier that his 'word was pledged ... with a family of distinction' after 11 July. The large caravan that Whymper had seen Carrel escorting on 9 July should have aroused his suspicions about Carrel's intentions.. At this point events took a turn that led to a fateful set of circumstances. 'By a series of chances, which I shall never cease to regret, I was first obliged to part with Croz, and then to dismiss the others, and so, deviating from the course that I had deliberately adopted, which was successful in practice because it was sound in principle, became fortuitously a member of an expedition that ended with the catastrophe that brings this book and brought my scrambles amongst the alps to a close.'

For well over a century there has been no lack of comment about the drama which followed the first ascent of the Matterhorn on 14 July 1865. It is not intended, in this chapter, to indulge in any polemics, or to pretend that the last word can be unequivocally declared about the whole affair. But it is worth re-examining the facts. On 11 July Whymper found himself the victim of a surreptitious local plot at Breuil. Guideless, and denied the services even of porters, he grew more determined than ever. Bad weather continued, and he decided that he must move quickly to Zermatt to make another attempt from the east; and, if that failed, to return to Breuil to ascend the old route ahead of Carrel's heavily encumbered expedition. While his iron will and courage demand respect it is difficult to avoid feeling that Whymper, blinded by ambition, was clutching at straws with such naïve plans. But luck was on his side. At midday, plunged in deep gloom by enforced inactivity, he encountered Lord Francis Douglas who had just come over the Théodule pass from Zermatt accompanied by Joseph, the younger son of his guide Peter Taugwalder. Six days earlier, Douglas had made the first ascent of the Wellenkuppe, followed on 7 July by the second ascent of the Ober Gabelhorn, the first from Zinal by its north ridge, accompanied by Taugwalder and Joseph Vianin. (Note 9) It is believed that Douglas had come to Breuil to try to obtain the services of Carrel for an attempt on the Matterhorn, upon which he had set his heart in the final week of his alpine holiday. He was a younger brother of the

Marquess of Queensberry, and had been elected to the Alpine Club in 1864 at the age eighteen; this was his third alpine season, and he had developed into a competent mountaineer. A year earlier, in the Dolomites, Douglas had made the second ascent of Antelao (3283m), first climbed in 1863 by Paul Grohmann. He possessed keen physical skills combined with an instinct for challenging ventures. Whymper and Douglas agreed to join forces for an attempt on the Matterhorn from the Swiss side, a route about which Douglas' guide Taugwalder, who 'had lately been beyond the Hörnli' had reported favourably (a remark which seems to imply that Taugwalder might have made a second examination of the Hörnli route, following his winter visit in 1862 with Kennedy). Whymper's reference to his partnership with Douglas is characteristic: 'Lord Francis Douglas expressed a warm desire to ascend the mountain, and before long it was determined that he should take part in the expedition.' Seizing his chance to outwit Carrel, Whymper packed his bags and departed in haste from Breuil accompanied by Douglas, whose porter Joseph Taugwalder carried Whymper's effects; the latter included Whymper's tent and all his ropes, which were deposited at the Schwarzsee near the foot of the Hörnli ridge in readiness for their climb the next day. Arriving in Zermatt on 12 July, they met, outside the Hotel Monte Rosa, Michel Croz, who was now in the service of Reverend Charles Hudson following the illness at Chamonix of John Birkbeck, his original employer. Croz stated that Hudson intended to set out the following day to attempt the Matterhorn. After dinner at the hotel they met Hudson and his friend, who 'had returned from inspecting the mountain'.

Hudson, aged 37, was then Vicar of Skillington in Lincolnshire. He had taken up hill-walking at the age of seventeen, and he began his alpine 'excursions' in 1852. He was considered to be one of the leading amateurs of the day, having built an excellent record, which included the first ascent of the Dufourspitze, the highest summit of Monte Rosa, on 1 August 1855 with John Birkbeck, Edward Stevenson and the brothers Grenville and Chrystopher Smyth. A fortnight later, with the same companions, excluding the first two but including Edward Shirley Kennedy and Charles Ainsley, he made the first guideless ascent of Mont Blanc, and the first by a route from St Gervais over the Aiguille and Dôme du Gouter to the Grand Plateau. In the same year he made the first ascent, solo, of Mont Blanc du Tacul. In 1858, he made the first completed passage of the Mönchjoch, and was the first to reach the Col de Miage in 1861. In 1862, he made the second ascent of the Aiguille Verte, the first by the Moine ridge, with Thomas Stuart Kennedy and Reverend George Hodgkinson, accompanied by Michel Croz, Michel Ducroz and Peter Perren.[3] Hudson was in some ways a forerunner of modern alpinism: a pioneer of guideless climbing, unafraid of taking risks, and interested in searching for new routes up mountains which he had climbed. His experience and natural skills placed him in the forefront among his contemporaries. His generous nature, and a run of successes in his mountain campaigns had led him, perhaps, to adopt a rather easy-going attitude. This was demonstrated by his seemingly casual invitation to several friends, including TS Kennedy, the Reverend J McCormick, John Birkbeck, and two others less experienced, to join him in 'having a shot' at the Matterhorn; all of whom, for various reasons, had to withdraw.

Since it seemed 'undesirable that two independent parties should be on the mountain at the same time with the same object' Hudson and Whymper agreed on a merger of forces, or, as Whymper chose to put it, 'Mr Hudson was invited to join us, and he accepted our proposal'. Hudson introduced his companion, Douglas Hadow, an athletic nineteen-year-old, whose only serious climb had been an ascent of the standard route up Mont Blanc one week earlier. Hudson responded to Whymper's doubts with: 'I consider he [Hadow] is a sufficiently good man to go with us.' The admission of the young and inexperienced Hadow as a member of the party was the first major error. The hastily-constituted group which set out from Zermatt on 13 July to ascend the Matterhorn, included the guides, Michel Croz, aged thirty-seven, one of the strongest and boldest of Chamonix men, and Peter Taugwalder, aged forty-five, with his elder son 'young' Peter, aged twenty-two, both employed by Lord Francis Douglas.

To attempt to apportion blame in any one direction, or to suggest that the tragic loss of four lives on the descent resulted from sinister motives, as Whymper initially implied, would be to ignore much of the factual evidence. The accident was the outcome of a series of mistakes. The conclusions of the four-man Court of Enquiry

---

[3]Apart from his short book, *Where there's a will there's a way*, jointly authored with Edward Shirley Kennedy and published in 1856, Charles Hudson wrote little about his climbs. The Smyth brothers also, though active as climbers, were reticent as writers.

summoned from Visp, and conducted in Zermatt, stated that the accident had resulted from a combination of human error and inexperience: the concluding sentence of their verdict was: 'There is to be no sequel to the foregoing enquiry, but a decision of no grounds for prosecution.' (Note 10) An overriding urge to race Carrel to the top had clouded Whymper's judgement. Whymper and Carrel were both determined men. Carrel's conduct, though disingenuous, was not dishonest. He was acting on his home ground, and had warned Whymper in advance that his services were committed to others. The original plans for an ascent of the Matterhorn by an Italian expedition had been settled two years earlier, when Carrel was called to Biella in 1863 for discussions with Quintino Sella, a leading politician, and Felice Giordano, a distinguished scientist. Both men were prominent among the founders of the Club Alpino in that year, and they had targeted an Italian ascent of the Matterhorn as one of the new Club's principal objectives, selecting Carrel as leader of the expedition.

The untried route on the Swiss side of the Matterhorn turned out to be much easier than expected. The party camped on the east face at about 3350m, 90m above the present Hörnli hut, and at 3.40am the next day, they set out to ascend mostly easy-angled rocks leading to the prominent 'Shoulder'. 'For the greater part of the way there was, indeed, no occasion for the rope' – this ambiguous phrase in Whymper's account left open the question of whether the party was roped together during the initial part of the ascent; during a press interview in Zermatt thirty years later Whymper stated clearly that they were not roped. Above the prominent Shoulder a difficult section was encountered, where the climbers traversed out on to the north face at an angle of about 35-40° across slabby rocks occasionally glazed with ice. Whymper's narrative implies that the party roped up after reaching this section, but he is imprecise about the order of roping, and the type of rope(s) used. Croz went into the lead, followed by Whymper and Hudson. 'Sometimes, after I had taken a hand from Croz, or received a pull, I turned to offer the same to Hudson; but he invariably declined, saying it was not necessary. Mr Hadow, however, was not accustomed to this kind of work, and required continual assistance.' After a climb lasting around eight hours, excluding halts, the top of the Matterhorn (4477m) was reached at 1.40pm on 14 July by all seven climbers. In spite of perfect weather and conditions, the slow pace of the party is not surprising owing to its size, the unequal skills of its members, and the fact that they were treading unknown ground. Whymper and Croz, casting off the rope, raced up the last few metres, arriving 'about ten minutes' ahead of the others in a burst of anxiety to confirm that they had outwitted Carrel. Spotting him and his friends on the Italian side of the mountain some distance below, they yelled themselves hoarse, hurling down stones from the summit.

An hour was spent on top. The intoxication of the party's triumph, led to a fatal neglect of safety precautions for the descent. Joint leadership had been tacitly agreed between Hudson and Whymper, the two most experienced members. 'Whatever responsibility there was devolved upon us.' Departing from normal practice, in which the strongest climber should occupy the last position on the rope when descending, (a point stressed by TS Kennedy in a letter he wrote to *The Times* on 28 July 1865 relating to the accident) Hudson and Whymper agreed that Croz, the strongest, should go first with Hadow, the weakest, directly behind him. This was the next major error: their two positions, at the least, should have been reversed. Hudson wished to be third. Lord Francis Douglas was placed next, followed by his guide, old Peter Taugwalder. Whymper states that he: 'suggested to Hudson that we should attach a rope to the rocks on our arrival at the difficult bit, and hold it as we descended, as an additional protection. He approved the idea, but it was not definitely settled that it should be done. ... The suggestion was not made for my own sake, and I am not sure that it even occurred to me again.' (Note 11) Whymper was sketching on the summit when Croz, using one of two hundred-foot lengths of strong manilla rope, tied on Hadow, Hudson and Douglas who were placed with him in the front. A second hundred-foot length of rope of the same quality appears to have been used by Whymper who tied on behind, with young Peter as last man. The remaining rope available was 150 feet of a heavier type, and about 200 feet of lighter rope, 'of a kind that I [Whymper] used previously'. All these ropes had been provided by Whymper, and neither Whymper, Hudson, or Croz, troubled to observe that Old Peter picked up the lighter rope when attaching himself to his employer Douglas, who, apparently, did not remark upon it. The type and number of ropes used for the descent, or even the actual need for a third rope, have been the subject of much debate chiefly because, it must be said, Whymper's own accounts were never specific – perhaps to conceal any remorse that he might have felt personally over his failure to check Taugwalder's use of the weakest of his ropes. (Note 12)

Shortly after the descent began Douglas turned to Whymper requesting him to join his two-man rope to old Peter for added security. The party was then spread out on the exposed upper rocks of the north face, comprising seven climbers of unequal skills joined together by rope-links of unequal strength. Before commencing the descent, Hudson and Whymper, as co-leaders, overlooked the placing of fixed belays, failed to determine the safest order of roping, and omitted to ensure that only the two hundred-foot lengths of sound manilla rope were used. Given the party's general feeling of elation on reaching the top of the Matterhorn, and their elementary knowledge of roping techniques, the ease with which such errors were committed seems all too obvious. The failure to fix belay-ropes was the reason why, when the inexperienced Hadow apparently slipped, knocking Croz out of his steps, the two inevitably dragged down Hudson and Douglas to whom they were attached. Old Peter, instinctively securing the loose portion of his rope to a rock, was able to hold firm to his position at the moment of the slip but, on receiving the weight of four falling men, the weak rope linking him to Douglas broke, before the full strain could have been felt by Whymper (although Whymper's account refers to the rope between him and Taugwalder being 'taut ... the jerk came on us both as on one man'.) Had the seven-man party been linked together by ropes of equal strength, it seems almost inevitable that – without a fixed belay – a slip by one member would have resulted in seven deaths. Alternatively, had a belay-rope been securely in place, the experienced Croz, closely attending to Hadow, and reacting instantly, would have been adequately secured to arrest his slip. In an article published by *Graphic* magazine on 6 October 1894 Whymper wrote: 'The accident took place on a spot where rope ought to have been fixed, and if it had been fixed no accident would have happened.'

From Interlaken on 25 July 1865, Whymper addressed to E von Fellenberg of Bern, an original member of the SAC of which he was then Secretary, a letter intended as an authentic account of the accident for the information of the Club and the Swiss press; he addressed a similar letter to the Secretary of the Club Alpino in Turin which was published in their *Bollettine*. In the final paragraph he added: 'No blame can be attached to any of the guides; they all did their duty manfully, but, I cannot but think, that had the rope been tight between those who fell as it was between myself and Taugwalder, that the whole of this frightful calamity might have been averted.' A false assumption. Whymper modified his views three weeks later, when he wrote his first official account, published in *The Times* on 8 August 1865: 'If the rope had not broken you would not have received this letter, for we could not possibly have held the four men.' Old Peter's evidence at the Zermatt enquiry revealed that at the moment of the accident: 'to be more secure I turned towards the rocks and as the rope which was between Whymper and myself was *not taut* [my italics] I was fortunately able to wind it round a projecting rock, which then gave me the necessary life-saving anchorage.' Taugwalder's quick reaction saved the lives of Whymper, himself, and his son. In a letter dated 9 August 1865 to W Wigram (who made the first ascent of the Dent Blanche with TS Kennedy in 1862) Whymper wrote: 'there is not the slightest reason for suspecting that there was any foul play with the rope ... it is an absolute certainty that it broke freely.' (Note 13) In the same letter he added: 'I have no idea why he [old Peter Taugwalder] did not use the stronger ropes. Still I have no reason to suspect even that this was done intentionally.' Which would seem to add greater injustice to Whymper's subsequent behaviour towards old Peter Taugwalder. Without a shred of direct evidence he implicitly held him guilty of the deliberate use of a weak rope, part of his own equipment. The charge, though clearly false, was never publicly retracted.[4]

After their shattering vision of the disaster, the descent for Whymper and the two Taugwalders of the exposed upper part of the mountain, must have been a frightening experience. They descended with extreme caution: 'we were able to do that which should have been done at first, and fixed rope to firm rocks, in addition to being tied together. These ropes were cut from time to time and were left behind.' Whymper's narrative leaves little doubt that the nerves of their little party were severely on edge. His personal sense of shock appears to have given him a distorted view of the attitude that he attributed to the Taugwalders which, he stated later in a letter to a friend, filled him with fears for his life. His suspicions of an intended

---

[4]It is curious, in his account in *Scrambles,* that Whymper should have expressed surprise when he recognised old Peter's broken rope as the weak one; testifying to his failure to identify the rope when he tied his own to old Peter only a short while earlier at Douglas' request.

plot by father and son seem exaggerated. His account in *Scrambles* admits that the guides 'spoke in *patois* which I did not understand'. In fact any coherent conversation between him and his guides would have been impossible, and subject to serious misunderstandings. A dispute about payment of their fees is cited by Whymper as a source of contention between him and the Taugwalders. Whymper's reactions need to be judged in the light of his initial uneasiness over the cause of the accident, his apprehensions about the consequences, and the explanation that he, as the sole English survivor, would be expected to provide. Strong feelings of bitterness appear to have developed on both sides. It is regrettable that with the passage of years Whymper, in whose power it lay to promote a reconciliation with the Taugwalders, did not do so. Whymper, although young in years in 1865, possessed in many ways the mature characteristics of a much older man, and he preferred to dwell under the shadow of the tragedy. It is impossible to tell whether he was troubled by some personal sense of remorse. (See Bishop Browne's remarks in Note 12)

Entering the Monte Rosa hotel alone on 15 July, evidently under great physical and mental strain, Whymper retreated alone to his room. Although understandably shaken by the accident, his self-imposed silence did him little credit; his reasons were obscure, and were never fully explained. But he acted promptly and honourably when he set out from Zermatt at 2am on 16 July fifteen hours after his return, to reach his fallen companions. He headed a rescue party which included three other Englishmen, Reverend J McCormick, the English chaplain at Zermatt, Reverend J Robertson of Cambridge, and JS Phillpotts, Rector of Bedford school – the first two were among those whom Hudson had invited to join his party – accompanied by five guides, Josef-Marie Lochmatter and his brother Alexander from Saint-Niklaus, Franz Andermatten from Saas, Frédéric Payot and Jean Tairraz from Chamonix: Zermatt guides, under compulsion to attend mass on Sunday morning, were excluded. The shattered bodies of Croz, Hadow and Hudson were found lying close to each other on the Matterhorn glacier at the foot of the 1100m north face of the mountain, with the tattered remnants of their clothing and boots spread across the ice. They were placed inside a freshly-dug hollow in the glacier, and Reverend McCormick recited part of the burial service, reading from the prayer-book found near Hudson's body. The body of

Lord Francis Douglas was never found. Three days later the authorities despatched twenty-one Zermatt men, including two of Peter Taugwalder's sons, young Peter and Joseph, to recover the three bodies which were placed in plain wooden coffins and buried in the village.

Prior to the Matterhorn ascent, old Peter Taugwalder appears to have had only two first ascents to his credit, Pollux in 1864 with J Jacot, and in 1865 the Wellenkuppe, followed by the second ascent and first traverse of the the Ober Gabelhorn, both with Douglas. He had also taken part in the first traverse of the Allalinhorn in 1860 with a party that included Leslie Stephen. He climbed the Ostspitze of Monte Rosa in 1851 with the brothers Adolph and Hermann Schlagintweit, and had gained some renown as a Monte Rosa guide, having made numerous ascents of the Dufourspitze. Although not in the foremost rank of Zermatt guides, and probably getting past his prime by 1865, he deserves credit for having reported favourably to his employer Douglas about the north-east side of the Matterhorn, having been among the first to examine the route as one of TS Kennedy's two guides in the winter of 1862. Partly as a result of his having been falsely impugned for his rôle in the 1865 tragedy, his guiding activities declined after the accident. (Note 14) Peter Taugwalder refused a request by the young Paul Güssfeldt two months later to accompany him on the Hörnli route of the Matterhorn, which he never climbed again. But, with his son Joseph, he accompanied Güssfeldt to within 500m of the top of the Matterhorn from the Italian side. Smarting under imputations and criticisms from fellow guides, he left for America in 1874 where he lived for four years. He died at the Hotel Schwarzsee in July 1888 at the age of 68.

Young Peter Taugwalder, who died in his eightieth year, started climbing with his father as an assistant guide in 1859 at the age of sixteen, making ascents of the Weisstor, Monte Rosa and the Cima di Jazzi between 1859-62. In 1863 he made the fifth ascent of the Weisshorn with J Birkbeck Jr and F Biner. In 1865, a few weeks after the Matterhorn accident, he was employed by EN Buxton, Grove and R Macdonald, whose Chamonix guides J Cachat and M Payot, refused at first to set out with him, owing to the highly-coloured reports spread about the Taugwalders by Croz's brother JB Croz. The two were dismissed, and after their replacement with Jakob Anderegg, Cachat later agreed to rejoin the party. Peter Taugwalder *fils* was regularly employed from 1866 onwards; the entries in his *führerbuch*, written mostly by members of the Alpine Club, testify to the high opinion in which he was held. His climbs included many of the classic routes in the Valaisian, Bernese, and Bernina alps, as well as ascents in the eastern alps, including the Gross Glockner, Ortler, and Dachstein. In 1870 he was employed by Lord Queensberry, brother of Lord Francis Douglas, whom he led across two passes. In 1872 after traversing the Cols d'Herens, Bertol, and Collon with Leslie Stephen, he climbed Mont Blanc with two Americans, who noted in his *führerbuch* that he 'sustained his reputation as one of the best guides in Switzerland ... [he] is well known and largely respected among the rival fraternity of guides here, and during the ascent today our Chamonix friends yielded him the privilege of leading the way.' In the same year he returned to the Matterhorn, which he traversed from Zermatt to Breuil with R and W Pendlebury, C Taylor, F Imseng and G Spechtenhauser, shortly after that party's first ascent of the great eastern face of Monte Rosa. He is said to have ascended the Matterhorn 125 times altogether. In 1917, at the age of seventy-four, he was asked to provide a narrative containing his version of the events of the 1865 ascent of the Matterhorn, a copy of which was published in volume 61 of the *Alpine Journal*. There are, inevitably, lapses of memory, and differences in detail between his and Whymper's accounts, such as his reference to the party roping up at the very start of the climb, and the statement that above the 'Shoulder' the lead climbers on the rope were Croz and Hudson. On the descent he describes the rocks on the north face as being 'entirely free from snow' although Whymper refers to the 'snow-filled interstices of the rock face ... at times covered with a thin film of ice'. But the principal differences between his account and Whymper's relate to his resentment, and vigorous denial, of the discussions over pay that are alleged by Whymper to have taken place on the mountain after the accident. It was he who conversed with Whymper in French, having acquired a smattering of the language during military service in the French-speaking canton of Vaud. He added: 'various expressions which he [Whymper] put into our mouths were absolutely without foundation.'[5] He described the vision of two

---

[5]Whymper's account stated that the guides did not want him, on behalf of their dead employer, to pay their fees, and asked him to publicise their names whereby they hoped to gain more clients.

crosses in the sky following the accident, which forms a striking frontispiece to *Scrambles amongst the Alps*, as an invention of Whymper. While there are no startling revelations in young Peter's account, he emphasised the fact that his father's firm stance – referred to by Whymper as his 'wonderful feat of strength' – at the moment of the accident, saved Whymper's life. His words leave little doubt about his bitterness towards Whymper, whom he regarded as unfriendly, ungenerous, and as the source of unwarranted accusations against his father.

While Whymper triumphed on 14 July, hurling down torrents of rocks and stones into Italy from the summit of the Matterhorn, one can imagine Carrel's crushing sense of defeat when he recognised his old employer standing there on the crest of the mountain. The party that he led comprised Jean-Joseph Maquignaz, a stonemason by trade on his first major alpine ascent, César Carrel, and Charles Gorret, brother of *l'abbé* Gorret. Jean-Antoine had refused Felice Giordano's request to join the party because he feared that the inclusion of a *'voyageur'* (tourist) might delay them. The latter waited anxiously at Breuil, relaying messages to Quintino Sella at Turin. At 1.40pm on 14 July the Italians were not far from Pic Tyndall, about 330m below the top. In Carrel's words: *'J'en suis affecté au delà de toute expression.'* (It is impossible to describe my feelings of despair.) A sense of shock extinguished his will to continue. Had he done so, his party might well have reached the top that day. Instead, the defeated group descended to Breuil the same evening carrying down all their equipment. 'You must set off again,' said Felice Giordano. Starting from Breuil on 16 July, a four-man party which included *l'abbé* Gorret and Jean-Augustin Meynet, opened the Italian route on the Matterhorn on 17 July 1865 when Jean-Antoine Carrel and Jean-Baptiste Bich reached the summit. On the final stretch to the top, Carrel and Bich followed a difficult and exposed *galerie* across the Z'mutt (Swiss) face of the mountain. When they returned safely to Breuil at midday on 18 July the whole valley, roused to an intense degree of pride, celebrated the event with rapturous joy, in sharp contrast to the atmosphere of despair and humiliation prevailing on the other side of the mountain. Thus ended the rivalry between two men and the Matterhorn. Was it a twist of irony, or the hand of fate, that Whymper's ascent was followed by mourning in Zermatt, while Carrel's success three days later was celebrated with rejoicing in Valtournanche?

On 14 August 1867, Carrel and Bich guided F Craufurd Grove up their route, to make the second ascent from Breuil. On 13 September of the same year Jean-Joseph Maquignaz with his brother Pierre, accompanied by César Carrel and two others, made the third ascent from Breuil, the first by a new and less exposed route up the final head-wall entirely on the Italian side of the mountain. Two weeks later, on 2 October, the two Maquignaz brothers led W Leighton Jordan up their route. The brothers accomplished the first traverse of the mountain with Professor Tyndall on 28 July 1868 from Breuil to Zermatt; and one week later the first traverse from Zermatt to Breuil accompanying two Geneva climbers, O Hoiler and F Thioly. In 1866 and 1867 Hoiler had failed to persuade Zermatt guides to accompany him up the Swiss route. On 9 August 1868 Paul Güssfeldt, with the St Niklaus guides Peter Knubel and Jean-Marie Lochmatter, ascended the Matterhorn by the Swiss route and returned to Zermatt in a day. Thirty years after the first ascent from the Italian side, the very exposed final section of Carrel's original route had been climbed only three times; it is rarely used now. Jean-Joseph Maquignaz became one of the leading Italian guides, with a reputation equal to that of his friend Jean-Antoine Carrel. It was J-J Maquignaz, with his son Jean-Baptiste and his nephew Daniel, who spent four days in July 1882 hammering fixed aids into the rocks in order to ascend the Dent du Géant. He made the first winter ascents of the Lyskamm, and Monte Rosa. Jean-Antoine Carrel enjoyed a glorious career as a guide, which included his pioneer climbs in Ecuador with Whymper in 1879-80. His fame continued to grow in his native valley and elsewhere; he made fifty-three ascents of the Matterhorn, including the first winter ascent in 1882, accompanying the great photographer Vittorio Sella then aged twenty-three, a nephew of Quintino Sella. On 25 August 1890, twenty-five years after his first ascent, Carrel died at the foot of the Matterhorn, within sight of the pastures of Breuil, at the end of a desperate twenty-hour struggle in a terrible storm on his cherished route, after safely guiding down his client Leone Sinigaglia, a law student from Turin. Upon his death, Whymper opened a subscription in England which raised a substantial sum for Carrel's family. Three years later, a small iron cross was raised by Sinigaglia at the very place where Carrel died, situated about 100m above the position of the Rionde Hut.

At the age of twenty-five, Whymper withdrew from the alpine climbing scene. Apparently his decision to do so was not a sudden one. He had told friends earlier that once the Matterhorn was climbed there would be no further challenge to stimulate his interest. His book *Scrambles amongst the Alps*, published in 1871, has been described as an artistic masterpiece. It was in that year that Stephen's *The playground of Europe,* and Tyndall's *Hours of exercise in the Alps* also appeared, engravings to illustrate both books having been provided by Whymper. He worked for the best part of six years in preparing his own book. Great trouble was taken over every word and every sentence, analysing, correcting, and rewriting. A lifelong victim of insomnia, he wrote mostly at night while living at Town House, Haslemere, where his father had moved in 1859 on account of his stepmother's ill-health in London. In June 1869 he wrote to Reverend J Robertson: 'The book is entirely personal, all ego.'[6] About the book's magnificent collection of 115 illustrations, Whymper wrote: 'The preparation of the illustrations has occupied a large part of my time during the last six years. About fifty have been drawn on the wood by Mr James Mahoney ... Twenty of the remainder are the work of Mr Cyrus Johnson ... The illustrations have been introduced as illustrations and very rarely for ornamental purposes. We have subordinated everything in them to accuracy, and it is only fair to the artists who have honoured me by their assistance to say that many of their designs would have ranked higher as works of art if they had been subjected to fewer restrictions.' Nonetheless it is assumed that Whymper accepted as permissible some degree of artistic licence in his sketches. Exaggerations, intended to create a greater impact, certainly did occur in some illustrations; Croz standing on the very tip of a cornice on the Moming pass, and Almer's leap on the Ecrins ridge come to mind as two examples, apart from the famous frontispiece. 'Scrambles' was clearly not a term used at the time to describe minor mountain adventures light-heartedly undertaken. Whymper's book describes the events of a series of courageous, resolute, carefully-organised alpine expeditions, which provide plenty of exciting material. In his preface Whymper wrote: 'These scrambles amongst the Alps were holiday excursions ... They are spoken of as a sport, and

---

[6]An honest confession. Later generations of climbers do not shrink from admitting that it is egotism which provides one of the most compelling motives.

nothing more.' The book's strength lies in the emphasis on action; and on the author's ambitious approach to the challenges that he set himself. Whymper omitted some facts from his story, giving undue importance to others; and he had a tendency, not uncharacteristic, to magnify his own rôle. In the course of a lengthy review in the *Alpine Journal*, of which he was then editor, Stephen described the book as 'the congenial record of the most determined, the most systematic, and ... the best planned series of assaults that were made upon the High Alps during the period', adding: 'his [Whymper's] career in 1865, up to its most disastrous end, was by far the most brilliant ever carried out in the Alps ... He was clearly the most advanced, and would, but for one melancholy circumstance, have been the most triumphant of us all.' The review concludes: 'The most enduring merit of the book [is] the admirable quality of the illustrations ... Mr Whymper's woodcuts seem to bring the genuine Alps before us in all their marvellous beauty and variety of architecture.' (Note 15) Half a century later, in 1923, Geoffrey Winthrop Young wrote in the *Cornhill Magazine*: 'He (Whymper) wrote under an inspiration which we feel to have been greater than himself, and which probably he himself only understood for a short space of his youth. ... Leslie Stephen has had many imitators. His recipe book has been plundered of everything but the light unerring touch that mixed the inimitable proportions. Whymper founded no school. No one has succeeded in imitating anything but his egoism.'

The drama of the Matterhorn tragedy turned Whymper into something of a legend, a rôle which, with his crusty exterior, he filled to perfection. *Scrambles* contains some colourless sections. There are over forty pages of comment about the action of water and ice upon the beds of rivers and glaciers; thirty-four pages dealing with the construction of the Mont Cenis tunnel and railway – Whymper having been one of the invited guests during the first passage through the tunnel from France to Italy in September 1871. There are in addition fourteen pages describing the population of bouquetins, and the prevalence of cretinism, in the Aosta valley – each subject is treated with meticulous detail. In an age that preceded mountain photography, the book's illustrations are a masterly tribute to the engraver's art, based upon Whymper's own detailed sketches and the professional skill of his craftsmen. A direct result was the pre-eminent rôle subsequently acquired by Whymper's artistic services with a growing demand for alpine illustrations. Whymper tended to overdraw certain situations – Almer's leap on the Ecrins was the subject of a bitter controversy with Coolidge, who had commented that the leap was pure invention. An enraged Whymper called a special committee meeting of the Alpine Club, when he stated unequivocally: 'that Christian Almer made the jump; that I witnessed it; that every member of our party made it, and that the illustration is, to the best of my belief, a fair and is substantially an accurate representation of the incident.' Horace Walker, a member of the Ecrins party, confirmed that a leap did take place. The frontispiece of Whymper's book, showing an apparition in the sky with crosses seen after the accident on the Matterhorn, inevitably raised questions. The caption reads: 'The Taugwalders thought that it had some connection with the accident.' Young Peter, as we have seen, denied the existence of the crosses. Carrel's party, descending the Italian ridge of the Matterhorn on 17 July, saw at the same late hour from a similar height a 'mirage' in the sky above the Lyskamm. Whymper's 'fog-bow, ' to use his term, is likely to have been an over-dramatised rendering of a Brocken spectre showing a magnified shadow of his little party thrown across a bank of cloud by a low evening sun. It is impossible not to enthuse over the dramatic quality of certain other illustrations, such as the midnight storm on the Matterhorn, and the crossing of the *bergschrund* on the Dent Blanche. Whymper's illustrations were, in a sense, the forerunners of modern photography, in which striking examples of the photographer's art are often made to appear slightly larger than life.

Whymper was generous in his praise of the best guides. Of Croz he said: 'We had made many expeditions together, and I think I may say we had the greatest confidence in and liking for each other ... he had the strength and courage of a lion, joined to a skill and sagacity rarely to be met with.' During the crossing of the Col de Pilatte in 1864 with Moore, Walker, and Almer, Whymper wrote: 'I cannot close without paying tribute to the ability with which Croz led us through a dense mist down the remainder of the Glacier de la Pilatte ... he went on with the utmost certainty, and without having to retrace a single step; and displayed from first to last consummate knowledge of the materials with which he was dealing ... he cut steps down one side of a *sérac*, went with a dash at the other side, and hauled us up after him ... ridiculing our apprehensions, mimicking our awkwardness, declining all help, bidding us only to follow him.' Of Christian Almer: 'The temper of Almer it was impossible to ruffle; he was ever obliging and enduring – a bold but a safe man. That which he lacked in fire – in dash – was supplied by Croz, who in turn was kept in place by Almer.' Of Carrel: 'He is the finest rock-climber I have ever seen ... I would that [he] could have stood with us at that moment [on the summit of the Matterhorn].' Yet, with his aloof nature and iron will, Whymper adopted an autocratic attitude towards his guides. He was never a generally popular figure with them, and did not acquire a real degree of friendship with any, except perhaps Croz. He devised the plans, they led him up and down the climbs, in a mutual arrangement which suited both sides.

A year after the Matterhorn ascent Whymper wrote: 'I have done with the Alps.' In the summer of 1866 he spent about two weeks at the request of Professor Forbes examining the veined structure of the ice in the depths of the Stockji glacier below the Col de Valpelline, accompanied by Franz Biner, with whom he climbed the Tête de Valpelline. In 1867, and again in 1872, he spent a few months travelling among the glaciers of Greenland. Unaccompanied, it was impossible for him to achieve very much, and apart from limited geological and glaciological explorations he regarded both expeditions as failures. In 1872, he was elected Vice-President of the Alpine Club. Whymper returned to the Swiss side of the Matterhorn in 1874, when he made the seventy-sixth ascent accompanied by the powerfully guided team of Carrel, Bich and Josef-Marie Lochmatter; photography appears to have been one of his chief objects. A night was spent with eighteen others in a diminutive *refuge* built on the north-east ridge: 'the floor was mainly composed of ice and the door was off its hinges.'[7] Whymper and his guides took four hours to complete the ascent, following a cairned route somewhat different from that of his original ascent. He remarked on the fixed ropes, adding that those at the place of the fateful accident, appeared to be in poor condition. His diary comments include the prediction: 'Soon the biggest duffers will be able to go up.' (Note 16) Two years later, he walked up from the Schwarzsee to visit his 1865 campsite.

On 23 July of the same year an English schoolmaster, A Cust, with AH Cawood and JB Colgrove made the first guideless ascent of the

[7]The first Hörnli Hut was established in 1880.

Matterhorn. All three were experienced climbers, and they were careful to choose a day when the weather was favourable. Cust reported later that they departed from Zermatt: 'without an encouraging word from anyone, on an enterprise apparently regarded by others of a rash or dubious nature.' A night was spent in the primitive hut on the Hörnli ridge, from which they departed before 4am. Small cairns were built along the route to facilitate their return. 'It is astonishing what a difference there is in the consumption of time between following the trail of guides ... and picking one's own hesitating way amid unknown and various details not without doubt and discussion.' They were not record-breakers and the ascent and descent, occupying twelve hours, was a tribute to their individual skills and care.

Whymper made his last major alpine ascent in 1894, when he spent two nights in the Janssen observatory, erected that year below the summit of Mont Blanc from where he was able to witness the sunrise on a brilliantly clear morning. One year later at the age of fifty-five, accompanied by César Carrel, his son, and two other guides, Whymper set out from Breuil to ascend the Matterhorn by the south-west ridge, the scene of so many of his youthful hopes and defeats; but it was an object that remained unfulfilled. The frosts and storms of thirty years had taken their toll, and he found familiar features much altered, with certain rock sections almost unrecognisable. After reaching the overcrowded Italian hut below the Great Tower, the party retreated in the face of stormy weather. (Note 17)

By 1874 Whymper had begun to develop an interest in the physical and psychological problems of human existence at high altitudes about which very little was known. When his plans to visit the Himalaya had to be abandoned owing to political restrictions, he decided to organise an expedition to the mountains of Ecuador. Departing from England in November 1879, accompanied by Jean-Antoine Carrel and his cousin Louis, Whymper planned his expedition, which was to last about seven months, with his usual meticulous attention to detail. There were numerous local difficulties, and long spells of bad weather with bouts of heavy rain and snowfall, including a period of fifteen days when the sun was not seen at all. Whymper, then in his fortieth year, had done no regular alpine climbing for almost fifteen years; he was principally interested in exploring the country, conducting high-altitude observations, and studying the customs of the people. He tended to treat the Carrels as porters for his scientific equipment on mountain ascents which involved few challenges of interest to skilled climbers; he appears to have been singularly insensitive to their complaints, and there were frequent disagreements. Despite frustrations, including the generally unfavourable weather, trying for Whymper and probably a good deal more so for his guides, the expedition produced excellent results. Ten mountains were climbed, including Chimborazo (6310m) (twice), which was one of the first 6000m mountains to be climbed by Europeans. Three high camps were set up the highest at 5300m, and in the long and exhausting final climb through soft snow Louis Carrel's feet were frostbitten; the wind speed on the summit was measured at 80km per hour. Among other mountains ascended were Cayambe (6163m), Antisana (5895m), Carihuairazo (5035m), Corazon (4837m - second ascent), and Cotopaxi (5980m - fifth ascent) where the last camp, placed about 75m from the crater, was occupied for twenty-six hours; at one point the rubber floor of the tent showed signs of melting from the heat while the outside temperature measured minus -8°C. On a moonlit night, Whymper peered into the crater to see: 'its lower part illuminated by glowing fires.' Whymper's intention to climb Chimborazo amazed the local people, who believed it to be inaccessible; suspecting that he was searching for buried treasure, they besought him to divide the spoils with them.[8] Whymper recorded meteorological details, and the physical effects of oxygen-lack after thirty-six nights spent above 4250m.

On his return to England, he wrote numerous articles for newspapers and magazines, and was much in demand as a lecturer. His talk to the Alpine Club on 1 February 1881 was a tremendous success; it was held in the theatre of the Royal Institution before an audience of over nine hundred including the Prince of Wales, later King Edward VII. His book about the expedition, *Travels amongst the great Andes of the Equator*, appeared over ten years later – a very comprehensive volume including maps and appendices. Apart from descriptions of exploratory travel, the scientific records added a good deal to contemporary knowledge about conditions at high altitudes.

---

[8] Over forty years ago when travelling in an isolated region of Kohistan in north-west Pakistan, I can recall having been asked similar questions by my porters about my reason for coming to their 'inhospitable' mountains; they could not believe that financial gain was not my motive.

Although the book received excellent reviews, it lacks something of the compelling power of *Scrambles* written during the vibrant years of Whymper's youth. A generous tribute was paid to the Carrels: for their 'zeal and industry upon all occasions ... the laborious duty of transporting (scientific) instruments devolved upon J-A Carrel. In consequence of his extreme care, no breakages occurred.'

Between October and December 1900, Whymper was invited to give a series of lectures across North America. In 1901, at the invitation of the Canadian Pacific Railway, he spent the first of three summers in the Canadian Rockies exploring, climbing and photographing mountains in areas served by the railway in a drive to promote tourism. He took with him four Swiss guides, Christian Klucker (a career schoolmaster and leading guide, among whose clients were William Edward Davidson, John Percy Farrar and Paul Güssfeldt), Josef Pollinger, Christian Kaufmann and Joseph Bossonay. During three months, between June to September, seven first ascents were made, Whymper participating in four of the smaller climbs including Mounts Whymper (2845m), Marpole (2997m) and Collie (3116m), and several passes were crossed. Whymper was responsible for the planning, but, at the age of sixty-one, he had lost his zest for climbing and lacked the robust health of his early years. His preference for walking and fishing created a good deal of discontent among his guides, who were obliged to act as porters, and whose suggestions to attempt more challenging mountains such as Assiniboine (climbed later that year by Reverend J Outram with the guides C Häsler and C Bohren) and Robson were rejected. His later visits to the Rockies in 1903 and 1904, troubled by then with rheumatism, were occupied mostly with minor excursions and walks. Two further short visits to Canada were made in 1905 and 1910, the first to discuss with the directors of the Canadian Pacific Railway his reports and photographs, the second to attend a Camp at Lake O'Hara as a guest of the Alpine Club of Canada. By 1912, under the leadership of the Swiss guide E Feuz Jr a new mountaineering era opened in the Canadian Alps centred at Golden in British Columbia.

Around 1892 Whymper, shrewdly perceiving a profitable market, commenced work on his Chamonix and Zermatt guide books. With his personal knowledge and wide experience he began methodically to amass information from a wide variety of sources. The work entailed annual summer visits to the Alps, during which long distances were covered on foot, while copious details were gathered and recorded. No climbing was involved. The Chamonix guide was published in 1896 and the Zermatt guide in 1897[9], offering to burgeoning crowds of British and other tourists the first real alpine compendium. Both guides sold well, running into sixteen and fifteen editions respectively. They provided Whymper with a useful source of income in addition to that obtained from lectures, articles, and the sales of his two books. Whymper's guide books contained lists of the main peaks and passes, names and tariffs of guides, facilities offered by railways and hotels, detailed suggestions concerning excursions of every grade of facility and difficulty, and a good deal about the political, social and mountaineering history of the respective regions.

The earliest records in existence relating to Zermatt, under its former name Praborno, are dated 1280AD; and it was probably a flourishing little village when the Swiss Confederation was founded in 1291, the canton of Valais being one of the last three, in 1815, to accede to the Confederation. Chamonix is mentioned under *Le Prieuré de Chamonix* in a deed dated 1091AD although the original *prieuré*, destroyed by a fire in 1758, was said to have dated from 1062. The valley was held under tutelage for several centuries, its proprietorship alternating between ecclesiastical and political groups, and its inhabitants occasionally rebelling violently against various forms of persecution. It was not until 1786 that the valley was delivered out of feudal servitude; and it was only in 1860 that it was ceded by the Duchy of Savoy to France. A census taken in 1896 recorded the valley's total population as 3438, with the Commune of Chamonix accounting for 1923 persons; by that time over 15,000 annual visitors were recorded, and up to 1886, a hundred years after the first ascent of Mont Blanc, 1000 ascents had been made. During the next twenty-four years up to 1910 a further 1500 ascents were recorded. The 1910 edition of the Chamonix guide lists almost three hundred members of the *Compagnie des Guides*. The Zermatt guide quotes the 1888 Cantonal Census for Valais as recording a population of 101,790, with 100,925 heads of cattle, emphasising its essentially pastoral character, with the cow providing almost exclusively the basis of existence. The geographical pattern of this mountainous canton, like some others,

---

[9]*Chamonix and the range of Mont Blanc: a guide* and *The valley of Zermatt and the Matterhorn: a guide.*

tended to keep populations isolated and parochially minded. The first *auberge* in Zermatt was opened in 1839 by Herr Joseph Lauber the village doctor, who offered three double-bedded rooms in his house to tourists. The house was bought in 1854 by Alexandre Seiler who extended and converted it into the Hotel Monte Rosa which opened in 1855 on 1 August, Switzerland's National Day. Seiler's name soon became synonymous with the growth of tourism in Zermatt; he acquired the Mont Cervin hotel in 1867, and later set up hotels at Riffelalp and Schwarzsee. By the end of the nineteenth century there were twenty hotels and *pensions* in existence in Zermatt, with tariffs ranging from four to eight francs per night. The railway service from Visp, which was opened in 1891, was electrified in 1898; and in the same year the Gornergrat line was opened, becoming the first rack-and-pinion mountain railway in the country. The 35km length of road from Visp to Zermatt was not infrequently blocked by avalanches during the spring and autumn – an occurrence which is not uncommon even now; the last notable one having occurred in 1991, when on 8 and 18 April two successive falls of earth and rock crashed down the west slopes of the Mattertal, blocking the valley around Randa, damming the river, and obliterating the motor-road and the railway line. Heavy rainfall occurring between June and August of that year caused flooding, and greatly delayed the restoration of communications. (Note 18)

Whymper's guidebooks, translated into French and German, and regularly updated during his annual visits to the Alps, undoubtedly boosted the tourist appeal of both resorts. In 1900 Coolidge wrote: 'It is really unnecessary to dwell much on Zermatt, once a favourite climbing "centre", but now abandoned to the noisy tourist.' (Note 19) Grindelwald also had become a popular tourist destination with the opening in 1892 of the railway from Lauterbrunnen. The esteem, and even regard, in which some British mountaineers were held in the Alps did not extend to the expanding numbers of British tourists some of whom, because of their demanding ways and arrogant manners, were often overcharged by their hosts.[10] Among the sale outlets that Whymper used for his guidebooks were the tourist-frequented hotels at the respective resorts, where he adopted the

---

[10]In the current alpine environment, dominated by European tourists, the attitudes and manners of British visitors continue to stand apart.

practice of calling personally to collect his share of the sale proceeds. Acrimonious disputes were not uncommon. He was almost always accorded a cordial welcome at Zermatt's Monte Rosa hotel, where he was given a complimentary room. Yet his diary records a visit made in late October 1905: 'It was dark when I got to Zermatt, and very cold. Not a soul at the station to carry my things. Turned into the first place where I saw a light, in a little café about 100 yards from the station, and passed the night on two benches, under my railway rugs.' Whymper was then sixty-five years old.

Guido Rey, author of a classic book about the Matterhorn, an honorary member of the Alpine Club London, and a nephew of Quintino Sella, had a chance meeting with Whymper in 1895. 'I was descending from the Theodul. Half-way between the Col and the Jomein I saw coming slowly up to me a fine, tall old man, with a ruddy countenance, clean-shaven, clear-eyed ... his face bore the impress of an iron will; his body straight as a dart ... was full of vigour; his long, rhythmical gait testified to his familiarity with mountains.' After they had passed each other, Rey's guide told him that it was 'Monsieur Whymper, and he pronounced the name in a tone of respect. I had never seen Whymper ... I at once turned round to look at him. He had stopped too and was looking at the Matterhorn, whose aspect was one of marvellous grandeur from this point. I cannot describe how much I was impressed by that meeting in that spot ... They were there, the Matterhorn and Whymper ... He was looking at it, and was perhaps recalling the deeds of daring he had performed on the stubborn peak in the vigour of his youthful years.'

Writing about him in 1897, friends whom he had visited described Whymper as 'one-third hero, one-third old bachelor, one-third mysterious man of business and lecturer'. (Note 20) Throughout his life he had formed no sentimental attachments, nor made any lasting friendships. He was self-centred, and women formed no part of his ambitions. Spiritually, he was a lonely person but in September 1899 at Chamonix he met a Miss Charlotte Hanbury, ten years older than himself, who attracted him because of her personal charm, her physical energy (she was an active walker and loved mountains), and her literary talent. Their friendship ripened during the year that followed, but was marred by tragedy. In October 1900, during his lecture tour of America, he received news of her sudden death, writing to his sister Annette Whymper: 'My beloved friend gone. I hardly know how I carry on.' That Whymper was deeply moved by her death seemed clear to the few who knew him closely. His querulous and aloof nature did not improve as he grew older; yet despite his imperfections he remained a heroic figure, reflecting the physical courage and strength of his earlier years. He was always regarded, even by close family and relations, as rather awesome although he appears to have possessed a kindly streak in his character, which would sometimes surface unexpectedly. At the age of sixty-six, Whymper married Edith Mary Lewin aged twenty-one; the ceremony was conducted by Canon James McCormick, who had assisted him after the Matterhorn accident. The marriage, which was an unhappy one, broke up four years later, and Edith Whymper died shortly after. Their daughter, Ethel (Blandy), inheriting her father's qualities as an alpinist, did some fine climbs in Zermatt and elsewhere – a tradition carried on by the second and third generations of the Blandy family.

In 1894 Whymper was elected to Fellowship of the Royal Society of Edinburgh. In the same year he was proposed for election to the Royal Society London; although he failed to secure his Fellowship, it was something of a distinction for a man who had not had any formal scientific training. He was elected to honorary membership of three European Alpine Clubs: Switzerland, France and Italy, also of the Sierra Club. He took an interest in the latest climbing developments, and often lectured to climbing clubs in an honorary capacity. Before his lecture to the Yorkshire Ramblers Club in October 1906 he wrote to the President: 'I should like to make a substantial addition to the funds of the Yorkshire Ramblers; and although members might very well be admitted free, I think you would do well to make outsiders pay.'

William Augustus Brevoort Coolidge, born in 1850, belonged to an old Boston family one of whose members became the thirtieth President of the United States in 1923. He was taken to Europe as a weakly youth of fourteen accompanied by his mother and sister, and his aunt Miss Meta Brevoort aged thirty-nine. At the age of fifteen, with his aunt, he crossed the Strahlegg Pass (3454m). They engaged Christian Almer as their guide in July 1868 when, from Belalp, they climbed the Nesthorn (third ascent) and the Aletschhorn. Miss Brevoort was an accomplished and determined climber who acquired an impressive list of ascents. Coolidge and his aunt pursued an energetic series of travels and climbs throughout the Alpine chain, particularly in the Dauphiné, where their pioneering ventures encouraged its development as a mountaineering centre. (Note 21) After his aunt's sudden death at the age of fifty-one, Coolidge continued his explorations and climbs across the Alps, accompanied by Almer and his sons Ulrich and Christian. During his thirty-year alpine career, between 1865-95, Coolidge built up a record of 1700 separate expeditions, which included the first winter ascents of the Jungfrau, Wetterhorn and Schreckhorn, and several notable ascents in the Dauphiné including the second ascent of the Meije. With a poor physique, he was not a naturally-gifted climber and relied heavily upon the skill of his guides, denouncing those who had the temerity to climb without guides. Apart from his editorship of five volumes of the *Alpine Journal* between 1880-1889, he edited with fastidious attention to detail about two dozen guidebooks covering practically every alpine region. He was elected to Fellowship of Magdalen College Oxford in 1875; and he took Holy Orders in 1882. He is remembered as a great alpine historian, and an unchallengeable authority on the Alps. His publications included over twenty volumes covering the early history of the Alps, a biography of his friend Frederick Gardiner, and a variety of travel and mountaineering guides. His writing style, although dry and dull, was always clear, precise, and invariably accurate. At the age of forty-six he retired to Grindelwald, where he dwelt during the last thirty years of his life in a chalet overflowing with an unrivalled library of 26,000 volumes, representing a collection of over half a century. His biographer titled his book *An eccentric in the Alps*. With an encyclopaedic knowledge and a pedagogic urge to correct any and every inaccuracy, he indulged in – often inflammatory – polemics, delighting in controversy and censure, sparing none of his multitudinous correspondents, and acquiring an intimidating reputation. After his death, an obituary in *The Times* referred to his adeptness 'at the gentle art of making enemies ... a man who regarded a hatchet not as an instrument for burying but for use'. He was the only member of the Alpine Club ever to have resigned his honorary membership.

Whymper and Coolidge had crossed swords on many occasions, passions having risen to fever pitch when Coolidge stated that Almer's leap during the descent of the Ecrins ridge, illustrated in an engraving in *Scrambles amongst the Alps,* had never taken place. Towards the end of Whymper's life, the two men were reconciled, and appear to have corresponded regularly, each having intuitively detected some thread forming a curious link between their respective temperaments. Whymper agreed to visit Coolidge at his chalet. 'When I come,' he wrote, 'I shall come in the old style. Shall walk up, not order rooms in advance ... If none can be had, I shall camp out.' On 3 September 1911, the two men spent almost an entire day together conversing, reminiscing, perhaps experiencing unexpectedly some kinship of spirit. From Grindelwald, Whymper travelled via Geneva to Chamonix, where he fell ill on 12 September, writing in his diary: 'Did not feel at all well towards the end of the day.' Lately, he had suffered from attacks of faintness and failing sight. He retired to his room at Couttet's hotel, where he remained alone, refusing all aid, and died there on 16 September.

There is plenty of drama to be found in *Scrambles amongst the Alps,* but an early chapter describing an ascent of Mont Pelvoux in 1861 reveals a more appealing picture of Whymper filled with youthful spirits and the enjoyment of simple pleasures. He was accompanied by Reginald Macdonald, Jean Reynaud of La Bessée, and Pierre Sémiond, (Note 22) an old peasant from the Ailefroide valley, or the Val D'Alefred as Whymper called it. They made the second ascent of the highest Pelvoux summit (3946m), which Victor Puiseaux of Besançon had first climbed alone in 1848, his guide Pierre-Antoine Barnéoud having accompanied him part of the way. Whymper's account recalls all the enthusiasm and delight which the expedition clearly aroused in a twenty-one-year-old on his 'first serious mountain scramble'.

CHAPTER SEVEN
ALBERT FREDERICK MUMMERY
1855-95

Such precipices are among the most impressive as well as the most dangerous of mountain ranges; in many spots inaccessible with safety either from below or from above; dark in colour, robed with everlasting mourning, forever tottering like a great fortress shaken by war, fearful as much in their weakness as in their strength, and yet gathered after every fall into darker frowns and unhumiliated threatening ... to the utmost desolate; haunted only by uninterrupted echoes from far off, wandering hither and thither among their walls, unable to escape, ... and, sometimes, when the echo has fainted, and the wind has carried the sound away, and the mouldering stones are still for a little time,- a brown moth, opening and shutting its wings upon a grain of dust, may be the only thing that moves, or feels, in all the waste of weary precipice, darkening five thousand feet of the blue depths of heaven.

John Ruskin, *Modern Painters,* Part IV
Thoughts on contemplating the Rochers des Fys
above the Col d'Anterne

Albert Frederick Mummery occupies a prominent place among the alpine pioneers. The early period of the Golden Age, which virtually came to an end after the ascent of the Matterhorn in 1865, was succeeded by a new and more challenging phase of activity involving climbs once regarded as being beyond the limits of possibility. Mummery was ten years old when the Matterhorn was climbed, and a decade and a half were to pass before his exploits began to make an impact in the alpine world, placing him in the forefront of alpine climbers during the later years of the Golden Age by his adoption of a new style of mountaineering. His relatively short life spanned the heyday of the Victorian era, and he was outlived by several mountaineers whose earlier achievements were responsible for the foundation of the new sport in the 'playground' of the Alps.

Mummery was an innovator, revolutionising established ideas, crossing new frontiers in pursuit of climbs which demanded greater technical skills; and he accelerated the start of guideless climbing. Like most innovators he was ahead of his time, and his methods, not unnaturally, attracted criticism. His influence set a high-level mark in climbing circles for over forty years after his death. It is not surprising that he was regarded as a heretic by some of the older generation comprising the nucleus of the early Alpine Club whose membership, dominated by scientists, scholars, and professional men, reflected a more conservative outlook. When Mummery's application for membership of the Alpine Club was rejected in 1880, it was almost certainly an expression of disapproval of his style, and resentment over his achievements. (Note 1) Following his ascents of the Grépon and the Aiguille Verte in August 1881, Mummery replied on 3 November to WAB Coolidge, then editor of the *Alpine Journal*, 'I am extremely sorry to be unable to promise you a paper ... I trust you will understand that my refusal is the unavoidable result of the action of the AC'. Again, on 26 January 1882, he wrote: 'I am conceited enough to think that I can do quite as well without the AC as the AC can without me. But it is different with my guides. Burgener does not appear to be very much injured by the almost total loss of his AC "Monsieurs" ... but Venetz suffers so severely from his connection with me that the most skilful young rock climber in the Alps seems likely to be forced into some other employment.' (Note 2) Mummery was offended by the rejection of his membership application which had been approved by the committee, having been sponsored by Douglas Freshfield and Clinton Dent, two later presidents of the club. The incident reveals a good deal about the narrowness of Victorian attitudes, and the power of particular cliques to manipulate membership applications, which they did by means of the balloting system then in existence. Eight years later, Mummery's application was put forward again, and he was duly elected. By then he was launched on the final spell of his mountaineering career devoted almost wholly to a series of technically difficult climbs without guides, accompanied by small groups of friends who shared his outlook and his skills.

Mummery was born into a well-to-do family in Kent. His father, William Rigden Mummery, had settled in Dover around 1850 where he acquired a tannery, and during the 1860s he was elected thrice to the mayoralty of the town. The Mummery family resided at Maison Dieu House, an old Jacobean mansion adjoining Dover Town Hall, which later housed the Public Library. As a young man Mummery joined the family firm, in which he and his brother became partners, later inheriting the business, which provided him with comfortable private means. During the last few years of his life he had decided to unburden himself of his business interests in order to devote his mind to economic questions, the investigation of which had begun increasingly to fascinate him. Mummery had collaborated with the economist JA Hobson, a classical master at an Exeter school, in the joint authorship of a book on economic science, *The Physiology of Industry*, published in 1889. Although the principles it advanced seemed chimerical at the time, three or four decades later they became a touchstone of economic orthodoxy. The book was praised by John Maynard Keynes.

A major part of Mummery's life was dedicated to mountains, his active involvement with mountaineering covering twenty-four of his thirty-nine years. 'At the age of fifteen the crags of the Via Mala and the snows of the Théodule roused a passion within me that has grown with the years, and has to no small extent moulded my life and thought.' The youth, who had crossed the Théodule pass at the age of fifteen, climbed Monte Rosa at seventeen, and the Matterhorn at eighteen. In later years he wrote about his first impressions of the Matterhorn seen from the Théodule. 'I remember, as if it were yesterday, my first sight of the great mountain. It was shining in all the calm majesty of a September moon, and, in the stillness of an autumn night, it seemed the very embodiment of mystery and a fitting dwelling place for the spirits with which old legends people its stone-swept slopes.' Physically Mummery had an unathletic appearance being tall, thin, and bespectacled; he often removed his spectacles when walking, making his movements appear clumsy. He had a powerful will, tireless energy and a charismatic presence.

Mummery's passion for mountains did not conform to the conventions of his time. While the pioneers of the preceding generation explored glaciers, crossed high passes, and climbed new peaks, Mummery was an explorer of climbs. He was deeply sensitive to the majesty of mountains. In their presence, he delighted in the physical and technical skills required to overcome the challenges that they seemed to invite, and he was undaunted by the risks. One ascent of a mountain, or a single route up it, was not sufficient. 'I am fain to confess a deplorable weakness in my character. No sooner have I ascended a peak than it becomes my friend, ... and in my heart of hearts I long for the slopes of which I know every wrinkle, and on which each crag awakens memories of mirth and laughter and of friends of long ago ... Each memory has its own peculiar charm, and the wild music of the hurricane is hardly less a delight than the glories of a perfect day ... It is true the crags and the pinnacles are the same, but their charm and beauty lies in the ever-changing light and shade, in the mists which wreath around them, in the huge cornices and pendant icicles, in all the circumstances of weather, season, hour ... on one day [the climber is struck] by the tingling horror of the precipice, the gaunt bareness of the stupendous cliffs ... on another day he notices none of these things, lulled by the delicate tints of opal and azure, in the graceful sweep of the wind-drifted snow, or even in the tiny flowers wedged in the joints of the granite.' Lyrical musings such as these are rare; Mummery's prose is characteristically facetious and lively, reflecting the intense enjoyment that he derived from his climbs. He was a brilliant rock-climber, and an excellent ice-man. With a dynamic personality, he was a persuasive leader in search of the sort of challenges that deterred lesser men. Martin Conway describing Mummery at the age of about thirty, wrote: 'He had great muscular strength in arms and legs, and little weight of body for them to raise. He knew by instinct or long experience whether his points of adhesion were sufficient for momentary safety. I doubt if he ever slipped. He was always completely confident. Nothing flurried or hurried him. He could endure any amount of cold, and would sit out through a night in the open at any level.'

Mummery's outspoken criticism of established ideas labelled him as an outsider, outraging some of his contemporaries less skilled or adventurous than himself. It is easy to see why. 'To the (self-dubbed) mountaineers, the right way up a peak is the easiest way, and all other ways are wrong ways. Thus ... if a man goes up the Matterhorn to enjoy the scenery, he will go by the Hörnli route; if he goes by the Z'mutt ridge it is, they allege, merely the difficulties of the climb that attract him. Now, this reasoning would appear to be wholly fallacious.

Among the visions of mountain loveliness that rise before my mind, none are fairer than the stupendous cliffs and fantastic crags of the Z'mutt ridge. To say that this route, with its continuously gorgeous scenery is, from the aesthetic point of view, the wrong way, while the Hörnli route, which, despite the noble distant prospect, is marred by the meanness of its screes and its paper-besprinkled slopes, is the right, involves a total insensibility to the true mountain feeling.' Brushing aside the blinkered attitude of some of his contemporaries, Mummery climbed the Matterhorn seven times, by four different routes.

John Ruskin first visited the Alps in 1832 at the age of thirteen, and continued to do so at regular intervals until he was sixty-nine, spreading a message of their sublime beauty in an age when the upper regions of rock and ice were regarded as hostile. Ruskin's attitude to mountains was singularly illogical or, at the least, ambivalent. He declared that 'the real beauty of the Alps is to be seen, and seen only, where all may see it, the child, the cripple, and the man with grey hairs', and he regarded mountaineers who scaled the peaks as intruders. Yet he seems to have possessed a vision all too familiar to the climbers whom he condemned. In 1863 he wrote from Chamonix in a letter to his father: 'That question of the moral effect of danger is a very curious one; but this I know and find, practically, that if you come to a dangerous place, and turn back from it, though it may have been perfectly right and wise to do so, still your character has suffered some slight deterioration; you are to that extent weaker, more lifeless, more effeminate, more liable to passion and error in the future; whereas if you go through with the danger, though it may have been apparently wrong and foolish to encounter it, you come out of the encounter a stronger and better man, fitter for every sort of work and trial, and nothing but danger produces this effect.' (Note 3) An over-riding motive in Mummery's relationship with mountains was the element of challenge, clearly sensed by Ruskin, attainable only through close encounters with danger. Like Ruskin, Mummery was sensitive to the beauty of mountains. Unlike Ruskin, Mummery's intimacy with every aspect of the mountains, enabled him to identify himself more closely with them. To Ruskin's taunt, directed at the new wave of climbers, if not actually at himself, 'The Alps ... you look upon as greased poles in a bear garden which you set yourselves to climb', Mummery commented, 'Putting aside the question of grease, which is offensive and too horrible for contemplation in its effects on knickerbockers – worse even than the structure-destroying edges and splinters of the Grépon ridge – I do not see the enormity or sin of climbing poles. At one time, I will confess, I took great delight in the art ...'.

Alexander Burgener, born in 1846 in the village of Eisten in the Saas valley, was a man of dominating character, stocky, broad-shouldered, his face 'half hidden in a beard'. To his immense physical strength was added a tenacity and ingenuity far in excess of normal. He was at heart a chamois hunter, who never lost his interest in hunting. Stalking a herd of chamois at the age of sixty-three, he shot four animals then carried two of them across his shoulders, their feet bound across his chest, during a four-hour descent to the valley on the same day. Burgener began his career as a guide at the age of twenty-two, and each summer, from 1868 to 1878, he was engaged by Clinton Dent with whom he made the first ascent from the Trift glacier of the Zinal Rothorn in 1872; the east face of the Taschorn in 1876, and in 1878 the Grand Dru, which Burgener considered to be one of his greatest exploits. (Note 4) In 1879 Mummery, aged twenty-three, met Burgener in front of the Monte Rosa hotel at Zermatt. Mummery wished to climb the Z'mutt ridge of the Matterhorn. Burgener replied that to go on such an expedition with a Herr of whom he knew nothing would be a *verfluchte Dummheit* (an utter stupidity). Impressed by the honesty and confidence which the answer implied, Mummery interpreted it as the opinion of a man possessing boldness and unflinching determination. After four days of 'trials', including ascents of the Fletschhorn and Sonnighorn and the crossings of Laquinjoch, Mischabeljoch and Ried passes, the two were ready at the end of August to begin their attempt on the unclimbed Z'mutt ridge. They learnt that William Penhall, a twenty-one-year-old English medical student with his guides, Ferdinand Imseng and Louis Zürbriggen, had left Zermatt a day earlier with the same intention; the weather was fair which augured well for their chance of success. Mummery decided to switch his plans, intending to cross the Col Durand and try a new route on the Dent Blanche as an alternative. Approaching Staffelalp they encountered Penhall's party descending, a sudden change in the weather having caused them to delay their plan. Mummery and Burgener, with Johann Petrus and Augustin Gentinetta, continued to the Stockji glacier, but the guides believed that the weather was hopeless. 'I was much too young and too eager to dream

182

of returning, and being wholly ignorant of all meteorological lore I was able to prophesy fair things with such an appearance of knowledge that Burgener was half convinced.' As the weather worsened, Burgener's confidence began to waver: 'and I felt more than a tremor of doubt myself ... but the die was cast so I kept a cheerful countenance and declared that we should have fair play from the weather. Burgener was impressed ... My persistence suggested occult knowledge.'

Mummery was asleep in the late afternoon when Burgener woke him with a 'jubilant air and a thump, intended to convey devout appreciation of my astounding wisdom'. Mummery and his guides set out in the improved weather, camping that night on a ridge of rock leading to the foot of the snow arête at the start of the Z'mutt ridge, somewhat below Penhall's earlier camp. Setting out at 4.15 the next morning, the third of September, they benefitted from tracks left on the snow-ridge by Penhall and his guides, but the rock pinnacles of the next section caused much delay. The consistent steepness of the rocks that rose beyond provided a climb that tested their combined skills. On the final stretch they passed J-A Carrel's famous 'corridor', reaching the summit after over nine hours of continuous effort.

Penhall and his guides were not to be outdone. Leaving Zermatt at ten o'clock in the night, they chose what was intended as a shorter variation of their first route by following a steep couloir on the west face which presented great technical difficulties, and was, moreover, threatened by ice and rockfall, causing much time to be lost before they were able to reach the rock pinnacles beyond the initial snow ridge. (Note 5) Penhall and his guides reached the summit one hour and a half after Mummery, returning to Zermatt at ten o'clock that night – a very impressive performance. Both ascents were of a high quality. (Note 6) That Mummery and Penhall harboured no unfriendly rivalry before or after their respective ascents of the Z'mutt ridge is borne out by their joining forces four days later with their guides to make the first tourist ascent of the Dürrenhorn (also written Dirruhorn), situated at the north-west end of the Nadelgrat. Although it measures 4035m, it was a fairly easy mountain for such a powerful team, and had perhaps been ascended earlier by local chamois hunters. (Note 7)

Mummery made another ascent of the Z'mutt ridge on 27 August 1894 with Norman Collie, Josef Pollinger, a young apprentice guide from St Niklaus, and the Duke of Abruzzi (Prince Luigi Amadeo Savoia, brother of the King of Italy), famous for his pioneer explorations and climbs in the Arctic, Alaska, Africa and the Karakoram. In threatening weather, the fitness and competence of the party enabled them to accomplish the ascent in the rapid time of six hours and ten minutes from a bivouac at the foot of the snow ridge. Exceptional performances such as these made by climbers over a century ago contrast sharply with current climbing 'advances'.[1]

The Mummery-Burgener partnership accomplished some remarkable first ascents, and made several notable attempts, including two on the Dent du Géant in 1881 by its south-west and north faces. Mummery left a cairn, with a card inside, at his highest point on the north face, about 245m from the top. The card was found by the first ascensionists in 1882 led by Jean-Joseph Maquignaz, who installed a series of fixed ropes up the face. Mummery had written on his card, 'absolutely inaccessible by fair means'. In 1880, Mummery and Burgener crossed the Col du Lion (3580m), 'than which no more difficult, circuitous, and inconvenient method of getting from Zermatt to Breuil could possibly be devised'. Nine years earlier, Moore studying the Col from the Tiefenmatten glacier wrote: 'If any gentleman wishes to achieve the reputation of having made the most impossible-looking pass in the alps, let him try to climb this couloir. If he succeeds, I shall have great pleasure in congratulating him; while if he fails and comes to grief into the bargain, it will afford me equal satisfaction to observe that it served him right.' (Note 8) Mummery and Burgener had reached a critical point in a narrow and tortuous couloir about half-way up the route when 'Burgener took the lead again, and soon found that he had no ordinary work before him. The ice was bare and as hard as well-frozen ice can be; it was, moreover, excessively steep. So evil did it look above, that he halted and gazed anxiously at the rocks of the Matterhorn to see if we could escape in that direction. It was, however, obvious that we should encounter prolonged difficulty on them; besides which it would leave the problem of the couloir unsolved. Once more he turned sullenly to the wall of ice, and foot by foot hewed out a way. The projecting rocks on our right, ever tilting the slope outwards, forced us to the left into a

[1]Josef Pollinger, after years of strict training under his father Alois, was Mummery's choice although he obtained his guide's badge only two years later. During his forty-one-year career he gained a high reputation becoming the regular guide of WE Davidson, EL Strutt and RW Lloyd. He joined EA Fitzgerald's expedition to Aconcagua in 1896, and was one of Whymper's guides in Canada in 1901.

sort of semi-circular recess in the cliff. Suddenly the step-cutting ceases. *Der Teufel* [the devil] is apostrophised in soul-curdling terms, and half the saints in the Romish calendar are charged, in the strongest language known to the German tongue, with the criminal neglect of their most obvious duties. Burgener's axe had broken! Midway in an ice-couloir two thousand feet high a single axe alone stood between us and utter helplessness. I untied and carefully lashed my axe to the rope and sent it up to Burgener.'

After a desperate struggle, they reached the Col, where they set to work thawing frozen fingers and repairing other physical damage acquired during the relentlessly steep and icy ascent. After an hour seated on the Col, they raced down the slopes to Breuil, arriving an hour and forty-five minutes later. The young guide Benedikt Venetz awaited them, and the three then proceeded to Chamonix from where on 15 July they climbed the south-west face of the Aiguille des Charmoz. Venetz, whose suppleness and natural skills complemented the physical strength of Burgener, was often given the doubtful honour of tackling the delicate work out in front. The face was climbed by the main Charmoz-Grépon couloir, parts of the upper section in stockinged feet; the difficulties were increased by icy conditions. The northern summit (3431m) was reached and an ice-axe was planted on top; it was the highest point of the lower section of the crest. During the descent of the couloir: 'Burgener tried to fix one of our wooden wedges; but, do what he would, it persisted in evading its duties, wobbling first to one side and then to another, so that the rope slipped over the top. We all had a try, driving it into cracks that struck our fancy, and even endeavouring to prop it up with ingenious arrangements of small stones. Someone then mooted the point whether wedges were not a sort of bending the knee to Baal, and might not be the first step on those paths of ruin where the art of mountaineering becomes lost in that of the steeplejack. Whereupon we unanimously declared that the Charmoz should be desecrated by no fixed wedges, and finding an insecure knob of rock we doubled our rope round it, and Venetz slid down.' Five years later, the highest point of the Charmoz (3445m), was climbed by a party that included H Dunod, P Vignon, F & G Simond and F Folliguet who recovered Mummery's axe. In 1892 Mummery made a guideless ascent of the Charmoz, as leader of a party which included two ladies, finding his original route easier owing to 'the extraordinary diminution of ice' in the main couloir.

The day following the Charmoz ascent, Mummery, Burgener and Venetz walked from Chamonix over the Cols de Balme and de la Forclaz, reaching Martigny in time to take a train to Visp. The next day, they set off to attempt the Furggen ridge of the Matterhorn. Threatened by stonefall and in deteriorating weather, they climbed the lower part of the slabby east face reaching: 'the gap between the two towers seen from Zermatt ... The final peak looked very formidable, and, in such weather, could not have been assailed with any reasonable approach to safety.' The wind was driving missiles of ice and rock down the face which was swept by waves of snow. Undertaking an exposed and avalanche-threatened traverse as speedily as possible across the smooth rocks on the upper part of the face they were able to make their escape to the shoulder above the north-east ridge, and to complete the ascent of the mountain by the Swiss route. Mummery's account of this adventurous climb includes an episode which occurred during the pre-dawn approach to the foot of the east face. Burgener, a prey to superstition, swore that a moving light he had seen in the far distance was a *geist* (ghost), and that anybody seeing one was certain to be killed within twenty-four hours. He and Venetz counselled immediate retreat. 'I pointed out that ... there could be no advantage in turning back, for, either they were ghosts, in which case we must be killed, or they were not ghosts, in which case we might as well go on.' They went on; but Mummery, being the only member of the party sceptical about the ghost theory, was allotted the post of leader. (Note 9)

Mummery's association with Burgener, which had begun on the usual basis of a Herr-guide relationship, developed into a partnership of equals with mutually dedicated aims. Burgener's opinion of Mummery is summed up in an incident when Julius Kugy, the great pioneer of the Julian Alps, descending the Théodule Pass with Burgener, saw a tall, thin man wearing spectacles and riding on a small donkey, his long legs reaching the ground on either side. 'Who is that poor fellow,' asked Kugy. 'It is Mummery,' replied Burgener, 'he climbs better than I do.' A second quotation from Kugy is worth adding. 'When I got back from the Matterhorn [in 1886] I was asked by Paul Güssfeldt, who was in Zermatt, how I found it. "Difficult," I said, without hesitation. "Thank God!" he exclaimed, "at last here's someone brave enough to call the Matterhorn difficult."' Several years later RLG Irving, who once met Burgener in the Festi Hut, remarked that 'his voice broke when he spoke of his beloved "Herr Mommerie".' Some of Mummery's best climbs with Burgener were done in 1881. On 30 July they made the first ascent from the Charpoua glacier of the Aiguille Verte, a route that is rarely climbed now owing to the danger of stonefall; they traversed the mountain, descending by the Whymper couloir. From the Charmoz the previous year Mummery thought that the east (Mer de Glace) face of the Grépon looked feasible. After spending eight hours on the face, he and Burgener decided to rule out further attempts from that side. Two days later, joined by Venetz, they moved over to the other side. On the Nantillons glacier, at the foot of the couloir leading to the Charmoz-Grépon col, they met a party heading for the Blaitière led by a 'well-known' Oberland guide. 'The Oberlander first giving Burgener much good advice and ending by strongly advising him to abandon the attempt, "for," said he, "I have tried it, and where I have failed no one else need hope to succeed." Burgener was greatly moved by this peroration, and I learnt from a torrent of unreportable *patois* that our fate was sealed, and even if we spent the rest of our lives on the mountain (or in falling off it) it would, in his opinion, be preferable to returning amid the jeers and taunts of this unbeliever.' The ascent was accomplished without the use of a single piton. But Mummery was not satisfied that the North summit of the Grépon, which they had reached, was higher than the further rock tower forming the South summit (the latter is four metres higher). Within thirty-six hours the climb was repeated. A tricky manoeuvre was required to ascend the final tower. 'It was certainly one of the most forbidding rocks I have ever set eyes on. Unlike the rest of the peak, it was smooth to the touch, and its square-cut edges offered no hold or grip of any sort. ... Added to all this a great rock overhung the top, and would obviously require a powerful effort when the climber was most exhausted. Under the circumstances, Burgener and I set to work to throw a rope over the top, whilst Venetz reposed in a graceful attitude rejoicing in a quiet pipe. After many efforts, in the course of which both Burgener and I nearly succeeded in throwing ourselves over on to the Mer de Glace, ... we decided that the rock must be climbed by the fair methods of honourable war. To this end we poked up Venetz with the ice-axe (he was by now enjoying a peaceful nap), and we then generally pulled ourselves together and made ready for the crucial struggle.

Burgener ... stood ready to help Venetz with the ice-axe so soon as he should get within his reach, whilst my unworthy self, ... was able to assist him in the first part of his journey. So soon as Venetz got beyond my reach, Burgener ... jamming the point of the axe against the face of the rock, made a series of footholds of doubtful security whereon Venetz could rest and gain strength for each successive effort. At length he got above all these adventitious aids and had to depend exclusively on his splendid skill. Inch by inch he forced his way, gasping for breath, and his hand wandering over the smooth rock in those vague searches for non-existent hold which it is positively painful to witness. Burgener and I watched him with intense anxiety, and it was with no slight feeling of relief that we saw the fingers of one hand reach the firm hold offered by the square-cut top. A few moments' rest, and he made his way over the projecting rock, whilst Burgener and I yelled ourselves hoarse.'

Eleven years later, the Grépon had received only two further ascents, both by the less exacting southern ridge. In the same year, Mummery made the first guideless ascent, following his original 1881 route as leader of a party that included Geoffrey Hastings, Norman Collie and Charles Henry Pasteur; they traversed the peak, descending by the southern ridge – 'a rollicking self-confident party can dodge falling stones, and dance across steep slabs in a manner and at a pace which is impossible to anxious and disheartened men.' In August 1893, Mummery made the third ascent of his route on the Grépon, also guideless, with Hastings and Lily Bristow. (Note 10) Mummery described his 1893 ascent of the Grépon as 'amongst the hardest I have made' owing to the accumulation of ice and snow in the cracks and gullies. In a letter home Lily Bristow wrote: 'Fred is magnificent, he has such absolute confidence, I never once had the faintest squirm about him even when he was in the most hideous places, where the least slip would have been certain death, and there were very many such situations.' Norman Collie, Cecil Slingsby and Brodie simultaneously ascended the southern ridge of the Grépon, and the whole party descended together by that route. In 1892 Mummery made a determined attempt to climb the north face of the Aiguille du Plan with Cecil Slingsby[2] and Ellis Carr: 'I can still shut my eyes and

[2]Apart from his alpine ascents with Mummery, and his rock climbs on British hills, William Cecil Slingsby gained renown as a pioneer mountaineer in Norway in the 1880s and 90s. He was Vice President of the Alpine Club from 1906-8.

see Carr toiling like a giant at the endless slopes of ice, and can still feel the blank chill that shivered through us when night chased the last lingering streaks of daylight from the slopes. The songs still ring in my ears with which he sought to keep us merry and awake through the icy hours, as we sat huddled on a tiny ledge. And when, despite all efforts, sleep stealthily approached, Slingsby's strong arm wrapping round me and holding me on to my narrow perch – there was nought between my back and Chamonix, eight thousand feet below – still seems a sure defence from peril.' The north face was not climbed until 1924 by a strong French team of J Lagarde, H de Ségogne and J de Lépinay.

Mummery returned to the Aiguille du Plan in 1893 with Slingsby, Collie and Hastings and suceeded in opening a new route from the west. The same team made the first ascent on 25 July of the Dent du Réquin; three years were to pass before a second ascent was made. Mummery, Hastings and Collie also climbed the Aiguille Verte, making the second ascent of the south-west ridge (the Moine). In 1894, Mummery, Collie and Hastings made the first crossing of the Col des Courtes from Chamonix to Courmayeur. They followed that with the first guideless ascent of the Brenva face of Mont Blanc. Adopting a variation of Moore's route, they ascended a rib of rock situated between it and the route followed in 1927 by Frank Smythe and Graham Brown via the *Sentinelle Rouge*. Forced into a bivouac below the final *sérac* barrier, they spent a very cold night before finding a difficult passage through it the following morning. The expedition had taken forty-eight hours from Courmayeur over the top of the mountain and down to the Grands Mulets. In 1891, Mummery spent ten days climbing in the Dauphiné with Pasteur, G Morse and JH Wicks. Between 1891 and 1894, Mummery carried out an exceptional series of guideless climbs. Also, in order to test his technique and route-finding skills, he made a few solitary excursions, notably over the Schreckjoch, the Triftjoch and the Col du Géant.

Pasteur, describing the atmosphere around Chamonix in the 1890s, wrote: 'The most interesting personality was undoubtedly Albert Mummery ... wherein lay his great superiority is a difficult question to answer ... he was a clumsy walker and no one who had not seen him at work would credit him with his outstanding powers as a climber and a leader. He was a man of will-power and energy tempered with a marvellous patience ... his temperament allowed him to enjoy every minute of his day's climb whether he got to the top or not. He was always happy on a mountain, and that is what made him such a delightful companion ... If [Mummery] had made up his mind that a climb was possible nobody could persuade him that it was not.' (Note 11) Mummery was fascinated by the 'gaunt bareness of the stupendous cliffs' that tower above Chamonix, as he was with the inaccessible aspect of the Matterhorn's ridges. His genius for seeking challenging new routes is likely to have kept him well ahead of his time at the turn of the nineteenth century exploring the 'problems' that occupied alpine climbers of a later generation. 'No feeling,' he wrote, 'can be more glorious than advancing to attack some gaunt precipitous wall [with staunch friends] ... Nothing is more exhilarating than to know that the fingers on one hand can still be trusted with the lives of a party, and that the lower limbs are free from all trace of knee-dissolving fear, even though the friction of one hobnail on an outward shelving ledge alone checks the hurtling of the body through thin air' – chilling thoughts, but an anachronism today with the use of sophisticated modern methods of protection.

At the age of twenty-seven, Mummery married Mary Petherick, aged twenty-four, daughter of JW Petherick, an Exeter solicitor. They had one daughter. Family archives are very scarce. Apart from those described in his book, Mummery left practically no record of his climbs, and he disliked being photographed. Mrs Gray, their daughter, who donated to the Alpine Club three family photographs, two of which comprise the only known portraits of her father, stated that no diaries, notes or letters were found after his death; and for many years the subject of mountaineering was too distressing to be discussed with her mother. Her own and her mother's personal relics perished in 1942 during the Exeter blitz. It is known that 'thirty short notes' of Mummery's climbs were presented to the Alpine Club in 1943 by Mrs Mummery, who died in 1946 aged eighty-seven, but they have not been traceable. (Note 12)

Mummery's alpine activities appear to have fallen into three separate periods. The first, between 1879 to 1882, included all his climbs with Burgener and Venetz. The second period, following his marriage in 1883, included joint expeditions with his wife, who was a natural and enthusiastic climber, (like her brother WJ Petherick a member of the Alpine Club) to the Maritime Alps in 1884-5 following Freshfield's travels in those areas seven years earlier, and to the Swiss Alps in 1886-7 when their climbs included the Jungfrau, Ober Gabelhorn, Matterhorn traverse from Breuil to Zermatt, the first ascent of the Teufelsgrat on the Taschorn (of which more later), and other ascents, as well as the crossing of passes, occasionally without guides. In 1888 Mummery visited the Caucasus, where he made the first ascent of its second highest peak, Dych Tau. The year 1889 saw the publication of his book on economics, *The Physiology of Industry*, jointly authored with JA Hobson.

The last phase of Mummery's alpine career from 1891 to 1894, before his departure for the Himalaya, was filled with a brilliant series of guideless climbs accompanied mostly by friends, principally Collie, Hastings, Slingsby and Pasteur. In adopting the practice of climbing without guides Mummery was not seeking personal glory. He was well aware that his methods were likely to be denounced by the climbing establishment, who believed that to climb without guides was dangerous and irresponsible. The earliest practitioners of guideless climbing were the Reverends Girdlestone and Hudson, TS Kennedy, F Gardiner, and the brothers Smyth, Parker and Pilkington. At an Alpine Club meeting in 1870 a minute had been recorded deprecating the practice fairly strongly. 'It was agreed without a single dissentient that ... the neglect to take guides on difficult expeditions ... when the party is not exclusively composed of practised mountaineers, is totally unjustifiable and calculated to produce the most lamentable results.' That view seemed specially severe since a few of the early climbers, with the exception of Girdlestone who was notoriously careless as a mountaineer, had all achieved some success without guides and without accidents.[3]

The period around 1870 was a sensitive one for the Alpine Club, still smarting under criticism and even ridicule from diverse quarters, striking at its very *raison d'être*. Mummery's activities took place during a later period, when he and his companions had few equals in skill and experience. Mummery, never a slave to convention, had his own reasons for his actions, and his spirit was shared by his climbing friends. 'We had learnt the great truth that those who wish really to enjoy the pleasures of

[3]During the mid 1880s an Alpine Club member is reported to have remarked facetiously that guides were responsible for a large proportion of bottles marking the route up many well-known mountains, and that the assistance of these signposts made possible the rise of guideless climbing.

mountaineering must roam the upper snows trusting exclusively to their own skill and knowledge. ... when I start in the morning I do not want to know exactly what is going to be done, and exactly how it is all to be carried out. I like to feel that our best efforts may be needed, and that even then we may be baffled and beaten ... the essence of the sport [of mountaineering] lies not in ascending a peak, but in struggling with and overcoming difficulties, ... this struggle involves the same risk, whether early climbers attacked what we now call easy rock, or whether we moderns attack formidable rock, or whether the ideal climber of the future assaults cliffs which we now regard as hopelessly inaccessible. ... The true mountaineer is a wanderer ... who loves to be where no human being has been before ... I do not pretend to be able to analyse this feeling, still less to be able to make it clear to unbelievers. It must be felt to be understood.' Mummery practised what he believed; he also showed that the climber of hard routes is not necessarily insensible to natural beauty; and that those who regularly return to the mountains are usually attracted by their beauty as well as their challenges. His writings leave little doubt that he derived genuine delight from merely being in the mountains, commenting, as he did once during a bivouac, 'In no other way can one see wind-enchanted shapes of wandering mist, and exquisite effects of fading light playing among fantastic pinnacles of tottering ice.' A few years after Mummery's death, his close climbing companion Collie wrote: 'Amongst the most pleasant recollections I have of the Alps are those connected with our camps ... and I may say that during all the years I spent climbing with Mummery only twice have I slept in a hut with him. ... When I look back and think of all the various places where Mummery, Hastings, Slingsby and I have slept out in the open, and remember how we enjoyed ourselves, I for one would go back year after year to the Alps if those times could be brought back again.' (Note 13)

Mummery's alpine climbs led inevitably to more ambitious plans. Before his first journey to the Caucasus in July 1888 there had been few visits by English climbers. (Note 14) Mummery travelled without an English companion, accompanied only by the Meiringen guide, Heinrich Zurfluh, who did not seem altogether happy in a foreign environment; a fairly helpful Tartar porter was engaged to accompany them. Mummery and Zurfluh made the first ascent of Dych Tau, (5198m), on 24 July by its south-west ridge, which they accomplished in the remarkable time of eight hours and a quarter from a camp on the Bezingi glacier below the great south face of the mountain. After overcoming the difficulties of the face, they reached the upper part of the mountain where Mummery and his guide engaged in a hard struggle along the final ridge. 'After contemplating Zurfluh's graceful attitudes and listening to his gasps as he battled with the desperate difficulty, it was borne in upon me that the second peak of the Caucasus ought not to be climbed by an unroped party ... I mildly suggested these fears to Zurfluh. He asked me whether I would come up for the rope or whether he should send the rope down to me. For some hidden reason a broad grin illuminated his face as he strongly recommended the former course, pointing out that the ledge on which I was huddled was not a convenient place for roping operations. Despite this advice I unhesitatingly decided on the latter alternative, and when the rope came down, successfully grappled with the difficulty of putting it on ... a moment earlier I could have sworn ... that the cliff in front was absolutely perpendicular. Yet no sooner was the rope firmly attached than the cliff tilted backwards till it barely exceeded a beggarly sixty degrees.' This was a brilliant ascent, with difficulties sustained to the very end. Forty-seven years were to pass before a second ascent was made in 1935 by an Austro-German party. Russian climbers currently classify it under their Grade 5A, and it is normally done with one intermediate camp.

Mummery's and Zurfluh's performance had been closely watched by their porter seated on a rocky outcrop above the glacier. On descending to their camp: 'We soon discovered that instead of consuming the whole of our provisions, the porter had not even had a crust of bread. We urged him to take a preliminary lunch, or rather breakfast, while the soup was cooking, but he refused, and seemed in no hurry for dinner. He manipulated the fire with much skill, making the vile wood burn in a really creditable manner, and only pausing from his efforts to award me an occasional appreciative slap on the back. It being early, 4pm, Zurfluh expressed a strong desire to strike camp and descend; but ... I refused to move. ... A camp at one spot is practically as comfortable as at any other, and in consequence, so soon as one feels inclined to sit down and laze, the day's work is over and one postpones the screes and moraines to the sweet distance of tomorrow. It is, indeed, a rare delight to sit at one's ease in the early afternoon and gaze at the huge cliffs amongst which one has been wandering, free from all the thought of hurry, of moraines, or of darkness.' – enchanting thoughts. Mummery's 1888 visit to the Caucasus included travel through some interesting semi-explored country. There are delightful descriptions of his journey across passes and glaciers – 'an unknown ice fall shrouded in impenetrable cloud is indeed enough to rouse the sporting instinct in any mountaineer' – and through the lush valleys of the Suanetia, where he was royally entertained and quartered by a village headman in a guest-house: 'situated in an open park-like country. Splendid trees and rippling watercourses were all around us, whilst above towered the great white pyramid of Tetnuld. In the other direction the rocky crest of Ushba just showed above the lower ridges. The flickering sunlight through the leaves suggested a delicious feeling of freshness and home.' A note about this journey which he sent to the *Alpine Journal* included the following: 'No other holiday has afforded me half the pleasure. I found the travelling much easier than I had expected. ... I became great friends with the old chief at Bezingi, who gave me several dinners in his private apartments. I in turn provided tea and sugar for himself and his numerous relatives and friends.'[4] Mummery returned to the area two years later with his wife's brother WJ Petherick, when they explored a number of valleys south of the main mountain chain, but he has left practically no record of their travels, and no notable ascents appear to have been made.

Mummery had long been attracted by the idea of climbing among the world's highest mountains, and he had planned several times to visit the Himalaya. There had been only two earlier expeditions of any note to those great unexplored regions. (Note 15) In 1894, Mummery's Himalayan plans finally crystalized; getting together his old climbing companions, Hastings and Collie, he decided to make an attempt on Nanga Parbat. In an Introduction to the 1908 edition of her husband's book Mrs Mummery wrote: 'The year 1894 was a momentous one ... during its passage all the varied energies of his life seemed to gather themselves up in one great effort towards outward expression.' His alpine season that summer had included an ascent of the Aiguille Verte from the Charpoua glacier, his second ascent of the

---

[4]One month after Mummery's visit Clinton Dent visited the Caucasus, when two members of his party, WF Donkin and H Fox, died during an attempt on Koshtantau.

Z'mutt ridge of the Matterhorn with the Duke of Abruzzi, and the first guideless ascent of the Brenva face of Mont Blanc. Mummery had decided by then to relinquish most of his business interests in order to devote more time to the study of economic issues, which had formed the subject of his book five years earlier. At the same time he was busy working out final plans for his Himalayan expedition. Then, fortunately, 'One winter's evening he threw down on to the table a bundle of papers and ... announced his intention of writing an account of his climbing experiences.' Had he not done so, few details would have been known about his alpine climbs, or his personal reflections. In a short preface, Mummery addressed his book 'to those who think with me, who regard mountaineering as unmixed play'. On 20 June 1895, one week after the publication of *My Climbs in the Alps and Caucasus,* Mummery started out on his journey to the Himalaya. His book soon ran to a second edition; but, sadly, he was not destined to appreciate the impact that it created. There were very few critics. A notable one was Edward Whymper who, after the appearance of the 1908 edition, wrote a contentious review in the *Sphere* on 20 January 1909, wholly insensitive to the effect on Mrs Mummery of the malicious remarks which he chose to make about her late husband.

Mummery's letters to his wife, written during his journey across India and at camp below Nanga Parbat, provide a valuable personal account of his impressions during the expedition. In a later edition of her husband's book, Mrs Mummery was persuaded to include extracts from some of the letters dated between 10 July, after his arrival in Kashmir, and 23 August, the day before he departed for his final climb. Mummery had invited Bruce[5] to join the party in India, and he brought with him two Gurkha soldiers, one of whom, Raghobir, had previously travelled with him in the mountains. In Bruce's book, *Himalayan Wanderer,* published in 1934, there is a chapter describing the two weeks that he spent with Mummery's party, although he was mostly unwell with an incipient attack of mumps. Collie provides a detailed account of the expedition in his

---

[5]The Honourable Charles Granville Bruce was then aged twenty-nine and serving as a major in a Gurkha regiment. He retired from the army with the rank of general in 1920. He was appointed leader of two British expeditions to Mount Everest in 1922 and 1924, and was elected President of the Alpine Club in 1923.

book *Climbing on the Himalaya and other mountain ranges* published in 1902. Collie, a professor of chemistry and something of a mystic, was passionately devoted to mountains. He started climbing in Skye in 1886 at the age of twenty-seven, later becoming one of the leading pioneers of rock-climbing in Scotland, and making the first ascent of the Tower Ridge of Ben Nevis. He climbed extensively in Britain, the alps, Norway and Canada and retired to Sligachan at the age of eighty, where he spent the last three years of his life amidst his beloved mountains. He once remarked: 'If anyone ever happens to write an obituary of me I want two things said – I first discovered Neon, and I took the first X-ray photographs.'

Mummery's expedition was based initially at Tarshing on the south side of the mountain, which the party reached on 16 July twenty-seven days after leaving England. Ten days later he wrote from there to James, later Lord, Bryce (President of the Alpine Club 1899-1901) 'Thanks to your help we are having a splendid time. The Government have helped us in every way imaginable, and not only so but the different officials with whom we have come in contact have gone right out of their way to give us personal aid and assistance. So far we have not exceeded 19,000 feet (5790m), but our last expedition (from the Diamarai valley back here) involved some exceedingly difficult rock climbing of the Chamonix Aiguille sort at a height of 17,000 feet (5180m), and we found ourselves as 'fit' as in the Alps, so I have good hopes that we shall get up Nanga. On our first pass, the Mazeno, we felt very bad, partly, I think, from heat, partly from interminable loose stones, and partly from rarity of the air, but we seem to have entirely got over these troubles.' It soon became obvious that the steep Rupal face of Nanga Parbat offered them no prospect of a feasible route. Crossing over the Mazeno Pass to examine the Diamir[6] side, Mummery felt confident that he had spotted a route that would 'go'. The base of operations was then shifted to the west side of the mountain. While porters and baggage traversed the Mazeno

---

[6]The name Diamir is in current use, although the form used by Mummery has been retained in the quotations. In his book, *Himalayan Wanderer* published in 1934, Charles Bruce describes this crossing: 'After about seventeen hours of climbing ... we began descending the steep ice slopes leading actually to our own side of the Mazeno Pass, and there on a little outcrop of rock Collie, myself and the Gurkhan Raghobir, at some 19,000 feet (5790m) above the sea, spent a chilly but safe night. Mummery and Hastings were located rather higher up in the same kind of bivouac. No food, no clothes, but lucky for us no wind.

Pass, Mummery with Collie and Hastings, seeking what they believed to be a more direct route, first on the way back to the Rupal base from the western exploration, and again a few days later moving over to the new Diamir base, became involved in some difficult climbing into and out of unsuspected valleys between the Mazeno and Rupal glaciers. The first trip involved an anxious bit of exploration lasting almost two days. The party's reaction on returning to the comfort and plenty of the Tarshing base was ecstatic after forty hours of thirst, hunger and fatigue. Memories often linger in remote places; in 1929 an English army officer crossing from Tarshing over the Mazeno Pass encountered an old Chilasi man who spoke reverently of *Mahmuli lat sahib* (*lat* being a jumbled version of the English word lord) whose feats of daring had greatly impressed him. The final crossing from Tarshing to the Diamir glacier, an experience shared by Bruce and Raghobir who by then had joined the party, involved a twelve-hour climb to a gap on the Mazeno ridge followed by a bivouac without provisions or equipment. Raghobir collapsed, having neither drunk nor eaten anything for forty hours; and the entire party suffered from various degrees of exhaustion. Mummery and Hastings, notwithstanding, ascended a peak of about 6400m situated on the Mazeno ridge. Both adventures indicate an obvious failure to appreciate the difference in scale between the Alps and the Himalaya. Food supplies began to run low on two occasions, replenishments having to be arranged first from Buner by the cook, and a week later by Hastings from Astor. In the interval an ascent was made of Diamarai Peak, situated north-east of the Mazeno Pass. The climb took a whole day, and was carried out alpine style, with a pre-dawn start by lantern-light and a return to camp after dark. The party comprised Mummery, Collie, Raghobir and a Chilasi porter (perhaps the man encountered in 1929?). The standard of difficulty was regarded in places as similar to that on the Aiguille du Plan or the Grépon. Collie comments: 'We had climbed between 6000 and 7000 feet, and Mummery had led the whole way. The last 3000 feet had been very severe, for at first most of the steps had to be laboriously broken, and later we had to win our way by the use of the axe. But Mummery was perfectly fresh and could have gone on for hours, ... neither was Raghobir any the worse for his climb; Lor Khan and I had slight headaches.' Lor Khan whose feet were wrapped in skins, country-style, proved his mettle on the ascent when his foot slipped on an icy slope and 'he never lost either his head or his axe'. 'As we sat on the top ... Mummery and I debated ... How should we feel if we ever ascended to 26,000 feet? Mummery reasoned that it would chiefly depend on our state of training at the time. Had I not been dreadfully ill at 18,000 feet crossing the Mazeno La, whilst here we were all right at 19,000 feet?[7] Had we not ascended our last 3000 feet with hardly a rest and at exactly the same pace as if we had been climbing in the Alps?' In emphasising the 'state of training' Mummery was partly right, and his remark might easily be translated today to mean their state of acclimatization, namely the process by which the body slowly adapts to working in an atmosphere with diminished oxygen. Scientific knowledge was non-existent at the time about the causes of high-altitude stress, or about the process whereby climbers acclimatize to heights up to around 7500m; nor about the irreversible process of physical deterioration above that height, which is believed to be caused principally by bodily dehydration resulting from prolonged exposure to oxygen deficiency. Twenty-five years later Norman Collie, aware by then of the limitations involved wrote: 'Above 20,000 feet (6100m) a cubic-foot of air contains less than half the amount of oxygen than it does at sea-level. As the whole metabolism of the body is kept in working order by the oxygen supplied through the lungs, the obvious result of high altitudes is to interfere with the various processes working in the system. The combustion of bodily material is less, the amount of energy produced is therefore less also, and so capacity for work is diminished progressively as one ascends.'

For the attempt on the Diamir face of Nanga Parbat, a camp was placed at the head of the glacier at 3660m below a series of three prominent rock-ribs. The difficulties began directly above that camp. Two rucksacks of supplies were carried up to a second camp, placed above the second rock-rib, and a night was spent there. The third rock-rib was then climbed, and a high point of c6100m was reached, which gave access to the icy face forming the upper part of the mountain in a line directly below the summit and seemingly less

---

[7]Current heights are 5377m (17,642ft) for the Mazeno Pass, and 5568m (18,268ft) for Diamarai peak, the second ascent of which was made by an Austrian party in 1939.

steep. Collie wrote: 'The climbing, Mummery admitted, was excessively difficult. ... I shall always look upon it as one of his finest climbs. Part of it I know from personal experience, and from Mummery's description of the upper half there must have been some magnificent climbing surrounded by an ice world such as can be seen nowhere.' Mummery's tactics for the ascent, briefly spelt out in a letter to his wife, were thoroughly sound. 'Collie and I took up [supplies] to a point 17,000 feet [5180m] yesterday ... we shall make another expedition next week and push [supplies] to about 20,000 feet [6095m] ... then a third expedition ought to get [the supplies] to the base of the final peak at about 23,000 feet [7010m].' From that point Mummery intended to launch his summit attempt – overlooking the critical need to ascend and descend over 1000m of steep ice slopes in a day from a camp at 7000m, and failing to recognise the exposure of his route to avalanches which threatened the rock-ribs from three separate *sérac* zones poised above. The dangers became obvious to Mummery during his third ascent of the route. His climbing companion was Raghobir, who unfortunately fell ill; or, more likely, had been weakened by insufficient food, having carried none of his own to the upper camp. On descending from their high point of about 6100m Mummery found that their tent and supplies had been carried away by an avalanche, making it clear that further attempts from this side would have to be abandoned. But he was not ready yet to give up, deciding to attempt an examination of the northern side of the mountain.

In a letter to his wife dated 26 July Mummery wrote: 'I feel fairly confident of getting up' followed on 9 August by, 'We find Nanga a tough nut to crack. The way up is easy enough, but it is very difficult to get our camps fixed, and the air certainly does effect one.' His final letter was written on 23 August. 'Our chances of bagging the peak look badly enough ... you must not be disappointed about Nanga. I have had some slap-up climbs, and seen cliffs and *séracs* such as the Alps and Caucasus cannot touch.' For the move round to the north to reach the Rakhiot glacier, Mummery wished to avoid 'the interminable scrambling over loose stones' which he would have to endure if he travelled round the mountain with the rest of the party. (Note 16) It occurred to him that a more direct passage to the upper Rakhiot glacier might be found via an unexplored northern branch of the Diamir glacier leading to a depression or col at about 6230m on the ridge between Ganalo Peak and Nanga Parbat. Provisions for two to three extra days were deposited on the lower part of his projected route in case a return should be necessary if the crossing proved to be impracticable. Since Collie was not keen on attempting the 'pass', and Hastings was suffering from the effects of a damaged heel and a chill, Mummery chose the two Gurkhas, Raghobir and Goman Singh, as his companions, although he was unable to speak a word of their language. He wrote to his wife: 'They are first-rate climbers and good men, but cannot afford the help of a real AC man.' Mummery and the Gurkhas parted from their companions on 24 August, and were not seen again. Disaster is likely to have struck during their ascent of the branch glacier, which flows through a narrow avalanche-swept valley overhung on both sides by *sérac*-laden walls. In the unlikely event of their having reached the top of the dividing ridge, they would have discovered exceedingly steep cliffs of ice and rock, subsequently observed by Collie, which appeared to provide the only means of descent to the Rakhiot glacier on the northern side.

Setting out from the Diamir base, Collie and Hastings travelled for about two days to reach a 5000m-pass which led them to the Rakhiot valley. Collie wrote: 'From the top of the ... pass ... we could see the great face down which Mummery and the Gurkhas would have had to come had they reached the Diama Pass. It seemed to us quite hopeless. I spent about half an hour looking through a powerful telescope for any traces of steps cut down the only ridge that looked at all feasible. I could see none.' Suspecting the possibility of an accident, a return was made to the Diamir valley. Hastings entered the branch glacier up which Mummery had gone, finding it highly dangerous with avalanches falling continuously. Proceeding up it as far as he dared, he retrieved the reserve rucksacks of food which were found exactly as Mummery had left them. There was no possible outlet from the narrow glacier except via the proposed 'pass' at its head. Given Mummery's temperament, and his skills, his choice of an apparently shorter and more challenging route over to the northern side of the mountain was entirely in character. But clearly he failed to appreciate the hazards posed by the unpredictability and scale of Himalayan avalanches; and he was guilty of a serious error of judgement in planning to cross, alpine-style, an unreconnoitred glacier pass to the unknown Rakhiot side with two technically untrained climbers as companions. Collie wrote later of the destructive power of Himalayan avalanches. 'That which in winter on a Scotch hill would be a slide of snow, and in the Alps an avalanche, becomes amongst these giant peaks an overwhelming cataclysm shaking the solid bases of the hills, and capable with its breath alone of sweeping down forests.'

Forty-four years after Mummery's disappearance, an Austrian party comprising Peter Aufschnaiter, Heinrich Harrer, L Chicken and H Lobenhofer, approached his route on the Diamir face, discovering a piece of firewood near the top of the first rock-rib. The climbing was found to be of a high technical standard consisting of continuously steep sections of ice and rock. A high point of c6000m was reached, but the route was abandoned owing to serious avalanche danger. Aufschnaiter looked at the narrow northern branch of the Diamir glacier leading to Mummery's proposed 'pass' which he described as 'swept cross wise in many places by avalanches from both sides'. His party then explored a section of the Diamir face further to the north, seemingly less hazardous, on which they climbed to about 6190m. (Note 17) The summit of Nanga Parbat was first reached after a solitary climb by Hermann Buhl in 1953 from the Rakhiot side, after four attempts had been made by German/Austrian parties between 1932 and 1938 from that side during which ten Europeans and fifteen Sherpas lost their lives.

In 1961, an attempt to climb the Diamir face via Aufschnaiter's 1939 route ended at c7175m. The following year, a strong Austrian party succeeded in making the first ascent of the Diamir face, and the second ascent of Nanga Parbat, when A Mannhardt, S Löw and Toni Kinshofer reached the summit on 22 June 1962 after a climb of sixteen hours from their high camp at c7100m. After an open bivouac in a storm 100m below the summit they started to descend, unroped, in stormy weather the next morning. At about 7500m, Löw slipped and fell, sustaining serious injuries from which he died that night in the arms of Kinshofer who watched over him, Mannhardt having descended to summon help. Kinshofer climbed down alone the following day having endured fifty-six hours of savage conditions without rest or nourishment. Two years later Kinshofer died aged thirty from injuries sustained after a fall while climbing at a *klettergarten* (rock climbing centre) in Baden-Baden. Mummery's route on the Diamir face of Nanga Parbat is said to have been used on the descent by the brothers Gunther and Reinhold Messner in 1970, when the former was killed, apparently by an ice avalanche, near the foot of the face.

Mummery's book, *My Climbs in the Alps and Caucasus,* retains a high place among mountaineering classics. That it should have made a strong impact when it first appeared in 1895, is not at all surprising. Compared with the alpine literature of the day, it was unique, describing the opening of a new mountaineering era, and declaring without fear of criticism or reproach the articles of faith of a new style of mountain climber. The book contains sharply-etched accounts of a few of Mummery's ascents over a period of almost twenty years, revealing the determination and courage with which they were carried out, despite a breezy style that often underplays reality, and has sometimes been criticised as facetious. The fact that Mummery's style glows with a sense of fun, and in many cases with unmistakable joy, is the purest evidence of the measure of happiness that he derived from his climbs. The happiness did not spring solely from his ability to master the physical challenges of a particular ascent, but out of a genuine passion for the power which mountains exercised over his whole being. Mummery was no seeker of fame or fortune, either from his climbs or from his writings. He regarded mountaineering as 'unmixed play'. The sport of tackling a difficult mountain ascent, represented a fair challenge carried out 'by fair methods', in an environment of 'steep cliffs and fantastic crags' in which Mummery delighted.

A chapter in Mummery's book, written by Mrs Mummery at her husband's request, contains a description of the first ascent of the *Teufelsgrat*, the 2km-long south-west ridge of the Täschhorn, on 16 July 1887, with A Burgener and J Andenmatten. The party started from the Täschalp at 1.30am and reached the top sixteen hours later, returning to the village of Randa at 5.30 the next morning, having experienced a series of difficulties and trials on the climb, including a cold and stormy bivouac above the tree-line on the descent. Early in the ascent, a rock-fall crushed Burgener's right thumb. Half-way along the ridge: 'Andenmatten ... advanced to the attack. The base of the tower went well, and little by little the difficulties seemed to be yielding. Our leader's face beamed with pride and pleasure as he stormed crag after crag, but alas! he forgot the well-worn proverb

"Pride goeth before destruction, and a haughty spirit before a fall." Solomon was once more to be justified, and the joyful Andenmatten was to be the victim. A last small, rocky tooth impeding his progress, and not being able to find sufficient hold, he summoned Burgener to his aid. The suggestion that he should take off his knapsack was treated as an insult, and a minute later, aided by a friendly shove, he had not merely got good hold on the top of the tooth, but was actually resting his arms on it. The tooth was to all intents and purposes climbed, when, to our horror, we saw his arms sliding off, and with a last convulsive effort to find grip for his fingers, he toppled outwards and plunged head downwards over the cliff ... we saw him, heels uppermost, arms outspread, knapsack hanging by one strap, and hat rolling into space, on a sloping ice-glazed rock some fifteen feet below us. Burgener, with admirable readiness, had caught hold of the rope as Andenmatten was in the very act of falling, and his iron grip, luckily for us, had stood the strain.' Two-thirds of the climb had been accomplished when: 'Suddenly our leader [Mummery] came to a halt, and though Burgener urged him to proceed, he utterly refused, and after a few moments summoned Alexander to the front. I could not see his usually expressive face, but the words *Herr Gott unmöglich!* (Good God, impossible!) reached my ears, and I hurried forward to see what new peril threatened us. ... the ridge by which we had been ascending appeared to end abruptly, – immeasurable space yawned in front. ... No wonder, then, that black horror seized us. Return was not to be thought of, and advance seemed impossible. There we four stood, absolutely powerless, our teeth chattering with the bitter cold, and the damp, cruel mist ever driving across, threatening to add obscurity to our bewilderment.' Mummery and Burgener, sharing the lead, worked their way out of this and other difficulties, and the party stepped on to the summit of the Täschhorn with storm-clouds gathering around them.

The great guide Alexander Burgener died in July 1910 at the age of sixty-four while leading two German clients from the Alsace, assisted by his sons Adolf and Alexander, and three guides from Grindelwald. The party was engulfed, about 10m below the door of the Bergli Hut, by a powder-snow avalanche which killed seven including the guide Christian Bohren who had come out of the Hut to greet them. There were only two survivors, both badly injured, one of whom was Burgener's younger son, Alexander. Clinton Dent, one of Burgener's earliest employers, wrote: 'If at the end he fell a victim to the mountains, we may feel sure that it was from no lack of prudence or foresight....He had identified himself so thoroughly and for so long with the mountains that at last they had just claimed him as their own.' (Note 18)

In her Introduction to the 1908 edition of *My Climbs in the Alps and Caucasus,* Mrs Mummery provides a rare personal glimpse of her husband. 'Much might be written of his social and domestic life, for it was here that his individuality was most strongly marked, and here also, as among the peaks, it was absolutely impossible for him to walk in "the beaten tracks". For society and its conventionalities he cared little, and although by no means an ascetic, he loved most of all, during his leisure hours, to surround himself with books and maps, and even now the lines traced on his maps testify to projected journeys and ascents that he had hoped to carry through in future years.' Douglas Freshfield, addressing members in December 1895 as Alpine Club President, said: 'I had never climbed with Mummery, but I regarded it as one of the greatest compliments ever paid me that he asked me to go to the Himalaya with him. ... I knew something of the man, and, as we all did, I thoroughly liked and trusted him. He was not only fearless and brilliant as a climber; he possessed an original, strong, and keen intelligence. ... He was a stimulating companion.'

The final chapter of Mummery's book contains what would have been regarded at the time as a daring piece of public moralising, in which deeply-felt opinions are expressed about technical and ethical aspects of mountaineering – although Mummery was almost certainly aware that his views would meet with general disapproval except by a minority of the active climbers of his day. Much of what he wrote over a hundred years ago reveals a remarkable prescience about possible future mountaineering trends. In the concluding paragraph of *My Climbs in the Alps and Caucasus* Mummery wrote what might have been his own epitaph. [The mountaineer] 'gains a knowledge of himself, a love of all that is most beautiful in nature, and an outlet such as no other sport affords ... gains for which no price is, perhaps, too high. It is true the great ridges sometimes demand their sacrifice, but the mountaineer would hardly forego his worship though he knew himself to be the destined victim.'

CHAPTER EIGHT
AN UNEXPECTED SUCCESS

Mais les vrais voyageurs sont ceux-là seuls qui partent
Pour partir; coeurs légers, semblables aux ballons,
De leur fatalité jamais ils ne s'écartent,
Et, sans savoir pourquoi, disent toujours: 'Allons!'

True travellers are those who travel
For travel's sake, their hearts light as a balloon,
Caring little for the future
And, unthinking, simply say: 'let's go!'

Baudelaire, *Le Voyage*

Apart from Antoine de Ville's seige-like ascent in the Vercors of the striking-looking Mont Aiguille, which was made under royal edict in 1492,[1] the backward and neglected alpine zone comprising the mountains of Dauphiné rising south of Grenoble had remained virtually untouched by mountaineers until after the middle of the nineteenth century. The name derives from the Counts of d'Albon, owners of an area of land extending from Grenoble to Briançon, who assumed the family title of Dauphin in 1183. Their lands and title passed under the sovereignty of Charles V of France in 1349, who ceded both to his eldest son and heir-apparent in 1368. Records dated 1673 show that apart from sporadic crossings of a few glacier passes, practically nothing was known about the mountains which cover the major part of the region. It was not until 1749 that the first surveys were undertaken by the French geographer, Bourcet, whose maps, published over the next five years, outlined the main mountain groups. Bourcet's maps identified the Ecrins as Mont d'Oursine, Ailefroide as the Grands Pelvoux, and La Meije (a name adopted in 1830) as the Aiguille du Midi de La Grave, or de la Meidje, the *d* being sounded in the local dialect; the height given for the first exceeded 4000m and the last fell just short of that. Over a century was to pass before the Dauphiné began to attract the interest of mountaineers.

[1]Described in Chapter 1.

205

In 1828, two members of an official party under Captain A Durand were appointed to carry out a new survey of the region, when they reached one of the lower summits of the Pelvoux, the Pic de la Pyramide or Pointe Durand (3932m). In 1839, two local hunters, attracted by the sightings of chamois on the upper rocks of the Aiguilles d'Arves, are known to have climbed the Central Peak (3509m); a lower point of the North Peak (3363m) is also believed to have been climbed by local hunters a few years later. During Moore's Dauphiné expedition in 1864 with Walker and Whymper (see Chapter 5), the party crossed a col between the South and Central peaks of the Aiguilles d'Arves with their guides Croz and Almer, and climbed one of the peaks of the Aiguilles de la Saussaz north of La Grave. From its summit they had a view which Moore describes. 'Straight in front of us was the great mass of the Meije, the second mountain in the Dauphiné, one of the finest walls of mingled crag and glacier in the Alps. There is no one distinct summit, but many pinnacles crown the ridge, three of which appeared to be (almost) equal in height ... The glacier (de Tabuchet) is a continuous ice-fall ... but its ascent would be quite practicable, and by it we thought that it might be possible to get very high up, if not to the summit of the Central Peak. On to the highest point of that superb mountain mass there did not appear to us any possibility of arriving from this side. In fact, I have rarely seen such hopelessly impracticable precipices.' Whymper, from the same viewpoint, provides a more dramatic picture. 'The Meije deserves more than a passing notice. It is the last – the only – great Alpine peak which has never known the foot of man, and one cannot speak in exaggerated terms of its jagged ridges, torrential glaciers, and tremendous precipices.'

A spectacular view of almost the whole north side of La Meije can be seen from the road which runs between Grenoble and Briançon. Of its three principal peaks the Eastern (3890m) is the lowest. A long ridge stretches from the Central Peak (3974m) to the Western, or Grand Pic (3983m), containing four rock pinnacles of varying degrees of sharpness. In 1877, it was the last important mountain still unclimbed; and when it was eventually ascended later that year it was considered to provide the most difficult *voie normal*, or first ascent route, of any alpine mountain. Until then, mountaineering in the Dauphiné had a relatively short history. Victor Puiseaux appears to have been the first mountaineer to take a serious interest in the area when, in 1848, he reached the highest summit of the Pelvoux (3946m) alone, his guide having stopped short of the top. Apart from Professor Forbes' early visit to La Bérarde, the earliest visitors to the mountains of Dauphiné were William Mathews, Thomas George Bonney and Francis Fox Tuckett, who, between 1860-3, carried out some interesting exploration, and made attempts to climb the Pelvoux and the Ecrins with the brothers Jean-Baptiste and Michel Croz of Chamonix. On Whymper's first visit there in 1860, he commented: 'The district is still very imperfectly known ... [although] it contains some of the highest summits in France and some of its finest scenery.' In 1861, together with Reginald Macdonald, Whymper made the second ascent of Pelvoux's highest summit. In 1864, Whymper described La Bérarde as 'a miserable village, without interest, without commerce, and almost without population'. This was as Coolidge and his aunt, Meta Brevoort, must have found it six years later when, with Christian Almer and his son Ulrich, they began a decade of systematic exploration and climbing in the area, making the first ascent of the Central peak of La Meije. From its summit they were disappointed to find the Grand Pic rising above them to the west; but Almer, viewing the sheer cliffs on all sides, dampened any hopes that they might have had about proceeding further along the ridge. Coolidge, aware that the whole region was relatively untouched and a paradise for pioneers, returned to it year after year with his aunt and the Almers making several ascents including Les Bans (3669m), Le Rateau (3809m), La Grande Ruine (3765m), Pic Coolidge (3774m), and in 1884 the third ascent and the first traverse of the Ecrins ascending the south face and making the first descent of the north face. Coolidge's expeditions were, in a sense, responsible for the opening up of the Dauphiné as an important new arena for mountaineers. But the Grand Pic of La Meije, on which repeated attempts were made, continued to defeat all efforts. In 1876, a few months before her death, Brevoort wrote to her nephew who was then climbing with the Almers in the Dauphiné: 'Give my love to all my dear old friends now in your sight and specially to that glorious Meije and ask her to keep herself for me.'

There were others apart from Coolidge interested in ascending the Grand Pic of La Meije. The advance in climbing skills, and the steady expansion of alpine climbing after 1866, when over twenty new mountains were ascended each season, meant that every important summit in almost every region of the alps had been reached. F Gardiner, C Taylor and the brothers R and W Pendelbury made a determined attempt in 1873 to climb the Grand Pic of La Meije, but succeeded only in making the second ascent of the Pic Centrale. Their guide, Hans Baumann, expressed his opinion that one Herr and two guides might get up if they never cared to come down again. (Note 1) The following year a French party with J Manuel made the third ascent of the Pic Centrale, but failed to reach the Grand Pic. Several fresh attempts were made during 1875. The first was by an Italian climber A Martelli, who was followed by G Devin and H Cordier, whose attempt was foiled by bad weather. (Note 2) Shortly after, another strong team comprising J Eccles, T Middlemore and J Oakley Maund were on the scene, although their attempt like the others was unsuccessful. Further attempts were made that summer by Lord Methuen, JE Montgomrey and Lord Wentworth, and by Coolidge with Almer.

In August 1875 the French climber Henri Duhamel, then aged twenty-one, teamed up with a seventeen-year-old student, Henri Emmanuel Boileau, whom he had met the year before at Chamonix after both had been foiled by violent storms in their respective attempts on Mont Blanc. Their guides were Alexandre Tournier, and the brothers François and Léon Simond of Chamonix. In view of the many failures to reach the summit ridge of the Grand Pic from the south, they decided to start from La Grave in an attempt to reach it from the north. It turned out to be a lengthy and strenuous expedition, involving four nights spent in a tent on the Rocher de l'Aigle (3439m), where the réfuge of the Club Alpin Français was later placed. After crossing the Col des Corridors, they made the first ascent of the Tête des Corridors. But they found the rocks on the north face of the Meije excessively steep and coated with a thin film of ice. In his account of the climb Duhamel commented that he thought the route might be climbable only in winter. The party then made the fourth ascent of the Pic Central, but were unable to proceed any further; their guides, like Almer and Baumann earlier, judged the connecting ridge to the Grand Pic to be too dangerous. They then crossed the Brêche de la Meije and descended to La Bérarde, where Duhamel had to depart. Boileau set out the following day with the guides Alexandre Tournier and Léon Simond to climb the Ecrins. Leaving La Bérarde at 4.35am they arrived at the Col des Ecrins two hours later, and at 11.45am the three men stood on the highest point of the Dauphiné. Hastening down the mountain in a race against the weather, they crossed the seemingly endless Glacier Blanc, but before they could reach Ailefroide they were struck by a heavy storm, seeking refuge inside a deserted hut where they sheltered for the night. They had made the seventh ascent of the Ecrins, Tournier having made the fourth ascent with Georges Devin the year before. Boileau completed that season in the Dauphiné with his guides by crossing the Col du Sellar (3067m), and the Col de la Muande (3059m).

At the age of eighteen Boileau had developed a strong will of his own, and had acquired sound mountaineering experience, confident that he could compete with the best. Appreciating the unspoilt beauty of the Cevennes where he lived with his parents in his youth, he used to take long walks across the moors, hunting in the hills and forests, and climbing the highest peak in the region Mont Aigoual (1565m). He had an unusual background, being descended from a Protestant family, owners of important lands in the Languedoc region to which he succeeded with the title of (eighteenth) Baron de Castelnau. The family's gallant deeds in battle and in the affairs of state could be traced back to the thirteenth century when one of his ancestors, Etienne Boileau, took part in the seventh Crusade, and became in 1256 provost-marshall of Paris where he is commemorated with a statue that stands in the Hôtel de Ville. It was at the Boileau family estate in 1704 that 'count and lord' Roland, generalissimo of the Protestant rebellion in France, established his Camisard headquarters, and where he was betrayed and killed. It was said that his disciples, bold and hardy men of the mountains, would 'mystically put a grain of wheat among the pewter balls with which they charged their muskets'. Members of the Boileau family suffered many tragedies, fighting and dying for their faith. One of them, Charles Boileau, fled to England where he settled, and a member of the British branch of the family was later knighted.[2] Emmanuel's father, Baron Charles Boileau, a doctor of law, held a position as judge in Nîmes. As a protest against the illegal seizure of power by Louis-Napoleon in

[2]Early in the nineteenth century Sir John Boileau married Lady Catherine Elliot, a sister of Lord Minto who in 1830 had made the third ascent of the Zermatt Breithorn.

1851, he resigned his post, although he was then married with a small son. With a modest capital he was able to purchase a piece of marshy land in the area between Nîmes and Montpellier, where he worked with dogged persistence draining the ground, ploughing the soil, and succeeding in producing cereal crops; later he planted vineyards which began to flourish. Emmanuel, the only son and a delicate child, was educated at home, mostly by his mother, until her death when he was fourteen years old. His father, whom he described as 'a good, upright, just, but hard man', then sent his son to Paris to study for the *baccalauréat* at the Ecole Polytechnique, and to prepare for a profession either as a lawyer or a pastor, though his son's desire was to enter the Military Academy of St-Cyr to train as an army officer. At this period, books about exploratory expeditions to the polar regions, Africa, and Asia, of which he became an avid reader, interested Emmanuel greatly. When he was taken by his parents for a holiday to the Pyrenees at the age of thirteen and expressed an eagerness to do some climbing, they engaged a guide with whom he ascended the Pic de Néthou and the Maladetta; a strenuous beginning at his age, which however resulted in a perceptible improvement to his health.

Two years later in 1872, Emmanuel and his father visited Switzerland, the latter agreeing to his son's wish to climb mountains, requiring only that he should keep him informed of his whereabouts. At the age of fifteen Emmanuel was 'allowed to do exactly as I wished, and [my father] followed me by train while I ascended the peaks. Either he did not realise what dangers I had to face, or he had great confidence in me; the latter is more probable, I think. I was not yet sixteen, yet I travelled by myself according to my own plans, selecting my guides, paying my hotel bills, and ascending the most difficult peaks, which made everybody at the hotels stare at me in amazement. I am extremely grateful to my father, for that sort of education did me a great deal of good both physically and morally. I had been a sickly child, and I had grown into a tall, hardy, young man.' It should be added that not many French climbers were to be seen in Switzerland at that time. Between 1872-5 Boileau's climbs included the Jungfrau, Finsteraarhorn, Matterhorn, Dent Blanche, Gran Paradiso, Mont Blanc (four times, including one non-stop ascent in twenty-four hours) the Ecrins, and several other Dauphiné peaks; he also traversed the Théodule pass, Col du Géant, Mönchjoch, and Oberaarjoch.

Boileau recorded his ascents in his journals two of which, for the years 1874-5, were shown by his son in the late 1940s to the alpine historian Claire-Elaine Engel who was able to obtain from the family the use of unpublished documents, as well as a good deal of personal information about Emmanuel's early and later life. The diaries reveal his clear-headedness and independence. On his mountain expeditions he was indisputably the leader – calm, bold, fully committed, and the main moving force behind his guides.

After studying for his *baccalauréat* in Paris, Boileau spent the summer of 1875 in the alps where, as mentioned, he and Duhamel made a determined attempt on the Grand Pic of Meije from the north. The following year he decided to continue his exploration of the Dauphiné. On the recommendation of a friend Boileau met and engaged Pierre Gaspard, a sturdy mountain peasant aged forty-two with extensive local knowledge acquired from years of experience as a shepherd and hunter. It was only after 1877 that Gaspard was officially registered as a professional guide, and during the years that followed, usually accompanied by his son, he guided several clients on expeditions, making a number of first ascents, and gaining a reputation as the leading guide in the Dauphiné. During four weeks, between 21 August and 19 September 1876, Boileau with Gaspard and his son Pierre made five first ascents, of the Tête des Fétoules (3465m), Tête de l'Etret (3563m), the Aiguille de l'Olan (3383m), which was traversed, the Tête de Graou (3168m), and the south peak of the Cavales. They also crossed the Col du Plat (3115m) (first), the Col de la Grande Ruine (3140m), the Col des Aiguilles (3084m) (first), the Col de la Lauze (3512m), and they traversed a ridge to the west of the Col de la Mariande. Attempts to climb the Grand Pic of La Meije continued during that summer. Henri Duhamel tried three times from La Bérarde placing a cairn at his highest point. (Note 3) An attempt was also made by HG Gotch which ended, like many others, on the Pic Centrale. In 1877 La Meije seemed to be under seige. Henri Cordier made an unsuccessful attempt early in June, one week before his ascent of Le Plaret, on which he died. There was another attempt later in June by two Germans; and between 27-29 June Lord Wentworth, who had tried the peak two years earlier, made fresh attempts from the North. During July attempts were made by two French climbers, P Guillemin and F Fayolle. During the same year Coolidge, after a successful season in the area with four first ascents, including Pic Coolidge (3774m), failed once again in a fresh attempt to reach the Grand Pic with the Almers, departing from La Bérarde in high dudgeon.

The defeat of repeated attempts by a number of experienced climbers prior to 1877 to reach the Grand Pic of La Meije is not surprising. At the time climbing methods and equipment were still rudimentary, and not many hard alpine rock climbs had been successfully achieved. Jean-Antoine Carrel's finish on his ascent of the Matterhorn in 1865 was one outstanding example of what a highly-skilled climber was able to accomplish. He later confided to Edward Whymper that it was the hardest single bit of climbing he had ever done. In 1871, describing Carrel's route, Whymper wrote: 'it was not only more difficult ... but *much* more difficult than ours.' F Craufurd Grove, who was the first to repeat Carrel's route in 1867, accompanied by him and JB Bich, described the final part as 'a passage of great difficulty and danger', and of the *galerie* Carrel he wrote: 'I thought the ledge decidedly dangerous, and should not like to set foot on it again.' The final variant on the headwall of the Matterhorn, pioneered by the brothers Maquignaz in 1867 (today festooned with ropes) entered a similar category of difficulty at that period, the route having followed a series of steep clefts and gullies. In the Dolomites, the Austrian mountaineer Dr P Grohmann climbed the Grosse Zinne (Cima Grande) in 1869, and ET Compton with A de Falkner and the guide BB Nicolussi climbed the Cima di Brenta in 1871. Ascents of increasing difficulty were beginning to be achieved from Chamonix. The Aiguille de Rochefort (4001m) was climbed by J Eccles with the Payots in 1873; the Aiguilles de Blaitière and Triolet, both in 1874 by English parties; and in 1876 Les Droites and Les Courtes by Cordier, Middlemore and Oakley Maund. (Note 2) But the Grand Dru was not climbed until 1878, when Clinton Dent and J Hartley, with Alexander Burgener and Kaspar Maurer, succeeded after their eighteenth attempt. The Petit Dru was climbed by the Chamonix guide-team of Charlet-Payot-Folliguet in 1879; and in the same year Mummery and Burgener, Penhall and Imseng, climbed the Z'mutt ridge of the Matterhorn. It was not until 1880 that Mummery and others opened a new phase in alpine rock climbing, with ascents of the Aiguilles des Charmoz and Grépon. However, in 1881 Mummery failed 'by fair means' to climb the Dent du Géant, which was ascended the following year by Jean-Joseph Maquignaz and the Sella brothers after the cliffs had been equipped with ropes and pitons; and by WW Graham with A Payot and A Cupelin.

By 1877, at the age of twenty, Boileau, starting his seventh alpine season, was tough and determined having gained wide knowledge of the Dauphiné mountains. It was not surprising that he should set his sights on the unclimbed Grand Pic of La Meije. During the second fortnight in July, accompanied once again by Pierre Gaspard *père* and *fils*, he carried out a number of preparatory expeditions, making the first crossing of the Col des Aigles (3220m), and the second crossing of the Col de Clochâtel (3100m); also the first ascent and traverse of the Dôme de Neige des Ecrins (3980m), and the first ascent of the Tête du Roujet (3421m). They made the first crossing of the Col des Bans (3380m), and climbed successively all the Pelvoux summits, making the first ascent of the Petit Pelvoux (3762m), after which they descended to La Bérarde via the Col de Coste-Rouge (3152m) arriving there on 1 August. Their series of successes had emboldened Boileau and his guides, strengthening their resolve to launch an attempt on the Grand Pic. 'Each one of us', Boileau wrote, 'was now able to judge our capabilities.'

Spending the night of 3 August at the Châtelleret bivouac Boileau and Gaspard ascended the Brêche de la Meije, from where they continued up the ridge, reaching the cairn which Duhamel's guides had placed at their high point the year before; they found themselves standing at the foot of a steep rock face. Duhamel wrote in the *Club Alpin Français Bulletin* in 1876 that beyond this point: 'I would say that a few centuries are likely to pass before anyone will be able to proceed beyond the place where my courageous guides set up a cairn.' Taking an initial look at the way ahead, Gaspard demurred at first, but when Boileau decided to tackle the problem anyway, the two of them climbing in bare feet, inched their way up helping each other over about 20m of the hardest bits. They reached the top of the rock face late in the day and, encouraged by the prospect above, fixed a rope-length of about 12m by which they descended, leaving the rope in place for their return, and spending a second night at Châtelleret. Their reconnaissance was followed by a delay owing to bad weather, and because of a visit to Grenoble by Boileau who had developed a severe toothache. On 15 August at 11pm Boileau, accompanied by Gaspard and his son, set out once more from La Bérarde with a porter Jean-Baptiste Rodier heavily laden with provisions and 350 feet of rope. Reaching Châtelleret at 2am on the 16th they halted for some food and drink and began their ascent at 4.20.

Boileau's detailed account of their climb, appears in Volume 4 1877 of the *Annuaire du Club Alpin Français*, providing a vivid picture of the physical and mental struggles in their battle against the difficulties encountered during their ascent and descent of the Grand Pic. 'At 9.15 we reached M Duhamel's cairn. The rope we had left in place helped us to get up the vertical pitch which we had found so dangerous before. The wall still offered serious enough difficulties. We could only move one at a time, and our advance was desperately slow. We could not relax precautions as the wall was almost vertical. We got ourselves into a couloir from which we could not escape, and saw ourselves momentarily having to beat a retreat; morale began to suffer. I can record that without taking a moment for rest we took 2 hours 45 minutes to get to the top of the 150m wall to reach the glacier du Doigt, (glacier Carré.). We left the glacier on our right to re-join the west ridge from where we could see the houses and meadows of La Grave.' They halted there forty minutes for some food, leaving the porter Rodier, who was slow and incompetent, to await their return. Boileau and the Gaspards resumed their climb at 12.45. It took them three-quarters of an hour to cut steps across the 45° glacier slope, in places on bare ice. Emerging from it they reached a col which fell in a vertical couloir on the north side down to the valley. 'Turning to the right, and keeping always on the south face of the mountain we climbed the rocks of the peak proper very fast and without any difficulty. Victory seemed ours when, only 12m from the summit, an unexpected obstacle made us doubtful of success. The summit rocks overhung on all sides: in other words, the slope was a curve and we were in its concavity. Our efforts at first were fruitless. Gaspard *pére* got up about 3 or 4m, and found himself unable either to advance or to return. He called for help which I was able to supply by standing on his son's shoulders, but only just in time as his strength was giving out. I then tried, but met with no great success. Gaspard *fils* succeeded in getting a little higher, but he put us in such danger helping him down that I was ready to order the retreat. He was so exhausted by his efforts that on his return he could not move his limbs, and the nervous stress had been so great that he dissolved in tears. All three of us were pale and trembling. The biting cold paralysed our forces. The weather had been deteriorating for the last hour. We were enveloped in cloud whipped across by a violent wind which threatened to tumble us. We descended a little way ready to retreat after having been within 12m of the summit when Gaspard, furious at finding his efforts ineffective, proposed that we try to turn the obstacle on the North face. With much difficulty we crossed a horrible section, and this time our perseverance was rewarded by success. At 3.30 we set foot on the summit after spending 2 hours in climbing the last few metres. What gave Gaspard the greatest pleasure was to find enough stones to build a cairn there; he and his son collected stones and built two cairns about 5 feet high. Gaspard repeated that no-one would believe our story unless a cairn was there to prove it. The thermometer registered minus 2°C. ... It was all very well to have climbed La Meije, but we still had to get down. This thought was neither pleasant nor re-assuring.'

'We set off at 3.55. The difficulties were many and frightening. The pitch immediately below the top was impossible; we had to fix one of our ropes to a spike of rock and slide down it until we could find a stance on a ledge. This ledge was 20m lower; we had to cut the rope and abandon this length. Once past this section we descended to the Glacier du Doigt without too much trouble; but after crossing the glacier, picking up Rodier, and regaining the west ridge, the difficulties reappeared; a fixed rope was again necessary and another 20m had regretfully to be abandoned. Night was falling; the vertical rocks, scarcely practicable by daylight, became more and more dangerous in the dark. We got down another two or three very difficult pitches, almost without seeing them, but when only about 18m above M Duhamel's cairn we were stopped on a shelf and found ourselves unable to proceed. We had to resign ourselves to awaiting the morning on this narrow rock landing ... huddled together against the cold, we were prepared for a long and terrible night.' The four men secured themselves as best they could, with 600m of empty space below, facing squalls of snow and hail, unable in the restricted area to move their limbs. There was no food or drink left, and the thermometer recorded minus 11°C while the falling snow, melting on touching their bodies, re-froze into a coating of ice. 'Gaspard did not let go of me for a moment; we stayed with arms enlaced around each other's bodies or knees throughout the storm. ... Nobody spoke, except occasionally to ask the time.' At 2am on 17 August the wind dropped. A first attempt was made to start at four, but it was not until six, with the return of the wind and fresh snowfall, that they realised it was imperative to start moving at once. 'The rocks, covered with hail and verglas, offered no sure hold so that to reach M Duhamel's rock we had to rope down for the third time. ... This was the last pitch to give us trouble ... the rest of the descent was easy.' Speeding down in rain they reached their bivouac at Châtelleret at 9am where they built a fire 'under the rocks out of the rain, and ate with a terrible appetite'. They had neither drunk nor eaten for almost twenty-four hours. Returning in pouring rain to La Bérarde at midnight, Boileau slept for sixteen hours.

Boileau's ascent of La Meije in 1877 was a heroic achievement. As a rock climb it was of a technical quality equal to the best climbs yet accomplished, and it could be regarded as one of the earliest in a series of technically difficult rock ascents which, around then, had began to proliferate in other parts of the Alps. The subsequent history of ascents of La Meije had its share of success and tragedy. In 1878 the Grand Pic was twice ascended, first by Coolidge with the Almers, and again by H Duhamel, P Giraud-Lézin and F Gonet. The fourth (the first guideless) ascent of the Grand Pic was made by those redoubtable pioneers of guideless climbing Frederick Gardiner with Charles and Lawrence Pilkington in 1879. (Note 4) In 1885 one of the great guideless teams of the nineteenth century comprising Ludwig Purtscheller and the brothers Otto and Emil Zsigmondy made a complete traverse of the Meije summits, following that with a daring attempt on the south face on which Emil died. Emmanuel Boileau's climb aroused the envy of others, and the resentment of at least one bitter rival. Coolidge felt cheated after several failed efforts to be the first, and he might even have harboured doubts about the veracity of Boileau's account of his ascent. All doubts vanished, however, when he himself reached Gaspard's summit cairn with the Almers one year later. Coolidge expressed his opinion that it was the 'longest continually difficult climb in the Alps.' (Note 5) Boileau, who had joined the Club Alpin Français in the year it was founded, was elected to the Alpine Club London in 1878, having been proposed by Coolidge and seconded by Freshfield. However Coolidge was not one to forgive and forget. His resentment of Boileau's achievement on La Meije resurfaces in a gratuitous remark which appears in his book *The Alps in Nature and History* published in 1908: 'The Meije fell by a kind of accident to a young Frenchman who was a chamois hunter rather than a peak hunter.'

Boileau, who was introduced to mountaineering at an unusually early age, appears to have been attracted to it as a sporting challenge; there is nothing to suggest that he was driven either by aesthetic motives, or competitive ambitions. The pleasures that he derived from the sport were 'physically and morally' uplifting; and in the fullness of his youthful vigour he enjoyed the risks and the dangers. That he grew into a man who would seek other challenges can be judged by aspects of his subsequent career, a few details of which were obtained from his family. It had been thought that Boileau gave up alpine climbing after 1877, but that does not appear to be the case since the *Annuaire du Club Alpin Français* for 1879 mentions him as having been among the active climbers of that year with a few summits to his credit; but details of his climbs from his notes and diaries for the later period are untraceable. He was a man of wide-ranging enthusiasms and hobbies, and other interests began successively to occupy his life in place of mountaineering, which had dominated his sporting activities between 1870 to 1877.

In the autumn of 1877, still under twenty-one, Boileau requested his father's permission to enter the army. Although his father agreed, he did not help to make his son's army career easy, by advising his commanding officer that Boileau had a wilful character which required to be disciplined – apparently his own efforts in that direction having been unsuccessful. Boileau's brief military period in Tarascon was a grim experience, not least because his father's advice had been too rigorously applied by the officer concerned. On leaving the army after about a year, Boileau spent some months in Heidelberg in order to study German. His diary records: 'I was disgusted by the student life and the necessity for fighting duels ... I left for Stuttgart where my grandfather had emigrated. [During the French Revolution] I did not work much though I matriculated as a *Kunststudent*; life was a succession of balls, parties, and receptions. The

Würtemberg ladies were most partial to Frenchmen, I got engaged to God knows how many girls. ... I mostly lived with the American colony ... they practised many sports ... I was taken into a foot-racing team and had to race every day. I was massaged, rubbed with lemon juice, given unknown drugs to drink [a timeless practice?] and I let them do what they wished, with the result that I was entered for the great Mile Race in Germany ... and I won it.'

A new period of his life opened when Boileau entered the Faculty of Medicine in Paris, where he appears to have passed a series of examinations, although he did not write his thesis and he never practised medicine. By his mid-thirties, after a life that could have been described as anything but dull, he developed fresh enthusiasms, some of which may have been regarded as uncharacteristic for someone with his background. He became a keen bicyclist, a sport that was still considered as something of a novelty. In 1898, one of the first years when bicycle racing began to be organised in France, he entered for the Paris–Tours race, and finished second. Boileau had become acquainted with some of the earliest builders of motorcars, Peugeot, Panhard, de Dion and Bolée, whose primitive vehicles, resembling horse-drawn carriages, were subject to frequent breakdowns. He learnt not only to handle them, but to cope with the many mechanical failures to which they were prone. Amédée Bolée once travelled by train laden with spare parts, from one point to the next, ahead of Boileau who was conducting trials of one of his new models. Car makers were constantly searching for improvements, and Boileau once took to Peugeot the draft-plan for a new engine he had designed which, however, the latter refused to build because it was said to be capable of a speed of sixty kilometres per hour, and he did not wish to be held responsible for his friend's death. In 1895, when he was thirty-eight, Boileau entered the first *Tour de France Automobile* finishing fifth. A year or two later he became attracted to flying, trying out hot-air balloons, as well as the perilous wood and canvas contraptions in which Louis Blériot and others carried out experimental flights.

During his late forties, Boileau began to be increasingly troubled by asthma. He was married, and lived on his estate in Languedoc with his wife, son and daughter, devoting the major part of his time and interest to agriculture, experimenting with new methods for the

Caucasus party 1874: (left to right) FC Grove, H Walker, AW Moore & F Gardiner.

Mont Blanc and Brenva glacier. Moore's route follows prominent rock and ice rib right of centre.

Rotten-Verlag Brig

Leading Italian guides: (left to right) Josef Maquignaz, J-A Carrel, Pierre Maquignaz & JB Bich, by E Perotti, 1867.

Alpine Club London

Matterhorn from Breuil. Col and glacier du Lion (left). SW ridge on left skyline leads to Pic Tyndall. Summit above, left Italian (4478m), right Swiss (4477.5m). Photo: WF Donkin, 1885.

Grindelwald, 15 January 1874: (left to right) Christian Almer, Meta Brevoort, Tschingel, WAB Coolidge & Ulrich Almer.

Alexander Burgener.

Melchior Anderegg.

E Whymper with Dr James Hector at Glacier House, BC Canada, 1903.

Matterhorn from the south; Z'mutt ridge (right), Hörnli ridge (left),
North face (centre).

Aiguille du Grépon.
Photo: CD Milner, 1938.

Matterhorn from Hubel above Zermatt. NE ridge (centre) leads to Shoulder and North face (scene of accident). East face in the sun. Furggen ridge on far left skyline.

Camp at Tarshing, July 1895: (left to right) Raghobir, Major CG Bruce and AF Mummery.

NE arm of Diamir glacier showing Mummery's intended 'pass'.

Diamir face of Nanga Parbat. Mummery's three rock ribs stand out in the centre lower half of the picture.

improvement of his vineyards which had begun to acquire a high reputation in the district. In 1923 he began dictating his memoirs to his daughter, but he fell ill soon after, and died at his home in his sixty-sixth year.

A touching account has been provided by Boileau's son of the meeting in 1914 near La Bérarde between his father and his former guide Gaspard, then an old man of eighty. They had not seen each other since their ascent of La Meije thirty-seven years earlier. 'We noticed on the little path a man driving a small flock of sheep; he was slightly bent, and leaned on a stick. He had a long grey beard and, under a wide-brimmed hat, one could see shining black eyes under shaggy eyebrows. My father had stopped, and waited for him. Gaspard looked intently at us while drawing near and then, when he came within a few steps, he recognised my father. He stopped short and then my father and he rushed to meet each other and embrace. I think Gaspard was weeping and my father looked deeply moved. They remained long embracing ... hopping and turning round and round. Gaspard's little sheep dog was yelping with fury, while my sister and I were almost as terrified as the dog.' (Note 6)

CHAPTER NINE
THERE WERE
MANY OTHERS

Doubtless the climber's craving is a compensation, the pursuit
of a release from things ... that are unnatural and warping in
useful life. Perhaps too, for some climbers the sport is
symbolical: an ascent may enact something that a day's work
does not clearly show. Perhaps again, the very inutility of
climbing, in an over-all view of it, gives a special relish to the
real plain usefulness of a saving hold. It is easy to raise plenty
of unanswerable questions about any passion. What would
have happened, most climbers have asked themselves, if what
was put into mountaineering had gone into something else ? ...
You could equally ask: Where would you have been without
what you believe you have gained from the hills ?

Dorothy Pilley, 1935

LEADING LADIES
In the mid-Victorian era when men were railed at for their alpine
adventures, the prejudice against lady climbers is best illustrated by
the expressions of horror from Lady Bentinck in 1879 about her
grand-niece (later Mrs Aubrey Le Blond), exhorting her mother to:
'Stop her climbing mountains; she is scandalising all London and
looks like a Red Indian.'

An eighteen-year-old girl Maria Paradis, owner of a village stall in
Chamonix, became the first woman to reach the top of Mont Blanc
in 1808. She was not eager to make the climb and did not enjoy it, but
was persuaded into it by her friends, local porters and guides, because
the notoriety would help to boost her trade, which it did. Thirty years
later Comtesse Henriette d'Angeville, donning plenty of flannel and
tweed clothing, heavy woollen stockings, fur-lined gloves, a bonnet
and a straw hat, and carrying an alpenstock but without a veil or dark
glasses, made the second ascent of Mont Blanc by a lady. As many
other climbers did in her day, she made her will before starting out,

and was filled with deep misgivings, experiencing '*une telle angoise, une telle anxiété, une si complète insomnie, une tension de nerfs si fatigante*' (Such anguish and anxiety, the inability to sleep and an exhausting nervous tension). At the age of forty-four the expedition appears to have caused her no special difficulty; she dined heartily at the *Pierre à l'Echelle*, and after her tent was erected, sketched and listened with pleasure to the singing of her nineteen guides headed by Jean-Marie Couttet. Her courage during the ascent won the admiration of her escort, who raised her on their shoulders at the summit. Her achievement gained her some celebrity in Paris social circles. She did not give up climbing; it was something that she obviously enjoyed. Over the next twenty-five years she made twenty-nine further mountain ascents, including one in winter, carrying out her last climb, of the Oldenhorn, at the age of sixty-nine.

The names of the first British women climbers on record are those of the Parminter sisters of Devon, Jane, Elizabeth and Mary, who ascended Le Buet in 1786. In 1822, a Mrs and Miss Campbell are known to have crossed the Col du Géant, but they did not carry out their announced intention of climbing Mont Blanc. In 1854, a Mrs Hamilton climbed Mont Blanc with her husband, becoming the first Englishwoman to do so. In 1860, the Empress Eugénie accompanied her husband the Emperor Napoleon III on a visit to Montenvers, apparently with a troop of sixty-eight guides.[1]

The most striking of the early lady climbers were the Pigeon sisters, Anna and Ellen, who began their alpine careers in their mid-thirties and, during the next eight years, climbed sixty-three peaks and crossed seventy-two passes. Tough, spirited, and courageous, attired always in voluminous skirts, they often slept out prior to undertaking a major climb. In 1873 they achieved the first female traverse from Breuil to Zermatt of the Matterhorn accompanied by Jean-Antoine Carrel, Victor Maquignaz and Jean Martin. A spectacular adventure was their crossing on 12 August 1869 of the Sesiajoch (4296m) from Riffel to Alagna, a difficult expedition conducted in bad weather. Moore and George, the first to cross the pass from the opposite

[1]Although the royal presence barred the area to all other visitors, Edward Whymper aged twenty on his first alpine journey succeeded with characteristic determination in slipping past a cordon of *gendarmes* placed around the approaches and reached Montenvers as the Imperial party was leaving.

direction in 1862, initially expressed scepticism, but later acknowledged their achievement as a very daring exploit. The sisters were accompanied by Jean Martin, their young guide from the Val d'Anniviers (employed in 1864 on the Moiry glacier by Moore who described him as nervous and unskilled) and an incompetent porter. The party left Riffel at 3am intending to cross the easier and lower Lysjoch to Gressoney. When the guide lost the way the elder sister saved the demoralised party by her skill and courage acting as an anchor during the roped descent of the steep (average gradient 62°) south-east precipices of Monte Rosa. Anna Pigeon, who became vice-president of the Ladies Alpine Club in 1910, had one of her feet frostbitten as a result of the Sesiajoch expedition. In 1885, the sisters published a slim volume *Peaks and passes* containing diary accounts of their expeditions between 1869-76.

An early Alpine Club member, well known for his stand-offish manner and autocratic views – who numbered among his climbs, between 1875-1915, two hundred and fifty ascents of the Riffelhorn – held very strong views against the presence of lady mountaineers. In spite of the male prejudice which they faced, and which lasted into the 1890s, there were three outstanding ladies who showed the way. Of these, Lucy Walker (1835-1916) was probably the most accomplished, and as the first regular lady mountaineer in Europe she became almost a legend. She and Meta Brevoort (1825-76) between them accounted for most of the important ladies' ascents made during the decade commencing in 1860. They were followed shortly after by Mrs Aubrey Le Blond (1861-1934), one of the principal movers in the founding of the Ladies Alpine Club in 1907.

Lucy Walker did not allow the problem of dress to interfere with her alpine activities, persisting in her attire of a 'white print dress' as her climbing costume. There is a rare vignette of her provided by the Belgian economist and author Emil de Laveleye who, while visiting the hut on the Théodule pass in the late 1870s, was: 'extremely surprised to see creeping into that dark den a young woman endeavouring to dry her garments soaked with water and crisp with frost in front of a wretched fire ... the guides said she was going to climb Monte Rosa ... we watched her moving off roped to her guides ... she walked quickly and was soon out of sight behind a thick mist and sheets of drizzle driven by the blizzard.' Following the example of her father Frank and her brother Horace, Lucy took up climbing, an activity quite different from any other, because she was attracted by the isolation of the alpine environment and the physical challenge. Her introduction was an ascent to the top of the Théodule pass in 1858 followed by a visit to the Monte Moro pass. Thereafter, alpine holidays were taken every year by the family, the father, daughter and son carrying out climbs from bases in Zermatt, Grindelwald, Chamonix, the Dauphiné and elsewhere, the mother providing support in the valley with victuals, clothing and mail. In 1859 Lucy met Melchior Anderegg at the Schwarenbach Inn below the Gemmi pass where he worked. From there they climbed the Altels, an ascent which marked the beginning of a twenty-one-year partnership between Melchior Anderegg and the Walker family. He was also much sought after as a guide by others, including Leslie Stephen, Charles Mathews, Charles Hudson, E Noel Buxton, F Craufurd Grove, Reginald Macdonald, Francis Fox Tuckett, and it was not long before he acquired a reputation as one of the two or three top guides during the Golden Age. Lucy Walker's personal record, which few men could have surpassed, was ninety-eight expeditions, of which only three were unsuccessful. She climbed almost all the major peaks in the Swiss and French Alps, and a few in the Dolomites and Bavarian Alps. Practically all her climbs were first ascents by a lady. She climbed the Matterhorn on 17 July 1871, three days after her ascent of the Weisshorn, Melchior Anderegg narrowly managing to thwart Meta Brevoort's ambition to be the first lady to do so. Regrettably, none of the family wrote much about their climbs, apart from occasional contributions by Horace to the *Alpine Journal*. Lucy's skills were equal to those of her brother, and both continued to climb regularly after their father's death. Lucy is said to have suffered throughout from mountain sickness; one wonders whether her preferred diet of sponge cake and champagne could have been a cause rather than a cure for her affliction. Asked once why she never married, Lucy Walker is said to have replied: 'I love mountains and Melchior, and Melchior already has a wife.' She had an unassuming, unpretentious nature, and a dislike of publicity. Under doctor's orders she stopped climbing in 1879, but continued to visit favourite places in the Alps almost every summer, meeting old friends and calling at the home of the Andereggs. At the age of seventy-six she became the second President of the Ladies Alpine Club in 1912. She attended the Club's London Dinner in 1913 when, although requiring assistance to rise to her feet, she thrilled a new generation of lady climbers with a spirited speech about early days in the alps.

When doctors in America advised that WAB Coolidge, a weakly youth, should spend the winter of 1864-65 in the mild climate of the Mediterranean, his mother and sister journeyed there with him from New England, accompanied by his mother's thirty-nine-year-old sister Margaret Claudia (Meta) Brevoort. The Coolidge family, one of whose members became the thirtieth President of the United States in 1923, had emigrated from Holland to America in the mid eighteenth century. Meta Brevoort possessed a strong character combined with an innate exuberance and vitality, and her nephew grew strongly attached to her. It was her example, and her genuine enthusiasm for mountain travel and exploration, that led him to devote his life to the alps as a climber, explorer and historian, outliving her by fifty years. Brevoort visited Switzerland in 1865 taking her nephew with her, when the fifteen-year-old accompanied her across the Strahlegg pass, and walked to the Hörnli from Zermatt, which had not fully recovered from the Matterhorn disaster two months earlier. They hired mules to visit Gornergrat, and it was reported that she did not hesitate to beat mule-drivers whom she saw ill-treating their animals.

Following their first visit Brevoort and her nephew were regular summer visitors to the alps. At Grindelwald in 1868 they were able to engage Christian Almer, then well established in his career. Although he knew nothing about the pair, he felt that 'after a day's walk (he) could soon tell how they would go'. It was the beginning of a very fruitful partnership. During that year and the next they carried out a series of classic ascents in Switzerland and France. In 1870 they went to the Dauphiné. Coolidge commented later: 'I am not quite sure what made us choose the Dauphiné as our battleground but I believe it was ambition. There was a whole world for us to explore there and that was enough for us.' They had entered an area practically untouched – and lacking in any amenities. From La Bastide Brevoort wrote to her sister: 'The floor of our room was as black as the ace of spades, a bag of flour and a sieve in one corner. No means of washing ... no pillows, sheets like dish-cloths ... we made some tea and had boiled eggs, but neither milk nor butter as the cows are away. Fleas without end.' The only available map was Bourcet's, dating from the eighteenth century. A golden opportunity for pioneers, and they used it well. In that first season their climbs included the first ascent of the Pic Centrale of La Meije, and the second ascent of the Ecrins. During their next five seasons there with Almer, they explored the Dauphiné Alps thoroughly, making a series of important ascents: Grande Ruine, Le Râteau, Les Rouies, Pic de la Grave, Grandes Rousses, Roche de la Muzelle, to name a few. As a direct result of their exploration the mountains of the Dauphiné became a focus of attraction for several well-known climbers. One summit, the Grand Pic of La Meije eluded Brevoort, and it was to remain for her an unfulfilled ambition. Among her list of alpine ascents, which included seventy major peaks and several first ascents, were the first traverse by a lady of the Matterhorn from Zermatt to Breuil on 5 September 1871; two winter ascents in 1874, the first by a lady, of the Wetterhorn and the Jungfrau; and a new route on the Bietschorn in 1871 about which she wrote an article for the *Alpine Journal* 'A Day and a Night on the Bietschorn' – which appeared under her nephew's name owing to the exclusion of women from the Club and its publications. Her character may be judged by the warm congratulations – despite her deep personal disappointment – with which she greeted Lucy Walker who became the first lady to climb the Matterhorn in July 1871. Her last alpine climb, the first ascent of the Gross Füsshorn, was made on 21 September 1876 with W Little, M Salzmann and two porters. She died suddenly a few months later aged fifty-one. Coolidge was deeply distressed by his aunt's death, all his early enthusiasm for the Alps having been inspired by her. Although his interest in mountains did not diminish the emphasis had changed. He travelled more widely, always accompanied by Christian Almer and his sons, with a view to gathering information for a work which he had conceived about the history of the Alps. His travels ended in 1895, and a year later he settled in Grindelwald where he died aged seventy-six.

Mrs Le Blond, born Elizabeth Hawkins-Whitshed from an old Irish family, had a wide range of interests. Physically delicate, she was advised at the age of eighteen to spend a summer at a Swiss health resort. There were not many to choose from, and they were fairly primitive. In 1879 she went to St Moritz, accompanied by the husband she had just married, FC Burnaby, a Guards officer nineteen years older than herself. She stayed in the Engadine for several months, her health gradually improving. From Pontresina, armed with a tall alpenstock, she walked up to the Diavolezza pass (2575m) where she was struck by the beauty of the mountains and decided to take up mountaineering, to which she devoted the next twenty years of her life. After her husband's death on active service in Egypt in 1884, she married a Mr DF Main, who died in 1892.[2] Her third marriage was to Mr Aubrey Le Blond. In one of her nine books including an autobiography, which were published variously under her three married names, she wrote that she owed 'a supreme debt of gratitude to the mountains for knocking me from the shackles of conventionality'. She practised what she believed, which was that she saw absolutely no reason why women should not climb mountains on equal terms with men. She wore breeches for climbing, with a skirt over them which was removed once she was out of sight of civilisation. A strong sense of independence, a love of adventure, physical bravery and a cool head were the hall-marks of her character. With her health quite restored, she was able to enjoy to the full the pleasures of mountaineering. She chose excellent guides, from whom she learnt the required skills, developing into a competent climber. Her favourite guides were Edouard Cupelin of Chamonix, and Joseph Imboden (who had accompanied WW Graham to the Himalaya in 1883) and his son Roman. She also climbed with Emil Rey and Alexander Burgener, with whom she ascended the Matterhorn. In addition to making most of the classic ascents, she carried out some remarkable winter ascents, which included the Aiguille du Tour, traverses of Piz Palu and Piz Bernina and (first in winter) ascents of Piz Zupô, Piz Sella and Disgrazia, the last in February 1896 in a round trip from the Forno hut occupying fifteen hours. In the summer of 1882 she climbed the Grandes Jorasses, the Dent du Géant, and Mont Blanc. In January 1883, with Cupelin she made the first crossing of the Col du Tacul, followed by crossings of the Cols du Chardonnet and d'Argentière. A month later she joined forces with Vittorio Sella, who had made the first winter ascent of the Matterhorn the year before, for a winter attempt on Monte Rosa, when they were turned back at 4200m by a violent storm. In 1884, she

[2]According to Swiss records Elizabeth Main is credited with having taken the first brief ciné films in the Engadine in 1899 illustrating the growing popularity of winter sports. See also Chapter 2, page 47 with reference to Arthur Conan Doyle's activities in the Engadine in 1894-95.

made the first ascent of the north-west (lower) summit of Piz Roseg. She was greatly distressed by Roman Imboden's death in a disastrous accident on the Lyskamm.[3] Although she stopped climbing in the Alps, she spent a few summers climbing in Norway with Roman's father. She was a keen traveller, visiting the Middle East, Manchuria, China, Siberia and Russia. Mrs Le Blond moved easily and gracefully in social circles. During World War I she was actively engaged in voluntary work for ambulances and hospitals in Britain and France, and in helping to raise funds for auxiliary services. Upon the founding of the Ladies Alpine Club in 1907 she became its first President, and was an efficient organiser and speaker. In 1933, she accepted a second term as President, one year before her death. Mountaineering exercised an important influence upon her life, and formed the subject of several of her books.

Of other lady climbers who belong to the same and slightly later periods, all demonstrated a similar courageous and independent outlook, rejecting the popular belief that mountaineering was an exclusive male preserve. Four deserve special mention. Isabelle Straton, a wealthy Englishwoman, began climbing at the age of twenty-seven and in 1865 embarked on a series of climbs and travels in the Alps and the Pyrenees with the Chamonix guide Jean Charlet. Her frequent companion was Emmeline Lewis-Lloyd of Wales, with whom she made an attempt on the Matterhorn in 1869. They made the first ascent of the Aiguille du Moine in 1871, and the first women's ascent of Monte Viso. Miss Straton climbed the Aiguille du Midi and the north summit of the Aiguille du Blaitière. The Pointe Isabella, of which she made the first ascent in 1875, bears her name. She made four ascents of Mont Blanc, including the first winter ascent on 31 January 1876, accompanied by Jean Charlet, Sylvain Couttet and Michel Balmat. She married Charlet a few months later and set up home in Chamonix, where she spent the remainder of her life. Their two sons, anticipating their future careers, climbed Mont Blanc at the respective ages of thirteen and eleven and a half.

Mrs EP Jackson, who built up a record of 140 *grandes courses*, was described by Mrs Le Blond as 'one of the greatest women climbers of

---

[3]He died with his employer Dr Max Günther, and a second guide Peter Ruppen, on 10 September 1896 in a fall from the east ridge resulting from a broken cornice. On 6 September 1877 a similar tragedy had occurred when a cornice on the east ridge of the Lyskamm collapsed, causing the deaths of two English climbers WA Lewis and NH Paterson and their guides, three members of the Knubel family.

her time'. Her list of climbs, which were made mostly with Alois Pollinger, reflected the higher technical standards that were beginning gradually to emerge; they included the Dru and the Charmoz, first ascents of the east face of the Weissmies, the west ridge of the Dom, and in 1884 the first descent of the unclimbed west (Ferpècle) ridge of the Dent Blanche with Alois Pollinger and Johann-Josef Truffer. One of her most remarkable achievements was her series of winter ascents during January 1880 when, accompanied by Ulrich Almer and Emil Boss, she climbed the Lauteraarhorn on the fifth, the Klein Fiescherhorn on the sixth, and the Grosses Fiescherhorn on the eleventh. On the sixteenth she traversed the Jungfrau from the Bergli hut to the Guggi glacier where, owing to a forced bivouac, both she and Almer were frostbitten. Her account of these winter adventures, written at the request of the Alpine Club, appears in the *Alpine Journal* under the title 'A Winter Quartette'.

Katharine Richardson (1854-1927), frail-looking but exceptionally tough, started climbing at the age of seventeen when she ascended Piz Languard and Piz Corvatsch in the Bernina alps. She enjoyed a very active eleven-year alpine career, during which she made 116 major ascents, which included six first ascents, and fourteen first ascents by a woman. In one week from Zermatt she climbed the Zinal Rothorn, Weisshorn, Matterhorn and Monte Rosa. In 1888, accompanied by the great guides Emil Rey and Jean-Baptiste Bich she made the first direct ascent of the south ridge of the Aiguille de Bionnassay, descending the east ridge to the Col de Bionassay and traversing the entire ridge of the Dôme du Goûter. In the same year she made the first north-south traverse of the Ecrins by a lady. Also in that year she made the first lady's ascent of the Grand Pic of La Meije, starting from La Bérarde at 9pm with her guides Jean-Baptiste Bich and Pierre Gaspard *péré*, and returning there at 5.30 pm the next afternoon. In 1889 she traversed the Petit and Grand Dru, as well as the five summits of the Grands Charmoz. In the Dauphiné she often teamed up with the well-known French climber Marie Paillon, with whom she climbed the Central peak of the Aiguilles d'Arves, and a peak in the Pelvoux group, the Pointe Richardson, which bears her name. She joined the Ladies Alpine Club in 1908, and was described by prominent co-members as 'a magnificent mountaineer'.

At a slightly later date, when the presence of women on alpine peaks was no longer a rarity, Lily Bristow established a reputation as a very skilled and daring climber. She was the first woman to make difficult guideless ascents accompanying the leading male climbers of her day, which included the north-south traverse of the Grands Charmoz in 1892 with Mummery and Carr; the north ridge of the Zinal Rothorn with Mummery in 1893; a traverse of the Matterhorn with Mummery, Collie and Hastings, ascending the Hörnli ridge and 'chased from its shattered crest down the Italian ridge [to Breuil] by the mad fury of thunder, lightning and snow'. She climbed the Petit Dru with the same team, leading sections of the climb. In 1894 she made the first descent of the Z'mutt ridge of the Matterhorn with Joseph Pollinger and Matthias Zurbriggen. In 1895 she made the first ascent by a lady of the Grépon (which was no 'easy day for a lady' – a phrase coined by Mummery in another context) and the second traverse of the mountain with Mummery, Collie, Hastings and Slingsby. The limited records of her climbs reveal that Mummery did not exaggerate when he commented about her performance on the Grépon, 'Miss Bristow showed the representatives of the Alpine Club the way in which steep rocks should be climbed.' Mrs Mummery, a keen climber, accompanied her husband on several major ascents. Extracts from her lively account of a difficult climb on the Täschhorn in 1887 are quoted in Chapter Seven.

Gertrude Bell (1868-1926) cannot be excluded from this illustrious group of early lady climbers. Better known as an archaeological scholar, traveller and writer on the Middle East, she enjoyed an active six-year career in the alps, which she visited for relaxation and in pursuit of adventure. In 1899 from La Grave she traversed the Pic Central of the Meije and climbed the Ecrins. A year later from Chamonix she carried out a traverse from the Grand to the Petit Dru. In 1901, after climbing the Schreckhorn she spent a fortnight in the Englehorner climbing seven peaks. The following year she set her sights on the unclimbed north-east ridge/rib of the Finsteraarhorn, an impressive wall of 1070m. This turned out to be her greatest alpine adventure, which was defeated at a tower 250m below the top in a storm. After a forced bivouac, the descent was made in an unceasing blizzard under extreme conditions. She and her guide Ulrich Fuhrer returned safely after an outing of fifty-seven hours, the latter filled with praise and wonder over her skill, bravery and coolness.[4]

[4]The north-east ridge of the Finsteraarhorn was climbed on 16 July 1904 by the Swiss climber Gustav Hasler and his guide Franz Amatter. Fifty-two years later only four further ascents had been made. It was Franz Amatter who led Yuko Maki's party during the first ascent of the Mittelegi ridge of the Eiger on 10 September 1921.

In 1904, she climbed the Dent Blanche, Lyskamm, Monte Rosa, and traversed the Matterhorn from Breuil to Zermatt. In 1920-21, with her extensive knowledge of the local people and the politics of the region, Gertrude Bell was appointed Oriental Secretary to the British Commissioner in Baghdad during negotiations for the setting up of the independent state of Iraq.

EMINENT EUROPEANS

Practically all the earliest European mountaineers were men who dwelt within the shadow of mountains. They were a physically tough minority, attracted by the unknown, and their pioneer climbs and travels were motivated by curiosity. They seldom recorded their adventures, and such of their writings that exist often relate to natural phenomena. The ascent of Mont Blanc in 1786 formed a watershed marking the birth of mountain climbing for its own sake, which fulfilled the dual purpose of satisfying a personal challenge while exploring an untouched world. The opening chapter of this book has referred to mountain ascents made as early as the thirteenth century by small numbers of devout men. By the nineteenth century the curiosity of scientists to explore the origin of mountains became an interesting subject for study – much as current exploration of the planets seeks to reveal hidden secrets of the universe.

The ascent of the Gross Glockner by five men of Heiligenblut on 28 July 1800 which marked the birth of alpinism in the Austrian Alps, represented the fulfillment of a desire to ascend the highest mountain in the region, a first attempt in 1799 from a hut constructed on the southern slopes having ended on the Kleinglockner. A variety of interesting routes on the mountain were fully explored during the latter part of the nineteenth century. Perhaps one of the best-known was the Pallavinci couloir on the east face, first climbed on 18 August 1876 by Count Alfred Pallavinci and his guides G Bäuerle, J Kramser and J Tribusser, the last named cutting 2500 ice-steps in seven hours, neither crampons nor pitons having been used. Other hard routes on the mountain were opened by Dr Guido Lammer and others during the 1890s. The first winter ascent of the Gross Glockner was made by WA Baillie-Grohmann with four guides on 2 January 1875. One of the first Tyrolean climbers possessing a genuine love of mountains was the priest Peter-Carl Thurwieser (b1789) teacher of Oriental languages at Salzburg, who is believed to have reached seventy summits between the years 1820 to 1847 including the Angkogel and Watzmann. Among his pioneer ascents were Strahlkogel (3290m) in 1833, Fernerkogel (3300m) in 1836, and Schrammacher (3416m) in 1847. An outstanding Austrian explorer and climber, and a founder member of the Oesterreichischer Alpenverein in 1862, was Paul Grohmann (b1838), a leading pioneer of Dolomite climbing between 1863-69. Among his climbs were Tofana's three summits, Antelao, Marmolada, Cristallo, Sorapiss, Grosse Zinne and Langkofel, an outlier of which 'Grohmannspitze' bears his name. It was after his series of ascents that the region began to attract wider attention. A period of brilliant ascents, although not free from fatalities, continued in later years. Prominent in that later period was the famous guideless trio Ludwig Purtscheller and the brothers Emil and Otto Zsigmondy. Mountaineering in the Dolomites really began to grow after the amalgamation in 1874 of the Deutscher and Oesterreichischer Alpenverein, the strength of both clubs with expanding membership making possible the construction of pathways and huts, also the installation on steep rock of wire-ropes, ladders and stanchions, forerunners of the currently popular *via ferrata*. There were some who felt that the latter were excessive, and they were deplored by a few leading climbers of the period.

From the hardy mountain peasants of the pioneering years grew several families of great guides, chief among whom were Siorpaes, Dimai, Nicolussi and Innerkofler. After the expansion of roads and transport in the early years of the twentieth century, the valleys began to emerge from their former isolation and a new era of popular tourism opened.

Two months after the ascent of the Matterhorn in 1865, the young Paul Güssfeldt, later a professor at Berlin university and a leading climber, approached Peter Taugwalder in Zermatt with a view to repeating the climb; the latter refused but, with his son Joseph, he accompanied Güssfeldt in an attempt from the Italian side. Güssfeldt made two first ascents in the Bernina alps, the Biancograt on Piz Bernina (4049m) in 1878, and Piz Scerscen (3971m) in 1877. In 1876 with Alexander Burgener he repeated Mummery's crossing of the Col du Lion but in the opposite direction starting from Italy. His winter ascents included the Grandes Jorasses and the Gran Paradiso.

In 1892, Güssfeldt made the fourth ascent of Moore's route on the Brenva side of Mont Blanc with Emil Rey and two other guides, adopting a shorter variation which avoided the lower rock arête, and approaching the ice-ridge from the central bay of the Brenva glacier by what became known as the Güssfeldt couloir. Several of his notable climbs, including his winter ascents were done with his favourite guide Rey. (Note 1) Probably his finest expedition, when he was over fifty-two in 1893, with Rey and Christian Klucker, lasting eighty-eight hours and requiring two bivouacs, was the ascent of Mont Blanc via the Brenva glacier, the Aiguille Blanche de Peuterey, and Mont Blanc de Courmayeur.

Other exceptional Austrian and German climbers were Hermann von Barth (1845-79) who carried out a number of solitary climbs in the Karwendel and Wetterstein areas, and is reported once to have remarked, 'who goes with me must be ready to die'. Georg Winkler (b1869) had a brief and sensational career. At eighteen, he climbed the Winklerturm solo, the most difficult of the Vajolet towers in the Dolomites. In 1888, two days after making a solitary ascent of the Zinal Rothorn, he disappeared during a solo attempt on the north face of the Weisshorn.

Ludwig Purtscheller (b1849) made an almost unrivalled number of 1700 ascents, including forty peaks over 4000m. Among his first ascents was Kibo (5895m) the highest point of Kilimanjaro in Tanzania, which he climbed in 1889 with the geographer Hans Meyer of Leipzig. He climbed regularly with the brothers Emil and Otto Zsigmondy of Vienna, forming an exceptionally strong and successful guideless team. Apart from their many noteworthy climbs in the Dolomites, they achieved the first guideless traverse of the Matterhorn from Switzerland to Italy, the first traverse of the Meije, the first ascent from the south of the Bietschhorn, and the first guideless ascent of the Marinelli couloir on the south side of Monte Rosa. Purtscheller published a guide to the eastern Alps in two volumes in 1894 which was expanded to four volumes in its fourth edition published in 1911. His book *Uber Fels und Firn* containing accounts of his climbs was published in 1901, one year after his death.

Emil Zsigmondy (b1861) in Vienna, a doctor by profession, was a brilliant and very daring climber often taking risks which his brother Otto and his friend Ludwig Purtscheller considered unjustifiable. One of his early climbing companions Julius Kugy (b1858) gave up climbing with him because of his rashness. Between 1875 to 1884 he was involved in fifteen accidents in the mountains. He wrote a book, *Gefahren der Alpen*, which was translated into French *Dangers des Alpes,* and published, ironically, shortly before his death outlining safety methods and avoidance of danger in mountaineering. He died in a fall during an attempt on the south face of La Meije in 1885. His intended route was climbed twenty-seven years later by the great Dolomite guide Angelo Dibona with the brothers Guido and Max Mayer of Vienna, and Luigi Rizzi.

Vittorio Sella (1859-1943) the great mountain photographer, who had begun experimenting with dry photographic plates in 1880, combined his photographic skills with his interest in mountaineering. In 1882 he made the first winter ascent and traverse of the Matterhorn. Setting out from Breuil with J-A and J-L Carrel at 11pm, they reached the Col du Lion at 6am and the summit at 2pm, descending to the Swiss hut where they arrived five and a half hours later. On 26 January 1884, he made the first winter ascent of Monte Rosa (Dufourspitze) with Joseph and Daniel Maquignaz after a night spent on the Grenz glacier, and a second very windy night after the climb between the Gorner and Théodule glaciers. Sella made several other winter ascents of 4000m peaks in the Valais, Bernese and Bernina alps, and the Graians. He considered Alpine winter conditions 'when the great cold cleanses the air' as the finest for photography. He accompanied the caravan of Queen Margherita of Italy to the top of Punta Gnifetti on Monte Rosa in 1893. His many expeditions abroad resulted in superb collections of photographs; to the Caucasus in 1889-90; with the Duke of Abruzzi to Mount St Elias in 1897, the Ruwenzori in 1906, the Karakoram in 1909; and with Douglas Freshfield in 1899 on his journey round Kangchenjunga. Vittorio Sella's career as an explorer and climber was complementary to his pre-eminence as a mountain photographer.

GREAT GUIDES

What appears to be the first recorded account of the work of alpine guides relates to a party of pilgrims returning from Rome in January 1129, who were blocked by heavy snow at the foot of the Grand St Bernard pass. A group of local men, equipped with long wooden batons, and with iron spikes fitted to their boots, offered to clear a pathway by which they succeeded in leading the pilgrims across the pass into Switzerland. There is a story about the Count of Villamont in 1588, who may have been one of the first persons to be assisted up a mountain by guides, being all but lifted to the top of Rochemelon (3538m) by two sturdy peasants carrying wine and food with which to refresh him, fixing spikes to his shoes, and acting as human crutches under his armpits when required. Professional guiding developed as a natural consequence of the inborn skills and toughness of alpine peasants who acquired experience through solitary explorations of the upper forests and glaciers in search of game, precious metals and crystals. A regular demand for their services existed in the Middle Ages during the north–south trade conducted by caravans across the alpine passes. By the nineteenth century with the arrival of increasing numbers of travellers and tourists the profession began to provide a regular source of income in the summer, although some of the early guides might be forgiven for having regarded foreigners who wished to climb mountains as men with more money than sense. It was at Chamonix in 1821 that the first Register of professional guides was established. Some family names, which became well known, are still found on the present Register. In Switzerland men of the Haslital were usually available at the Grimsel hospice ready to guide parties across glaciers at the beginning of the nineteenth century. Melchior Anderegg was one of those who began his career there before 1850. Others were Johann Jaun (1806-60), Jakob Leuthold (1807-43) and men of the Abplanalp family. Although it was only in 1856 that a professional guide's organisation was established in Grindelwald there were a few men such as Peter Baumann (1800-53), and Hildebrand Burgener (1792-1867) who had been conducting visitors to the mountains as early as the 1820s. The guiding careers of men from Saas, St Niklaus, and Zermatt achieved prominence during the Golden Age, and there are Imsengs, Lochmatters, Imbodens and Biners still active today.

Leading mountaineers of the Golden Age relied upon the local knowledge of their guides, and some admit to having learnt their skills from them. Several close employer-guide relationships were built, and the best guides were valued as much for their personal qualities as for their professional skills. During the early period of the Golden Age among the best men were Auguste Balmat (b1809), Johann-Joseph Bennen (b1819), Ulrich Lauener (b1821), Christian Almer (b1826), Melchior Anderegg (b1827), Jakob Anderegg (b1827), Jean-Joseph Maquignaz (b1828),[5] Jean-Antoine Carrel (b1829), Michel Croz

---

[5] Also his son Baptiste, nephew Daniel and brother Pierre.

(b1830), Ferdinand Imseng (b1845), Emil Rey (b1845) and Alexander Burgener (b1845), the last six of whom died in the mountains. All of them possessed a high degree of courage and resource; three acquired exceptional records, which included first ascents of major peaks or new routes up them, and the crossings of new passes. Melchior Anderegg is credited with fourteen of the former and six of the latter; Christian Almer with eighteen and fifteen; Alexander Burgener with about two dozen of the former as well as climbs in the Caucasus. In an age when there was a growing demand for their services, the best guides acquired special merit and the vocation frequently passed from father to son. Melchior Anderegg passed on to four of his eight sons the principles and skills of his profession, as he did to two of his *protégés,* Andreas Maurer (1842-82) and Johann Jaun (1843-1921). Christian Almer's five sons all adopted their father's profession, and two of them, Ulrich and Christian, became worthy successors to their father. Josef-Marie Lochmatter (1837-82) one of the leading guides of St Niklaus was the founder of a famous dynasty. He joined Whymper in the search for the victims of the Matterhorn accident in 1865, and made the second ascent of the mountain from Zermatt with Reverend JM Elliot. He died on the Dent Blanche at the age of forty-five with his eldest son aged twenty-one and his employer WE Gabbet. His five other sons all became guides, the most illustrious of whom was Franz (1878-1933) described as *primus inter pares* among the guides of his generation. He and his brother Joseph achieved a series of remarkable ascents with VJE Ryan. He accompanied CF Meade to the Himalaya in 1912, and Dr and Mrs Visser on three visits to the Karakoram between 1922-30. He died at the age of fifty-five as a result of a slip in a relatively easy place while descending the Weisshorn. Another leading guide from St Niklaus was Peter Knubel (1833-1919), who made the second ascent of the Matterhorn from Zermatt in 1868 with Elliot and Lochmatter. Among his first ascents were the highest summit of Elbruz during AW Moore's Caucasus expedition in 1874, and the south ridge of the Dent Blanche in 1876 with Frederick Gardiner. His son Josef (1881-1961) gained fame as Geoffrey Young's guide, ascending the Mer de Glace face of the Grépon with him in 1911 in nailed boots without the use of a single piton. Josef Knubel later climbed with Graham Brown and Alfred Zurcher. It was said that he used three pitons during his entire career.

It should not be supposed that even during the Golden Age guiding provided even the leading men with adequate financial means. At best, the most sought after among them obtained engagements for about four months in the summer. Practically all of them relied on agriculture, cattle-farming, hunting, forestry, carpentry and other skills, to provide a livelihood for themselves and their families. Over one hundred years later in Nepal, the Sherpas gaining a reputation for hardihood and skill as mountain porters, and later benefiting from educational schemes and the massive growth of tourism, have achieved popular success as climbers, guides, and tour operators, in a much shorter time than their alpine counterparts. A Swiss climber recently remarked that although the leading mountaineers of the Golden Age enjoyed a high reputation, their guides, whose climbing skills were in many cases superior, were not accorded a fraction of the glory. That is not wholly true. The leading amateurs of the era were unsparing in praise for their guides. There are, besides, two important books which deal, almost in panegyrical terms, with the careers of the great guides of the early and middle periods, *The pioneers of the Alps* (1887) by CD Cunningham and Sir William Abney and *Pioniere der Alpen* (1946) by Carl Egger. Since it often happens that a teller of his own tale acquires a higher degree of popular fame, it is a pity that men like Christian Almer, Melchior Anderegg and Jean-Antoine Carrel never sat down to relate their adventures. They, and many others, shared equally in the success of the climbers who shone brightly during the Alpine Golden Age. To quote Leslie Stephen, the successes of the pioneers may be attributed largely to: 'the skill and courage of Swiss guides and the ambition of their employers.'

PART THREE
20ᵀᴴ CENTURY

CHAPTER TEN
BEYOND THE
BEGINNINGS

Fifty years ago it was still possible for us to deny that competitive mountaineering was anything but a rare and regrettable phenomenon, and we have continued ever since to record sincere but completely unavailing protests against the exploitation of mountaineering successes in the interests of national aggrandisement. Continental historians, it is true, have sometimes implied that even if we did not blow our own trumpets we breathed down them with considerable effect.

Arnold Lunn, 1957

On my first visit to the Alps in August 1948, I arranged to meet my guide Arthur Lochmatter in the Visptal at St Niklaus, then still a relatively unspoilt village, where I was hospitably received in his home. The next day, after a hot climb of 750m to the last alp below the Ried glacier, my guide led me to a primitive chalet, occupied only during the summer, where a solitary peasant family offered me a large glass of cold uncreamed milk to appease my raging thirst. We slept at the Bordier hut, of which we were the sole occupants, setting out at 4am, traversing the Nadelgrat and descending to the Dom hut late in the afternoon. The following day we traversed the Dom, ascending the Festigrat and descending the north face. On both days there were no climbers other than ourselves on the summits. Zermatt bore the character of a mountain village, with small shops and hotels lining the main thoroughfare, where walkers and climbers made way for the occasional pack-mule or horse-drawn carriage. Traversing the twin summits of Castor and Pollux above the Grenz glacier we met no one; on top of the Rimpfischhorn, we met only two others; on Monte Rosa's Dufourspitze we found ourselves part of a summit crowd of six. Later, crossing two cols and ascending five peaks, I had the thrill of experiencing an other-worldly atmosphere. Once, in poor weather, after two nights alone at the Coaz hut in the Bernina alps, I climbed Piz Corvatsch and Piz Chapütschin, and made a lonely crossing of the

Fuorcla Surlej pass, descending the long winding tracks to Champfersee near St Moritz – there was no cable-car then. Those were memorable days in a magical alpine environment still relatively free from signs of over-development.

In 1992, reclining blissfully on green slopes above conifer forests with the giant curve of the Aletsch glacier visible to the east, it was not difficult for me to understand why John Tyndall had fallen in love with Belalp, from where he used to climb the Sparrhorn for the simple joy of the scramble and the sweeping views from the summit. Scrambling to the top of the Dent d'Oche, a prominent mountain situated above Evian in the Savoie, the view from which Leslie Stephen praised lavishly, I was alone as he was on a day of impeccable weather with the vast lake spread out below and a glistening array of peaks filling the horizon in every direction. On a railway journey in 1948 from Brig to Geneva after over two weeks in the Alps, I was embarrassed by disapproving glances from fellow-passengers at my travel-worn clothes, peeling sunburn, and pre-war climbing kit. In the years directly following the end of World War Two, the prosperous Swiss dwelling in their picturesque land provided a striking contrast to the immediate post-war austerity of England. Such glimpses from the past illustrate how rapid were the changes that had begun, by the turn of the second half of the twentieth century, to shape the future course of mountaineering.

Recalling alpine delights of yesteryear poses the question whether they have been replaced by something better. The answer depends upon the individual point of view: which, in turn, revolves around the question why people climb mountains. For many climbing is a form of recreation, a physically and morally challenging experience yielding uniquely personal rewards. For some it is an egocentric exercise in risk-taking, involving a deliberate attempt to tread on the edge of perceived limits. For others it is a sporting activity; although 'sport' is currently regarded as a means of acquiring recognition and reward, with an increasing number seeking to turn the hobby into a profession. Since it is now possible to indulge in the activity more easily and with increased security thanks to advances in equipment, mechanical facilities and rescue services, there has been an enormous expansion in various forms of mountain activity. The transformation of popular regions following increasing exploitation of natural resources, has created a variety of problems. How does one reconcile conflicting interests? There are no simple solutions to mutually exclusive objectives such as protection of the environment, and expansion of resorts, especially when the latter is backed by strong economic incentives.

Long ago, when the Alps first cast their spell, personal satisfaction seemed a sufficient reward for those who reached the summits of the great peaks by routes which are now often regarded as dull. They faced up to the challenges, and they did their best. An uncovered secret loses some of its attraction, or lacks the same degree of interest. But the discoveries of a few often throw the field wide open to many, who may seek to repeat or enrich a particular experience. There are innovators and followers in every field: the latter carry forward the process of change by the introduction of different standards and practices. New horizons, mental and physical, are open to all who seek them. And who is to say whether the challenge faced by a disabled person attempting to walk or climb in the mountains demonstrates a lesser or greater degree of courage than that of an alpinist performing a star-turn. During the latter part of the twentieth century, scientific and technical advances combined with changing ideologies have altered our lives immeasurably. A surge of more open, arbitrary, and indulgent ideas has given birth to fundamental changes. Every form of sporting activity has been profoundly affected almost imperceptibly, through various stages, from condemnation yesterday to disapproval today to acceptance tomorrow. The common denominator for all mountaineers, representing the special quality of the sport, is the challenge, and the risks involved. John Hunt described the relationship between risk and safety as: 'the use of personal judgement in matching skill and experience against dangers of which you are fully aware.' He added: 'We seek an equation ... between ourselves and the mountain which, hopefully, will be marginally favourable to ourselves. It is in coolly measuring the width of that margin, sometimes reducible to a knife-edge, without pushing one's luck too far, that lies the fascination of our sport.' As President of the Alpine Club during its Centenary year in 1957, Hunt referred to the contrasting, even conflicting, attitudes relating to the new climbing trends, just then beginning to spread across the mountain world – the artificial techniques, acrobatics, speed, the urge to compete, the application of such words as 'attack' and 'conquest'. Also to 'the failure to preserve a free and objective spirit, and to distinguish the mountains in their entirety'.

Risking a charge of over-simplification, it seems almost possible to define, in broad terms, the categories into which the sport appears to have developed at the start of the twenty-first century.

'Mountaineers' are naturally attracted to mountains. They pursue an unremunerative (not, as some believe, useless) pastime for the sake of pleasure – whether adventurous, physical, moral, or spiritual – which springs from a love of mountains. Respecting the dominating force which the mountains represent, they measure their minds and skills against calculated risks, competing only against themselves. They are indifferent to the trappings of glory. A mountaineer descending from a successful ascent is aware that the mountain he has been privileged to climb is never 'conquered'; his reward is the satisfaction of having overcome a personal challenge in a magnificent environment. 'Climbers' (or alpinists) approach mountains with bolder and more aggressive intentions. They are generally driven by a desire to test their skills to the limit. Equipped mentally, physically, technically and materially to meet extreme conditions, they take comfort from the knowledge that in an absolute emergency a rescue can be counted upon. Driven by the search for a personal limit to risk-exposure, their dedication to the sport is total; and public acclaim is often part of their reward. 'Performers' – who might have passed through one or other of the first two stages – fall into two groups. The first comprises alpinists motivated by a quest for spectacular deeds, record-breaking, and star-rating. Often dependent upon sponsorship, they are impelled to demonstrate exceptional performances. Reckoning that the end justifies the means, they are not troubled by any criticism that their methods might invite. Their commitment amounts to a way of life to the exclusion of all else.[1] Their courage and skill, well bolstered though their efforts might be, demand respect. Striding along a knife-edge, eternally driven by the need to boost their image, their chief danger is the creation of an illusive sense of power over forces more powerful than themselves. The second group of performers runs no such risks, and their pastime does not require the presence of mountains. They belong to a new generation devoted to storming man-made walls, which they ascend by means of a pre-ordained system demanding physical strength, acrobatic skills, daring, and suitable security

[1] The uninitiated might be forgiven for regarding some aspects of their activity as an exercise in masochism.

safeguards, exhibiting astonishing performances. Theirs is a competitive spectator sport, accompanied by prize-giving ceremonies, providing a strong athletic appeal to supple, youthful limbs. It is reported that there are close to five hundred climbing walls in Britain today. Wall climbing appears to be growing as a form of entertainment.[2] It does not follow that devotees of this sport acquire a taste for mountaineering, given the basic differences which distinguish the two activities – the one involving exposure to the unforgiving elements of nature, the other contact with contrived obstacles in a controlled environment. (Note 1)

There is, of course, another category which has been in existence since the dawn of tourism, encompassing those who with the benefit of expanding facilities are able to approach remote regions and undertake unimagined ventures in order to sample special thrills, or to leave their footprints in once-hallowed places. Today's staggering growth of tourism from its beginnings about a century and a half ago is hailed justifiably as a commercial success in many of the world's mountain regions and among some who live there. The positive side of current developments is strong, creating unmatched opportunities for greater numbers, especially the young, to appreciate and enjoy the mountains, to develop new skills, and to overcome unusual challenges, opening up an entirely new world of adventure and understanding.[3] Between January and July 2003 official figures published in Switzerland reveal that fifty deaths were recorded in the mountains against twenty-eight and twenty-seven deaths recorded in the same period during the two preceding years. This probably resulted from several factors: principally increased numbers, inexperience, inattention to the weather, also the exceptionally high summer temperatures which rendered several routes unusually dangerous. It cannot be denied that immoderate expansion of tourist facilities has a negative side, and could lead to permanent damage at the existing rate of exploitation. Voices have been gaining strength in recent years about the need for greater awareness and restraint, and the application of measures necessary for protection of the special quality of mountains.

[2] The SAC awarded their 2001 Cultural Prize to a team performing dances on a climbing wall to musical accompaniment.

[3] To quote one example, the *Naturfreunde Oesterreicher,* founded in 1895, the second largest Mountain Club in Austria with interests largely in tourism and trekking, has 150,000 members and owns 170 mountain huts.

There are high achievers who, having acquired at a relatively youthful age fame, fortune and the status of an *éminence grise,* appear to have transferred their enthusiasms to other fields, leaving one to wonder whether their mountain passion flows from a love of mountains, or of themselves? There are exceptions of another sort – and exceptional people. HW Tilman took up climbing at the age of thirty-two when he traversed Mount Kenya with Eric Shipton in 1930. His subsequent expeditions, mostly with Shipton, opened a new pioneering era in the Himalaya and Karakoram. After distinguishing himself during World War Two working secretly with resistance fighters in the mountains of Albania and Italy, he picked up the threads of his pre-war activities between 1947-50 with travels in Central Asia and Nepal, being almost the first foreigner to be granted permission for mountain exploration in the latter country, and the first to examine the southern approaches to Mount Everest. Crossing the rubicon of his fiftieth year, he came regretfully to the conclusion that his physical capacity for mountaineering had seriously diminished ('start slowly and slow down as you go along', he remarked wryly). His adventurous spirit found new challenges, which became a dominant driving force to the end of his life. Acquiring the first of three sailing boats, he skippered voyages to distant regions, usually with the goal of some moderate climb in remote mountain country. At sea he began to feel at home as he had always felt at home in the mountains, knowing how to adjust and to live in relative comfort in a harsh environment. During his final mountaineering years he had written: 'I felt uncommonly happy at trekking ... over a road and country new to me ... with the promise of [many] days ahead. I felt I could go on like this forever, that life had little better to offer than to march day after day in an unknown country to an unattainable goal.'

An early mountaineer, William Cecil Slingsby, who shared many daring ascents with Mummery (see Chapter 7), wrote: 'The high mountains are the natural playground of those who are endowed with health and strength ... All who are worthy of being termed mountaineers, in contra-distinction to climbing acrobats, find that year by year their love of mountains increases, and so too does their respect and veneration.'[4] The romantic age of mountaineering ended

---

[4]WC Slingsby is regarded as the father of mountaineering in Norway in the nineteenth century where his climbing career extended over forty years.

before the start of the twentieth century. Succeeding generations introduced fresh ideas designed to advance the achievements of their predecessors, seeking more challenging routes on the great peaks of the Alps, and searching for new mountains to climb beyond the Alps. The development of new techniques and safety practices led to a rapid advance in the quality of climbs that mountaineers felt competent to undertake. During the first decade of the twentieth century the practice of guideless climbing, which had been adopted by a few exceptional climbers twenty-five years earlier, was not general. It was felt that professional skill in a party was desirable if hard climbs were to be attempted. With the use of nailed boots, and largely without the use of mechanical aids, some remarkable climbs were achieved during the period before World War One. The south face of the Täschorn, first climbed in 1906, was regarded as a very hard climb by four leading Swiss climbers who made the second ascent thirty-seven years later using superior equipment. When GW Young climbed the Mer de Glace face of the Grépon with Josef Knubel in 1911, a route first attempted by AF Mummery with Alexander Burgener in 1880, he wrote: 'The hazard of the ascent ... removes the climb outside the class of those that can be justifiably, or even sanely, led by more than two or three men now living.'

Major advances took place during the twenty years between the end of World War One and the start of World War Two. It was an era that marked also the beginning of large nationally backed expeditions to the highest Himalayan peaks; seven went to Everest, four to K2, three to Kangchenjunga and five to Nanga Parbat. The development of new equipment, techniques, and increased skills led to the general adoption of guideless climbing in the Alps. Standards soared, and routes previously regarded as unassailable were climbed: the north face of the Matterhorn in 1931, the north face of the Dru and the Croz spur on the Grandes Jorasses in 1935, the north-east face of the Badile in 1937, and in 1938 the north face of the Eiger and the Walker spur, to name a few in the Alps, in addition to several exceptional ascents made in the Dolomites. What were the motives of the alpinists, principally French, Italian, German and Austrian, who achieved those ascents? The satisfaction of a personal challenge, certainly; a search for notoriety, perhaps; a competitive urge? The harsh words of EL Strutt, editor of the *Alpine Journal* during that period, although representing ideas of the 'old-school', carried a ring of truth. 'A wave of recklessness and folly is spreading through the Alps. The irrational desire and competition for new routes has degenerated into a mad striving for notoriety ... The new alpinist's ambition is to incur the maximum of danger ... Of rational pleasure, of interest, there is no question. It is a gamble of unadulterated danger from first to last.' An unfavourable aspect of that period, a symptom of social and national unrest, was the tendency of some groups to treat an attempt to climb a mountain as a death or glory struggle against the mountain, to be pursued 'until one or the other was vanquished'. In 1968 Anderl Heckmair, one of the four men who first climbed the north face of the Eiger, wrote: 'What does fame mean to climbing? The true climber seeks his fulfillment in the limitations set to him personally by the forces of Nature. Whether this fulfillment is found in walking amongst mountains or in conquering extreme routes, it is all the same in the end. With luck, climbing will never become a 'competitive' sport ... climbing is, and remains, a very egocentric and personal activity.' A lot has changed since that was written, and yet much remains fundamentally the same. The talented mountaineer Patrick Bérhault died tragically on 29 April 2004 at the age of forty-six shortly after commencing his descent from the summit of the Täschhorn. He and his companion Philippe Magnin had spent the previous sixty days climbing sixty-four Alpine peaks above 4000 metres. When asked, as a young man of twenty-five, why he climbed mountains he replied, 'I climb to achieve harmony of spirit, because it enables me to live every moment intensely, because it is a form in which I can express myself ethically and aesthetically, because I seek total freedom of body and mind. And because the sensation of movement provides me with intense joy.'

It struck me as strange to hear three leading Swiss climbers proclaim in 1947 that the 'last great problems' of the Alps, barring one or two, had been solved. On the Matterhorn, the Furggen ridge was climbed in 1941, but it was not until 1962 that a complete ascent of the west face of the mountain was achieved. The central Freney pillar on Mont Blanc was climbed in 1961, the west face of the Petit Dru in 1952 and its south-west pillar in 1955. When the French climber Pierre Allain, who with R Laininger climbed the north face of the Dru in 1935, he wrote about the west face: 'the perfect example of the impossible ... only supports fixed in the rock ... would be of any use (to the climber). But that would no longer be mountaineering, but construction work – for which everything is possible.' That forecast, made over sixty-five years ago, is a reality today for certain types of climbs where mechanical aids fixed to a mountain are used as the only means of ascending extreme routes. Walter Bonatti, who made a solitary ascent of the south-west pillar of the Dru in an epic five-day struggle in 1955, was as honest as anyone could be about his motives. He summarized his articles of faith during an era when traditional methods were still generally respected. 'Any climb ... must be above all a justification for living in the fantastic mountain world in order to experience the most intense feelings and sensations by *the conquest of nature* [my italics] and the sense of victory over oneself ... Someone had suggested that K2 had done for me. [Bonatti believed that he had been slighted and ignored on the successful 1954 Italian expedition] ... Then one day a mad idea occurred to me. I would return to the Dru and *conquer* it alone and prove to myself that I was not finished.'[5]

By 1960, in conformity with an evolutionary pattern that seems to re-emerge every couple of generations, significant changes had taken place in the climbing world; the 'old school' was replaced by a rising generation filled with ambitious ideas. The relentless search for harder ascents imposed the need for freer use of safety devices; higher climbing standards demanded the invention of new types of equipment. This marked the start of what was to develop into technical, or artificial, climbing, the sophistication of current climbs having advanced hand in hand with the sophistication of climbing equipment. Fundamental changes in ethical attitudes during the 1970s and 1980s arose from the urge to move the frontiers of possibility relentlessly forward. Alpinism has drifted towards the greater mountain ranges of the world from its traditional birthplace in the European Alps, the attractions of which have, to some extent, diminished for some leading climbers.

To dwell only upon controversial aspects of modern mountaineering would be to provide an unbalanced picture. There are many positive developments. Perhaps central to these is the introduction of the younger generation to the mountain world. Co-ordinated by the

---

[5]At the age of thirty-one, at the peak of a brilliant career Walter Bonatti, like Edward Whymper one hundred years earlier, virtually withdrew from serious mountaineering following a tragic expedition on Mont Blanc in 1961 which resulted in the deaths of four companions.

International Mountaineering and Climbing Federation, better known as the UIAA, and conducted under trained and dedicated leadership, group courses have been increasingly set in motion in several European countries, making it possible for young people to gain the required knowledge and understanding of mountains. There can be little doubt that the spirit of the pioneers is still alive when a mountaineer of our day feels able to express unaffectedly why he climbs. 'Perhaps the lure is the savage grandeur and beauty of snow-capped summits reaching to the sky. Mountains, like nothing else, throw out a challenge to our spirit of adventure.' That a keen pioneering spirit continues to guide the modern mountaineer is exemplified by a growing search for unexplored regions and unclimbed mountains.

The Himalayan Golden Age dawned in 1950 with the ascent of the first mountain above 8000m, and extended over the next fifteen years when all the main 8000m summits had been reached, including a number of important 7000m peaks. Of the fifty-six new ascents recorded in the Himalaya between 1907-57, over half were achieved after 1947. The methods adopted for practically all the early expeditions, which were often nationally sponsored, left as little as possible to chance. The ' seige ' attitude tended to be adopted as a general pattern, the publicity attracted by early successes acting as a spur for those who followed. With the dramatic expansion that began to take place by the mid 1980s, and has continued ever since, the time was ripe for the birth of commercial expeditions, boosted by every conceivable modern facility, human and material, including bottled oxygen, which brought in their wake a lowering of mountaineering practices. The present situation on Mount Everest recalls a remark made by Edward Whymper in 1874, on viewing the cairns and ropes placed on the north-east ridge of the Matterhorn, when he predicted correctly, 'soon the biggest duffers will be able to go up'. But it would be inaccurate to regard such a trend as universal. Small independent groups have shown that there still exists plenty of scope for mountaineering in less accessible places, where the dwindling bounty of a remote environment has been allowed to preserve its character.

In a polemic published in the *Alpine Journal* a few years ago, comparing the exploits of the pioneers with those of modern climbers, an opinion was expressed that: 'One era is no better than another ... the [climber's] business is the same.' A half-truth. And remarkable for its failure to recognise that those who spearheaded the opening period in the Alps, almost without exception, were amateurs engaging in an enjoyable pastime – 'unmixed play' to quote Mummery – while today notoriety and professional advancement are more likely to dominate the aspirations of their modern counterparts. In a complex modern society there appear to be few limits imposed by the demands of sponsorship. Fully equipped with the latest technology, the modern climber on his mountain perch in the Himalaya provides live broadcasts and interviews to distant lands, and communicates by e-mail from his portable lap-top, issuing digital images of the day's climb to be transmitted by satellite telephone. Half a century ago, Eric Shipton, reflecting on changing practices compared with his own efforts a couple of decades earlier, expressed the feelings of many. 'If we are wise we shall reflect with deep gratitude that we seized our mountaineering heritage, and will take pleasure in watching younger men enjoy theirs.'

Mountains possess an unusual power to attract and inspire; differences of degree in appreciation of their qualities, and of the passions that they arouse, are the main distinguishing factors between mountaineers, climbers and performers. Personal motivation derives from several different sources. The boldest exploits of some of today's high achievers might result from the search for a personal outlet, or simply 'to find a wild place where climbing is the most intense'. The hard men who seek the excitement of facing extreme risk and danger, do so as a means of satisfying themselves with some inner proof: an elusive craving that one of them has defined as a 'search for authenticity and identity'. Dorothy Pilley wisely observed: 'It is easy to raise plenty of unanswerable questions about any passion.'

Brief sketches drawn from a personal selection of a few mountaineers who achieved prominence during the second-half of the twentieth century, shed some light upon individual aspirations, revealing that despite different periods and circumstances the primary motives contain many common elements. Challenge, risk, and ambition provide the main incentives ever since mountains were recognised as regions of beauty and wonder over two hundred years ago.

Wilfrid Noyce fell to his death in 1962 at the age of forty-four when descending from the summit of Garmo peak (6030m) in the

Pamir. John Hunt said about him that to describe him: 'simply as a great mountaineer would present a quite incomplete impression of the man ... His true worth was in himself, as a person.' Mountains were the focal point of his life. As a schoolmaster teaching modern languages, he married at the age of thirty-three, raised a family, and was beginning to gain increasing distinction as a writer. Two serious accidents while rock-climbing in Britain (the degree of protection used at the time was minimal) had not diminished his mountain passion. He regarded the mountains as greater than the people who climb them, and his devotion took the form of a personal relationship. Like George Mallory he was a naturally talented climber, possessing exceptional stamina and endurance. He was reticent about his achievements never referring even by implication to his own share in any ascent. Accompanied by the Chamonix guide Armand Charlet in 1937, his first alpine climbs at the age of twenty included a traverse of the Aiguille Verte from the Charpoua glacier, the Mer de Glace face of the Grépon and the Route Moore on the Brenva face of Mont Blanc: the last two were both done in the remarkable times of three and a half hours. Twenty-two years later, guideless in 1959, he climbed the north face of the Dent d'Hérens, and made the fourth direct ascent of the Furggen ridge of the Matterhorn, reaching the summit after five hours of difficult climbing above the Shoulder. Posted to India during World War Two he spent short periods climbing in Garhwal and Kashmir. When I met him in Sikkim in 1945 after his ascent of Pauhunri (7127m) accompanied by Angtharkay, I was struck by his self-effacing manner, quiet assurance and personal charm. About his recent climb he spoke mostly of Angtharkay's skill and resolve. After his marriage in 1950 he seemed for a while to have settled comfortably, deriving simple enjoyment from introducing his pupils to British hills. When in 1952 he hesitantly accepted John Hunt's invitation to join the Everest expedition, it marked a turning point in his life. He proved to be one of the fittest climbers in the party, opening the route to the South Col with Annullu, his Sherpa companion. Hunt said of him later: 'Without doubt he could have reached the summit and I know, from a quiet uncomplaining word to me at Base Camp on May 8 after I had explained the plan for the assault, that he felt this, too. It was some comfort to us both that we were to have made a third attempt together, if such had been needed.'

Some of his best climbs followed. Apart from those which he made in the Alps in 1959 already mentioned, he went twice more to the greater ranges. In 1957 he and David Cox stopped about forty-five metres short of the top of the unclimbed Machapuchare in Nepal after a long and technically demanding climb. The mountain, regarded as sacred, has since been closed to climbing parties, and has not been (officially) attempted since. In 1960 he led a small party of six to an unnamed and unknown Karakoram peak of 7732m in the Distaghil Sar group. The final climb to the summit 660m above the top camp, which was placed in a crevasse, was both difficult and arduous occupying fourteen hours. In 1961 Wilfrid Noyce gave up teaching in order to devote his interests more fully to literature and mountains. He possessed a charismatic quality, both of character and intellect. He always insisted on walking over the tops at the end of a British rock climb. His tireless energy was often a source of encouragement to other members of an exhausted party at the end of a long day in the mountains. As a mountaineer his motives, in his own words, were: 'The mountain itself, action upon it, companionship, and an indefinable sense of greatness.'

When Peter Boardman took over in 1978 as director of the International School of Mountaineering in Leysin, Switzerland, his reputation as a mountaineer was already established; he had qualified as a guide the year before, and two years later became president of the British Association of Mountain Guides. His alpine climbing, which began in 1968 with a number of classic ascents, very soon spread to a wider field with expeditions to the Hindu Kush, Alaska, the Caucasus, the Polish Tatra and Kenya. He came into prominence at the age of twenty-four, after climbing Everest by its south-west face on Chris Bonington's 1975 expedition, when he waited for one and a half hours below the south summit with his companion Pertemba for Mick Burke, who made a conscious choice to attempt to reach the summit alone in the face of threatening weather, and failed to return. In 1976, he and Joe Tasker made their first joint ascent climbing the formidable 1380m West wall of Changabang, initially regarded by some as a 'preposterous idea'. The venture had been prepared with meticulous care, and the ascent was carried out under frugal and demanding conditions, vividly described in his book *The Shining Mountain*. Two brilliant climbs followed in 1979: the third ascent of Kangchenjunga, the first from the north, with Doug Scott and Joe

Tasker in May, and the first ascent of Gaurisanker's south summit in November by a lengthy and technically difficult ridge. Boardman was keen to add K2 to his list of ascents. Apart from the attempt on the west ridge in 1978 as a member of Bonington's party, he made a determined attempt in 1980 via the Abruzzi ridge, when he, Joe Tasker and Dick Renshaw were very lucky to survive an avalanche which fell during the night almost burying them in their bivouac high on the mountain. The ascent of Kongur in China followed in 1981. Whatever misgivings Peter Boardman might have felt about the long north-east ridge of Everest in 1982 – and he certainly had some – the attempt involving a small group of well-tried climbers appealed strongly to him because it offered such an immense challenge. Boardman was no idealist or dreamer, and his joy at facing a mighty objective in a thrilling arena was tempered by feelings of uncertainty about the outcome. He was a lover of life; his work as a climbing instructor in Leysin gave him deep satisfaction, he was happily married, he was full of future plans, and he had taken up writing, for which he had shown a particular talent – his second book appeared posthumously. On Everest in 1982 he was a skilled mountaineer who took nothing for granted, and would not have embarked on anything without carefully weighing the risks. When Joe Tasker, his regular climbing companion for six years, and he failed to return, his wife Hilary resolutely refused to accept that he was the victim of an accident. Ten years later, she was proved right. His body was found high on the upper part of the ridge, seated as though he had fallen asleep. At the age of fifteen, walking and scrambling over Corsican hills, Peter Boardman expressed for the first time what was to become his lifelong passion for 'the freedom of moving, lightweight, through mountain country carrying shelter, warmth, food, and fuel on my back'. He possessed human warmth, and the boyish gift of an elfin-like charm. The mountains he not only loved, but also respected. He belonged to the 'modern' generation, but he was a mountaineer in the classic mould. Once he had fixed an objective he took immense trouble to learn everything about it from those who had preceded him, acknowledging the value of their pioneering efforts. Driven by ambition, he was well aware that the force which impelled him forward had directed his life along a dangerous course. It was not his desire to throw away the life he loved so deeply, not even in a hero's death. He accepted the rewards gratefully; his card to me from Kathmandu, after Kangchenjunga, said simply, 'Doug, Joe and I stood just below the top at 5pm on 16 May to watch the sun descending ... a beautiful unspoilt area, altogether a very satisfying expedition.' Early in March 1982, the day before his departure from Leysin, he and his wife Hilary came to see us in Lausanne. There seemed something uncharacteristic about his detached mood; and when we wished him goodbye I could not suppress a strange feeling that perhaps I might never see him again. He was thirty-one, and in the prime of life.

It seems inconceivable that so many leading climbers with brilliant records have died in the mountains. There appears often to be a degree of similarity in the circumstances. The Himalaya, where major objectives invite major risks, have provided the scene for many tragedies. Perhaps excessive reliance is placed on the efficiency of modern equipment; or perhaps luck, which seems so constant, simply runs out. It is not the way of experienced climbers to devalue the mountains; but in rare cases personal skills have perhaps been overestimated. One thinks of Hermann Buhl on Chogolisa in 1957 who, when descending a ridge obscured by cloud, stepped to his death through a large cornice which he could not have failed to observe on his ascent of the same ridge only a few hours earlier. Dougal Haston, regarded as one of the top alpinists of his generation, died at the age of thirty-seven while skiing off-*piste* on a steep slope above Leysin in Switzerland in the winter of 1977. Undertaking a challenge that he had set himself on that particular slope, he was clearly aware of the risks, and would not have treated them lightly. The slope – posted with a danger warning – avalanched, burying him under waves of powder snow. Uncannily, he enacted in real life the precise rôle that he had created for the hero in his semi-biographical novel completed just prior to his death. In the book, *Calculated Risk* published in 1979, his hero survived the avalanche.

Pierre Beghin, attempting with J-C Lafaille a new route on the south face of Annapurna in 1992, was killed when a protective anchor pulled out. Beghin was motivated, in his words, by '*ma passion d'alpinisme*'. Personal challenge was the source of his passion, unalloyed with any desire for notoriety or commercial gain. He had a deep respect for the power of the mountains, and he measured carefully the risks involved in every new venture. He was not a professional mountaineer but a practising engineer, specialised in the mechanics of snow and avalanches, working with the Civil Research Institute at Grenoble; also a technical adviser on mountain equipment, and author of three mountain books. He had an extensive record of hard alpine climbs. In 1977, at the age of twenty-six, he made the first winter ascent of the Bonatti direct route on the Grandes Jorasses. On his first visit to the Himalaya in 1980, the only one that he made as a member of a large expedition, he reached the top of the south-west pillar of Dhaulagiri at 7500m. On subsequent visits Beghin sought out pioneering ventures, often with a single companion. His primary interest was to climb alpine-style, and by 'fair' means, avoiding the use of aids. He was deeply disturbed by the harm being inflicted upon the environment – the final chapter of his last book is wholly devoted to a general plea for care and restraint. Personal publicity and involvement with the media were alien to his creed. He was a dedicated mountaineer in the purest sense. Although driven by the desire to overcome a challenge, he had the strength of will to turn back when the odds were clearly against him. His ascents of six 8000m mountains included the west face of Manaslu with B Muller in 1981, the south pillar of Dhaulagiri (Japanese route) with JN Roche in 1984, the north side of Jannu (Japanese route) in 1987. Among his finest climbs were a true solo ascent (in four days) of the south-west face of Kangchenjunga in 1983, and the four-and-a-half day solo traverse of Makalu in October 1989, ascending the south-west face and descending the north-west face, on which he was lucky to survive two avalanches. About the latter climb he wrote: 'In this venture I have experienced the hardest and most uncertain of my mountaineering adventures. There will be other climbs, but nothing that I undertake will be quite the same.' For his last great climb in 1991 he teamed up with Christophe Profit who, although of a different temperament,[6] was an ideal climbing partner during a five-day ascent of extreme exposure under difficult conditions on K2. They climbed the north-west ridge, placing a bivouac at 7950m above its junction with the north face. Starting from there at 7am on 15 August and traversing across the massive face of K2 on avalanche-

---

[6]In 1985 he climbed three difficult alpine north faces in twenty-four hours with wide media publicity.

prone slopes, they exited via a steep couloir on to the north-east ridge which led them to the summit at 6.50pm. Five years had passed since the last climbers had stood there. In gathering darkness, with the temperature estimated at –30°C, they began a dangerous and painful descent, reaching their bivouac at 11.30pm where they spent the next three hours trying to save fingers and toes from frostbite. On returning to their Savoia glacier Base they found that each had lost about 8kg in body-weight. Profit, climbing his first 8000m mountain, confessed that he was more exhausted than he had been four years earlier after his winter ascents of three north faces in twenty-four hours. I read with amazement and deep interest the objective and unaffected handwritten account which Pierre Beghin sent to me describing the climb. He possessed great personal charm; his quiet, gentle manner concealed the inner fires which drove him ever forward to seek the challenging ventures which he craved in order to engage his spirit and his skills.

When Wanda Rutkiewicz died on the north face of Kangchenjunga in May 1992 at the age of forty-nine, she was described by close climbing friends as the greatest ever female Himalayan climber. The claim is not exaggerated, and her record remains unsurpassed. Her climbing career among the world's great peaks began in 1975 when, as a member of an Anglo-Polish expedition, she climbed Gasherbrum III (7952m), then the highest unclimbed summit, on which Riccardo Cassin had carried out a reconnaissance in 1958. During the next seventeen years she was involved in twenty-two separate ventures in the Himalaya and Karakoram, climbing eight of the fourteen 8000m mountains. One year before her death she stated that it was her intention to climb the remaining six in a 'caravan to dreams' planning to attempt each summit in succession, while her body was acclimatised to the previous one. A very ambitious scheme demanding immense mental and physical powers, but overlooking the fact that no amount of willpower is able to overcome the body's inability to breach its physiological limits. She made the first complete female ascent of K2 in 1986 (a year of multiple disasters on that mountain), and she was the first woman to climb the British south-face route on Annapurna I in 1991, reaching the summit alone; earlier that year she had climbed Cho Oyu. In 1978 she made the first ascent of Everest by a European woman. She climbed Nanga Parbat in 1985, Shishapangma in 1987, Gasherbrum II in 1989, and Gasherbrum I in

1990. She was a totally dedicated climber, making ascents in Norway, North and South America, the Pamir, and Hindu Kush. Some of her alpine ascents stressed her enterprise for high achievement: the Mer de Glace face of the Grépon at the age of twenty-four, the north pillar of the Eiger by Messner's route, the first woman's ascent of the north face of the Matterhorn in winter. Courage, an immense determination, and great powers of endurance helped to fuel her ambitions. Her natural skills and strength had developed early among her home mountains in the High Tatra, where she climbed regularly in summer and winter. She possessed a creative and energetic personality, made several mountain films, and was an interesting lecturer. Her complete attachment to the world of mountains limited her private life. Although twice married and divorced, she had no children; nor did she devote a serious interest to her profession, although she had obtained a degree in science and engineering at Warsaw. Meeting her at a Convention in Pakistan, I sought her views about the tendency of a few climbers on high peaks to push limits excessively, heedless of weather signs, personal fitness or reserves. She stated her creed simply and unequivocally: strive for the highest objective, and pursue the challenge to the absolute limit. Her single-mindedness was striking, as was her resolute optimism over the powers of the mind and body to overcome factors which stretch beyond their limits. Wanda Rutkiewicz was last seen by her team-mate Carlos Carsolio on his descent alone of Kangchenjunga's north face at around 8pm on 12 May 1992. She was seated inside a snow shelter at about 8250m, her bivouac-sack wrapped around her body, having started from the top camp at 7900m that morning with one litre of water, but without sleeping bag, stove, fuel, or food. Her rate of ascent had obviously been slow, and she looked tired. She said that she was cold, but intended to try for the summit the next day. Under a clear sky and in freezing temperatures she made a calculated decision to stay where she was, approximately 350m below the summit. Long years of experience must have forewarned her of the dangers inherent in her situation. Buoyed by the strength of her ambitions, and with faith in her personal resolve, one cannot imagine it as likely that she would have acted otherwise.

Fame is something that Erhard Loretan has never sought. He has chosen to preserve the freedom to plan his ventures with the minimum of fuss and publicity, and without the pressures of sponsorship. He believes that mountaineering is uniquely different from competitive sports, being driven by a love of mountains and the will to master a personal challenge. During an exceptional thirty-year career in the Alps, Himalaya, and elsewhere, he has provided practical proof of the integrity of his beliefs. He retains a special devotion for the Gastlosen, a striking group of limestone mountains in Fribourg, Switzerland, in whose shadow he grew up, where he began to climb at the age of eleven, establishing his first new route at the age of sixteen, and which became for him 'an arena of anguish and of glory ... from my chalet I always have them in view; in my absences I long to see them again'. Apprenticed to a carpenter, and acting as a part-time warden at the Fründen Hut, it became his ambition to qualify as a mountain guide, which he did in 1981. At the age of twenty-one he set out with two friends in 1980 for the Peruvian Andes where five summits above 6000m were reached, two of them by new routes. Loretan's association with the Himalaya began in 1982 as a member of the Swiss expedition to Nanga Parbat when he reached the summit from the Diamir side without the use of bottled oxygen, and discovered that his performance was practically unaffected at high altitudes. He returned every year to the region for the next thirteen years, learning to distinguish 'the narrow boundary between courage and inadvertence', and developing, despite a small and light body, exceptional stamina and strength. Some important successes were achieved – three 8000m peaks in fifteen days between 16 to 30 June 1983, three of Annapurna's summits along its 7.5 km-long east ridge, and descent by the north face, between 22-26 October 1984, a three-day ascent of K2's Abruzzi ridge in 1985, and the direct ascent and descent of Everest's 2500m north face in forty-three hours in 1986. There were also a few 'failures', but Loretan never sacrificed the simplicity of his style nor his ethical standards. When his 1990 ascent of Shishapangma ended on the lower central summit, he returned five years later to climb solo to the main summit (8046m) in a round trip of twenty-six hours. With his ascent of Kangchenjunga in 1995 he became the third climber to reach the world's fourteen highest summits. That had not been a focussed objective; other daring projects had intervened. For Loretan, a clear perception of the critical point at which to turn back is when the weight of experience really counts. There is no mystery about Loretan's high-altitude achievements. Based on extraordinary stamina and skill, he has adopted an ultra-lightweight technique combined with astonishing speed, enabling him to minimise the time spent at extreme altitudes. He has followed the same well-tried principles for his alpine winter ascents of thirty-eight major summits in nineteen days in February 1986, and thirteen north faces in thirteen days in January 1989; also for two brilliant solo ascents of unclimbed peaks in Antarctica in 1994-95. Loretan attributes his success to his physical and mental capacity, technical ability, choosing the right conditions – and luck. With his unpretentious manner Loretan believes that a mountaineer's deepest satisfaction derives from overcoming a personal challenge in good style. An attitude of respect, founded on a genuine passion for mountains, appears today to have been largely replaced by a quest for heroics. It is this, Loretan believes, that is one of the saddest aspects of modern alpinism. When guiding a client, he is constantly on high alert, aware that a minor error could have fatal consequences; and his greatest reward as a guide is to share his companion's joy in achieving an otherwise unattainable goal. In recent years, he has been sponsoring and accompanying free camping holidays in the mountains for deprived young people. Loretan follows his chosen course with full awareness of the perils and penalties. 'I have never questioned the validity of my passion, nor for a moment have I ever considered giving it up ... I have no wish to lose my life, but the manner of my death troubles me more than the prospect of death itself.' He regards as his most sublime experience the 'magical' hour-and-a-half that he and his companion Jean Troillet spent undisturbed, in flawless weather, on the summit of Everest after ascending its north face in 1986. During the 1987 Mountain Film Festival at Diablerets I was seated at the back of the hall watching the film portraying that ascent, when I noticed a hesitant figure standing at the entrance door. It was Erhard Loretan. Beckoning him into an empty seat alongside mine, I became aware of the real meaning of humility.

In the stillness of a spring morning, as I write, I look out across the garden, beyond the flowering trees, to a horizon filled with a line of glistening mountains stretching from Mont Blanc to the Bernese alps – which re-awakens the spell, and arouses memories of earlier challenges and delights. Whatever might be the future of mountaineering it is to be hoped that certain essentials will remain. Such as the first spellbound moment of a youthful spirit stepping across the threshold into an awareness of the mountain world, and the birth of a desire to preserve what it has discovered.

NOTES TO CHAPTERS

NOTE

1   Current scientific theories link evidence of global warming to emission of CO_2 gases by a heavily industrialised world. Without invalidating these conclusions it would not be unreasonable to question whether the adoption of means to prevent the process would be meaningful. Historical evidence of the earth's potential for climatic change is provided by the existence of a warmer climate during past centuries followed by a Little Ice Age. According to the Glacier Monitoring Service of the Swiss Academy for Natural Sciences in Zürich, 2244 Swiss glaciers were originally recorded in 1850, of which 249 (over 11%) have disappeared during the past 150 years. Satellite measurements of the overall glaciated surface of the Swiss Alps have revealed a loss of 20% during the period 1985-2000. In 2003, resulting from exceptionally high summer temperatures and lack of precipitation, measurements taken on the Trifit glacier have revealed a shrinkage of 150m, while the Turtmann, Breney, Otemma and Rhône glaciers have lost over 100m each. Not a single advance was observed. The degeneration of glaciers worldwide provides factual evidence that global warming probably began much earlier than is generally supposed, as part of a familiar pattern of global climatic change.

2   Comments, with some differences, that are still appropriate.

3   *Die Alpen*, first published in 1732, was inspired by his earliest excursion into the Alps in 1728. Eleven authorised editions of his poem appeared in Haller's lifetime and quite a few more afterwards. *Die Alpen* has been described as a didactic poem with an ideological framework. It is an idyll of rural tranquillity and simplicity, conveying an idealised picture of the beauty of the Alps, and the untroubled lives of its inhabitants. This theme created an immediate impact, revealing the Alps in quite a different light from its unpopular image as a bleak and harsh region that inspired fear. The work revealed Haller as the first major Swiss poet, who took an artistic delight in the beauty of the alpine world. It was translated into English, French, Italian and Latin, and was read all over Europe, encouraging artists and writers to visit the frugal paradise of the Alps. In a sense, Haller's poem heralded the birth of tourism in Switzerland, which began to expand dramatically a hundred years later.

4   Typical of the hardy men encountered by de Saussure in the upper alpine
     valleys was a young Savoyard hunter who told him: '*Mon grand-père est
     mort à la chasse, mon père y est mort, je suis si persuadé que j'y mourrai, que ce sac
     que vous voyez, Monsieur, et que j'emporte à la chasse, je l'appele mon drap
     mortuaire, parce que je suis sûr que je n'en aurai jamais d'autre, et pourtant si vous
     m'offriez de faire ma fortune à condition de renoncer à la chasse au chamois, je n'y
     renoncerais pas.*' (My grand-father died hunting, and so did my father. I am
     certain that I shall follow their example, and I regard this hunter's bag
     which I carry as the only coverlet that I shall have when I die. Yet, if you
     were to offer me a prosperous future provided I gave up hunting chamois
     I would not do so.) Passionate sentiments from a young hunter, whose
     prophecy was fulfilled – De Saussure learnt two years later that he had
     died in a fall from a cliff.

5   To Michel-Gabriel Paccard (1757-1827), village doctor of Chamonix,
     goes the credit of founding the spirit of mountaineering. After three years'
     careful study and exploration of a possible ascent route on Mont Blanc he
     became, at the age of twenty-nine, the first person to reach the summit
     late in the evening on 8 August 1786, displaying great courage in spite of
     reluctance by his companion during the final hours of the climb. He
     returned to Chamonix the next morning snow-blind and exhausted after
     a night's open bivouac. Paccard was driven by a sense of adventure, an
     eagerness to examine his physical reactions at unexplored heights, and a
     desire to take barometric readings from the top of the mighty mountain
     whose altitude had not yet been accurately determined. Accompanying
     him as a porter was Jacques Balmat aged about twenty-three, a crystal
     hunter from Les Pèlerins. The latter, on returning, lost little time in
     travelling to Geneva to collect the monetary award offered by de Saussure.
     A Geneva painter and writer Marc-Théodore Bourrit, frustrated in his
     own ambition to be the first to climb the mountain and blinded by
     jealousy, launched a deceitful campaign to discredit Dr Paccard, attributing
     wholly to Balmat the successful outcome of their ascent. De Saussure,
     who called to see Dr Paccard shortly after his ascent, and learnt from him
     the full story of the climb, could with his authority have stifled the false
     stories from the beginning, but he did not choose to do so, perhaps
     regarding the village doctor as a rival, because of Paccard's scientific
     probings resulting from his ascent. Bourrit's fable gained respectability and
     wider publicity following an account published by the French writer
     Alexandre Dumas in his book *Impressions de voyage en Suisse*. Dumas met
     Balmat, then aged about seventy, at Chamonix in 1832. At Dumas' request
     Balmat, well fortified with wine, expounded a tale laced with myth and
     fancy about his ascent with Dr Paccard forty-six years earlier.
     Astonishingly, over 170 years were to pass before complete and authentic
     details of Dr Paccard's ascent became generally known after painstaking
     research by Sir Gavin de Beer and Professor Thomas Graham Brown of
     early documents, including Dr Paccard's original notebook now held in
     the Alpine Club's archives. Their book *The First Ascent of Mont Blanc* was
     published in 1957, the centenary year of the Alpine Club London.

6   Edward Theodore Compton (1849-1921) belonged to a later period. Born in Stoke Newington, he died in the Carinthian Alps where he made his home during the last forty-seven years of his life. Known equally as a mountaineer and painter, his large output of mountain paintings in oils and watercolours captured with great clarity and perception the majesty of Alpine peaks and glaciers. His climbing companions were Karl Blodig, the first climber to ascend all the 4000m peaks of the Alps; also Ludwig Purtscheller and Emil Zsigmondy. A mountain hut in Carinthia has been named after him.

7   The height of the Niton stone, measured as 376.64m above sea-level, was used as a point of reference when the Bureau Topographique was set up in Geneva in 1838, and was adopted as a universal standard for calculation of all heights shown on the first official maps of Switzerland.

8   Professor Forbes has left a picture of the days when giant glaciers touched the lives of valley dwellers. 'An advancing glacier presses forward into the lower valleys, turning up the soil, and wrinkles the grass of the meadows like a tremendous ploughshare, bringing among the fields a wintry blast, overthrowing trees and stubble in its progress ... [peasants have seen] the full ears of corn touching the glacier ... [and have] gathered ripe cherries from the tree with one foot standing on the ice.'

9   In the final chapter of his book Viollet-le-Duc wrote: 'Nature is uncompromising in obedience to its laws. It does not restore the slope or the boulder that the traveller's foot has sent tumbling into the depths; it does not re-sow the forest that in our imprudence we have cut down, exposing bare rock and unprotected soil to be swept away by streams arising from rainfall and snow-melt; nor does it restore the lushness of the meadows whose disappearance we have caused by our improvidence. By your failure to understand the faultless logic of Nature's laws, you set in motion the destruction of that which you should conserve. So much the worse for the human race! Don't complain, therefore, if floods cause havoc in your valleys, or demolish your towns; and don't attribute such disasters to the warnings or vengeance of Providence. They are to a very large extent the result of your own ignorance, arrogance, and vanity.' The thoughtless expansion of tourist facilities often seen in the mountains, in defiance of perceived knowledge, is the work of short-term 'maximisers' who prefer to ignore long-term consequences.

10   During the politico-religious war of the Sonderbunds in 1845, General Dufour, appointed as leader of twelve Confederate cantons, led his troops to victory in a decisive battle at Fribourg on 14 November against seven Catholic cantons. The aftermath of that war led to Switzerland's final release from foreign tutelage and to its complete National Independence. In 1848 the country established its first Federal Constitution, and its status as an Independent Federal State was internationally recognised

based upon a policy of neutrality. In 1863 General Dufour was appointed chairman of a meeting in Geneva of international experts, which led to the establishment in 1864 of the International Red Cross.

11   John Auldjo (1805-86) made the 19th ascent, the first Scottish ascent, of Mont Blanc on 9 August 1827 accompanied by Jean-Marie Couttet, Julien Devouassoud and four other guides. The following year he published a book *Narrative of an Ascent to the Summit of Mont Blanc* containing eight graphic sketches of the climb. Three editions of the book were sold out which provided an important influence during the years preceding the birth of mountaineering as a sport. In a rambling hand he wrote a letter to his sister from the summit of the mountain, reportedly on the back of one of his guides: 'You can judge of the gratification I have in being above the habitable world - a thing I'v (sic) much desired'. The letter, originally presented to the Alpine Club London, is now held in the Geneva State archives. Auldjo was a skilled artist; he travelled widely in Italy, Spain and Greece before settling in Geneva in 1865. In 1870 he was appointed British Consul in Geneva where he lived until his death, and was a popular figure among the then small English community.

12   Puiseaux made the first ascent, also in 1848, of Mont Pelvoux, completing the last part of the climb alone. He was one of the first to start guideless climbing; and, with his son Pierre, also a notable climber, was among the founders of the Club Alpin Français.

13   The ascent of the Dufourspitze was a major achievement at the start of the Golden Age.

14   Some of his climbs are described in his book *Nouvelles Excursions dans les Alpes,* published in Neuchâtel in 1845.

15   The Rosenhorn was the subject of a study in 1997 by a Committee in Grindelwald for a scheme to set up on its summit a cable-car station and a panoramic restaurant, with a number of tele-ski facilities situated on the plateau above the Upper Grindelwald glacier. These environmentally insensitive plans for the exploitation of a relatively unspoilt and unique region of the Bernese Alps apparently received local support, but were condemned in Switzerland by the Alpine Club and Mountain Wilderness. The plans were invalidated when, in December 2001, UNESCO designated the Jungfrau-Aletschhorn-Bietschhorn region as an International Area of Natural Protection.

16   The ascent of Piz Bernina in 1850 by Coaz then aged twenty-eight with two local guides was an important achievement. A start was made at 6am from the Berninahaus, an inn situated at 2046m below the Morteratsch Glacier, and the summit was reached twelve hours later; the descent was made in darkness, the expedition having taken twenty hours. The

extensive pioneering work carried out by Coaz in the region is commemorated by a memorial plaque raised below the Boval hut in 1922 on the centenary of his birth. During 1850-51 Coaz acted as private secretary to General Henri Dufour. As Federal Chief Insepctor of Forests 1875-1914 Coaz was occupied with conservation of forests, protection of bird and wild life, and in devising safety measures against avalanches.

17 By 1880 the Matterhorn had been climbed 159 times: 132 ascents were made from the Swiss side and 27 from Italy. A direct ascent of the last of the four major ridges of the Matterhorn, the Furggen, was achieved in 1941 by Luigi Carrel with Enzo Perino and Giacomo Chiara.

18 A Swiss writer has described the whole period as the 'unveiling of the Alps'. Arnold Lunn in his book *A Century of Mountaineering* (1957) refers to the second phase as the Alpine Silver Age.

19 On 19 August 1890, Jean-Joseph Maquignaz, with his client the young Count Umberto di Villanova and the guide A. Castagneri, disappeared, it is assumed between the Dôme du Gôuter and the Aiguille de Bionnassay, during two days and nights of tempestuous weather on Mont Blanc. With Jean-Antoine Carrel's death at the foot of the Matterhorn on 26 August 1890, the Valtournanche lost, within one week, two of its greatest guides.

20 Valedictory address, 1970, by Sir Charles Evans, President, Alpine Club London.

CHAPTER TWO: ALFRED WILLS

1 Obituary notice by Arthur Milman, published in the *Alpine Journal*, Volume 27, 1912.

2 A description by de Saussure in *Voyages dans les Alpes* of his visit from Montenvers to the *jardin de Talèfre* in the eighteenth century illustrates the methods used then, as now, to ease the passage of mountain travellers. '*Les deux premières fois que j'ai passé là, on ne pouvoit placer son pied que sur quelques inégalitiés du roc; et si l'on avoit glissé, on seroit tombé dans le glacier qui est au-dessous à une assez grande profondeur. Mais en 1778 dès mon arrivé à Chamouni j'y envoyai deux hommes qui firent jouer quelques mines dans le roc et rendirent ce passage sinon très commode, au moins à peu près sans danger.*' (On my first two visits it was barely possible to obtain a footing on the uneven rocky surface, and a slip would have resulted in a fall to the glacier at a great depth below. In 1778 on arriving at Chamonix I sent two men ahead who, by blasting the rocky slopes, were able to render the route if not exactly pleasant, at least almost free from danger.)

3   Between 1865-66 a research station and living quarters were built on the Théodule pass where meteorological and glaciological observations were made by the French scientist Daniel Dollfus-Ausset, who financed the cost of construction and carried out the scientific work. He recorded the results in *L'Etude des Glaciers* published in Paris between 1863-70 in eight volumes. Today, the Théodule pass at 3317m forms the centre of a major ski-complex conducted jointly by Switzerland and Italy. One feels that Wills' old philosopher might have been dismayed rather than gratified by the scale of development at his chosen niche in the heart of the high Alps.

4   Earlier types of crampon, also known as 'Cramp Irons', comprised a four-pronged iron frame strapped to the instep or heel of the boot. Reference to a primitive type of crampon has been found in records as long ago as 1128, when the soles of boots were 'armed with iron spikes on account of the slipperiness of the ice'.

5   Of the two other peaks in the Wetterhörner, the Mittelhorn (3704m), highest of the group, was first climbed on 8 July 1845 by a Scottish medical student Stanhope Speer accompanied by K Abplanalp, J Jaun and J Michel. The Rosenhorn (3689m) was first climbed by E Désor on 28 August 1844. Both ascents were made from the Grimsel side. According to T Graham Brown, editor of the *Alpine Journal* (1949-53), Speer, who made the first ascent of the Mittelhorn in 1845: 'probably played a greater part in the beginnings of mountaineering as a sport than the part usually attributed to Sir Alfred Wills' ascent of the Hasli Jungfrau [sic] peak from Grindelwald in 1854. Speer's narrative received immediate and wide publicity. ... Wills brought in early recruits to the young sport; Speer's service was to prepare the way for the sport itself.' (*Alpine Journal* Volume 59, 1953)

6   In 1936 when Paul Bauer on his third visit to the Himalaya climbed Siniolchu he wrote: 'That we had reached the summit seemed a divine favour – our struggles on the slopes only deepened our reverence for God's creation.' (*Kanchenjunga Challenge*, 1955) In 1995 a young Swiss climber, reaching her first 4000m alpine summit, wrote: '*C'est bien vrai, j'y suis, je me trouve à 4274m. Je cache à peine mes larmes d'emotion face au paysage qui s'offre à moi.*' *(Bulletin Mensuel*, SAC, Section Diablerets) (It is true. I am really standing at 4274m. The spectacle moves me so deeply that I am unable to hold back my tears.)

7   Rudimentary roping practices of the period seem to have included conflicting views among guides about the use of the rope when descending; some regarding it as necessary – see chapters on Tyndall and Whymper – and others as suicidal in the event of a slip.

8   Her son, Lieutenant General Edward Felix Norton, leader of the 1924 expedition to Mount Everest was the first man to climb to 8570m across

treacherous snow-covered slabs on the north-east face of the mountain, solo and without bottled oxygen. He died in 1954, having won many distinctions during his army career.

CHAPTER THREE: JOHN TYNDALL

1   Forbes' portrait reproduced in this book, painted by Sir J Watson Gordon in 1860, was commissioned by the Royal Society of Edinburgh. His biographers wrote that when it was painted: 'he felt strongly the frail hold he had on life, and whatever his hand found to do he set himself to do it with all his might.' The Society commented: 'When we look at the portrait we see only the embers of that fire which blazed so brightly in Forbes when, as a younger scientist and athletic mountaineer, he had revelled in meeting the physical and intellectual challenges presented by his beloved Alps.'

2   *Life and Letters of James David Forbes* by John Campbell Shairp, Reverend Peter Guthrie Tait and Anthony Adams-Reilly, 1873.

3   *Principal Forbes and his Biographers* by John Tyndall, 1873.

4   Introduction by Sir John Lubbock (later Lord Avebury) to 1906 edition of *The Glaciers of the Alps* by John Tyndall.

5   A donation of four guineas, provided by an English traveller Charles Blair of Dorsetshire specifically for the purpose, saw the construction in 1779 of a small shelter at Montenvers, which bore the dignified inscription Chateau Blair, and was referred to by the local peasantry as *Chateau de Folie* (freely translated as the Madhatter's Castle). Built with the superb Chamonix granite it lasted for thirty-three years and was used by de Saussure among others.

6   An iron constitution was not one of Tyndall's natural gifts. He was a lifelong martyr to insomnia and dyspepsia, making his evident toughness and stamina seem all the more remarkable.

7   The chapter on Edward Whymper contains an account of the discussions held in Breuil between Tyndall and Whymper about a possible merger of forces. The incident was omitted from the first edition, but added to the second edition, of Tyndall's book *Hours of exercise in the Alps*. It was not mentioned in Whymper's *Scrambles*.

8   *The Matterhorn*, by Guido Rey, 1946. Guido Rey's book *Il Monte Cervino* (Milano 1904) was published in English in 1907 under the title *The Matterhorn*. Rey, a nephew of Quintino Sella, was a passionate lover of mountains and a keen mountaineer. He was intimately familiar with the

Matterhorn and was the first person, after AF Mummery in 1880, to attempt the forbidding Furggen Ridge. After three failures, he set out from Breuil in 1899 with three guides, Daniel, Antoine and Aime Maquignaz, one of whom climbed to the summit by the normal (Italian) route and threw down a long rope over the final overhang as far as the highest point reached on the Furggen Ridge previously, enabling Rey and his two other guides to overcome the final section to the top. The first unaided ascent of the Furggen ridge was made in 1941 by 3 Italian climbers.

9   On 13 September 1867 the brothers Maquignaz opened a new route up the final head-wall of the Matterhorn, making the third ascent from Breuil and the first wholly on the Italian side of the mountain. On 2 October of that year they guided WL Jordan up their new route to the summit, then traversed a short distance down the Swiss side to the approximate place of the 1865 accident (a point which Jordan had reached from the Swiss side about two weeks earlier with Jean-Marie Lochmatter and Peter Knubel) before returning to the summit and descending to Breuil.

10   The Reverend Julius Elliott aged twenty-seven was killed the following year by an act of folly during an attempt on the Schreckhorn when he refused the offer of a rope from his guide Franz Biner. He had acquired a reputation for boldness during four alpine seasons, ascending several 4000m mountains accompanied by Biner. He tended to spurn advice from his guides, and to adopt an over-confident attitude, bordering on arrogance, about his own skills. Had he followed Biner's advice and roped up on reaching the final ridge of the Schreckhorn, his single mis-step might not have resulted in a fatal fall 400m down the north-east face.

11   In 1866 Felice Giordano spent six nights on the Matterhorn in a tent at 3500m during a spell of bad weather with J-A Carrel, J-B Bich, and J-A Meynet. He made barometric observations, and studied the possibility of setting up a hut, which a year later was placed at the *Cravate*. (The first Savoia Hut was erected in 1893 at 3835m.) In 1877, at the age of fifty, Quintino Sella, one of the chief founders of the Club Alpino in 1863, climbed the Matterhorn with his two sons, accompanied by Carrel, Antonio Castagneri and Ferdinand Imseng. In a letter to a friend after the ascent, he wrote: 'I regretted somewhat having taken my sons with me, for as regards myself I have passed half a century, and there would not be much harm in ridding Italy of my person; but it would be a pity to lose vigorous youths. But they, too, were so happy, so enthusiastic over this stupendous spectacle. If you only saw their faces when they speak of it!' His nephew, the famous photographer Vittorio Sella, made the first winter ascent of the Matterhorn in 1882, at the age of twenty-three. Leaving Breuil at 11pm on 16 March he reached the top after fifteen hours and descended to the Swiss hut five hours later. In the same year the 'vigorous

youths' made the first ascent of the south-west summit of the Dent du Géant after Joseph Maquignaz, with his son and nephew, had set up a line of fixed ropes attached to pitons drilled into the rock.

12   Bennen's name has also been written as Johann-Josef Benen. I have adopted the form inscribed on his tombstone.

CHAPTER FOUR: LESLIE STEPHEN

1   *Cambridge History of English Literature* by Hugh Walker LLD Volume XIV, 1916.

2   *Leslie Stephen* by Noel Gilroy Annan, 1951.

3   Comment by George Mathews, Stephen's frequent climbing companion in the alps.

4   Careful choice of time and place yields similar winter pleasures in the alps even today.

5   The Jungfraujoch project, conceived in 1893 by the Swiss railway pioneer Adolf Guyer-Zeller, astonished his contemporaries who expressed strong misgivings, despite his conviction that it would succeed. His death in 1899 deprived him of witnessing its fulfillment. Construction, including the boring of a tunnel seven kilometres long through the Eiger to an altitude of 3455m, took over sixteen years between 1896-1912. The Research Station situated 100m above the *joch* was installed later.

6   Other entries were by E von Fellenberg who made the second ascent of the Bietschhorn, and by Meta Brevoort and WAB Coolidge with Christian Almer and his son, who made the fourth ascent in 1871. Also Lord Wentworth and S Siegen of Ried who made the first ascent of the north face on 15 July 1876, traversing the west ridge on the descent. In 1878 CT Dent records his first ascent of the south-east ridge and east face. The last two climbs were typical of those achieved when hard routes were being sought during the second period of the Golden Age. Other entries were 'Mr & Mrs Mummery on Aug 16 1886 from Belalp by Beich [sic] Grat without guides'; R and TG Longstaff in 1889, when the latter, aged fourteen, made the first of his twenty visits to the Alps. The Nesthorn Hotel in Ried, still one of the leading establishments in the valley, is now equally popular with winter and summer visitors.

7   Publication of the DNB continued during the 20th century, initially with 10-yearly and later 5-yearly supplements, of the recent dead. After its copyright had passed to the Oxford University Press in 1917 the latter published in 3 volumes a Concise DNB, prepared by Sidney Lee, of

abstracts of the full entries. Plans were later developed for a revised edition aided by Government funds secured through the British Library. Work on the *Oxford DNB* began in Oxford in 1992 with Colin Matthew appointed as editor. About 13,000 new subjects are being added to the original, bringing the total work to 50,000 biographies covering the 4th century to the year 2000. The editor is assisted by 450 associate editors, over 50 copy editors and proof-readers, and a data manager with a fully integrated computer system, and with about 10,000 contributors. Publication is scheduled for September 2004 simultaneously in 60 print volumes of a million words each and online, making the *Oxford DNB* one of the largest works ever to be published in the English language. Leslie Stephen could never have visualised such a sequel to the work that he began single-handed in his Victorian office at 14 Waterloo Place SW1 scattered with books of reference, ink-pots, and paper-strewn tables.

8   *George Meredith* by SM Ellis, 1920.

9   *Hours in a Library* by Leslie Stephen, 1877.

10   *Alpine Journal* Volume 5, 1872. Review by Leslie Stephen of Whymper's book, *Scrambles amongst the Alps*.

11   *Alpine Journal* Volume 17, 1895. Review of 1894 edition of Stephen's book *The playground of Europe*.

12   Loppé's original painting is held in the archives of the Alpine Club.

CHAPTER FIVE: ADOLPHUS WARBURTON MOORE

1   *Alpine Journal* Volume 28, 1910.

2   Thirteen years were to pass, and several attempts were made, before the Grand Pic of La Meije (3983m) was climbed. (see Chapter 8)

3   In 1538 the Zürich scholar and alpine traveller, Konrad Gesner, described the joys of a hay-bed: 'soft and fragrant hay, compounded of the most wholesome grasses and flowers. You shall sleep more sweetly and healthfully than ever before, with hay for a pillow under your head, for a mattress under your body, and spread over you for a blanket.'

4   The first on 12 July with Tuckett accompanied by Peter Perren; the second, joined by his elder brother JB Croz, on 26 August with Bonney and Mathews.

5   The stony plain on which they bivouacked, a former meeting place of the glacier Noir and glacier Blanc, is now the tourist-frequented *Pré de*

Madame Carle which has its place in alpine history. Geoffroi Carle, President of the Supreme Court of Justice of Grenoble in the early sixteenth century, purchased from a Lucerne family the castle of Vallouise surrounded by a large property. He had a son, Antoine, who died young; his widow, Dame Louise Carle, administered the estate on behalf of her children, and her name was given to the property.

6   One hundred and thirty-one years later, the SAC Hut situated at 2786m on the Arpitetta alp was awarded the 1995 Wilderness Prize for its exemplary ecological standards, facilities and maintenance.

7   *Scrambles amongst the Alps* by Edward Whymper.

8   ibid.

9   From Freshfield's manuscript Journal held by the Alpine Club. Today among the scattered republics situated in the mountains south-west of the former USSR, discontent and unrest are seldom far below the surface.

10   From Moore's diary.

11   *Forbidden Mountains* by P Sicouri and V Kopylov, 1994.

12   Obituary of AW Moore by Horace Walker, *Alpine Journal* Volume 13, 1887.

CHAPTER SIX: EDWARD WHYMPER

1   The battle of Solferino, fought on 24 June 1859 by French and Piedmontese soldiers against Austrian troops, resulted in 6000 dead and 40,000 wounded. A Geneva writer and philanthropist Henri Dunant, shocked by the scale of the massacre, became convinced of the need to organize bands of voluntary medical assistants. His efforts led to the formation of an international committee which held its preliminary meeting in Geneva in 1863 chaired by General Dufour. The following year, with the signing of an International Convention, the Red Cross was formally constituted.

2   They had arrived just below the '*cravate*', so-called because its long horizontal ledge resembled a white scarf when snow-covered.

3   Thomas Stuart Kennedy (1841-94) was one of the finest climbers of his generation. He was twenty-one when he climbed the Dent Blanche. Six months earlier, in January 1862, he was the first to make a winter reconnaissance of what he called the north, in fact the north-east or Hörnli, ridge of the Matterhorn. On 5 July 1865 he made the second

ascent of the Aiguille Verte, the first via the Moine ridge, with the Reverends Charles Hudson and GC Hodgkinson, accompanied by Michel Croz, Michel Ducroz and Peter Perren. A few days later he climbed Mont Blanc with Hudson and Douglas Hadow in four and a half hours from the Grands Mulets. It was intended that he would join Hudson later at Zermatt for an attempt on the Matterhorn. Among TS Kennedy's other first ascents were the Aiguille de Leschaux, the north summit of the Blatière, the Col des Hirondelles with Leslie Stephen; and in July 1872, with Jean-Antoine Carrel and Johann Fischer, a difficult new route on the west side of Mont Blanc from the Miage glacier, known today as *l'éperon de la Tournette*, and only rarely climbed. Some of his boyhood years were spent in the Carinthian Alps at Feldkirch; and he attended school in Geneva. He joined the engineering business in Leeds founded by his father, from whom he later inherited a moorland estate in Dumfriesshire.

4   In 1880 AF Mummery with Burgener and Venetz attempting the east side along the Furggen ridge reached a prominent shoulder below the final section, then traversed the steep upper part of the east face to the Shoulder on the Hörnli ridge, completing the ascent from there.

5   The Parker brothers' attempts are described in *Alpine Journal* Volume 68, 1963. The three brothers, who carried out a series of guideless expeditions in the 1860s, made the first guideless ascent of the Finsteraarhorn in 1865.

6   *Alpine Journal* Volume 1, 1863.

7   Three years later on 30 June 1868, Horace Walker, accompanied by Melchior Anderegg, Johann Jaun and J Grange, reached the highest summit of the Grandes Jorasses, the Pointe Walker (4206m).

8   Four years later in July 1869, Christian Almer agreed to make an attempt on the Matterhorn with Coolidge, then aged nineteen, and his aunt Meta Brevoort, whose ambition it was to be the first lady to make the ascent. A night was spent at the bivouac on the *Cravate* but the party retreated the next day owing to bad weather. In September 1871, Christian Almer, with his son Ulrich and Peter Knubel, led Miss Brevoort and Coolidge up the Matterhorn from Zermatt descending from the summit to Breuil. Miss Brevoort, whose original ambition had been foiled by Lucy Walker, whom she had met and congratulated in Zermatt six weeks earlier, thus became the first lady to traverse the Matterhorn. To quote John Tyndall, 'the addition of the psychological element to the physical' was undoubtedly responsible for the change in Almer's views, and for his later success on the Matterhorn.

9   On 6 July, a day ahead of Douglas, the first ascent of the Ober Gabelhorn was made by Moore and Walker with Jakob Anderegg via its east ridge from Zermatt.

10   The Board of Enquiry held their sessions between 21-23 July 1865, but their report was not released publicly until 1920, nine years after Whymper's death. A copy was printed in the *Alpine Journal* Volume 33. Under questioning, Taugwalder stated his original belief that Hadow slipped, pulling Hudson and Douglas down, and that Croz and he might have held all three had the rope not broken between him and Douglas. Whymper's evidence stated that Hadow's slip knocked Croz off balance, dragging all four down. Taugwalder altered his initial assumption in favour of Whymper's who, he said, stood above him, and may have had a better view. Both men stated repeatedly that they were unable with certainty to describe the exact circumstances of the accident, because a rock partly obscured all the victims except Croz.

11   In his evidence to the Zermatt Court of Enquiry on 23 July, Old Peter Taugwalder is on record as having stated: 'I said to the guide Croz before we reached the dangerous place that one ought for greater security to stretch a rope. Croz replied that it was not necessary.'

12   The apparent insufficiency of good rope for use during the descent may be attributed to a story supposedly related by Whymper to a friend privately, that, when he and Croz broke away from the rest in their race to the top, he himself cut their rope. A detailed analysis by DFO Dangar and TS Blakeney in the *Alpine Journal* Volumes 61 & 71 concludes that no convincing proof of this has ever been established, neither in old Peter's evidence at the Zermatt enquiry in 1865 nor in young Peter's written statement fifty-two years later, and 'hearsay of this sort must be regarded with suspicion'. Soon after he returned to England in 1865 Whymper visited Reverend George Forrest Browne (Alpine Club President 1905-08, and Bishop of Bristol). Browne is reported to have said that he was the only person who knew the truth about the accident. If so, he took the 'secret' to his grave. In his book *The recollections of a bishop* published in 1915, he referred to Whymper's visit. 'He came to consult me on two questions of casuistry, on at least one of which he did not take my advice. He never returned to the subject with me.'

13   Alfred Wills' account of the descent of the Wetterhorn in 1854, and John Tyndall's observations when descending the Finsteraarhorn in 1858 highlight the reluctance of guides to use a rope while descending, no really secure techniques having been devised at the time as to its use in an emergency.

14   While Whymper denied any malicious gossip about Taugwalder having cut the rope, he never lifted publicly his suspicion about the deliberate use of a weak rope, athough fully aware that the only alternative available was 150ft of a heavy type of rope. Yet, perhaps he regretted his initial imputations against old Peter. In a footnote on p.404 of the 1871 edition of his book Whymper wrote: 'Not only was his ... act at the critical

271

moment [of the accident] wonderful as a feat of strength, but it was admirable in its performance at the right time.'

15   All good Victorian story-tellers managed to contrive a happy ending to their epic. Whymper's book was different, ending in drama and tragedy, which caused a public stir and shed a curious combination of controversy and renown upon the author.

16   The days of the 'duffer' might be coming to an end. During the summer of 2002 the Zermatt Bureau of Guides introduced a compulsory climbing test for potential Matterhorn clients in the interest of mutual safety – a step that is also intended to reduce the gridlock occurring on several rock passages where only one climber can move at a time, and when the number of summer aspirants during a spell of good weather rises to 150 per day. In July 2003, owing to an exceptional dry spell, a major rockfall occurred on the notoriously loose slopes of the Hörnli route. About ninety climbers were air-lifted to safety, and the route was closed for almost a week in anticipation of further rock slides. In spite of around 1200 rescue operations per season, there is an average death toll on the Matterhorn of fifteen persons annually. The current cost of engaging a guide for the Hörnli route is about 1000 Swiss francs per person.

17   The displacement of every stone, boulder, and slab, on a mountain alters its character. The nature of some sections of the Matterhorn's south-west and north-east ridges may have changed to a marked extent with the footsteps of hundreds of climbers treading up and down them each year for over 135 years. It is impossible to say whether the original ascent routes were harder or easier when the pioneers first attempted to climb them without fixed aids.

18   Between 25-28 July 1855, five years before Whymper's first visit to the Rhône valley, a series of devastating earthquakes struck the area, of which he found numerous traces. Preceded by an almost total drought, which withered the summer crops, the tremors converted the town of Visp with its two churches into a mass of ruins. After-shocks continued through August and September to 28 October. The inhabitants and their cattle, encamped in the fields, experienced thunderstorms and heavy rainfall; rivers overflowed their banks, and the temperature of the mineral waters at Leuk increased by several degrees. St Niklaus suffered as badly as Visp, but Stalden, situated between the two, escaped with only slight damage.

19   The following comments are taken from a contemporary account of mountaineering in 1885. 'Probably more mountains have been ascended in the past season than in any previous one. The number of mountains of all kinds, good, bad, and indifferent, was larger than it had ever been before, and the holiday-makers filled every resort to overflowing. We have heard of a case in which two friends arriving at a mountain inn could

obtain no better bed than the billiard table, and one was charged 5fr for sleeping upon it, and the other 4 fr for sleeping under it. ... The Engadine was even more crowded than usual, and Zermatt and the hotels on the Riffel were crammed. So, too, Chamonix, and the hotel at the Montenvert was more popular than ever. ... Among tourists in general the passion for going up mountains seemed to be developed to a preposterous extent.' Although in geographical size, measured on a world scale, the European Alps occupy the thirty-eighth position they receive over one million visitors annually.

20   A comment by the writer Michael Fields quoted in *Alpine Journal* Volume 46, 1934. By then, Whymper's reputation was well established as a writer, lecturer and illustrator of alpine scenes.

21   They were probably the first outsiders to bring the delights of the Dauphiné within the orbit of the mountaineering world. Partly responsible for La Bérarde's transformation into a climbing centre, they were also responsible for the destruction of the character of the region as they had found it on their first visit in 1870.

22   A whimsical picture of old Sémiond is drawn by Whymper who, upon awakening after a night tormented by fleas, was consoled by him with: 'Ah! as to fleas, I don't pretend to be different to anyone else – *I have them'* An early traveller provides a vivid description of a night spent at a primitive inn in the Valsavaranche. 'I know it sounds like effeminacy to complain of any of the hardships one undergoes on an expedition of this kind and I hold that a man who cannot endure hunger and thirst, cold and heat, to have his nose blistered and his toes frostbitten, has no business in the High Alps. But you must draw the line somewhere, and I draw it at fleas. They, I maintain, are a grievance at which one may lawfully murmur. ... If you knew what it was, after a sleepless night, and with a mind as well as body in a state of furious irritation, to start a walk of fifteen hours, during perhaps eight of which your personal safety depends on your equanimity and coolness, you might, I think, agree with me in ranking this little animal with the crevasses and avalanches and other perils which beset the path of the mountaineer.' (John Ormsby, from his account in *Peaks, Passes and Glaciers,* of the first ascent of the Grivola in 1859.)

CHAPTER SEVEN: ALBERT FREDERICK MUMMERY

1   It was in that year that he crossed the Col du Lion and climbed the Aiguille des Charmoz with Alexander Burgener; a year earlier he had climbed the Z'mutt ridge of the Matterhorn; these were regarded as exceptional exploits.

2   Mummery–Coolidge correspondence, *Alpine Journal* Volume
        60, 1955.

3   Ruskin family letters Volume III.

4   In 1885, with the Austrian climber, Moritz von Kuffner, and the guides
        Josef Biner and Anton Kalbermatten, Burgener made an attempt on the
        Mittelegi ridge of the Eiger, which failed at the great rock tower 300m
        below the top. Two days later, with the same party, Burgener climbed the
        Eiger by the ordinary route, and succeeded in making the first descent of
        the Mittelegi ridge. The first complete ascent of the Eiger's Mittelegi
        Ridge was made thirty-six years later, on 10 September 1921, by Yuko
        Maki of Japan accompanied by the Grindelwald guides Fritz Steuri, Franz
        Amatter and S Brawand.

5   The Penhall couloir was the scene of an accident in 1887 when two
        Austrians, Dr Guido Lammer and A Lorria, attempting the west face of
        the Matterhorn without guides, were forced by a storm into a terrifying
        descent of the couloir, narrowly escaping with their lives after being
        engulfed by an avalanche.

6   In the summer of 1999 a metal-framed bivouac was installed at 2974m
        on the initial snow section of the Z'mutt ridge, and fixed aids were placed
        on difficult rock sections above. Financed by the Swiss Lonza group and
        supported by the Zermatt Guides Association, the object was to render the
        ascent generally 'safer' – easier. In December 2000 the bivouac was carried
        away by an avalanche, and has not been re-installed. Even with existing
        fixed aids the Z'mutt ridge is still considered a serious undertaking.

7   Five of the seven men who climbed the Z'mutt ridge on the third of
        September 1879 have died in the mountains. In 1881 Ferdinand Imseng
        was swept to his death by an avalanche, together with his employer D
        Marinelli, while attempting to make the third ascent of the Macugnaga
        (east) face of Monte Rosa; Imseng had made the first ascent of that steep
        and dangerous route in 1872 with the brothers R and W Pendlebury, C
        Taylor, and the guides, G Spechtenhauser and G Oberto. In 1882, William
        Penhall was killed by an avalanche on the Wetterhorn with his guide
        Andreas Maurer. In the same year Johann Petrus was killed together with
        his client FM Balfour, a young Cambridge professor, probably by a fresh
        snow avalanche, during an attempt on the Aiguille Blanche de Peuterey, a
        peak that was climbed three years later by P Seymour King and Emile
        Rey. In 1895, Mummery disappeared below Nanga Parbat. In 1910,
        Alexander Burgener was killed by an avalanche below the Bergli hut.

8   AW Moore, *The Alps in 1864*. Marcel Kurz, the Swiss mountaineer,
        topographer, and guide-book editor, described the Col du Lion as *'un des
        grands casse-cou dans les Alpes'* (one of the major death-traps in the Alps).

9   The first complete ascent of the Furggen ridge direct was made on 23 September 1941 by the Italian guide Luigi Carrel accompanying Alfredo Perino and Giacomo Chiara. In 1931, Luigi Carrel made the first ascent of the Matterhorn's savage south face accompanied by Enzo Benedetti and Maurice Bich. In 1947, Luigi Carrel and Carlo Taddei opened a route on the west face, but avoided a direct finish; the complete west face of the Matterhorn was not climbed until 1962.

10   The Bristows were family friends of the Pethericks in Exeter, and Lily Bristow, one of the most accomplished lady climbers of her day, was an old friend of Mary Petherick who became Mummery's wife. During the next decade Miss Bristow made several notable climbs, often with Mummery as leader.

11   *Alpine Journal* Volume 63, 1958.

12   *Alpine Journal* Volume 60, 1955. Some of the photographs have since been traced. The collection originally gifted by Mrs Mummery included slides and photographs together with some thirty short notes about future plans, and a set of snapshots, the only photographs Mummery ever took, formerly in the possession of Norman Collie.

13   *Climbing on the Himalaya and other mountain ranges* by Professor J Norman Collie, 1902.

14   In 1868, Douglas Freshfield, among the earliest mountaineers to go there, records how the people of the country reacted incredulously to his explanation that pleasure was the only reason why he travelled among their mountains. They suspected that he was exploring for minerals or looking for other sources of financial gain. Over half a century later early travellers to unfrequented regions of the Himalaya and Karakoram encountered similar attitudes among the local people.

15   The first person from Britain to go there with the object of climbing mountains was WW Graham in 1883, accompanied by the Grindelwald guides Emil Boss and Ulrich Kauffmann. They failed to penetrate the Rishi gorge towards Nanda Devi but were able to reach the lower part of the west ridge of Dunagiri, which a Swiss expedition followed to the top in 1939. Graham also ascended a peak in Sikkim, which he mistakenly identified as Kabru (7300m), but which is likely to have been Forked Peak (6110m), situated south-east of Kabru Dome. The next British expedition, a major one supported by the Royal Society and the Royal Geographical Society, went out nine years later when Martin Conway, the Honourary Charles Bruce, AD McCormick and O Eckenstein, accompanied by the guide, Matthias Zurbriggen of Saas, visited the Karakoram in 1892. They traversed the Hispar glacier to discover a plateau at its head which they called the Snow Lake, crossed the Hispar

Pass, descended the Biafo glacier, and explored the Baltoro glacier to its head, discovering two glaciers to its north and south, which they named the Godwin Austin and the Vigne. They reached the top of a 6650m mountain ('Pioneer' peak) in the 'Golden Throne' (Baltoro Kangri) group.

16   Mummery, who generally removed his glasses when walking, had a positive loathing for stony pathways, on which he tended to move clumsily. He must have found Himalayan moraines a nightmare.

17   On the outbreak of World War Two in September 1939, Aufschnaiter and Harrer were held in India as prisoners of war. In April 1944, they succeeded in escaping from an internment camp in Dehra Dun. Travelling secretly, they entered Tibet and had an eventful twenty-one-month journey to Lhasa where they arrived in January 1946, destitute and in rags. Harrer became a tutor to the present Dalai Lama, then a boy; and Aufschnaiter introduced a modern irrigation system in Lhasa. Both men left Tibet in November 1950 after the arrival of the Chinese army.

18   Clinton Thomas Dent was one of the first in 1870 to employ Alexander Burgener as a guide, and climbed with him for almost twenty years. In 1886, Burgener accompanied Dent to the Caucasus. Dent's tribute to Burgener appears in *Alpine Journal* Volume 25, 1910.

CHAPTER EIGHT: AN UNEXPECTED SUCCESS

1   The brothers R and W Pendlebury and Charles Taylor with the guide Ferdinand Imseng had made the first ascent of the forbidding eastern face of Monte Rosa the year before.

2   In 1876 Henri Cordier (1856-77), T Middlemore & J Oakley Maund with Jakob Anderegg, J Jaun and A Maurer climbed the Aiguille Verte via a steep couloir from the Argentière glacier, a route that was repeated only twice during the next fifty-five years. A few days later the same team climbed Les Courtes and Les Droites. Henri Cordier died in the Dauphiné the following year after making the first ascent of Le Plaret (3564m) accompanied by Jakob Anderegg and Andreas Maurer. On the descent, unroping at the foot of the Plaret glacier, he fell into a glacier torrent while glissading.

3   In 1878, H Duhamel co-authored with Coolidge and F Perrin *Guide du Haute Dauphiné*. In 1879 he was the first man to introduce skiing in France, at Grenoble.

4   While Frederick Gardiner hardly ever wrote about his climbs, Coolidge published in 1920 a complete account of his friend's alpine career six years

after his death at the age of forty-six. The Pilkington brothers, likewise, wrote very little; Charles, it is known, gave a lecture to the Yorkshire Ramblers Club in 1896, the year in which he was elected President of the Alpine Club. In an address to the latter about his 1879 ascent of the Meije, he said that the climbing became progressively more difficult as they approached the glacier Carré. 'This last piece of the wall will always remain in our minds as the most desperate piece of work we have ever done.' On the descent a beautiful moonlit night was spent on the glacier Carré in a large india-rubber bag. Three short books of Lawrence Pilkington's poems were published in 1924, 1930 and 1936.

5   Christian Almer's great qualities as a guide are beyond question, but there are two occasions when misgivings held him back until others had shown the way. The Meije was one, although it might be argued that his earlier failures with Coolidge could have sprung partly from his fears that the difficulties of the final section might be beyond Coolidge's powers. The other, was his remark to Edward Whymper in 1865, 'Anything but the Matterhorn', although six years later he led Meta Brevoort up the Swiss route and down the Italian side to Breuil which made her the first lady to traverse the Matterhorn from Zermatt.

6   In 1977, to mark the centenary of the ascent of the Grand Pic of La Meije a memorial was raised to Pierre Gaspard at his village St Christophe, below La Bérarde, and a graphic film *Gaspard de la Meije* was produced for French television re-enacting his ascent with Emmanuel Boileau.

Chapter Nine: There Were Many Others

1   Emil Rey, one of the greatest Courmayeur guides, died at the age of forty-nine in 1895 while descending unroped with his employer from the Aiguille du Géant. A master carpenter by trade, he had a brilliant guiding career which began at the relatively late age of thirty. Among his many noteworthy ascents on the southern side of Mont Blanc were those made with H. Seymour King, Lord Wentworth, M. de Déchy and others. His sons Henri and Adolphe, following their father's footsteps, became leading guides.

Chapter Ten: Beyond the Beginnings

1   Mechanically-aided ascents of rock cliffs of extreme difficulty, otherwise known as sport climbing, now increasingly popular in Europe and North America, have led to restrictions on climbers' access to protected areas, where it is considered that damage is being inflicted. Efforts to resolve this sensitive issue depend partly upon the adoption of greater

responsibility by climbers themselves to preserve the unspolit wildness of their playground. Among other countries, Switzerland has been prominent in installing protective devices on a number of popular alpine routes, representing a clear choice between the respective merits of challenge and security in favour of the latter. In certain regions of Switzerland, the fashion has grown for setting up *via ferrata*, namely rock routes equipped with chains and ladders, introduced originally in the Dolomites.

ALPINE FIRST ASCENTS
13TH-19TH CENTURY

ABBREVIATIONS

AIG	AIGUILLE	N	NORTH
C	CENTRAL	NE	NORTH-EAST
E	EAST	PTE OR PT	POINT
GR	GROSS (GERMAN),	S	SOUTH
	GROSSE (FRENCH)	SIG	SIGNAL
KL	KLEIN (GERMAN),	SW	SOUTH-WEST
	PETIT (FRENCH)	W	WEST

YEAR	MOUNTAIN	HEIGHT (M)	AREA	FIRST ASCENT BY
1286	Mt Ventoux	1912	Vaucluse	2 local shepherds
1358	Rocciamelone	3538	Mt Cenis	Rotario d'Asti
1492	Mont Aiguille	2086	Dauphiné	Antoine de Ville with 10 men
1518	Pilatus	2120	Préalpes	Vadian & 5 priests from Luzern
1536	Stockhorn	3211	Préalpes	Johannn Müller & 3 priests from Bern
1558	Niesen	2362	Préalpes	Benedikt Marti
1654	Karwendelspitze W	2385	Bavarian Alps	Unknown
c1694	Mt Thabor	3181	Cottian Alps	Unknown
1707	Piz Beverin	2997	Grisons	Unknown
1710	Piz Linard	3414	Grisons	JC Zadrell & party
c1742	Schesaplana	2964	Rhaetian Alps	N Sererhard & party of chamois hunters
1744	Titlis	3238	Central Alps	4 monks from Engelberg
c1762	Ankogel	3251	Gross Glockner	Unknown
1770	Mont Buet	3094	Mt Blanc Group	De Luc bros with local chamois hunters
1778	Triglav	2863	Julian Alps	Dr L Willonitzer with a hunter, Rosic & two young miners M Kos & L Korosec
1779	Mt Vélan	3731	Valais Alps	L-J Murith with Genoud (chamois hunter)
1782	Scopï	3200	Grisons	Unknown
c1784	Aiguille du Goûter	3835	Mt Blanc Group	F Cuidet & F Gervais
1784	Dom du Goûter	4304	Mt Blanc Group	F Cuidet & J-M Couttet
	Dent du Midi	3257	Valais Alps	J-M Clement
1786	Mont Blanc	4807	Haute Savoie	M-G Paccard, J Balmat
1787	Dent de Morcles	2969	Valais Alps	A Thomas
1788	Stockgrond	3422	Glarner Alps	Placidus à Spescha

Year	Mountain	Height (m)	Area	First Ascent By
1789	Pizzo Bianco	3215	Macugnaga	Unknown
	Rheinwaldhorn	3402	Adula Alps	Placidus à Spescha
1792	Oberalpstock	3328	Tödi Group	Placidus à Spescha
	Klein Matterhorn	3883	Valais Alps	HB de Saussure & J-M Couttet
	Theodulhorn	3468	Valais Alps	HB de Saussure & J-M Couttet
1793	Piz Urlaun	3359	Tödi Group	Placidus à Spescha
c1799	Gross Wiesbachhorn	3564	Gross Glockner	Unknown
	Watzmann	2713	Bavarian Alps	V Stanig
1800	Gross Glockner	3796	Gr Glockner Group	2 brothers Klotz
1801	Punta Giordani	4046	Monte Rosa	Dr Pietro Giordani
	Piz Aul	3121	C Grisons	Placidus à Spescha
	Piz Scharboden	3122	C Grisons	Placidus à Spescha
1802	Piz Terri	3150	C Grisons	Placidus à Spescha
	Mont Perdu	3355	C Pyrenees	Laurens & Rondo
1804	Ortler	3905	Ortler Group	J Pichler, J Leitner & J Klausner
1806	Güferhorn	3383	Central Grisons	Placidus à Spescha
1808	Terglou	2865	Julian Alps	V Stanig
1810	Aiguille de la Grande Sassière	3756	Graians	Unknown
1811	Jungfrau N summit	4089	Bernese Alps	JR Meyer II, H Meyer, A Volker & J Bortis
1812	Jungfrau S summit	4158	Bernese Alps	G Meyer, A Volker & J Bortis
1813	Breithorn	4165	Monte Rosa Group	H Maynard, J-M Couttet & 3 Valtournanche guides
1817	Mettenberg	3104	Grindelwald	Pastor F Lehmann with chamois hunters
	Rochebrune	3324	Dauphiné	Unknown
1818	Aig du Midi N	3832	Mt Blanc Group	A Malczewski, J Balmat & 5 other guides
1819	Pyramide Vincent	4215	Monte Rosa Group	J-N Vincent
1820	Zumsteinspitze	4563	Monta Rosa Group	J Zumstein, JN & J Vincent
1822	Ludwigshöhe	4342	Monte Rosa Group	Ludwig von Welden
1823	Grand Rubren	3340	Cottian Alps	Unknown
	Bristenstock	3073	Tödi Group	Franz Lusser
1824	Tödi (Russein)	3620	Tödi Group	P Curschellas & A Biscuolm (chamois hunters)
1825	Hafnereck	3061	Ankogel Group	Unknown
1826	Hocharn	3254	Ankogel Group	Unknown
	Dossenhorn	3138	Bernese Alps	FJ Hugi with guides
1828	Pelvoux (Pt Durand)	3932	Dauphiné	J-E Mathéoud & A Liotard
	Pizzo Tambo	3276	Grisons Alps	Unknown

Year	Mountain	Height (m)	Area	First Ascent By
1829	Finsteraarhorn	4274	Bernese Alps	J Leuthold & J Währen, guides of FJ Hugi
	Torrenthorn	2998	Bernese Alps	Unknown
1831	Kl Windgälle	2986	Tödi Group	G Studer & M Tresch
1832	Mt Clapier	3046	Alpes Maritimes	Unknown
	Hausstock	3158	Glarner Alps	Unknown
	Dachstein	2996	Bavarian Alps	Unknown
1833	Strahlkogel	3290	Stubai Alps	P Thurwieser
1834	Similaun	3606	Oetztal Alps	Unknown
	Altels	3629	Bernese Alps	Peasants from Frutigen
	Uri Rotstock	2928	Urner Alps	H Zeller & H Imfanger
1835	Oldenhorn	3122	Vaud Alps	G Studer
	Sasseneire	3254	Valais Alps	Surveyors
	Piz Palü (E Peak)	3888	Bernina Group	Oswald Heer & 4 local guides
	Piz Linard	3414	Rhaetian Alps	Oswald Heer & 4 local guides
1836	Mt Tenibres	3031	Alpes Maritimes	Unknown
	Gr Gstellihorn	2856	Bernese Alps	B Studer & E von de Linth
	Fernerkogel	3300	Stubai Alps	P Thurwieser
1837	Tödi (Glarner)	3582	Tödi Group	G Vögeli & T Thut
1839	Aiguilles d'Arves (Central Peak)	3509	Dauphiné	2 chamois hunters
1840	Schrankogel	3496	Stubai Alps	Unknown
1841	Sustenhorn	3503	Bernese Alps	G Studer with guides
	Ewigschneehorn	3329	Bernese Alps	E Désor with 2 guides
	Düssistock	3256	Tödi Group	Unknown
	Gr Venediger	3674	C Tyrol	A von Ruthner, J von Kürsinger & 22 others
1842	Dents du Midi (Cime de l'est)	3177	Valais Alps	Unknown
	Wandfluhhorn	3589	Valais Alps	JD Forbes, J Pralong & V Tairraz
	Signalkuppe (Pt Gnifetti)	4554	Monte Rosa Group	Giovanni Gnifetti, with J & J Giordani
	Riffelhorn	2927	Valais Alps	J Barwell, W & V Smith
	Lauteraarhorn	4042	Bernese Alps	E Désor, E von de Linth & C Girard with 5 guides
	Schärhorn	3294	Tödi Group	G Hoffmann
	Düssistock	3260	Tödi Group	E von de Linth
1843	Wildhorn	3248	Bernese Alps	Unknown
	Dossenhorn	3138	Bernese Alps	E Désor
	Gr Loeffler	3326	Zillertal Alps	Unknown
1844	Rosenhorn	3689	Bernese Alps	E Désor, D Dollfus-Ausset, J Jaun, M Bannholzer & M Dupasquier
	Wetterhorn	3701	Bernese Alps	M Bannholzer & J Jaun

Year	Mountain	Height (m)	Area	First Ascent By
1844	Wasenhorn	3246	Valais Alps	JD Forbes
	Johannisberg	3460	Gross Glockner	Unknown
1845	Hoch Ducan	3063	Albula Alps	Johann Coaz
	Flüela Weisshorn	2988	Albula Alps	Johann Coaz
	Mittelhorn	3704	Bernese Alps	S Speer, K Abplanalp, J Jaun & J Michel
	Galenstock	3583	Bernese Alps	E Désor, M Dollfus-Ausset Sr & Jr with 5 guides
1846	Weisskugel	3839	Oetztal Alps	2 peasants from Schnals
	Piz Kesch	3418	Albula Alps	J Coaz
	Piz Languard	3262	Bernina Group	J Coaz
	Piz Surlej	3188	Bernina Group	J Coaz
	Piz Aguagliouls	3126	Bernina Group	J Coaz
	Piz d'Esen	3120	Bernina Group	J Coaz
	Piz Lischana	3109	Lower Engadin	J Coaz
	Gross Mörchner	3287	Zillertal Alps	P Thurwieser
1847	Schrammacher	3416	Zillertal Alps	P Thurwieser
1848	Piz Quattervals	3165	Lower Engadin	J Coaz
	Mt Pelvoux (Main)	3946	Dauphiné	V Puiseaux
	Grenzgipfel	4596	Monte Rosa Group	V Puiseaux & Dr Ordinaire
	Ulrichshorn	3925	Valais	M Ulrich, J-J Imseng, S Biner, F Andenmatten & M Zumtaugwald
	Gr Windgällen	3187	Tödi Group	G Hoffmann
	Wildspitze (SW)	3686	Oetztal Alps	Unknown
1849	Tête Blanche	3724	Valais Alps	G Studer, M & S Ulrich
	Piz Krone	3192	Rhaetian Alps	Unknown
	Piz Mundin	3146	Rhaetian Alps	J Coaz
1850	Monte Leone	3553	Valais Alps	G Studer
	Diablerets	3210	Vaud Alps	G Studer, M & S Ulrich
	Piz Bernina	4049	Bernina Group	J Coaz with J & L Tscharner
	Il Chapütschin	3386	Bernina Group	J Coaz with J & L Tscharner
	Piz Tschierva	3546	Bernina Group	J Coaz with J & L Tscharner
	Piz Corvatsch	3451	Bernina Group	J Coaz with J & L Tscharner
	Piz Misaun	3248	Bernina Group	J Coaz with J & L Tscharner
1851	Combin de Corbassière	3715	Gr Combin Group	G Studer, J von Weissenfluh & JB Fellay
	Cima di Jazzi	3804	Monte Rosa Group	GM Sykes & M Zumtaugwald
1852	Hohe Wilde	3482	Zillertal Alps	Unknown

Year	Mountain	Height (m)	Area	First Ascent By
1852	Schwarzenstein	3370	Zillertal Alps	Unknown
	Hochschober	3240	Zillertal Alps	Unknown
1853	Tödi (Sandgipfel)	3390	Tödi Group	G Studer & M Ulrich
	Glockturm	3355	Oetztal Alps	Poltinger with survey party
	Brunegghorn	3838	Valais Alps	J & F Tantignoni & J Brantschen
	Fletschhorn	3996	Valais Alps	M Amherdt with 2 guides
1854	Strahlhorn	4190	Valais Alps	C, E & J Smyth, with F Andenmatten & U Lauener
	Ostspitze (Monte Rosa)	4596	Monte Rosa Group	C & J Smyth with F Andenmatten & U Lauener
	Rinderhorn	3453	Bernese Alps	Unknown
	Monte Vioz	3644	Ortler Group	Unknown
	Hochweisstein	2692	Julian Alps	Austrian topographers
1855	Wildstrubel	3243	Bernese Alps	Dr Schmid & J Tritten
	Mont Blanc du Tacul	4248	Mt Blanc Group	C Hudson, C & J Smyth, ES Kennedy & C Ainslie
	Dufourspitze	4634	Monte Rosa Group	C Hudson, C & J Smyth, J Birkbeck, EJ Stevenson, U Lauener & J & M Zumtaugwald
	Weissmies	4023	Valais Alps	J Heusser, P & J Zurbriggen
1856	Aig du Midi S	3731	Mt Blanc Group	F de Bouillé, A & J Simond & JA Devouassoud
	Mont Avril	3340	Valais Alps	CE & W Mathews & A Simond
	Allalinhorn	4027	Valais Alps	EL Ames, J Andenmatten & J-J Imseng
	Lagginhorn	4010	Valais Alps	EL Ames with 3 friends plus F Andenmatten & J-J Imseng & three guides
1857	Mönch	4099	Bernese Alps	S Porges, C Almer père et fils, U & C Kaufmann
	Tête Blanche	3422	Mont Blanc Group	A Wills, CH Russel, RE Welbey with A Balmat & F Cachat
	Punta Lavina	3317	Graians	Unknown
	Pointe de Garin	3489	Graians	Unknown
	Ciamarella	3676	C Graians	Unknown
	Levanna (E)	3564	Graians	Unknown
	Bessanese	3632	Graians	Unknown
	Aig du Croissant	4243	Grand Combin	W Mathews with guides
	Kleine Schreckhorn	3494	Bernese Alps	E Anderson, C Almer père et fils & P Bohren
	Trugberg (lower top)	3850	Bernese Alps	J Ball
	Pelmo	3169	Dolomites	J Ball with local guide

Year	Mountain	Height (m)	Area	First Ascent By
1857	Tête du Lion	3715	Valtournanche	J-A & J-J & A Carrel
	Rutor	3486	C Graians	Unknown
1858	Punta Bianca	3793	E Graians	Unknown
	Dôme de Miage	3673	Mt Blanc Group	T Coleman, F Mollard & J-J Jacquemont
	Tour Sallières	3227	Mt Blanc Group	Unknown
	Dom	4545	Valais Alps	JL Davies, J Zumtaugwald, J Kronig & J Brantschen
	Nadelhorn	4327	Valais Alps	J Zimmermann, A Supersaxo, F Andenmatten & B Epiney
	Eiger	3970	Bernese Alps	C Barrington, C Almer père et fils & P Bohren
	Piz Morteratsch	3751	Bernina Group	Dr Brugger
	Hinter Brochkogel	3635	Oetztal Alps	Unknown
1859	Grivola	3969	Graians	R Bruce, J Ormsby, WA Dayne, Z Cachat & J Tairraz
	Muttler	3294	Rhaetian Alps	JJ Weilenmann
	Combin de Grafenèire	4314	Valais Alps	CS Deville, D & E & G Balleys & B Dorsaz
	Rimpfischhorn	4199	Valais Alps	L Stephen, R Liveing, M Anderegg & J Zumtaugwald
	Aletschhorn	4195	Bernese Alps	FF Tuckett, J-J Bennen, P Bohren & J Tairraz
	Bietschhorn	3934	Valais Alps	L Stephen, J & A Siegen & J Ebener
	Piz Julier	3380	Bernina Group	J Sarratz
	Hochalmspitze	3355	C Tyrol	Unknown
	Rainerhorn	3561	C Tyrol	Unknown
	Piz Duan	3131	Albula Alps	Unknown
1860	Gran Paradiso	4061	Graians	J Cowell, W Dundas, M Payot & J Tairraz
	Grands Casse	3748	Vanoise	W Mathews with J-B & M Croz
	Sig du Mt d'Iséran	3241	Vanoise	Unknown
	Alphubel	4206	Valais Alps	L Stephen, T Hinchcliff, M Anderegg & P Perren
	Blümlisalphorn	3664	Bernese Alps	L Stephen, R Liveing, JK Stone, M Anderegg, P Simond & F Ogi
	Oberaarhorn	3637	Bernese Alps	L Stephen & M Anderegg

ALPINE FIRST ASCENTS

Year	Mountain	Height (m)	Area	First Ascent By
1861	Monte Viso	3841	Cottian Alps	W Mathews, FW Jaccomb, J-B & M Croz
	Mont Pourri	3788	Vanoise	M Croz
	Mont Gelé	3518	Valais Alps	FW Jaccomb, J-B & M Croz
	Tête Blanche de By	3418	Valais Alps	FW Jaccomb, J-B & M Croz
	Weisshorn	4506	Valais Alps	J Tyndall, J-J Bennen & U Wenger
	Nordend	4609	Monte Rosa Group	T & N Buxton, J Cowell & M Payot
	Castor	4228	Valais Alps	W Mathews, FW Jaccomb & M Croz
	Lyskamm (East)	4527	Valais Alps	J Hardy, J Hudson, F Gibson, A Ramsay, T Rennison, W Hall, C Pilkington, R Stephenson, K Heer, J Cachat, P & J Perren, F Lochmatter & S Zumtaugwald
	Schreckhorn	4078	Bernese Alps	L Stephen, C & P Michel & U Kaufmann
	Piz Grisch	2898	Albula Alps	Unknown
	Fluchthorn	3402	Rhaetian Alps	Unknown
	Wildspitze (NE)	3772	Oetztal Alps	Unknown
	Mont Pourri	3782	Vanoise	W Mathews with guides
1862	Pointe de Charbonel	3760	Graians	Unknown
	Besso	3668	Valais Alps	Guides J-B Epiney & J Vianin
	Dent Blanche	4357	Valais Alps	TS Kennedy, W Wigram, J-B Croz & J Kronig
	Täschhorn	4490	Valais Alps	JL Davies, JW Hayward, J & S Zumtaugwald & PJ Sommermatter
	Gr Fiescherhorn	4048	Bernese Alps	HB George, AW Moore, C Almer & U Kaufmann
	Weisse Frau	3650	Bernese Alps	E von Fellenberg, A Roth, C Lauener, J Bischoff & K Blatter
	Gr Doldenhorn	3643	Bernese Alps	E von Fellenberg, A Roth, C Lauener, J Bischoff & K Blatter
	Kl Doldenhorn	3475	Bernese Alps	E von Fellenberg, J Boalt, P Gosset, C Lauener & J Bischoff
	Monte Disgrazia	3678	Bernina Group	L Stephen, ES Kennedy, T Cox & M Anderegg

Year	Mountain	Height (m)	Area	First Ascent By
1863	Grandes Rousses	3473	Dauphiné	W & C Mathews, TG Bonney, M Croz & JB Simond
	Dent d'Hérens	4171	Valais Alps	W Hall, FC Grove, RS Macdonald, M Anderegg, P Perren & J-P Cachat
	Diablons (Main)	3609	Valais Alps	S Taylor, K Whatman, F Andenmatten & J Vianin
	Diablons (S Peak)	3538	Valais Alps	S Taylor, K Whatman, F Andenmatten & J Vianin
	Parrotspitze	4432	Monte Rosa Group	RS Macdonald, FC Grove, M Woodmass M Anderegg & P Perren
	Balfrinhorn	3796	Valais Alps	Mr & Mrs RS Watson, J-J Imseng, F Andenmatten & J-M Claret
	Silberhorn	3695	Bernese Alps	E von Fellenberg, H Baedeker & guides
	Basòdino	3273	Ticino Alps	P Jossi with local guides
	Helsenhorn	3272	Valais Alps	Unknown
	Bifertenstock	3425	Tödi Group	Unknown
	Claridenstock	3267	Tödi Group	E Rambert, E Streiff & G Stüssi
	Selbsanft	3029	Tödi Group	Unknown
	Piz Zupò	3995	Bernina Group	L Enderlin, P Serard, H Badrutt & local hunter
	Piz Roseg (NW)	3920	Bernina Group	FS Bircham, A Flury & F Jenny
	Piz Palü	3905	Bernina Group	EN Buxton with 4 others & 3 guides
	Piz Cambrena	3604	Bernina Group	Unknown
	Zuckerhütl	3507	Stubai Alps	Unknown
	Antelao	3283	Dolomites	P Grohmann
	Tofana di Mezzo	3244	Dolomites	P Grohmann
1864	Cima dei Gelas	3135	Alpes Maritimes	Unknown
	Pte des Ecrins	4101	Dauphiné	AW Moore, H Walker, E Whymper, C Almer & M Croz
	Piz Roseg	3937	Bernina Group	AW Moore, H Walker & J Anderegg
	Piz Kesch	3420	Engadine	English team
	Punta Rossa	3630	E Graians	Unknown
	Grande Motte	3640	W Graians	T Blanford & RM Cuthbert

Year	Mountain	Height (m)	Area	First Ascent By
1864	Dent Parrachée	3712	W Graians	T Blanford & RM Cuthbert
	Aig d'Argentière	3902	Mt Blanc Group	AA Reilly, E Whymper, M Croz, M Payot & H Charlet
	Aig de Trélatête (S)	3920	Mt Blanc Group	AA Reilly, E Whymper, M Croz, M Payot & H Charlet
	Mont Dolent	3823	Mt Blanc Group	AA Reilly, E Whymper, M Croz, M Payot & H Charlet
	Aig du Tour	3544	Mt Blanc Group	CG Heathcote with M Andenmatten
	Zinalrothorn	4221	Valais Alps	L Stephen, FC Grove, M & J Anderegg
	Bouquetin	3478	Valais Alps	AW Moore, C Almer & P Martin
	Pollux	4092	Valais Alps	J Jacot, P Taugwalder & J-M Perren
	Balmhorn	3669	Bernese Alps	FL & H Walker & J & M Anderegg
	Fleckistock	3417	Bernese Alps	Unknown
	Bärglistock	3655	Bernese Alps	P Egger & P Inäbnit
	Studerhorn	3638	Bernese Alps	G Studer, R Lindt, K & J Blatter & P Sulzer
	Gross Wannenhorn	3905	Bernese Alps	G Studer, R Lindt, K & J Blatter & P Sulzer
	Kl Fiescherhorn (Ochs)	3900	Bernese Alps	E von Fellenberg, P Inäbnit, U Kaufmann & P Baumann
	Gr Fiescherhorn	4048	Bernese Alps	E von Fellenberg, P Inäbnit, U Kaufmann & P Baumann
	Ofenhorn	3235	Valais Alps	Unknown
	Gr Ruchen	3133	Tödi Group	Unknown
	Monte Sissone	3360	Bernina Group	DW Freshfield, JD Walker & RM Beachcroft
	Königsspitze (Gran Zebru)	3859	Ortler Group	FF Tuckett, EN & HE Buxton
	Cevedale	3764	Ortler Group	Austrian team
	Presanella	3558	Alto Adige	DW Freshfield, JD Walker & RM Beachcroft
	Adamello	3554	Alto Adige	M Payer with Austrian team
	Marmolata	3344	Dolomites	P Grohmann, A & F Dimai

Year	Mountain	Height (m)	Area	First Ascent By
1864	Sorapis	3220	Dolomites	P Grohmann
	Tofana di Rozes	3241	Dolomites	P Grohmann
	Dammastock	3630	Bernese Alps	A Hoffmann-Burckhardt, A von Weissenfluh & J Fischer
	Lyskamm(W)	4479	Valais Alps	L Stephen, EN Buxton, J Anderegg & F Biner
	Bocca di Brenta	2562	Dolomites	J Ball
1865	Aguille Verte	4122	Mt Blanc Group	E Whymper, C Almer & F Biner
	Gr Rocheuse	4102	Mt Blanc Group	R Fowler, M Ducroz & M Balmat
	Gr Jorasses (W)	4180	Mt Blanc Group	E Whymper, C Almer & F Biner
	Aig de Bionassay	4052	Mt Blanc Group	EN Buxton, FC Grove, RS Macdonald, J-P Cachat & M Payot
	Aig du Chardonnet	3824	Mt Blanc Group	R Fowler, M Ducroz & M Balmat
	Matterhorn	4477	Valais Alps	C Hudson, D Hadow, F Douglas, E Whymper, M Croz, P Taugwalder père et fils
	Ober Gabelhorn	4063	Valais Alps	AW Moore, H Walker & J Anderegg
	Grand Cornier	3962	Valais Alps	E Whymper, C Almer, M Croz & F Biner
	Wellenkuppe	3903	Valais Alps	F Douglas, P Inäbnit & P Taugwalder
	Trifthorn	3728	Valais Alps	AW Moore, H Walker & J Anderegg
	Pigne d'Arolla	3796	Valais Alps	AW Moore, H Walker & J Anderegg
	Mt Blanc de Cheilon	3870	Valais Alps	J Weilenmann & J Fellay
	Ruinette	3875	Valais Alps	E Whymper, C Almer & F Biner
	Gr Grünhorn	4043	Bernese Alps	E von Fellenberg, P Inäbnit, P Egger & P Michel
	Lauterbrunnen Breithorn	3785	Bernese Alps	E von Fellenberg, P Inäbnit, P Egger, P Michel & J Bischoff
	Tschingelhorn	3577	Bernese Alps	WH Hawker, H Feuz, C & U Lauener
	Gr Nesthorn	3824	Bernese Alps	HB George, A Mortimer, C & U Almer
	Piz Medel	3210	Grisons Alps	Unknown

Year	Mountain	Height (m)	Area	First Ascent By
1865	Piz Roseg	3937	Bernina Group	AW Moore, H Walker & J Anderegg
	Piz Umbrail	3033	Bernina Group	Unknown
	Piz Pisoc	3178	Bernina Group	Unknown
	Piz Ela	3339	Albula Alps	3 Pontresina guides
	Piz Buin	3312	Rhaetian Alps	J Weilenmann, J-A Specht & G Pröll
	Silvrettahorn	3248	Rhaetian Alps	Unknown
	Punta San Matteo	3684	Ortler Group	English team
	Pizzo Tresero	3602	Ortler Group	English team
	Cevedale	3778	Ortler Group	Austrian team
	Fineilspitz	3561	Oetztal Alps	Austrian team
	Langtaufererspitz	3529	Oetztal Alps	DW Freshfield, Fox, Tuckett, F Devouassoud & P Michel
	Ruderhofspitz	3473	Stubai Alps	Austrian team
	Wilder Freiger Spitz	3418	Stubai Alps	Austrian team
	Cima Tosa	3159	Dolomites	J Ball
	Care Alto	3463	Adamello Group	English team
	Monte Cristallo	3190	Dolomites	P Grohmann
	Croda Rossa	3139	Dolomites	P Grohmann
	Hochfeiler	3520	C Tyrol	English team
	Gross Möseler	3479	Zillertal Alps	DW Freshfield, Fox, Tuckett, F Devouassoud & P Michel
1866	Bec d'Epicoun	3528	Valais Alps	J Weilenmann & J Gillioz
	Pointe d'Otemma	3403	Valais Alps	J Weilenmann & J Gillioz
	Mont Fort	3328	Valais Alps	Unknown
	Aig d'Eboulement	3599	Mt Blanc Group	CE Mathews, AA Reilly, M Balmat & M Ducroz
	Tête de Valpelline	3802	Valais Alps	E Whymper & F Biner
	Kl Wannenhorn	3706	Bernese Alps	Unknown
	Wellhorn	3192	Bernese Alps	E von Fellenberg, C Michel & P Egger
	Blinnenhorn	3374	Valais Alps	S Taylor, J Tännler & F Huntren
	Corno da Tinizong (Tinzenhorn)	3172	Grisons Alps	DW Freshfield, F Devouassoud, E Hauser, P Jenni & A Fleuri
	Piz Cengalo	3370	Bernina Group	DW Freshfield, CC Tucker & F Devouassoud
	Corno di Lago Spalmo	3341	Bernina Group	HP Thomas, FA Lewin, P Jenni & A Fleuri

Year	Mountain	Height (m)	Area	First Ascent By
1866	Corno di Campo	3305	Bernina Group	HP Thomas, FA Lewin, P Jenni & A Fleuri
	Piz Vadret (E)	3196	Engadine	DW Freshfield & F Devouassoud
	Gross Litzner	3109	Rhaetian Alps	Unknown
	Monte Zebrù	3740	Ortler Group	Unknown
	Tuckettspitze	3466	Ortler Group	Unknown
	Punta Taviela	3615	Ortler Group	Unknown
	Monte Rosole	3531	Ortler Group	Unknown
	Dreiherrenspitze	3499	Venediger Group	Unknown
1867	Gletscherhorn	3983	Bernese Alps	JJ Hornby & C Lauener
	Tour Ronde	3792	Mt Blanc Group	DW Freshfield, CC Tucker, JH Backhouse, TH Carson, D Balleys & M Payot
	Mont Collon	3637	Valais Alps	GE Forster, H Baumann & J Kronig
	L'Evêque	3716	Valais Alps	A Baltzer & C Schröder
	Le Pleureur	3703	Valais Alps	Unknown
	Jägerhorn	3975	Valais Alps	CE Mathews, F Morshead, C Almer & A Maurer
	Gross Spannort	3198	Uri Alps	Unknown
	Tödi (South)	3432	Tödi Group	Unknown
	Cima di Piazzi	3439	Valtellina	Unknown
	Piz Badile	3308	Bregaglia	WAB Coolidge, F & H Devouassoud
	Monte Rosso	3088	Bernina Group	WAB Coolidge, F & H Devouassoud
	Piz Vadret (W)	3221	Engadine	J Hartmann & J Fitch with local guides Jenni & Stiefel
	Piz Mitgel	3159	Grisons Alps	Unknown
	Palon della Mare	3704	Ortler Group	Unknown
	Olperer	3476	Zillertal Alps	Austrian team
	Civetta	3220	Dolomites	FF Tuckett, J & M Anderegg & local guide
1868	Grandes Jorasses	4208	Mt Blanc Group	H Walker, M Anderegg, J Jaun & J Grange
	Aig de la Tsa	3668	Valais Alps	P Quinodoz, G Gaspoz, P Beytrison & P & J Vuigner
	Grosshorn	3762	Bernese Alps	H Dübi, E Ober, J Bischoff & J Siegen
	Ebnefluh	3960	Bernese Alps	TLM Brown, P Bohren & P Schlegel

Year	Mountain	Height (M)	Area	First Ascent By
1868	Dreieckhorn	3810	Bernese Alps	TLM Brown, P Bohren & P Schlegel
	Krönten	3107	Uri Alps	English party with guides
	Tschingelhörner	2848	Tödi Group	Unknown
1869	Gspaltenhorn	3437	Bernese Alps	GE Forster, J Anderegg & H Baumann
	Breithorn Lötschental	3785	Bernese Alps	GJ Häberlin, A & J von Weissenfluh
	Gr Zinne (C) (Cima di Lavaredo)	2999	Dolomites	P Grohmann, P Salcher & F Innerkofler
	Dreischusterspitz	3152	Dolomites	P Grohmann, P Salcher & F Innerkofler
	Langkofel (Sasso Lungo)	3181	Dolomites	P Grohmann, P Salcher & F Innerkofler
	Watzespitze	3533	Oetztal Alps	Unknown
	Sonklarspitze	3467	Stubai Alps	Unknown
	Thurweiserspitze	3652	Ortler Group	Unknown
	Hohberghorn	4219	Valais Alps	RB Heathcote, F Biner, P Perren & P Taugwalder (son)
	Cima di Fradusta	2939	Dolomites	L Stephen
	Cima di Ball	2783	Dolomites	L Stephen
	Schinhorn	3796	Bernese Alps	GJ Häberlin, A & J von Weissenfluh
	Morgenhorn	3613	Bernese Alps	H Baedeker, U Lauener & J Bischoff
	Pizzo Rotondo	3192	Ticino Alps	Unknown
	Petit Paradis	3868	Graians	Unknown
	Surettahorn	3027	Grisons Alps	Unknown
	Piz Argient	3945	Bernina Group	Unknown
1870	Aig Rouges d'Arolla	3646	Valais Alps	JH Isler, J Gillioz & Brochez
	Central & North	3593	Valais Alps	JH Isler, J Gillioz & Brochez
	Aig de Trélatête N (Tête Blanche)	3892	Mt Blanc Group	AW Moore, H Walker, J Anderegg & J Jaun
	Meije (Pic Central)	3974	Dauphiné	M Brevoort, WAB Coolidge, C & U Almer & C Gertsch
	Ailefroide W	3954	Dauphiné	WAB Coolidge, C & U Almer, & C Gertsch
	Lenzspitze	4294	Valais Alps	CT Dent, A & F Burgener
	Wilder Pfaff	3458	Stubai Alps	Unknown
	Weissseespitze	3526	Oetztal Alps	Unknown
	Pizzo di Presolana	2521	Adamello (W)	Unknown

Year	Mountain	Height (m)	Area	First Ascent By
1870	Croda Rossa	3146	Dolomites	ER Whitwell, C Lauener & S Siorpaes
	Cimone della Pala	3192	Dolomites	ER Whitwell, C Lauener & S Siorpaes
	Cima di Vezzana	3191	Dolomites	CC Tucker, DW Freshfield & Bernard, guide of Campitello
	Cima di Rosetta	2743	Dolomites	ER Whitwell, C Lauener & S Siorpaes
	Piz Popena	3152	Dolomites	ER Whitwell, C Lauener & S Siorpaes
	Antelao	3263	Dolomites	FF Tuckett, C Lauener & S Siorpaes
1871	Pointe de Zinal	3791	Valais Alps	E Javelle, G Beraneck & J Martin
	Trugberg	3933	Bernese Alps	E Burckhardt, P Egger & P Schlegel
	Monte Stella	3260	Alpes Maritimes	Unknown
	Pointe Sommeiller	3350	Mt Cenis Massif	Unknown
	Monte Guisalet	3313	Mt Cenis Massif	Unknown
	Ciarforon	3643	Graians	Unknown
	Dent des Bouquetins	3838	Valais Alps	AB Hamilton, J Anzevui & J Vuigner
	Dent de Perroc	3675	Valais Alps	AB Hamilton, W Rickman, J Anzevui & J Vuigner
	Pointe du Mountet	3877	Valais Alps	JM Hall, J Martin & J Mooser
	Portjengrat	3654	Valais Alps	CT Dent, A & F Burgener
	Aig du Plan	3673	Mt Blanc Group	J Eccles, M & A Payot
	Aig du Moine	3412	Mt Blanc Group	Miss I. Straton, Miss E Lloyd, J Charlet & J Simond
	Mont Mallet	3988	Mt Blanc Group	L Stephen, G Loppé, F Wallroth & M Anderegg
	Piz Lucendro	2963	Uri Alps	Unknown
	Piz Blas	3018	Grisons Alps	Unknown
	Sandgipfel	3390	Tödi Group	Unknown
	Cima di Brenta	3150	Dolomites	ET Compton & A de Falkner with B Nicolussi
	Gr Geiger	3360	Venediger Gr	Unknown
	Simonyspitz	3488	Venediger Gr	Unknown
1872	Combin de Valsorey	4184	Grand Combin	JH Isler & J Gillioz
	Aig de Leschaux	3759	Mt Blanc Group	TS Kennedy, J Marshall, J Fischer & J Grange
	Agassizhorn	3953	Bernese Alps	WAB Coolidge, U Almer & C Inäbnit

292

Year	Mountain	Height (m)	Area	First Ascent By
1872	Grunerhorn	3439	Bernese Alps	EJ Häberlin, A & J von Weissenfluh
	Scheuchzerhorn	3467	Bernese Alps	EJ Häberlin, A & J von Weissenfluh
	Unterbachhorn	3554	Bernese Alps	M Brevoort, WAB Coolidge, A Fairbanks, C & U Almer
	Zapporthorn	3151	Grisons Alps	Unknown
	Thurnerkamp	3422	Zillertal Alps	English team
	Roter Knopf	3281	Hohe Tauern	Unknown
	Hofmannspitze	3721	Gross Glockner	Unknown
	Marmarole (E)	2961	Dolomites	WE Kelso, CJ Trueman & S Siorpaes
	Kesselkogel	3004	Dolomites	CC Tucker & guide Bernard
	Cima di Vezzana	3191	Dolomites	CC Tucker & DW Freshfield
	Becco di Mezzodi	2322	Dolomites	WE Kelso & S Siorpaes
1873	Aig de Rochefort	4001	Mt Blanc Group	J Eccles, M & A Payot
	Aig de Blaitière (N)	3507	Mt Blanc Group	TS Kennedy, JAG Marshall, J Fischer & U Almer
	Schwarzhorn (Corno Nero)	4322	Monte Rosa Group	M Maglioni, A de Rotschild, P & N Knubel & E Cupelin
	Schalihorn	3974	Valais Alps	T Middlemore, J Jaun & C Lauener
	Gr Wendenstock	3042	Uri Alps	TCV Baston
	Gr Greiner	3203	Zillertal Alps	Unknown
	Darberspitze	3390	Gross Glockner	Unknown
	Bessanese	3632	Graians	Unknown
	Punta d'Arnas	3540	Graians	Unknown
	Herbetet	3778	Graians	Unknown
	Grande Ruine (Pt Brevoort)	3765	Dauphiné	M Brevoort, WAB Coolidge, C Almer, P Michel, C Roth & P Bleuer
	Le Râteau (E)	3809	Dauphiné	M Brevoort, WAB Coolidge, C Almer, P Michel, C Roth & P Bleuer
	Montagne des Agneaux	3662	Dauphiné	WAB Coolidge, C Almer & C Roth
	Les Rouies	3589	Dauphiné	F Gardiner, WM Pendelbury, C Taylor, T Cox, H & P Baumann, P Knubel & J Lochmatter

Year	Mountain	Height (m)	Area	First Ascent By
1873	Roche Faurio	3730	Dauphiné	F Gardiner, WM Pendelbury, C Taylor, T Cox, H & P Baumann, P Knubel & J Lochmatter
1874	Pic de la Grave	3669	Dauphiné	WAB Coolidge, C Almer père et fils
	Grande Rousses S	3473	Dauphiné	Unknown
	Aig de Blaitière (C)	3522	Mt Blanc Group	ER Whitwell, C & J Lauener
	Aig de Triolet	3870	Mt Blanc Group	JAG Marshall, U Almer & J Fischer
	Ceresole	3777	Gran Paradiso	WAB Coolidge, C & U Almer
	Roccia Viva	3650	Gran Paradiso	Unknown
	Aig des Maisons Blanches	3418	Grand Combin	M Maglioni, D Balleys & N Knubel
	Rosengartenspitze	2981	Dolomites	English team
1875	Roche de la Muzelle	3464	Dauphiné	WAB Coolidge, C & U Almer
	Sass Maor	2816	Dolomites	CC Tucker, HA Beachcroft, F Devouassoud & B della Santa
	Gross Lohner	3048	Bernese Alps	Unknown
	Becca di Tribolazione	3360	E Graians	Unknown
	Levanna	3640	C Graians	Unknown
	Becca di Montandeni	3838	E Graians	L Vaccarone & A Castagneri
	Punta di Gay	3623	E Graians	L Vaccarone, A Castagneri & P Palestrino
	Dent d'Ambin	3382	Mt Cenis Massif	Unknown
	Cima Dodici (Zwölferkofel)	3094	Dolomites	M & J Innerkofler
2 January	1st winter ascent of Gross Glockner	3796		WA Baillie-Grohmann, M Innerkofler & P Groder
1876	Bric Bouchet	3003	Vanoise	Unknown
	Roche Taillante	3200	Vanoise	Unknown
	Aig du Plat	3596	Dauphiné	H Cordier, A Maurer & J Anderegg
	Aig de l'Olan	3371	Dauphiné	E Boileau & P Gaspard père et fils
	Tête de l'Etret	3559	Dauphiné	E Boileau & P Gaspard père et fils
	Tête des Fétoules	3458	Dauphiné	E Boileau & P Gaspard père et fils

Year	Mountain	Height (m)	Area	First Ascent By
1876	Grande Fourche	3611	Mt Blanc Group	HR Whitehouse & H Copt
	Tour Noir	3837	Mt Blanc Group	E Javelle, F Turner R & J Moser & F Tournier
	Petites Jorasses	3650	Mt Blanc Group	MA Guyard, H Devouassoud & A Cupelin
	Les Droites E	4000	Mt Blanc Group	H Cordier, T Middlemore, JO Maund, J Jaun & A Maurer
	Les Droites W	3984	Mt Blanc Group	WAB Coolidge, C Almer pére et fils
	Les Courtes	3856	Mt Blanc Group	H Cordier, T Middlemore, JO Maund, J Jaun, A Maurer & J Anderegg
	Aig de Blaitière (S)	3521	Mt Blanc Group	R Pendlebury & G & J Spechtenhauser
	Mont Brulé	3591	Valais Alps	A Cust with porter
	Gross Füsshorn	3627	Bernese Alps	M Brevoort, W Little & M Salzmann with porters
	Gr Engelhorn	2781	Bernese Alps	HS Hoare, J von Bergen & K Streich
	Kl Spannort	3140	Uri Alps	J Cattani, J Furger, J Hess & E Ochsner
	Gr Windgälle	3187	Uri Alps	Unknown
	Pizzo del Ferro (W)	3276	Bregaglia	L Held
	Pt di Castello	2891	Adamello Group	Unknown
23 July	1st guideless ascent of Matterhorn			A Cust, AH Cawood & JB Colgrove
31 Jan	1st winter ascent of Mt Blanc			Miss I Straton, J Charlet, S Couttet & M Balmat
1877	Bric Froid	3302	Cottian Alps	Unknown
	La Meije Grand Pic	3983	Dauphiné	E Boileau & P Gaspard pére et fils
	Pic sans Nom	3914	Dauphiné	J Colgrove, R Pendlebury & G & J Spechtenhauser
	Grande Sagne	3660	Dauphiné	WAB Coolidge & C Almer père et fils
	Pic Coolidge	3774	Dauphiné	WAB Coolidge & C Almer père et fils
	Cime de Clot Châtel	3563	Dauphiné	WAB Coolidge & C Almer père et fils
	Sirac	3440	Dauphiné	WAB Coolidge & C Almer père et fils

Year	Mountain	Height (m)	Area	First Ascent By
1877	Le Plaret	3564	Dauphiné	H Cordier, J Anderegg & A Maurer
	Pic des Aupillons	3505	Dauphiné	F Gardiner, C & L Pilkington
	Punta Ondezana	3498	Graians	Unknown
	Dôme de l'Arpont	3611	Vanoise	Unknown
	Grand Nomenon	3488	Graians	Unknown
	Aig Noire de Peuterey	3773	Mt Blanc Group	Lord Wentworth, E Rey & J-B Bich
	Piz Scersen	3971	Bernina Group	P Güssfeldt, H Grass & C Capat
	Küchelspitze	3144	Arlberg	Unknown
1878	Piz Bernina (Biancograt)	4049	Bernina Group	P Güssfeldt, H Grass & J Gross
	Cima di Nasta	3108	Alpes Maritimes	DW Freshfield & F Devouassoud
	Brec de Chambeyron	3390	Monte Viso	Unknown
	Pic de la Font Sancte	3387	Cottian Alps	Unknown
	Grande Aig Rousse	3482	C Graians	Unknown
	Les Bans	3670	Dauphiné	WAB Coolidge & C Almer père et fils
	La Meije (E summit)	3890	Dauphiné	H Duhamel, Giraud-Lézin & F Gonet
	Pic Gaspard	3883	Dauphiné	H Duhamel, P Gaspard père et fils & C Roderon
	Pointe du Vallon des Etages	3564	Dauphiné	F Perrin, A Salvador & P Gaspard père et fils
	Pic des Arcas	3478	Dauphiné	WAB Coolidge & C Almer père et fils
	Aig du Soreiller	3339	Dauphiné	E Rochat & P Gaspard père et fils
	Aig d'Arves N	3510	Dauphiné	English team
	Aig d'Arves S	3206	Dauphiné	English team
	Aig de Peclet	3562	Vanoise	Unknown
	Pointe de Galise	3344	S Graians	Unknown
	Roc du Mulinet	3444		Unknown
	Mont Maudit	4465	Mt Blanc Group	WE Davidson, HS Hoare, J Jaun & J von Bergen
	Grand Dru	3754	Mt Blanc Group	CT Dent, W Hartley, A Burgener & K Maurer
	Aig des Glaciers	3816	Mt Blanc Group	ED Carretto, F Gonella, L Proment & G & A Henry
	Mittaghorn	3897	Bernese Alps	C Montandon, A Ringier & A Rubin

Year	Mountain	Height (m)	Area	First Ascent By
1878	Cima Undici (Elferkogel)	3092		M Innerkofler
	Sasso Rigais (Geislerspitz)	3025	Dolomites	Unknown
	Croda da Lago	2701	Dolomites	Austrian party
	Pala di San Martino	2939	Dolomites	J Meurer, A di Pallavinci,
			Dolomites	S Siorpaes & A Dimai
1879	Punta della Argentera	3290	Alpes Maritimes	WAB Coolidge & C Almer père et fils
	Monte Matto	3087	Alpes Maritimes	English party
	Aig de Chambeyron	3410	Cottian Alps	English party
	Pte Haute de Mary	3206	Cottian Alps	English party
	Tête des Toillies	3176	Cottian Alps	English party
	Le Pavé	3824	Dauphiné	WAB Coolidge & C Almer père et fils
	Pic du Says (S)	3421	Dauphiné	WAB Coolidge & C Almer père et fils
	Pointe de Verdonne	3327	Dauphiné	F Gardiner & L Pilkington
	Pic de Bonvoisin	3480	Dauphiné	F Gardiner & L Pilkington
	Tête de Lauranoure (C)	3323	Dauphiné	A Charbonnier & P Gaspard père et fils
	Punta di Forzo	3296	Graians	Italian party
	Grand Serraz	3552	Graians (Grivola)	English party
	Aig de Talèfre	3730	Mt Blanc Group	J Baumann, FJ Cullinan, G Fitzgerald, E Rey, L Larnier & J Moser
	Petit Dru	3733	Mt Blanc Group	J Charlet-Straton, P Payot & F Folliguet
	Pointe de Bricola	3657	Valais Alps	C Socin & E Peter
	Sonnighorn	3487	Valais Alps	AF Mummery, A Burgener & A Gentinetta
	Dürrenhorn	4035	Valais Alps	AF Mummery, W Penhall, A Burgener & F Imseng
	Mitre de l'Evèque	3659	Valais Alps	A Cust with J Martin & P Beytrison
	Gr Vernel	3210	Dolomites (Marmolada)	W Merzbacher &. guide Bernard
	Cima di Canali	2939	Dolomites	CC Tucker & M Bottega
	Cima di Lavaredo (Zinne W)	2320	Dolomites	G Ploner & M Innerkofler
	Elferkofel (Cima Undici)	3092	Dolomites	G Ploner & M Innerkofler

Year	Mountain	Height (m)	Area	First Ascent By
1879 3 Sept	Zsigmondyspitze Z'mutt ridge of Matterhorn climbed	3089	Zillertal Alps	Unknown AF Mummery, A Burgener, J Petrus, A Gentinetta & on same day by W Penhall & F Imseng
27 Jan	1st winter ascent of Schreckhorn			WAB Coolidge, C Almer père et fils, C, U & F Deutschmann
1880	Aig des Grands Charmoz (N) Pointe	3431	Mt Blanc Group	AF Mummery, A Burgener & B Venetz
	Aig des Petits Charmoz	2867	Mt Blanc Group	JA Hutchinson & guides
	Geisshorn	3740	Bernese Alps	WAB Coolidge, A Walden & guides
	Cima d'Ambiez	3096	Brenta Group	Unknown
	Füssstein	3380	Zillertal Alps	R Starr, H Lechner & J Ebel
	Grohmannspitze	3126	Dolomites	M Innerkofler
	Gross Furquetta	3027	Dolomites	Unknown
	Cinque Torri	2362	Dolomites	Unknown
	Innerkoflerturm	3072	Dolomites	Unknown
February	Winter ascent of Piz Bernina			CEB Watson, Parnell, C Grass & V Kessler
1881	Dôme de Rochefort	4015	Mt Blanc Group	J Eccles, M & J Payot
	Aig du Grépon	3481	Mt Blanc Group	AF Mummery, A Burgener & B Venetz
	Herbetet	3778	Graians	G Yeld, GP Baker, Almer & J Jossi
	Le Fifre	3698	Dauphiné	WAB Coolidge & C Almer père et fils
	Cima di Lavaredo (Zinne E)	2853	Dolomites	M & J Innerkofler & D Daimantidi
	(Zinne C)	2999	Dolomites	M & J Innerkofler & D Daimantidi
	(Zinne W)	2973	Dolomites	M & J Innerkofler & D Daimantidi
	Watzmann (E face)	2713	Bavarian Alps	O Schück & J Grill- Kederbacher
	Vajolet Tower	2821	Dolomites	W Merzbacher & guide Bernard
	Sasso di Mur	2554	Dolomites	D Diamantidi, L Cesaletti & B Mariano

Year	Mountain	Height (m)	Area	First Ascent By
1882	Torre di Brenta	2980	Dolomites	ET Compton, A de Falkner & M Nicolussi
	Aig du Géant (SW)	4009	Mt Blanc Group	A, A, C & G Sella, J-J, B & D Maquignaz
	Aig du Géant (NE)	4013	Mt Blanc Group	WW Graham, A Payot & A Cupelin
	Piz Prievlus	3610	Bernina Group	B Wainewright, JRP Legh, H & C Grass
16-17 Mar	1st winter ascent of Matterhorn and traverse from Italy to Switzerland			V Sella with J-A, J-B, & L Carrel
1883	Aig de la Varappe	3518	Aig Dorées	H Guttinger, E Thury, L Wanner & G Coquoz
	Sattelhorn	3723	Bernese Alps	K Schulz, A Burgener & J Rittler
	Piz Bacone	3244	Bernina Group	T Curtius, C Klucker, J Eggenberger & L Bernus
	Monte Ferro (E)	3293	Bernina Group	A & LV Bertarelli & G Rigamonti
1884	Crozzon di Brenta	3123	Dolomites	K Schulz & M Nicolussi
	Croda del Lago	2716	Dolomites	R Eötvös & M Innerkofler
	Galmihorn N	3517	Bernese Alps	A Barbey, L Kurz & 2 guides
	Galmihorn S	3486	Bernese Alps	A Barbey, L Kurz & 2 guides
	Schönbuhlhorn	3854	Bernese Alps	A Barbey, L Kurz & 2 guides
	Teufelshorn	3680	Gr Glockner Group	M von Kuffner, C Ranggetiner & E Rubesoier
26 Jan	1st winter ascent of Monte Rosa (Dufourspitz)			V Sella with J & D Maquignaz
1885	Aig Blanche de Peutérey	4108	Mt Blanc Group	H Seymour King, E Rey, A Supersaxo & A Anthamatten
	Aig des Grands Charmoz	3445	Mt Blanc Group	H Dunod, P Vignon, F & G Simond, F Folliguet & J Desailloux
	Grand Darrey	3514	Mt Blanc Group	L Kurz & F Biselx
	Dent de Perroc (Pte des Genevois)	3677	Valais Alps	A Tschumi, W Kündig & J Quinodoz

Year	Mountain	Height (m)	Area	First Ascent By
1885	Testa di Tribolazione	3642	Graians	G Yeld, H Séraphin, J Jantet, WAB Coolidge & C Almer
	Grivoletta	3514	Graians	G Yeld & H Séraphin
	Campanile Alto	2960	Dolomites	G Merzbacher & B Nicolussi
	Cima del Lago (SE)	3188	Dolomites	T Curtius & C Klucker
	Eiger Mittellegi Ridge descent			M von Kuffner, A Burgener, J Biner & Kalbermatten
	La Meije first complete traverse			E & O Zsigmondy & L Purtscheller
2 Mar	First winter ascents Gran Paradiso	4061	Graians	V Sella, S Aitken & J & D Maquignaz
22 Mar	Lyskamm	4527	Valais	V Sella, C & A Sella, J Maquignaz & P Gugliermina
1886	Pte Sud de Moming	3963	Valais	H Seymour King, A Supersaxo & A Anthamatten
	Dent de Perroc (N)	3651	Valais Alps	JA Vardy with J & P Maître
	Cima della Madonna (Sass Maor W)	2751	Dolomites	G Winkler & A Zott
1887	Aig Rouges d'Arolla (Sud)	3584	Valais Alps	WC Slingsby, HW Topham, A Macnamara & J Maître
	Bouquetins (Pte Barnes)	3612	Valais Alps	GS Barnes, WC Slingsby, Miss Oliphant & M Vuignier
1888	Aig de l'A Neuve	3753	Mont Blanc Gr	A Barbey, L Kurz, J Bessard & J Simond
	Aig Rouges du Dolent (Pte Kurz)	3680	Mont Blanc Gr	A Barbey, L Kurz, J Bessard & J Simond
	Sciora di Dentro (Sciora Dadent)	3275	Bregaglia	T Curtius, R Wiesner, with C Klucker
1889	Grande Lui	3509	Mont Blanc Gr	V Attinger, E Colomb, L Kurz with F Biselx, J & J Bessard
	Aig de la Lex Blanche	3697	Mont Blanc Gr	V Attinger, L Kurz, with J-B Croz & J Simond

300

Year	Mountain	Height (m)	Area	First Ascent By
1890	Petit Combin	3672	Valais	C de le Harpe, EW Vollier with J Bessard
	Pic du Gl Carré	3857	Dauphiné	A Holmes with M Gaspard & B Andenmatten
	Petit Darrey	3508	Mont Blanc Gr	V Attinger, A Barbey, H Pascal with J & J Bessard
	Aig Purtscheller	3478	Mont Blanc Gr	L Purtscheller (solo)
	Pic Sans Nom	3791	Mont Blanc Gr	E Carr, GH Morse & JH Wicks
1891 14 Jan	Grandes Jorasses 1st winter ascent			P Güssfeldt, E Rey & D Proment
1892	L'Eveque	3469	Mont Blanc Gr	C, I & M Pasteur, E Carr & C Wilson
1893	Dent du Requin	3422	Mont Blanc Gr	AF Mummery, JN Collie, G Hastings & WC Slingsby
1894	Combin de la Tsessette	4141	Gr Combin group	EFM Benecke & HA Cohen
	Bouquetins (S Peak)	3670	Valais Alps	AG Topham, J Maître & P Maurys
27 Mar	Matterhorn first winter ascent			C Simon, A Burgener & A Pollinger

BIBLIOGRAPHY

Agassiz, L. *Etude sur les Glaciers*. Neuchâtel; Jent & Gassmann,1840.

Alpine Club London whose Library and Archives contain a complete source of information about the Alpine pioneers.

Annan, NG. *Leslie Stephen*. London; MacGibbon & Kee, 1951.

Ball J. *Peaks, Passes and Glaciers*. London; Longman, Brown, Green, Longmans and Roberts, 1859.
    Alpine Guide – The Western Alps. London; Longmans, Green, 1898.

Bell, Q. *Virginia Stephen* Vol I. London; The Hogarth Press, 1972.

Bonjour, E, Offler, HS & Potter, GR. *A Short History of Switzerland*. Oxford; Clarendon Press, 1952.

Browne, GF. *Recollections of a bishop*. USA; Smith, Elder, 1915.

Bruce, CG. *The Passing of Mummery*. Himalayan Journal Vol III, 1931.
    Himalayan Wanderer. London; Alexander Maclehose, 1934.

Clark, RW. *The Victorian Mountaineers*. London; Batsford, 1953.
    The Day The Rope Broke. London; Secker & Warburg, 1965.
    An eccentric in the Alps. London; Museum Press, 1959.

Collie, JN. *Climbing on the Himalaya & Other Mountain Ranges*. Edinburgh; Douglas, 1902.

Conway, WM. *The Alps from End to End*. London; Constable, 1905.

Coolidge, WAB. *Les Alpes*; London; Payot Lausanne, 1913.
    Alpine studies. London; Longmans, Green, 1912.
    Swiss Travel and Guide-Books. London; Longmans, Green, 1889.
    The Alps in Nature and History. London; Methuen, 1908.

Coulson, M. *Southwards to Geneva*. Gloucester; Alan Sutton, 1988.

Cunningham, CD & Abney, W. *The Pioneers of the Alps*. London; Sampson Low, Marston, Searle and Rivington, 1887.

de Beer, GR. *Early Travellers in The Alps*. London; Sidgwick & Jackson, 1930.
    Travellers in Switzerland. London; Oxford University Press, 1949.

de Beer, GR & Brown, TG. *The First Ascent of Mont Blanc*. London; Oxford University Press, 1957.

de Ségogne, H. *Les Alpinistes Célèbres*. Paris; L Mazenod, 1956.

Dent, CT & others. *Mountaineering*. London; (Badminton Library) Longmans, Green, 1892.

Désor, E. *Nouvelles Excursions dans les Alpes*. Neuchâtel, Kissling, 1845.

Dumas, A. *Impressions de voyage en Suisse* Vol I. Paris; C. Lévi, 1881.

Eckenstein, O. *Seitenpfade um Saas-Fee*. Zürich; Orell Füssli, 1934.

Egger, C. *Pioniere der Alpen*. Zürich; Amstutz Herdeg, 1946.

Engel, C-E. *Le Mont Blanc*. Paris; Ed V Attinger, 1931.
    Histoire de l'Alpinisme. Paris; Ed Je Sers, 1950.
    They Came to the Hills. London; Allen & Unwin, 1952.
    History of Mountaineering in the Alps. London; Allen & Unwin, 1950.

Eve, AS & Creasey, CH. *Life and Work of John Tyndall*. London; Macmillan, 1945.

Evelyn, J. *The Diaries of John Evelyn* Vol 2, 1955.

Forbes, JD. *Travels Through the Alps of Savoy*. Edinburgh; Adam and Charles Black, 1843.
    The Glacier Theory. Edinburgh Review, April 1842.

Freshfield, DW. *The life of Horace Bénédict de Saussure*. London; Arnold, 1920.

Frison-Roche, R & Jouty, S. *Histoire de l'Alpinisme*. Paris; Ed Arthaud, 1996.

Gattlen, A. *Das Matterhorn*. Brig; Rotten-Verlag, 1979.

Girdlestone, AG. *The High Alps Without Guides*. London; Longmans, Green, 1870.

Godeffroy, C. *Notice sur les Glaciers, les Moraines et les Blocs Erratiques des Alpes*, Paris; Cherbuliez, 1840.

Gos, C. *Alpine Tragedy*. London; Allen & Unwin, 1948.

Hinchcliff, T. *Summer Months Among the Alps*. London; Longmans, Brown, Green, Longmans & Roberts, 1857.

BIBLIOGRAPHY

Hudson, C & Kennedy, ES. *Where there's a will there's a way*. London; Longmans, Brown, Green, Longmans & Roberts, 1856.

Imseng, R & Supersaxo, O. *Saas Fee Zweigespräch mit Dorf & Bergwelt*. Visp; Rotten Verlag, 1991.

Jeanneret, F & Maur, F. *Le Grand Atlas Suisse*. Bern; Kümmerly & Frey, 1982.

Keenlyside, F. *Peaks and Pioneers*. London; Elek, 1975.

Lukan, K. *Alpinismus in Anekdoten*. Wien; Neff Verlag, 1972.

Lunn, A. *A Century of Mountaineering*. London; Allen & Unwin, 1957.

 The Alps. London; Williams & Norgate, 1914.

 Switzerland & the English. London; Eyre & Spottiswoode, 1944.

Maitland, FW. *The Life and Letters of Leslie Stephen*. London; Duckworth, 1906.

Moore, AW. *The Alps in 1864* (2 Vols). Oxford; Basil Blackwell, 1939.

Mummery, AF. *My Climbs in the Alps and Caucasus*. Oxford; Basil Blackwell, 1946.

Noussan, E. *The Theodule Pass*. Valle d'Aosta; Arti Grafiche E Duc, 1998.

Oechslin, M. *Alpineum Helveticum* Vol I & II. Luzern; E Bachmann, 1948.

Pilley, D. *Climbing Days*. London; Secker & Warburg, 1965.

Rebuffat, G. *Cervin Cime Exemplaire*. Paris; Hachette, 1965.

Rendu, L. *Théorie des Glaciers de la Savoie*. London; Macmillan, 1874.

Rey, G. *The Matterhorn*. Oxford; Basil Blackwell, 1946.

Roch, A. *Exploits au Mont Blanc*. Lugano; Nuova Ed Trelingue, 1987.

Ruskin, J. *Modern Painters* Part IV. USA; Smith Elder, 1857.

Schuster, C. *Postscript to Adventure*. London; Eyre & Spottiswoode, 1950.

Senger, Dr M. *Wie die Schweizer Alpen erobert wurden*. Zürich; Büchergilde Gutenberg, 1945.

Shairp, JC, Tait PG & Adams-Reilly, A. *Life and Letters of James David Forbes*. London; Macmillan, 1873.

Shelley, PB. *Mont Blanc*. Letchworth; The Temple Press, 1936.

Smythe, FS. *Edward Whymper*. London; Hodder & Stoughton, 1940.

Stephen, L. *The playground of Europe*. Oxford; Basil Blackwell, 1936.

Swiss National Tourist Office. *Switzerland and her Glaciers*. Bern; Kümmerly & Frey, 1981.

Swiss Alpine Club. *Nos Cartes Nationales*. Bern; Stämpfli & Cie, 1979.

 Glaciers des Alpes. Bern; Stämpfli & Cie, 1988.

 Die ersten fünfzig Jahre. Bern; Stämpfli & Cie, 1913.

Swiss Academy of Sciences. *La Géographie en Suisse*, 1980.

Tallantire, PA. *Edward Theodore Compton*. Privately printed, 1996.

Tuckett, FF. *A pioneer in the High Alps*. London; Arnold, 1920.

Türler, Professor H & others. *Lexikon de Schweiz* (7 vols). Neuenberg; Attinger, 1921-1934.

Tyndall, J. *The Glaciers of the Alps*. London; JM Dent, 1906.

 Mountaineering in 1861. London; JM Dent, 1906.

 Hours of exercise in the Alps. London; Longmans, Green, 1906.

 Principal Forbes and his Biographers. London; Longmans, Green, 1873.

Viollet-Le-Duc, E. *Le massif du Mont Blanc*. Paris; Baudry, 1876.

von Haller, A. *The Alps*. Dübendorf; De Clivo Press, 1987.

Weiss, R. *Die Entdeckung der Alpen*. Frauenfeld; Verlag von Huber, 1934.

Wills, A. *Wanderings Among the High Alps*. Oxford; Blackwell, 1937.

Wills, J. *The Alfred Wills Letters*. Wills family archives, 2003.

Whymper, E. *Scrambles amongst the Alps*. London; John Murray, 1871.

 Guide to Zermatt & the Matterhorn. London; John Murray, 1903.

 Guide to Chamonix & the chain of Mont Blanc. London; John Murray, 1900.

Williams, C. *Women on the Rope*. London; Allen & Unwin, 1973.

INDEX